# *Tales of Many M*

*What the critics have said*:

'A stirring human document, written with verve and wit' – *The Mail on Sunday*

'Enthusiasm, humour and sheer doggedness . . . this wonderful tale . . . very well worth reading' – *The Alpine Journal*

'There's nobody like him. His extraordinary achievements have earned him a place in climbing history.' Chris Bonington

'A superb tale, graphically told . . . a modest account of courage and determination which will be enjoyed by climbers and non-climbers alike . . . an inspiring read . . . this heart-warming journal.'

# *Tales of Many Mountains*

*by*

NORMAN CROUCHER

*Amanda Press*

Published by Amanda Press
8 Woodville Gardens, Ealing, London W5 2LG
Photoset by Quadraset Ltd, Midsomer Norton, Avon
Printed by Antony Rowe Ltd, Chippenham, Wiltshire

ISBN 0 9514337 0 9

# *Introduction*

I have taken here as my main ingredients passages from three books, *Shin Kicking Champion*, published in 1971 by Barrie and Jenkins, *High Hopes*, published in 1976 by Hodder and Stoughton, and *A Man and his Mountains*, published in 1984 by Kaye and Ward, so there are few new ingredients, but less fat; this is a more complete and balanced meal. I wish I had waited until now to write my first mountain book, and here is what I would have written.

You need not be a country dweller to appreciate a book on country life, nor a climber to enjoy tales of mountain adventures. So this book is not written exclusively for mountaineers, and though it has not been possible to avoid climbing terms entirely, the few which are used are explained in the short Glossary, which is followed by a simplified description of climbing techniques.

# *Contents*

# 1

# *The Early Days*

The year was 1960. I wanted to climb but had lost my legs below the knees in a railway accident. People said it was a crazy idea, to think about climbing with artificial legs, but that hope was cherished throughout convalescence.

''E's gone bonkers,' my mother said, but two days on a rock climbing course before I lost my legs had planted the strong seeds of enthusiasm. 'The Cornwall Youth Committee has kindly agreed to subsidise the cost of the course, the charge for those attending will therefore be 12/6d,' said the leaflet, which I still have. That course was months before, as if in another life.

Experiments with various sporting and leisure pursuits soon showed that plenty of active pastimes were still available. The popular dance of the time was the Twist; I found to my pleasure one night that the dance was possible, although there was one drawback – when I got home I discovered that some of the rivets had popped out of my legs! Skating was hard and I seemed to spend more time on my back on the ice than actually skating. Riding a motor-scooter: not difficult. After falling off one day I finished up with a large dent in one leg; if the leg had been real it would have been broken, or very painful. A camping and hitch-hiking holiday took me through France, Belgium, Germany and Luxemburg. Gliding and cycling proved to be possible, too, but always, always on my mind was climbing. So, one day I scrambled awkwardly over a rough grey rock on a beach. Yes, climbing was on, so I wrote to a climbing instructor, Jim Smith, and we arranged to meet. He was thin and agile, in his forties. As we sat in his car, ready to drive the few miles from his home to the sea cliffs, I mentioned my legs for the first time and said I would like to climb. It was likely that he would refuse to help.

'Legs can be very handy when you're climbing,' he remarked, 'but we can soon find out what you can do.' Then away we went to the cliffs. It seemed that the question of saying no had not entered his head.

Jim was calm, patient, thoughtful, and above all sufficiently skilled to be confident that he would choose relatively safe situations for me to experiment in; to go with an expert was the way to find out without too much danger, so we started on little bits of rock only sixty or seventy feet high. The faces were steep, but easy because of plentiful holds for hands and feet in the form of ledges, cracks and jutting knobs of grey granite. I was a real beginner; two days on a rock climbing course before I lost my legs helped me to decide that I could still climb, but when it came to performing the movements I had to start almost from scratch.

It was essential to look down frequently at my boots to make sure that they had not moved, as they were inclined to slip from small toe holds. Steadiness of movement was of the essence, even more than for an able-bodied climber. Another minor problem was that if I raised a foot to a hold only as high as a chair seat I lacked the leg strength to step up. Arms had to provide so much of the power, whereas the usual climber gains most power from the legs. A further difficulty was the limited bend of the knees, not much over ninety degrees. Most frustrating of all was my inability to move the feet from the ankles to left or right, up or down, to fit nicely on holds. The feet just stuck out rigidly at attention, pointing straight forward. In addition, I lost several inches in reach through not being able to stand on tiptoe.

So there were several hindrances which could have been used as excuses if I did not want to climb, but none which truly precluded the sport. Rather than prevent participation, my physical condition only set limits on the difficulty of the routes which I could manage, and obviously progress would be very strenuous by comparison with other climbers. What would have happened if Jim had said no when first I asked for his help? I might not have climbed at all, so I was very grateful, for largely because of him the adventure had begun.

Over the next few years I was drawn to a few cliffs in Britain. In those early, tentative years on rock it seemed that while many cliffs and outcrops were accessible, mountains put up barriers which might for ever exclude me. It was not that the climbing was hard on mountains, for often the reverse was true; but the journeys were long. The combination of a march from the nearest road followed by a lengthy climb seemed too ambitious to contemplate. So nine years of rock climbing went by with hardly a thought about mountains, except for nagging regrets that they were not for me. Then, one day in 1969, on a sketch map of Snowdonia, the name and position of a mountain caught my eye. The peak, Tryfan, was marked as just over 3,000 feet high (c. 900 metres), and from the roughly drawn map I judged the summit to be within a mile and a half of the nearest road. Could I climb long enough to reach the summit? And descend safely? It seemed possible, just possible. There was one fact in my favour at the time: the month was February, snow lay deep on the mountain, and cold conditions suited me because the stumps of the legs were less inclined to injury when cool and free of perspiration. If I attempted Tryfan I could decide as I went along whether I should climb the mountain or merely see how far I could go. Ambition had to be tempered with caution in those early days of exploration.

'How about seeing if I can get up Tryfan?' The question was directed at Peter, a climbing pal.

'All right.'

We slept in Peter's mini-van in a lay-by at the foot of Tryfan. The night was so cold that our sandwiches froze hard, but the next day was fine and so we set off.

To start with there was half an hour's easy trudge through ankle-deep snow on the gentle lower slopes. We each had an ice-axe; they would be our brakes if we slipped. In places we crossed gaps where a slip would have sent us tumbling a long way, but the chances of such a fall were remote. Still, with a novice like me around we could not afford to take risks, and I felt the need for us to be roped together when we passed exposed spots. At such times Peter positioned himself so he could hold me on a rope if I fell. We call it 'belaying', which means to attach yourself to the rock and hold the rope for anyone who takes a tumble.

Each hour was punctuated by two short rests. As the hundreds of paces added up I expected pain to signal that the stumps had had enough, but they remained cool and uninjured. Six hours passed. Near the top I was so exhausted I could do no more than crawl on all fours through the snow for a few yards. Wedged between two rocks, I rested in a rock armchair with a soft snow cushion.

'Be all right in a couple of minutes, Pete.'

But hopes of making the summit faded considerably.

'I'll just scout ahead while you take it easy,' he said, tramping on. A hundred feet above he went out of sight behind a rock. Two minutes later he came into view again, shouting and waving his arms.

'It's only a couple of hundred feet to the top from where I'm standing. Just a walk!'

We hurried on to stand within five minutes beside Adam and Eve, the two big rocks which crown the summit. We grinned and giggled like schoolboys in a joke shop. It was a small mountain, but at least it was a mountain. I felt an elation which I was to be moved to seek again at the top of many peaks. It was then that Peter revealed that the secretary of a London climbing club had tried to talk him out of climbing with me, though she had shown a different and false face to me. I cursed her name; I think I was entitled.

We scurried back, part of the time slithering on our bottoms and controlling the slide with ice-axes. The whole descent took about two hours, in daylight all the way.

I could hardly believe I had climbed a real mountain. Suddenly, a whole new world opened up, though at the time I did not realise how much influence the mountains would have. This was a distinct watershed in life. Higher mountains beckoned, but it seemed advisable first to undergo some form of endurance training to improve my stamina on long treks. A few weeks later I made up my mind to walk the length of Britain, the near nine hundred miles from John o' Groats in the north of Scotland to Land's End in Cornwall.

It was frustrating to wait for the cool weather at the end of the year. Meanwhile, I looked round for sponsors who would donate money to Oxfam for each mile covered. A doctor friend said Oxfam should refuse to encourage my walk, but though I appreciated her concern such a cotton wool attitude would have suffocated rather than protected me. The walk was a critical stage in what was to become of me, and I needed to make it both physically and psychologically. I required the freedom to take my own risks, for good or bad.

Unlike many people who had undertaken the same walk, I travelled alone, without a support group, and with only £160 of my savings in a Post Office account for expenses. This was not a large amount, considering that if I could average only eight miles per day and took one rest day every two weeks I would be on the road for 120 days, allowing me only £1.6.8d per day for food, accommodation, repairs to footwear and all other expenses. If I bought camping equipment the weight would have been more than I wanted to take, so I would have to search for cheap meals and accommodation wherever I went.

September 18th, 1969. A sunny, windless morning at John o' Groats. I started to walk and eagerness led me to cover sixteen miles, causing my stumps to split open and bleed in half a dozen places by the end of the day, so I was very sore when I arrived at the town of Wick, looking for a place to stay for the night.

I rang the door bell at a guest house and when a woman answered I told her that I was walking from John o' Groats to Land's End and asked if she had any vacancies. The woman said she had only double rooms, and the throbbing pain in my stumps persuaded me to agree to pay for a double room, but the woman would not let me in. I suspected she was alone, and frightened of me.

'No, I don't want you in here,' she said.

'But I'll pay double,' I said. 'I've walked as far as I can today.'

Although it would probably have made a difference I was not prepared to tell her that I had artificial legs. The woman would not let me in, so I moved slowly away to look elsewhere for a bed. I was worried that this might be a sign of things to come when I quit the roadside each day. But I need not have worried; I noticed a caravan site across the road, and fortunately the people who ran it had a vacant chalet. They did not normally provide meals, but they took the trouble to bring me some food and tea. As it transpired, almost half of my accommodation was provided free of charge, by people who took me into their hotels, guest houses and homes and refused to accept any money because I was making the walk. In addition, at several places I was undercharged.

The following day was very hot. Within six miles the pain became almost unbearable and I had to call a halt. I felt sick with pain, and disappointed that it had taken more than five hours to move six miles. For someone who planned to walk 900 miles it was not an impressive performance.

The next day was no better; the state of my stumps was deteriorating and I was in a dazed condition all day long with exertion and pain. I decided to rest at a hotel for an extra night, and during the day I sat around while the manager, Mr. Mowatt, his family, staff and customers treated me with great kindness. To economise, I asked for a meat pie in the bar instead of having a meal. Within a few minutes Mr. Mowatt called me up to the bar and presented me with a tray bearing a bowl of soup, a pot of tea, and a plate of steak and vegetables.

'Get that inside you. Do you more good than a meat pie. And put that money away. There's no charge.'

Later I asked him if there was any shop open in the village where I could buy some antiseptic ointment and bandages.

'That will be difficult on a Sunday, but I'll see if someone knows of any place open.'

Five minutes later the receptionist turned up with the medical goods I needed, and refused to take any payment.

On Monday morning, when I was due to leave, Mr. Mowatt had left instructions that I was not to be given a bill.

The first two weeks of walking were filled with pain and the smell of antiseptic ointment. Then my stumps toughened to the punishment they received, though still they broke open now and then. The stumps set the limits. With the walking spread over daylight hours I maintained an average of ten miles a day. To make life easier I put my rucksack on a golf caddy-cart.

For more than a hundred miles the road weaved along close to the choppy sea until, south of Inverness, the highway climbed into wild mountain country. There was snow on the peaks.

Below the snow-capped heads of the Cairngorm Mountains I passed beautiful lochs surrounded by trees with leaves of rich yellows, bronzes, reds, browns and golds. After 170 miles on the road my stumps were still very sore by the time I had walked all morning, but the raw patches of flesh had benefited from daily application of antiseptic ointment, and were healed, or nearly so.

With the rucksack mounted on a golf caddy-cart I received much bewildered scrutiny while trundling up high streets and along lonely country roads.

Inevitably, one question recurred.

'I hope you don't mind me asking, but how did you lose your legs?'

In the planning stage of the walk I had anticipated that this would happen often, and I did not look forward to being asked.

'I was drunk when I was nineteen, and was run over by a train which cut off my legs.'

'Oh!'

The question had to be faced repeatedly, because, naturally enough, people were curious. The alternative was to retreat, to hide, to miss a large part of life itself, for the long walk proved to be a link in a chain which led to some delightful climbing experiences, so it had to be put into words, that the fault was mine; how ashamed I was to say that at first, but it was a comfort that as the fault was mine there was no reason for bitterness against any man. To come to terms with the physical and psychological consequences was up to me. The blame was mine and I just had to get on with living. What I would have given for it to have been the result of a respectable industrial accident or a sporting injury but, no, it had to be lived with. Adjustment, acceptance, were based partly on the thought that in a way it was fortunate that no one else was to blame, for bitterness would have been a great hindrance. I had my fair share of depression, but I simply could not feel bitter or self-pitying because my mind rejected these feelings and put the blame squarely with me. Before long I recognised I would have to come to terms with how it happened; that it had happened was not so difficult to accept. The challenge, psychologically, was greater because of the circumstances of the accident, and someone helped a great deal by saying, 'No one can make you feel inferior without your consent.' That took a long time to sink in, and I can't even remember who said it, but those words were a shield carried from John o' Groats towards Land's End, and quite soon I had no more need of a shield. I had had a small bit of limelight and survived. And above all, mine is a relatively minor handicap; that is a blessing.

On the day of the accident I had intended sleeping rough, partly because I liked the idea and partly because I did not have much money. During the day I found a suitable sleeping place for the night among some trees. When I returned there at night in my drunken stupor I must have walked too far in the darkness through the trees. An awful pain in my chest was probably accounted for by my falling down the embankment of the railway line which, unknown to me, ran through the trees. At some stage I came too, dazed, confused, but somehow not frightened.

My legs were severed, although I did not know it at the time. I realised, without any sense of horror, that something was wrong with me. The pain was no worse than if I had been lightly kicked on my ankle bones, but I felt helpless.

I called for help, and a schoolboy who was out late saved my life by telephoning the police. He had been, for the first time in his fourteen years, allowed to go to the cinema on his own. The film had broken for about ten minutes, so he was later home than he would have been; otherwise he would not have heard me and telephoned the police. They, and the ambulance service, moved quickly into action, and hospital staff worked to save my life.

There were vague patches of consciousness. I saw a white-coated, bearded man leaning over me and I heard him say, 'You'll be all right, son.' He had a glass syringe in his hand.

Later I was wheeled, lying on my back on a trolley, through an archway of red bricks. I felt cold. Then I was in a brightly-lit room. I was embarrassed when a nurse took off my trousers and underpants. She cut the material with scissors to make it easier to remove them. Snip, snip, snip, snip, and my lower half was naked.

It was confusing. Something was surely wrong, yet I could not understand what it was. People seemed to be concentrating their attention on my legs. When I tried to sit up they gently eased me back. There was pain, and that was the only connection this distant and dreamlike scene had with reality. I had been given drugs which reduced the ache in my legs to a bearable level.

Of the operation, naturally, I know only what I was told. The surgeon, Mr. Shields, had to work quickly as I had lost a lot of blood. While the operation was proceeding someone by mistake fetched a trolley from the mortuary to take me away. He was told not to be premature, and I was stitched up and taken to a ward.

After the operation my misty consciousness came back for only a few seconds at a time. A nurse sat at the bedside, watching. She smiled when my drowsy eyes opened. I was glad of her company. I vomited gently, as if I was full and just overflowing. She held a bowl to my lips to catch the black liquid which ran out.

My chest ached badly. The ache reminded me of the time I had indigestion after eating huge chunks of coconut one Christmas when I was about ten years old. I was not aware of much pain in my legs.

Every few minutes I woke up and noticed more of my surroundings. There were screens around the bed and I knew I was in a hospital ward. The nurse gave me a few sips of water from what looked like a small teapot, white, with the spout attached to one side instead of the front.

'Not too much,' she said. 'Just a few sips at a time. How do you feel?'

'Not too bad, thanks.'

At the bottom of the bed the blankets were supported by a tubular metal framework, like a miniature rigid tent frame, to keep them from resting on my legs.

Once I woke up vomiting a green liquid; the next time it was yellow. In this period of drifting into and out of sleep I gradually learned what was wrong with me. There was no definite point at which the fact became obvious, only a slow piecing together of bits of information in such a way that I was fairly aware of the nature of my injury long before I actually knew what it was. By the time breakfast was brought round, I knew for sure that my legs had been cut off below the knees.

The nurse announced that it was eight o'clock in the morning. The operation had been completed six hours earlier and we were in the Amesbury ward of the Odstock Hospital near Salisbury, Wiltshire.

Quite soon the nurse took the screens away from the bed.

'Be back in a couple of minutes,' she said, and left me.

Even though I wanted company I had been waiting to be alone for a few minutes. The patients close to me seemed to be asleep, and I raised the bedclothes and peeped under. There, neatly bandaged, were the two stumps, the strangers with whom I would have to learn to live. Lifting first the right one, then the left, I examined each more closely. It was fortunate that I had come to understand how bad the injury was before I saw the stumps. Although the shock at seeing them was unpleasant it was not as bad as it would have been had I not been prepared. I stared for a few moments until, exhausted, I lay back on the pillows and fell asleep.

Visitors came quite often during my weeks at the hospital. Some of my family drove 180 miles from Cornwall each weekend. Many of my visitors, particularly the older ones, were embarrassed at seeing me, but I was grateful that they took the trouble to visit, and I did my best to make them feel at ease. It is difficult enough for some people to visit a patient who has been seriously injured, but the fact that the majority of my relations were teetotallers made them feel even more awkward with someone who had nearly died as a result of being drunk.

As my body adjusted itself to its changed circumstances the stumps became quite painful. The blood had to find new pathways through which to circulate, since the routes it had taken for many years had been cut off. A feeling rather like intense 'pins and needles' stayed with me all day and night.

The strangest of all the new sensations to which I had to grow accustomed were the 'phantom' pains. I often felt a dull pain in my ankles, although I had no ankles, and it seemed as if the second toe on my right foot was curled underneath the big toe. I would lie in bed for long periods trying to straighten it.

Chats with the staff and patients, meals, cups of tea, bedpans, injections, dressings, books, fruit, the radio and visitors punctuated days which seemed short because I slept much of the time at first.

After several weeks at the Odstock Hospital I was transferred to a convalescent home at Perranporth, on the Cornish coast. The home, which consists of two houses, was set on a hill overlooking the town. There were generally thirty or more patients, over half of them confined to bed.

I had been looking forward to being in Cornwall again because I wanted to be near a girlfriend who lived there. She was eighteen years old, slim and pretty, and I was very fond of her. She had visited me at the

Odstock Hospital, and she became far more important to me than ever before. Would she stay by me after I had lost my legs, I wondered, and I had my doubts. She came to see me within a day or two of my moving into the convalescent home. She was friendly and relaxed. I imagined her helping me through the trials of learning to walk again, but it was not to be. She never came back. It would have been wrong to have expected her to have felt obliged to stay with me, and in hindsight it was a fortunate separation for both of us; but it was painful for me at the time.

My confidence was considerably undermined. I can see now that she must have found me inexperienced and immature, but I could not know if she had left me because of the accident. Uncertainty about how women would react to a disabled man was one of my great anxieties for a long period to come. I need not have worried, for if I was at ease so were they.

A few days later my mind was occupied with an important event. I was to be fitted with pylons, which would enable me to begin to walk long before I was fitted with artificial legs. The pylons were each to consist of a plaster cast fitted round the stump, and a metal extension rather like a peg leg. The opportunity to start to walk again could not come too soon, and it would be many weeks before my stumps were in a state to be fitted with artificial limbs.

My first attempt at walking down a ward at the convalescent home on crutches was a wobbly business after ten weeks in bed, but day by day the increases in the distance I could walk was noticeable. It was satisfying to find that it was impossible not to improve steadily with practice. Rather like cycling, the skill could not be unlearned.

It took two or three days of walking practice before I felt confident to tackle stairs. Concentration was important in walking, and was even more so in climbing or descending stairs. This was the time when I felt most like a mechanical man, ascending and descending with precise, considered movements. Again, continued practice helped, and being able to go up and down stairs brought the outside world within reach.

'You can go into town with the others today,' the sister said. I was surprised, having been practising on pylons for only a week. Four or five hundred yards each way was an exciting prospect. Two hours later I set off on my mini-marathon, with half a dozen patients who could walk quite well. A hobbling procession of men, some with walking sticks, wended its way down the road. Like several hens they clustered protectively around their one crutch-assisted chick. The march to the park took roughly ten minutes, and we sat by the boating lake on a fine August day for an hour, before retracing our steps.

That trip was easier than I expected and was the first of many excursions to the park. For two weeks we all went to the boating lake to hire rowing boats, and soon, instead of going to the park, we walked an extra hundred yards to the seafront.

One afternoon, on the way back from the beach, we passed a tree which looked inviting to climb. I scrambled over a small wire fence to reach the tree, and began. I had to do all the work with my arms and place my pylons carefully, very carefully. After a great struggle I rose only nine or ten feet above ground level, but an important idea was reinforced; when I had artificial legs I would climb.

For some weeks one of the surgeons who visited the convalescent home administered a psychological spur to my progress. He was a short, slightly-built man who looked very serious behind his spectacles. Despite his gruff manner he was kind.

'How far did you manage to walk yesterday?' he asked, shortly after I had been fitted with pylons.

'About fifty paces, sir.'

'I know a woman of seventy who has two pylons. She can walk a hundred paces,' he said, passing along the room to the next patient.

The following week he asked, 'Been up and down the stairs yet?'

'Yes, five times.'

'That old lady I told you about has been up and down some stairs five times as well, but the stairs she trains on are twice as long as these.'

Thus we went on, week by week, with his old lady progressing twice as quickly as me, until one morning in early September he approached me as usual.

'How far did you get yesterday, young man?' he asked.

Before I could reply the staff nurse interrupted.

'Ten feet,' she said. 'Upwards. Up a tree.'

The surgeon smiled and said 'Well done', and we never heard about his seventy-year-old lady again.

Unexpectedly, I was told I could go home. In a way this worried me, because I knew I would miss the companionship which I found at the convalescent home, but I had to go out and face life.

Now, back to the long walk. Day after day the ribbon of road stretched relentlessly away into the distance. When I had walked about 250 miles I met a man who had run from John o' Groats to Land's End, starting a few days before me. He had taken nineteen days and was hitch-hiking home when we met; he came up and introduced himself because he had heard that someone was pushing a caddy-cart to Land's End. Sitting on a window-sill of a derelict house, we had a long talk. His name was Eric Beard, and he was a mountaineer. We exchanged addresses in order to keep in touch and climb together in the Alps; he jotted my name and address in the front of his diary. Several days later he was killed in a motor accident and at the scene of the tragedy the police found his diary – with my name and address on the front page. My wife, Judy, was informed that I was believed to be dead. Fortunately, she knew where I was staying the night and was able to ring me. Just after midnight I was called to the telephone in the pub where I was staying. I heard Judy's voice.

'Norm?' she asked, urgently.

'Yes. It's me Jude.'

'Thank God,' she said, and broke down crying. My father took the phone from her.

'The police have just been here,' he told me. 'They thought you might have been killed in a car accident. Two men were killed this evening in a car which ran off the road.'

On the way up the high road over Shap Fell, in a gale, stinging rain made it difficult to see. It was a relief to retreat into the little wooden transport café at the top of the hill. Walking up to the counter, I was puzzled by a strange slopping sound. When I sat down and lifted one foot to tie a shoelace the cause became evident at once: water poured from the hollow leg. Driving rain had filled both legs, and the lady behind the counter gave me a very funny look as the water cascaded on to the floor! She could not have guessed where it came from.

I enjoyed tramping the quiet roads of the north of Scotland, but there was little romance in walking the verges of busy highways with traffic roaring by, in the south of Scotland and the north of England. But there were always compensations, like a pretty village here and a lake there, rolling hills in the distance, and attractive farmland.

I preferred to travel without publicity over the majority of the walk because I could move more quickly. It was encouraging to be recognised by well-wishers, but I succumbed too easily to the temptation of offers of cups of tea, pints of beer and meals, and lost time as a result. On one day I accepted twelve cups of tea, for the sake of being sociable, at houses and cottages along the way, and spent a long time behind bushes relieving myself. So I was content to be the anonymous stranger who was stared at as he wheeled his little cart down the road, and that was how it was over most of the walk.

Through Kendal, Lancaster, Preston and Wigan. On the way out of Wigan the right stump began to swell. After a mile I had to rest, then again after half a mile. Before long there were stops every fifty yards as the throbbing pain grew worse. On that day I managed only four miles, and had to rest the whole of the next day.

With two-thirds of the journey completed my stumps still split and bled at times, but less often than at the beginning of the walk. Through Tewkesbury, Gloucester, Bristol and Taunton I plodded at an old man's pace. The average daily distance remained at a little more than ten miles, although at times I pushed on for fourteen miles. Sometimes for a week or more there was no escape from the rain or from water splashed up by traffic.

On entering the county of Cornwall I had less than 100 miles to go. I ambled through the little village where my father was born and from where he was taken to live in the local workhouse as a boy, and soon I approached mid-Cornwall, where I had grown up.

Mount Hawke, St. Agnes, Cornwall is a pleasant country area close to the sea. Memory does not produce many details about the neat little whitewashed Meadow Cottage where I was born. The cottage was at the end of a rough hundred-yard farm lane, and I know you could pick oak-apples from a tree in the lane.

My mother used to take my elder sister's dinner to her at the nearby school. Once she made some stew which she put in a basin. We got ready to go out in the rain to the school, but mother knocked the basin from the stove on to the floor. She cried as she knelt and cleaned up the mess. We took another bowl to the school. When we got there the teacher said I could ride on the rocking-horse, and I did.

One day someone said an aeroplane had crashed, and all the men started running across the fields and climbed over hedges. I went after them but they disappeared over the hedges in the distance. I could not find the aeroplane, and had difficulty in finding my way home. Perhaps I was three then.

We had a tame rabbit which ran about in the garden. One afternoon a man came to the door holding it, limp and still. He told my mother that, thinking it to be a wild rabbit, he had shot it. We were all very sad, even though we soon acquired an Alsatian dog, kept in a kennel, which had corner posts stuck two feet into the ground. When guns sounded during the war that dog could drag the kennel on a chain to our back door.

I remember my elder sister and I were throwing stones down a mineshaft near our cottage when an air raid siren sounded. We ran home very fast because the Germans might shoot us or drop bombs on us from their aeroplanes. The Germans did bomb our village, my parents said, though they had been aiming for an aerodrome three or four miles away. The bombs fell in a line up a road and none exploded except the last, which landed in a field and killed a cow.

Some workmen left a pile of stones at the end of our lane. My younger sister and I got very dirty playing with them in our best clothes.

'Flipping kids,' wailed mum.

I am unable to fix any chronological order to these memories, which are almost the only ones I have of the years up till 1944, when we moved to live eight miles away at Truro, a city at that time of 10,000 inhabitants. I was approaching four years then.

My father, who was a driver in the Royal Army Service Corps when I was born, had bought a butcher's shop at Truro, some time after he was invalided out of the army, with extremely bad varicose veins.

We lived behind the shop in Lemon Street. It surprises me that I can remember so little of the seven years I lived in the city, yet I can walk along any of the streets and know where it leads. I am unable to remember being on that street, but I know I have been there. I know that with my macintosh draped over my shoulders and buttoned at the top like a cape I was Batman on some of the streets near home when it was dark. We were cowboys tracking Indians along River Street towards the playing fields at Hendra, where the battle would take place. We became aeroplanes to fly down Lemon Street, and trains to puff-puff up. The Germans were driven back along Charles Street in a tough fight; only one soldier out of five of us could be persuaded to be a German, so the lone German got all the glory in the end. But who was I at Falmouth Road, Daniel Street and Station Hill, and in dozens of other streets? My memory yields nothing about why I travelled most of the pavements, where I was going or what I was searching for. Perhaps I was just exploring; I think I always have been.

We moved to another butcher's shop (recently demolished to make way for a multi-storey car park) and our little back garden was home to many pets. I could take my tortoise from there for walks down Back Lane. Once we walked at least a hundred yards together on a hot summer day. He loved eating nasturtium and pansy flowers, so I sat on garden walls and secretly stuffed flowers in my trouser pockets to take home to Tort. I knew he would die one day, and when he failed to put his head out of his shell as I picked him up one afternoon I knew the end had come. I made a slate headstone which was erected after a funeral with the rest of the family in attendance. We sang 'There is a Green Hill Far Away'. I could never find out who 'Paintsy' was in that hymn. 'We may not know, we cannot tell, what Paintsy had to bear.'

I started with two mice. They did as nature dictated and soon I had dozens. I sold them for threepence each, then sixpence, but eventually tired of feeding and marketing the tiny things, and gave away the whole business to a friend.

A young crow with a damaged wing became my prized companion, partly because I had found and nursed it, but largely because when I took it into a field as soon as it had recovered it followed me home instead of flying away. It would sit on my shoulder. Probably it looked on me as some sort of mother, but unlike its real mother I did not know how to feed it properly, so it died.

The only lizard I ever kept had been rescued, tail-less and bitten, from our cat. I gave it a home in a big biscuit tin in the wash-house. It flitted from twig to twig and darted through the fresh grass and earth I put in the tin. One night it escaped, and I was lucky to find a slow-worm to take over its old quarters. Unfortunately, the cat, after many attempts, caught and killed the slow-worm. I came upon the body bitten in two on the wash-room floor.

A circus put a show on for a week in the Moorfield, a rough field at the bottom of our garden (and now the site of that car park). We children went to the circus and for many days after we had seen the animals, the talk was of circuses, lion-taming and performing dogs. I set about forming my own circus. Worms were useless; there was no trick which they could perform. Woodlice were not easy to handle and were unco-operative and flies always escaped. Caterpillars, however, had potential as performers. They could walk a tightrope, and rear on end on a tiny platform dangerously high above the sawdust ring. Ladybirds were agile and pretty, but were inclined to open their wings and desert their jobs. After a week I lost interest in the circus and set free the performers, even including Sybil, the fortune-telling spider.

Life was enriched by an ample supply of relations, particularly aunts and uncles. Dad had a car in which we took frequent trips to visit them and friends, and we often travelled around Cornwall. Living in a small city meant that we had people around us all day, and that suited me. There were adventurous companions close at hand with whom to go down to the river or to the park or through the woods.

My independence increased when I was given a bicycle, and it enabled me to explore the surrounding area. The beaches, the cliffs, farms, woods and moors became regular haunts. I tried trick cycling one morning, with the result that I was partially blind for a few days after landing on my head in the road. From that day I was an orthodox rider.

At the age of ten a friend and I had a craze for bows and arrows, catapults, spears and pea shooters. We attacked the next door neighbour's cabbages with an assortment of weapons during the day, and crawled into her garden at dusk to retrieve the arrows. Then one day I decided to use my bamboo pea shooter as a blow-pipe. It was simple to fix woollen flights to some pins, and I found that from five or six feet it was easy to hit a match-box with the improvised darts. I lay in bed one night, blowing sudden death at an orange at the foot of the bed. After several successful shots I increased the range. Setting the orange on the floor about ten feet away, I inserted a dart in my blow-pipe, took a huge breath, and blew hard. A woollen flight shot out of the blow-pipe, and fluttered to the floor three feet away. Holding the bamboo up to the light I looked through it. No pin. I coughed into my hand. No pin. I searched the bed and floor. No pin.

'Mum, I think I've swallowed a pin,' I called down the stairs.

'We'll have to search the bed,' she said. 'Flippin' kids!'

We searched the bed and the floor, but I was still one pin short in my armoury. My mother rang our doctor, who instructed her to give me a cotton-wool sandwich. Two pieces of bread with a cotton-wool filling are difficult to swallow, but I managed. My father drove me to the hospital at eleven o'clock that night and an X-ray confirmed that I had swallowed the missing pin.

I was admitted to the surgical ward right away. In order to keep the food firm in my digestive system I was not allowed any liquids for the five days I spent in the hospital. On the second day someone did give me a cup of tea, but I believe that was by mistake. Visitors were instructed not to give me juicy fruit, and my meals were examined to see that they did not contain much in the way of liquids. At first it was interesting to be in hospital, but thirst soon clouded my impressions. By the fourth day my throat and mouth were too dry for me to eat a piece of bread and butter. The crumbs remained dry when I chewed them, and I could not swallow. I was able later to make that day less unpleasant by surreptitiously sucking the water from my face flannel as I washed. The next day nature took its course and the pin was expelled.

The 11-plus examinations were not the ordeal I expected, and I gained a scholarship to the local public school, Truro School, where my first term began in September, 1952. The place frightened me from the start. The tradition was unfamiliar, the staff and most of the pupils seemed to come from social background distant from mine, and at the age of twelve I lacked the confidence and experience to handle the situation. I took the path of least resistance by conforming and working fairly hard.

At the end of my first year at Truro School my father decided to buy a farm, something he had wanted for a long time. He purchased one on Carn Brea, a 700-feet-high hill near Redruth in Cornwall. The farm consisted of thirty-three acres of land, on which my father kept dairy cattle, pigs and chickens. Carn Brea itself was an interesting hill, with granite outcrops rising from ferns and gorse, with a view of the sea, Stone Age circles, old tin mine workings and even a small imitation castle, used now as a restaurant but deserted most of the time we lived at Carn Brea. It was a place where the imagination of an embryo explorer could run riot, and I explored every inch of the hill, climbing the outcrops, none higher than a two-storey house, but mountains in my mind.

My scholarship to Truro School was for a pupil resident at Truro, so I forfeited the scholarship when we moved to Carn Brea, and entered the second year at the Redruth Grammar School.

Throughout my teenage years I grew more restless and those days of oil lamps, rock and roll, muddy lanes, pigs, manure and hay were clouded with loneliness which I attempted to forget in school books. I was often torn between staying at school to pass examinations, and leaving to begin a job. The advice I received on this matter from teachers was undoubtedly correct: it was better to stay. I knew this was true, but still I was impatient to get my years of study behind me so I could join the adult world. I liked Cornwall, but I yearned to travel to other places. The county was a pleasant backwater which I wished to leave for a few years.

Studious year followed studious year at school and I usually came in the first three in the top stream in the annual exams. My pursuit of knowledge was aimed at gaining higher marks at school and this approach rendered the subjects tasteless.

Outside the classroom were activities which I found healthier. For instance, the P.E. teacher ran a gymnastic club in his spare time. On two evenings a week about twenty of us practised and put on several displays in the district. I captained the team for a while, but I did not like taking any position of responsibility, because I was very shy.

Cross-country running and rugby were two enjoyable outlets for pent-up energy. Our school cross-country teams achieved good results and I particularly liked running. I was even presented with my county colours for a mediocre, no, poor performance in the South Western Counties cross-country championship.

The activities of the school's Air Training Corp squadron were broad and interesting, despite the fact that there was a tendency for the emphasis to be placed on the size of the squadron rather than the quality of the cadets. We fired guns, flew quite often, went to R.A.F. stations for two-week camps, and a small number of us went on a gliding training course where we gained A and B badges, entitling us to fly solo.

My instructor's words after my first kamikaze-style landing are embedded in my mind.

'Son, if you make another landing like that, you'll be sitting on your arse in the grass, in the middle of a pile of firewood,' he said. But I did improve, and his report said 'Worked hard'.

In the summer of 1956 I sat and passed eight ordinary level GCEs and stayed on at school to study for 'A' levels. The majority, in my opinion far too great a majority, of the pupils took science subjects at 'A' level. The trouble was that several people who were not very good at science were persuaded to take maths, physics and chemistry instead of subjects they were better at and enjoyed more. My preference was for English, French, history and geography, but I listened to the propaganda from some of the staff about science being the key to a secure and worthwhile career, and swallowed the bait. I half-heartedly joined the science course, and it was months before I finally accepted that I had made a wrong decision.

The best thing about this period was that I began to climb on a Youth Service course, and alone on the granite outcrops of Carn Brea, and at a flooded quarry near the farm. Going back to the quarry not long ago I was pleased to see that the steep brown wall above the green water looked quite hard. So, there really had been a budding climber inside me back in the days when legs were real. The wall was at the same time a harsh reminder of the agility, the physical ability, which was gone forever, snatched by drunkeness.

The school was restricting me when in the manner of most men I wanted to kill a lion, or win my spurs, or defend the tribe or shoot the rapids. I could not put up with being trapped at a desk or in laboratory. I had no need of an intellectual challenge; I needed a challenge which would stretch me near my limits to help me to grow up. My years at school had softened me, and made me too dependent on people and places that I knew. I had rarely been away from home and did not know how to look after myself.

Not long after I passed physics and failed mathematics and chemistry at

'A' level, I made a big decision. Ignoring any advice to the contrary, I left school and worked on a farm for a few weeks to make some money. Then, with a few pounds in my pocket and a small suitcase of clothing I left home.

I had no plans about where I would go except that I intended spending some time in London and some time abroad. To start with I worked as a labourer in a market garden in Exmouth and lived in lodgings, then after a few weeks moved on to work in a piston ring factory at Salisbury, in Wiltshire; I felt that experience of factory work would broaden my outlook. I had no friends in Salisbury as I was there for only four days, but I found plenty of company in the pubs. As it was summertime, I slept out to toughen myself up. I was looking for a lion to kill. In a way I suppose I found one, and it nearly ate me.

Judy and I met four times for weekends during the walk from John o' Groats to Land's End, and she took two weeks off from her job to accompany me through Cornwall. Each evening we were driven back to stay with my parents.

Finally, at Land's End. Fifty or sixty people waited, and as I took the last few paces over granite rocks to the clifftop by the hotel, their clapping and cheering signalled the end of the ordeal, which had lasted ninety days.

Oxfam's director and the chairman of the West Penwith Rural District Council were there to welcome me, the chairman of the Penzance Chamber of Commerce presented a certificate, and the congratulations of the Prime Minister and the Minister for Sport were conveyed by Lord Arwyn.

Jim Smith, my first climbing instructor, had been instrumental in organising a civic reception at the St. Ives Guildhall, where Judy and I were introduced to the Mayor and Mayoress. Then we were whisked of to the concert hall for a cheese and wine party at which the St. Ives band played. It seemed strange not to have to leave our hotel room next day and start walking, and for many a night I dreamed I still had a hundred miles or so to walk. But the walk was finished and my stumps were toughened sufficiently for me to contemplate climbing in the Alps.

Before we move on to my Alpine climbing, which began in 1970, I should tell you briefly what happened to me in the intervening ten years since I lost my legs.

Life came to a lull after I left the convalescent home at Perranporth and went home to wait for my artificial legs to be fitted. For two months the days were occupied with making a model aeroplane, reading, occasional trips around the locality by car or bus, and marquetry.

The day came when I was summoned to the artificial limb centre at Plymouth to be measured for my limbs. On 20th December 1959 I received the best Christmas present I have ever had, for that is the day on which my limbs were fitted, six months after my accident.

I spent the evening struggling from one piece of furniture to the next, tottering from a chair to the table three paces away, turning carefully, launching myself at the sideboard and so on, till I was exhausted and sore.

Gradually, I could take longer and longer journeys between the furniture, measured first in paces, three, four, five, and then tens of paces. In a day or two I made short expeditions out of doors with crutches. A few more days passed before I could launch myself away from the security of a wall or a door handle to totter without sticks or crutches along the rough lane which ran beside our house. I fell occasionally but came to no harm.

I was helped at Truro hospital by a physiotherapist, but after two sessions he decided I was getting plenty of practice on my own, and cancelled all further hospital appointments.

The light metal strap-on legs were uncomfortable to wear for long periods at first, so I took them off when I rested. As day followed day, walking became easier. I was fortunate in having a good sense of balance, and youth enabled me to adapt to the physical problems of learning to walk. When my stumps became damaged through too much walking they healed quickly.

Despite difficulty in finding anyone prepared to insure me – in the end I paid a double premium – I bought a motor scooter. That little green machine greatly increased my independence, but I still walked quite a lot for practice.

I took two temporary jobs, one as a laboratory assistant, the other as a clerk in a slaughterhouse, while I waited to see if I had been accepted on a teacher training course. The first of those jobs, started eight weeks after my legs were delivered, took me away from home into digs in another Cornish town. The move to digs was deliberate, forcing me to manage without people fetching and carrying for me all the time.

I had found the first job after an unsuccessful try at the local Labour Exchange.

'As a disabled person,' the man there had told me, 'you could be a lift operator, a car park attendant, a tailor or a watchmaker.'

It must have been obvious that the limited choice offered was not received with enthusiasm, and I think the man took offence. Whether by mistake or in retaliation I don't know (I suspect the latter), but a week later a green card from the labour exchange came by post. It informed me that there was a vacancy I might be interested in, quite close to home – as a hod carrier on a building site! It was a rather ambitious prospect for one so recently disabled.

Shortly after I had ceased to use walking sticks I contacted Jim Smith, and undoubtedly the highlights of that period were the weekends with Jim Smith and other friends on Cornwall's glorious sea cliffs, in fair weather and foul, on solid grey granite.

Soon after my interview with the principal at the Borough Road Teacher Training College at Isleworth, Middlesex I was informed that I had been accepted for a three-year course commencing in September, 1961.

Part way through the first term we were sent on a teaching practice. I spent three weeks in a junior school and found it difficult to cope with the standing and walking involved, and picking my way between the tiny desks and chairs and little feet was very tiring. At the end of the day I used invariably to get back to college, fall asleep in a chair and miss tea because I was sleeping. Whenever I am asked to counsel leg amputees, I remember those days; it takes time to become accustomed to artificial limbs.

I joined the college climbing club but was discouraged from taking part in their activities, so I climbed only when I went back home at weekends once or twice a term; several years later the secretary of the club contacted me to apologise abjectly for his attitude. How times have changed! Similarly I was refused permission to use the college gymnasium; it will be too dangerous, I was told. Weight-training, exercises – dangerous? Then came a fifty-mile walk during rag week. I can walk a few miles a day and cover the distance, I thought, but the organising committee rejected my entry. Since you already know of my subsequent long walk you will appreciate the irony of that little story. I mention these incidents not as a complaint but to illustrate how attitudes, including mine, have changed in a few years; I did not press my case.

One day a fellow student, John, asked if I would like to go to a party at Berridge House, a domestic science college at West Hampstead, where his girlfriend, Sue, was a student. I said yes. Sue was waiting with a friend called Judy. While John and Sue chatted, Judy and I went through the usual routine of polite questions like, 'What subjects are you studying?' and 'Did you enjoy your last teaching practice?' and 'What do you think of London?' Why she didn't faint with boredom, I don't know.

At the party, Judy wanted to dance. I told her to go ahead if she wanted to, but I would sit as I had slightly hurt my leg in an accident. We sat and talked all evening.

When Sue rang John at college they arranged to invite Judy and me out for the evening. Judy was rather upset at first because one of the students at her college told her about my legs in a very tactless manner. A sentence something like 'Imagine a little legless trunk rolling around' disturbed Judy more than learning of the nature of my disability. However, we had a nice evening, and over the next few days John's car could be seen nightly tearing along the North Circular Road bearing us to and from Berridge House.

At the end of the first year at college Judy went to her parents' home in Staffordshire and I went to Cornwall for the summer holiday. We wrote to each other regularly and arranged for her to spend two weeks in Cornwall at the end of the holiday.

In the meantime I found a holiday job selling home-made ice-cream in a shop near the beach at Perranporth. It was a pleasant labour selling cornets and lollies from two o'clock each afternoon till eight o'clock.

Judy arrived for her holiday. We had a grand time, travelling around Cornwall on my scooter, and at the end of her two-week stay we were both looking forward to returning to London so we could be near each other again.

After my second teaching practice, in a secondary school at Northolt, I decided I had made a mistake in choosing to teach. Hours of standing and walking created a very wearing pain in my right leg. Nowadays when I am tired I am reminded of the strain of my first two or three years of walking with artificial legs. I am glad that time is behind me; but I should point out that part of the trouble was that I was very active, and generally speaking anyone with a sedentary job will manage. As well as that, things get easier as the years go by, as you will see if you read on; and I know now that I could cope with the standing and walking which teaching would have required. On top of that, the pain in my right stump was not normal and could probably have been corrected surgically if I had abandoned my 'grin and bear it' attitude, and complained.

Near the end of my second year at the college the principal and I talked over the situation. He was considerate, and we agreed it would be best for me to leave college.

I was soon embarked on an entirely different course in life, as a social worker at St. Martin-in-the-Fields church in Trafalgar Square. It is tempting to cite examples of people who evoke a ready sympathy, for those were many, but the truth is that most of the smelly, inadequate, demanding, manipulative, insane, drunk, aggressive, violent, disorganised, confused people we dealt with would rapidly evaporate the sympathy of most who met them. And that was why we were there, to catch the people who had fallen through the network of our ability to readily understand and respond in sympathy, to try to communicate with those who were outside the normal regimes of employment, of housing, of social and health care. Though men and women often came just for a meal voucher or an item of second-hand clothing, we tried, whenever it was appropriate, to connect them with bodies such as hospitals, sheltered homes and specialist welfare organisations which had time for them, and expertise. Some were on the run from the police, many were mentally ill, a proportion were mentally handicapped, and a large number suffered from severe personality disorders. Many slept out all year long, under Charing Cross railway bridge, in parks, in doorways and in unoccupied buildings. They preferred such places rather than the dormitories where coughing, groaning, mumbling, screaming, snoring sleepers disturbed the night, and some just did not like being close to others in hostel dining rooms and dormitories. A few had been thrown out of the hotels because they were incontinent, and those who were on the run sought the anonymity they believed came from having no address.

As well as the homeless single people and hostel dwellers who came to the church, quite often families arrived as a result of referral by social workers, for food and other assistance which became necessary because of desertion, ill health, bereavement, and even fire damage. With vouchers we could supply railway tickets, clothing, accommodation, workmen's tools, medical and toilet goods and food.

Judy and I married in Staffordshire in 1967 and lived in the vicarage. We enjoyed being in such a central position and our windows at the top of the building gave a view of the meetings, demonstrations and celebrations which took place in the Square. Judy taught domestic science for a few months, then joined the Office of Population Censuses and Surveys, where she has remained for over twenty years.

After a couple of years at St. Martin-in-the-Fields I began to work more and more with the young people who drifted around the West End, particularly with the hippies and heroin and cocaine addicts; many of the latter were obtaining their drug supplies, at least in part, on prescription from a few general practitioners who prescribed indiscriminately for profit by making a charge for writing a prescription. By selling a proportion of the drugs so obtained, and in many cases through homosexual and heterosexual prostitution, by mugging (at that time referred to as 'rolling', but the same nasty crime) and sometimes by work, they raised sufficient for the next prescription charge. Soft drugs, as they were called, were widely taken as well.

I worked around Soho, Piccadilly Circus, Trafalgar Square, Covent Garden and adjacent areas by day and by night, with a small band of co-workers who mostly worked for six months in the West End. In any week in summer we were asked by parents, hospital staff and social workers to trace four or five young people who had gone missing. We made contact with about half of those we were looking for, which is as much as can be expected considering the circumstances we worked in, and remembering that many of the people we wished to find never in fact came to London.

Though we were instrumental in re-uniting scores of children with their parents, happy endings were not inevitable; but this was an important facet of our work. As well as that we generally tried to counsel young men and women about the hazards of the West End, sometimes we found them employment or accommodation, and we made arrangements for them to receive various forms of social and health care.

In one month three young people I knew died of drug overdoses. Two of them, both women, were buried in adjacent graves; I had escorted the mother of one of them to a mortuary for her to identify the body of her twenty-year-old daughter. I had come from a sheltered life in Cornwall, but work in London had made me grow up. I had seen too much of the ugly side of life, had witnessed much suffering, and at the end of four-and-a-half years at the church I was exhausted, partly physically, because of the peripatetic nature of my work, but mostly because of the emotional demands put upon me. I was depressed, but something good came of that, because depression spurred me into making a big change in my life. Judy was concerned, and patient, and needed to be, to go along with my next project, which was to walk from John o' Groats to Land's End.

While at the church I had climbed occasionally on rock outcrops near Tunbridge Wells, and with Peter, a colleague from St.-Martin-in-the-Fields, had climbed Tryfan. That ascent led me towards the thought that a long walk would be good preparation for more mountaineering, so when I felt the time to leave the church had come, the prospect of the John o' Groats to Land's End walk seemed more than just attractive, it seemed part of my destiny. The long walk served its purpose. It raised £1,140 for Oxfam and toughened me, and particularly my stumps, sufficiently to contemplate some lengthy mountain treks. If ever there was a time when alpine climbing was physically within my ability it was after my stumps had survived the harsh treatment they received over 900 miles; so I *had* to go to the Alps.

# 2

# *To the Alps*

Though his parents were against the idea, I talked a Cornish climbing friend, Mike, into coming to the Swiss Alps with me in the summer of 1970. We drove there in his mini-van.

A mountain railway carried us one morning up the steep track and through tunnels carved through mountain rock to the Jungfraujoch, a pass of over 11,000 feet, between the Jungfrau and the Mönch (Joch means pass). Built into the mountainside was a hotel, and a cheaper twenty-two bedded bunkhouse in which we stayed. From the Jungfraujoch climbers ascend many snow-covered mountains including the Jungfrau and the Mönch. Far, far above us stood the imposing Jungfrau, coated mostly in snow, but with small brown patches of rock showing. Rumbling avalanches slid down the steep eastern face from time to time, and at the base dark crevasses lay ominously across the glacier which had to be crossed to reach the mountain.

All the climbers we met were equipped with skis, and they explained that the snow was remaining soft later than in most years. Attempting to reach the Jungfrau on foot was out of the question, but we were told that the Mönch was accessible. The Mönch, 13,449 feet was close so we settled for that mountain. Allowing a full day to acclimatise to the rarer atmosphere, next day we did no more than walk a little way to inspect the glacier approach to the bottom of the route we hoped to take. There was no hesitation in our decision; the next day we would climb. The barometer was rising, and all the climbers in the bunkhouse looked forward to fine weather the next day.

When that day arrived we had breakfast at 3.30 a.m. and began to trudge to the Mönch at 4 a.m. Mist intermittently swirled around the mountain tops which could be seen easily in the bright dawn light. In thirty-five minutes we were at the foot of the south-east ridge, up which we intended to climb. How nervous, how excited I felt as we began to plod up the forty-degree snow slope at the foot of the ridge; after rising about 200 feet we crossed stretches of rock separated by snow.

We walked and climbed with no rope at first on the easy lower part of the mountain. The rocks were covered with good footholds and handholds, and until the sun had been shining on the snow for an hour or two our boots crunched with each step upward on the white carpet. As the morning wore on the snow softened and our soles sank deeper.

After three hours of steady progress we estimated that we were over half way up the mountain. We tied our rope on for safety, and moved one at a time while the stationary climber remained still, and tied to his ice-axe rammed deep in the snow. The comments of some climbers came back to me: the Mönch is not difficult to climb, but it is a little dangerous; if you fall you will fall a long way. In some places a slip, if not halted by rope or ice-axe, would have sent us tumbling and slithering five or six hundred feet.

Ahead of us on the mountain stretched the tracks of a party of three which took six hours the day before to reach the summit and return to the bunkhouse, and they had moved speedily on the lowest snow on skis. I estimated that their performance indicated that I would need twelve hours for the return journey, and that was rather long for me to keep going in those days.

At about 9.15 a.m. we struggled up a snow ridge which flattened out into a broad shoulder. We had been climbing and walking for five hours.

The slight mist cleared and the summit was suddenly visible, separated from us by a gently rising snow ridge. We slowly made our way in the direction of the top of the Mönch, a matter of a few minutes' walk away. We were within about three hundred feet of the summit when we halted. The ridge was corniced all the way, and I began to feel uneasy. The sun had been beating on the snow for several hours, and we were concerned that it was insecure. A painful decision faced us. The summit was about three hundred feet away and no more than fifty feet above us. The way was easy, but dangerous, and despite our intense desire to reach the summit, we felt unsure about going on. Ambition and enthusiasm tugged us upwards while caution and a feeling of risk pulled us downwards. We did what was sensible; we turned back. The Mönch is 13,499 feet (4,099 m) high. We reached about 13,450 feet, so we failed. But it was a successful failure, to climb almost all the way at a time of year when the snow was not in its best state. I was not greatly disappointed, for though we had not quite made the summit I had done enough to know that one day the Alps could be mine.

The final mile of snowfield on the way back was very soft. Our boots sank a foot with each stride, and once my right leg sank up to the top of my thigh. Eleven hours after leaving we were back in the bunkhouse.

'In three or four weeks the snow will be good,' several climbers told me. I could not stay that long because of the expense, and anyway Mike wanted to return to England immediately. But I made up my mind that one day soon I would try to climb the Jungfrau.

At home I felt very relaxed at first. My left stump took ten days to heal where the skin was broken, but that was a very small sacrifice for the thrill of the climb.

Within two or three days of arriving home Judy and I were planning another jaunt to Switzerland in August. For the first week of our holiday we intended to stay in the bunkhouse at Jungfraujoch while I climbed, and for the second week Judy could take the reins and lead wherever she wanted to go. No experienced climber I knew wanted to go to the Bernese Oberland in August, so I had to be prepared to pay for a guide if I could not find anyone else to climb with at Jungfraujoch.

Judy and I travelled overnight by train, arriving on 26th July at Grindelwald. I went straight to the mountain guides' office there that morning and asked about hiring a guide for the Jungfrau.

'The snow is still bad on the Jungfrau,' the girl in the office said. 'The bad winter has left a lot of snow and the hot weather has made it softer than usual. The guides are not taking people up there often this summer. It is too dangerous. The risk of avalanches is great.'

There was a sinking feeling in my stomach. My hopes were almost dead. I was dismal and it seemed a waste of time to ask if she could find me a guide. However, I pressed on, explaining about my legs and asking her to try to secure a guide who would take someone whose climbing would be very slow. The girl did her best, but the man she contacted was prepared to take me up a small local mountain and no further.

Judy and I dejectedly left the office and went for a cup of tea while we thought the situation over and tried to resuscitate my shrivelled expectations. It seemed that I would have to wait for another year, but we decided to go to the bunkhouse at Jungfraujoch for a few days in case the snow improved.

When we reached the bunkhouse several people said they had climbed the Jungfrau that day, and they had taken up to seven hours to complete the wearying journey on very soft snow.

The following three days we spent in walking through the snow and looking at the beautiful, clean mountain and glacier scenery and the brilliant blue sky. Over those three days we gleaned information from other climbers. We pieced together opinions and impressions and formed a picture of the state of the surrounding mountains. The Mönch return trip was as short as four-and-a-half hours for the speediest men, and that meant I had a good chance of climbing it right to the top. Even if I could not go up the Jungfrau I could attempt the mountain which just beat me a month before.

I could find no one in the bunkhouse to climb with, so on Thursday I asked the hotel manageress, Frau Sommer, if she knew any guides. Fortunately her husband, Ueli Sommer, the hotel manager, was prepared to act as a guide for me on the Mönch, and we arranged to climb early on Friday morning.

Friday came. I had breakfast at four o'clock and fifty minutes later the muscular, sun-tanned Ueli Sommer and I stepped out into light snow. I suppose Ueli was about thirty-five years old. He was chief of the local ski patrol at Kleine Scheidegg and knew the local mountains intimately.

The going was good over the gently sloping snow and while we took a brief rest at the foot of the ridge we were to ascend I thanked him for not refusing to climb with me.

'I have a friend with an artifical leg, and he goes all over the place around here,' he said.

'But I thought you might be a bit worried about guiding someone with two artificial legs.'

He raised his eyebrows and stared at me briefly.

'Two?'

'Yes, two.'

'Oh, I didn't know. I thought it was one. Anyway, we had better be on our way. Tie the rope on.'

The gently falling snow shower ceased, but the mist remained to hide the peaks. I was not interested in the view anyway as I toiled upwards over patches of snow and rock. Two or three times Ueli cut steps in the ice, but generally there was only rock or firm snow to climb.

By 6.30 a.m. it was warm enough for me to remove my jacket. We were making, for me, good progress and were about half way up the mountain. Ueli went ahead, up short steps of rock, and we reached the shoulder where the final long snow ridge started. Mike and I had stood there wondering whether or not we should continue, but this time there was no need to argue, for Ueli continued in his easy strides in the direction of the summit.

The final 200 yards to the top now looked firm, safe and innocent. We reached the spot where Mike and I had decided to turn back, and Ueli and I passed by.

I was carefully watching where I was placing my feet and long ice-axe when we came to a level patch of snow about the size of the floor of a large room. It looked like the summit.

Ueli stopped and slipped his rucksack from his shoulders.

'Is this it?' I asked, hardly daring to hope that it was.

'This is it.'

The mist was patchy and obscured the view, apart from occasional glimpses of the Mönch's snow-covered neighbours; but the future was bright and rosy in my mind, for I knew I would spend as much time as possible among these monarchs.

I sat on my rucksack for a ten-minute break. It was twenty minutes past eight, so in all we took three and a half hours. Not bad.

The next two days I rested. Climbers returned from the Jungfrau much more quickly than a few days previously. The weather remained good. My stumps were in fine condition. After climbing the Mönch I was acclimatised to the altitude. Everything had slotted into place to give me an opportunity to attempt the Jungfrau.

Ueli could not go, because he had already been engaged by another climber, but he contacted an older guide called Hans Almer. Hans, looking as weather-beaten as an old seaman, was a man of few words, but the words he said were sweet music for me.

'Yes, I can go up the Jungfrau with you. Start at two o'clock tomorrow morning.'

I awoke at one o'clock and dressed in darkness. Hans and I had breakfast and at two o'clock we were standing in the snow near the bunkhouse. In the flickering, yellow light thrown by Hans's candle lantern we looked around us. The sky was cloudy and it was raining. I was keyed up for action but the weather conditions were not good.

'We must wait two hours and see what the weather is like,' Hans said before going back to his bed in the hotel. Perhaps I would have to wait till next year after all.

Hans left me in the hotel lounge, where I could get some sleep, then sleepy-eyed and silent, he re-appeared to tie on the rope and lead me out into the weak daylight at 4.15 a.m. The weather was good.

We descended a steep slope of a hundred feet of snow, crossed a narrow crevasse by stepping over it, and started out on the hour-long walk south-westwards across the glacier. Within an hour we were strapping our crampons to our boots as several groups of climbers caught up with us. At the bottom of the thirty- to forty-degree snow slope were congregated about thirty quiet climbers in all.

For the next thousand feet in height we heaved our bodies up inclined snow which in one place steepened to sixty degrees or more. Two ice-axes helped me. A bergschrund, the name given to the large crevasse which forms between the mountaintop snowfield and the glacier it feeds, gave us no trouble because many people had already found a safe and easy way over its jumbled, broken chunks of ice. My hands began to ache with the effort of tightly gripping two ice-axes, but soon we were able to rest at the Rottal Sattel, a saddle between the Jungfrau and a nearby peak, the Rottalhorn. We were then 12,750 feet high.

Turning north-westwards from the Rottal Sattel, we walked along fairly level snow to the easiest ridge of the Jungfrau. When we arrived at a stretch of brown rock curving upwards into the distance, I grew excited. People had told me that there was a 200 feet length of gently sloping rock to climb just before the summit. I was panting, sweating and tired, and reluctant to ask Hans if we were on the last bit of rock because of the mental setback to be borne if we were not. I kept my eyes down on the rock immediately in front of me and pulled myself gradually higher.

I heard voices above me, and looked in their direction. Nearly thirty people sat in a group on the rocks fifty feet away. They were relaxed, eating, drinking and chatting, so I knew they were at the top.

Two minutes later I was beside them. After months of hoping and planning, I had climbed the Jungfrau. We were 13,642 feet (4,158 m) high, and had taken four hours and five minutes to get there. Hans seriously shook my hand and congratulated me.

It took nearly six and a half hours to descend carefully to the bunkhouse. I was touched to find that three holidaymakers from the north of England had waited, shivering in the cold air for a long time, just to shake my hand.

There was time then to relax. I decided I could now call myself a mountaineer, and that pleased me greatly.

From the first rock climb with Jim Smith in Cornwall to reaching the summit of the Jungfrau nearly a decade had gone by. It took that long to turn a disabled man into a mountaineer, and then only into a beginner. I thought at the time that I had reached a target and a terminus. But the call of the mountains is strong, and far from being at a terminus I was only a short way along the journey. I had dabbled with the peaks and now I found it hard to manage without them. My mountaineering life was just beginning.

Climbing became increasingly important and soon Judy and I agreed that my career would have to take a second place for a while to two ambitions; at the same time as progressing as a climber I hoped, particularly through writing, to do something towards creating opportunities for other disabled people in outdoor pursuits. I wanted them to have the chance to find the enjoyment I had found, not necessarily in climbing but in any outdoor activity they choose, like camping, rambling, angling, gliding or canoeing. Competitive sports for people with certain handicaps had been promoted for several years, but, with few exceptions, non-competitive sports had been neglected. It was time for suitable non-competitive sports to be promoted too, not instead of, but as well as, competitive games.

Judy remained in her civil service job while for a few years I was employed in the Post Office, at an accommodation agency, as a social worker, in the civil service, washing up in a hotel, at any work which would fit in with the timetable. Often I felt uncomfortable about this way of life but Judy rarely wavered in her conviction that for a few years climbing and the creation of opportunities for other disabled people should take precedence. She was patient with her restless husband over several uncertain years. A prime consideration was to allow sufficient free time in summer to train and if necessary to wait for the right weather conditions; the latter proved to be a key factor in the events which followed.

Looking back I can see that greater attention paid to earnings, career and security could have cost me the dearest ambitions, but it was not always easy to see that at the time. Similarly, if Judy had been more materialistic I might have failed in those ambitions. What a change it was from my former way of life, at St.-Martin-in-the-Fields Church. Now, periods of low wages meant that we had little money, but we saved what we could towards climbing trips. Our home was a bedsitter in Ealing, London. Perhaps we were materially poor at times, but only by comparison within our consumer society. Judy was happy with our arrangements, whereas many times I questioned whether I should place more importance on regular employment and career prospects. But mostly we felt as if we had no choice, that it was inevitable that our lives would take a certain course.

At the beginning of my climbing life rock climbs were graded according to their difficulty; Easy, Moderate, Difficult, Very Difficult, Severe, Very Severe. Modern equipment and techniques have led to the introduction in recent years of higher grades, so my efforts while climbing Severe and occasionally Very Severe routes would nowadays be seen as rather tame to hard climbers; but I do not mind if my efforts fail to impress them.

In the winter of 1970–1, Peter, with whom I climbed Tryfan, and I tried to decide on a satisfying alpine route which we could manage in the summer. By December the target was vaguely fixed; we would attempt a long, high alpine route involving at least two days of climbing. The Jungfrau was a high route, but it was not entirely satisfying because the climbing started at a high altitude. We believed that a long route, tackled slowly, could be undertaken by adapting normal climbing methods to my limitations. Many alpine climbs require a full day's activity for an able-bodied climber if he wishes to avoid spending a night in the open at high altitude. Generally, the mountaineer will in a day climb from a hut or some other shelter to the summit of his choice and back again to a bed. Some climbers plan to camp or bivouac at high altitudes so they have time to complete longer and harder routes. Bivouacking differs from camping because a normal tent is not used.

I decided that bivouac equipment could bring many mountain routes within my range and ensure that I never went too far in one day. The idea was to climb just enough in one day, without injury to the stumps, so climbing could be spread over consecutive days. Whenever the skin on the stumps split, further climbing brought very rapid deterioration. Bivouacs would change all that.

The mountain which eventually came to mind is well known: the Eiger. I had seen it many times when waiting to climb the Mönch and the Jungfrau. The three mountains stand together, and I had often felt a little disappointed that I could climb two of them, but not the third. The local story is that the Mönch, or Monk, protects the Jungfrau, the Virgin, from the Eiger, or Ogre. Now it looked as if that third mountain could be within reach. I could acclimatise at the Jungfraujoch, and we could start the climb from the Eiger Glacier station without a hot trek up through the alpine pastures from the valley. Also, I knew some guides in the area and felt that one or more of them might be prepared to climb with me.

I thought two days would be sufficient to scale the Eiger by an easy route in reasonable conditions. The route we had in mind was known as the west flank.

Alpine mountains lie in surrounding areas of very high pastures and forests, so to climb a mountain of 10,000 feet never involves climbing the full 10,000. Generally the mountaineer follows a trail or takes road transport, a mountain railway or a cable car to the highest convenient point before starting to climb. For this reason the height to be climbed on the Eiger west flank, which is over 13,000 feet high, is 5,400 feet. Below the starting point of the climbing are the mountain pastures and tourist walking trails, rich foregrounds to the lovely heights.

We bought bivi-bags, polythene sacks large enough to accommodate a person, for protection against wind and rain. Used in conjunction with warm clothing or a sleeping bag, a bivi-bag is adequate for quite harsh conditions. Bivouac experience was the next necessity, we decided, so in February we charged off to North Wales. Two days before there were radio announcements about roads blocked with snow in the area. We planned to tramp about the snowy mountains for hours and bivouac at night, but it was not to be. I had 'flu and spent two nights shivering in the bivi-bag under a rock, and one day sitting either on a rock in weak winter sunshine, or in a café. Hard-man aspirations thwarted, we returned home. One piece of equipment seemed to be mocking us on the drive back: sticking out from under a jumble of rucksacks, rope and clothing was an implement we had commandeered to speed up digging a shelter in the snow – my mother-in-law's coal shovel.

Amongst other places I visited for bivouac practice was Bleaklow Hill in the Peak District, where the land rises to about 2,000 feet above sea level. It was March 1971.

'Turn right just before the maggot farm,' a water-board man directed. This must be the most unusual direction I have been given.

'Maggot farm?'

'They breed them for zoos and pet shops.'

I strolled along a valley with a fast stream tumbling down the middle, the sort of valley where Lorna Doone might have walked, dreaming of a lover. When in mist I referred to a map and compass; only a few months previously I had been puzzled by some wildly inaccurate compass bearings I had taken while sitting on a rock in North Wales. The bearings just did not correspond with the map, and differed by as much as twenty degrees. It was some time before I realised the cause – the map was spread on my knees and whenever I held the compass near the map the metal in my legs made the needle deviate!

Above 1,800 feet there were patches of snow. I was soon at Bleaklow Head, 2,061 feet and the highest point around there. As night fell the wind grew fierce. I had a meal and huddled up in the bivi-bag. Daylight had almost gone, although it was still possible to see a few yards in the eerie, misty light. The wind screamed and buffeted the rocks. I was really alone, but I never feel lonely on mountains, or in wild country, though I am a gregarious man.

Peter was about to be engaged and it seemed to me that his girlfriend was very nervous about him accompanying me on the Eiger. Reluctance seeped slowly into his attitude, eroding his former enthusiasm, though he said nothing directly to me. His girlfriend did not climb, and I could understand that she might regard mountaineering as a pointless and dangerous pastime, and if so she was more than justified in hoping that he would not risk his life on a mountain, particularly with me. So one day I asked him if he really wanted to go, and he confessed that he had changed his mind. As well as the girlfriend, a friend whom Peter regarded as an uncle figure had dissuaded him from going. The man told me so himself some weeks later, adding that he was sure I realised he was correct. I refrained from pointing out that he had probably done Peter a great disservice by advising him on a subject about which he was ignorant, since Peter was an unconfident man who needed success.

I wrote to Ueli Sommer, whose reply arrived in May. He said he could go, and suggested taking a porter as well. So, if I didn't find another partner in time, I could go to Switzerland and climb with Ueli.

Someone from the South Wales Mountaineering Club offered me a lift to Switzerland; we had met by chance the year before at Jungfraujoch and had kept in touch.

'There are thirteen seats,' he said. 'The thirteenth one has been booked a few times but the lads who book it keep getting things like broken legs.'

'Sounds like it's intended for me. If I break a leg before we go I can change it.'

Although the legs were kept in a good state of repair by the fitters at Roehampton, I could not ignore the fact that breakages could occur on the mountain. I examined each artificial limb closely before and during each long climb, and to add strength I bound the metal legs with strong insulation tape around their weakest points, at the tops of the shins. They would stand up to any amount of walking but climbing put abnormal strains on the metal; by wrapping the insulation tape around in much the same way as you might to strengthen a pick handle, the effect was to protect the metal from cracks, and to slow the growth of any cracks which might form.

What other differences were there between me and an able-bodied climber? Well, each step would cost me more in energy, much more. I would be slower than an able-bodied man and my stumps would be injured if I went too far in one day – in a way the stumps were my Achilles heel. By planning to bivouac I was bringing the route within my personal limits. At least, that's what I thought.

* * *

The packing is finished. I've spent the past hour weighing things of kitchen scales so I can take the minimum possible weight of equipment.

'I'm off now, Ju.'

She doesn't try to stop me climbing. What would I do if she did? I don't know.

'I'm a bit worried, Norm, but I know how much climbing means to you.'

An hour later I was waiting at Victoria Station for the mini-bus hired by the South Wales Mountaineering Club. The vehicle arrived and thirteen people filled the seats and struggled to find room for rucksacks and ice-axes. Within half an hour we had a puncture, so out came the spare wheel. That had two large nails in it already, so we had to buy another at a garage.

At half past four the ailing vehicle was halted near Canterbury because one wheel was groaning. We couldn't find out why. Gloom descended on the company and the mini-bus crawled slowly into Dover. There an AA man inspected the complaining wheel while the seconds ticked away, bringing close the time of the boat's departure at seven a.m. It was a close thing. The AA man adjusted the wheel and while tightening the nuts fell on his head. He picked himself up and said the wheel was all right. There was no time to waste: we all scrambled back into the mini-bus and drove to the boat, leaving the AA man a little dazed and sucking his grazed knuckles. We owe him a tip.

In France we drove with hardly a stop until it was time to camp for the night at Vesoul, quite close to Switzerland. The next day we reached the outskirts of Basle before having another puncture. The tyre was old and useless, which is a polite version of the description applied by several people to the man who hired out the mini-bus. It took a time to find a garage which could supply another tyre on a Sunday, and it was while we were at the garage that one of the doors came adrift from its hinges.

I felt a bit like a rat deserting a sinking ship when I alighted at Zurich to take a train to Grindelwald, but Zurich was the last point from which I could travel conveniently. As I waved goodbye and the vehicle pulled away from the kerb I wouldn't have been too surprised if it had keeled over. In fact the mini-bus reached its destination on the outward journey and needed to be taken to a garage only once to prevent a wheel falling off. On the return journey the cylinder head gasket blew and the transport was abandoned at Dover by all hands.

I proceeded by train to Grindelwald, then took a ticket on the local mountain railway which has the Jungfraujoch Hotel at its terminus. The train clattered up a steep track where the gradient reached twenty-five degrees. Rhododendron bushes and pine slipped by the windows, then there were no more trees or bushes. Rich, green alpine pastures on both sides of the line were speckled with flowers of yellow, pink, red, purple, and blue which matched the sky. Cows nodded and their bells rang while they munched, ignoring the train; familiarity breeds contempt, even of the iron monster.

Kleine Scheidegg, 6,762 feet (2,061 metres), is the crowded interchange where you take another train for Jungfraujoch. From Kleine Scheidegg the train soon disappears into the four-and-a-half-mile tunnel cut right through the Eiger and Mönch. The railway tunnel, opened in 1912, begins at the Eiger Glacier station, a complex of a hotel, husky pens and railway buildings which sprawl along the line. A glacier crevasse was used as a refrigerator for the meat eaten by the hundreds of workers who helped to build the tunnel, and frozen red wine was sold to them by weight. Their labours over fourteen years, involving the deaths of several men, produced a tunnel through which the visitor can rise without effort from the Eiger Glacier station, 7,612 feet (2,320 m), to the Jungfraujoch, 11,333 feet (3,454 m), in less than three-quarters of an hour.

Emerging from the tunnel into the Jungfraujoch station is like drawing up in a long, rough-hewn cave about twenty yards wide. Thirty paces from the platform is the mountainside, which you can reach by walking through a lobby. An observation balcony overlooks the fourteen-mile-long Aletsch galcier, where two glacial moraines make dirty lines, perhaps 300 yards apart, down the centre.

'Must be wheel marks from a truck,' an American told his wife. Some truck! (If you don't know what a moraine is, have a look at the Glossary.)

The hotel hangs from the steep mountainside in the way that a fortress might: much of the building is inside the rock. For the visitor there is a man-made ice cave carved beneath the Jungfraujoch plateau, a souvenir kiosk, a post office, a small summer ski-school, husky dogs fighting each other and occasionally obliging by giving sledge rides, and a 367-foot lift ride to a prominent observation terrace at the top of a small peak.

Ueli came to the dormitory the next morning. I had been expecting to bump into him soon because he divided his time between the Eiger Glacier Station Hotel and the Jungfraujoch Hotel. His speech was slow and careful, and all his movements had that same deliberate quality.

'Ah, Norman. I was not expecting you for a few days.'

'I had a chance of a lift.'

'I am busy now, but we must talk soon.'

'Yes. There's no hurry. I'd like a day or two to acclimatise.'

Despite my eagerness to get on with the climbing, there was no sense in rushing into the headache, nausea and weakness which could result through attempting an exacting climb without being acclimatised. Two or three days would be enough to get reasonably used to the lower level of oxygen, one-third less at Jungfraujoch than at sea-level.

It was two days later that we had an opportunity to talk, in the restaurant.

'I think round about Tuesday it may be all right, if the weather is good,' Ueli said. That was five days away. 'On Tuesday there will be a good moon so we can start early. I will look for someone to go with us. I believe you should have two people with you. I think you may reach the summit in one day. Then we can come down and bivouac. Of course, we must wait for perfect weather.'

He left for a few minutes, then came back and introduced a young man in his mid-twenties.

'This is Treas Schlunegger. He can go with us. So it is all settled, if the weather is good.'

The days crept by, and hardly a cloud passed over Jungfraujoch without me glaring at it. On the whole the weather was good. Monday came, and at midday I began to pack my kit to take it by train down to the Eiger Glacier Station Hotel, from where we would start climbing the next day at about one a.m. Then Ueli came into the dormitory.

'I have just been on a rescue on the Eiger, on the west flank,' he told me. 'We had to bring down four people who were caught in a storm. I know them and they are good climbers. There is too much ice on the rocks at the top and it is very dangerous. I think we should not go now. Maybe if we have a week or two of good weather the west flank will be all right, but now it is too dificult. Even these good climbers had to be helped down. Luckily they were not hurt.'

I had been expecting bad news because the weather did not look good, but all the same it was a great disappointment.

'I must go now, and we can talk later,' Ueli said.

About four hours later, in the afternoon, I saw him again. He was wrapped in a duvet jacket and was on his way out of the hotel.

'I have to go to the Eiger again, to the west flank. Someone has been killed. We are going by helicopter.'

Next day Ueli told me about the rescue.

'An Englishman was killed and his three companions have been rescued. Conditions were terrible there. One of the men is in hospital in a very serious state. They were well equipped and I think they were good climbers.'

Back at home Judy had heard a news broadcast which said that an Englishman had been killed on the west flank of the Eiger. She knew that I was about to climb and she couldn't help thinking that the dead man might be me. The announcer gave details of the accident, weather conditions, etcetera, while she listened. It was only at the end of the news item that the victim's name was given.

'Now we must decide what you will do,' Ueli said.

'You think it will be a week or two before the west flank is in good condition?'

'Yes. Or perhaps more. It will take a long time for the ice to melt. You must decide what you want to do. It will be a long wait. Or you could try the Matterhorn.'

'I'd like to stay here.'

'All right. Stay as my guest. One person more or less won't make any difference.'

'I'd like to do some work in return. Washing dishes or something.'

'You can wash some glasses, and if you do that you can eat and live with the staff.'

That was very considerate of him, and work would help to pass the time. The routine of putting glasses through the glass-washing machine and drying them, slicing bread and washing spoons and dessert cups, kept me busy for about five hours a day. From the little room where I worked it was possible to keep watch through the restaurant windows on the weather. On the first day of work, Tuesday, it was misty, and on Wednesday and Thursday too. Friday was dull and cloudy and so it went on. The peace of Tuesday evening was broken by thunderous crashes as gigantic purple flashes illuminated the snowscape for miles around in a thunderstorm of frightening intensity. No wonder climbers who had been caught in lightning storms spoke of them with awe! I was scared, and I was in the bowels of the hotel, not at the top.

The next day there was another snowstorm. Time dragged by. It was all mist and long faces. The weather improved a little over a few days.

'But we must still wait until conditions are very good,' Ueli said. 'We must be careful.'

More glasses to wash, more bread to slice, more clouds to fill the sky, day after day. Wait, wait, wait. Improvements in the weather were short-lived. All I could do was wait. The only perseverance I needed had nothing to do with climbing, but with waiting. It was simple – if I did not wait I would not have a chance to attempt the climb that year. Nearly four weeks went by, and I waited. Four weeks! Often it rained or snowed or hailed. I waited still. Then the weather began to improve, and was fine for long enough for hopes to rise. Was this the time, at last?

'We must talk to Treas,' Ueli said one Monday. 'If he is available we can go to the Eiger Glacier station soon. If he is not free I will find somebody else.'

The weather remained good. Later that day I saw Ueli again.

'While the weather is good you must take the opportunity,' he said. 'I have seen Treas and he can go on Wednesday. Unfortunately I cannot go myself on that day, but Treas will find another guide.'

Treas and I sat in the restaurant to make plans the same day.

'We go to the Eiger Glacier station tomorrow,' he said. 'I will contact another guide to go with us.'

'He will have to understand that we will need to bivouac.'

'We will see. I have to go into the army the next day.'

'We climb on Wednesday and you go into the army on Thursday?'

'Yes.'

'But I can't get up and down in a day.'

'We will see. Maybe you will go very fast and go up and down in a day.'

'No. It will take me at least two days. It will be dangerous if I try to go too far in a day.'

'Perhaps the other guide can stay with you.'

'It's no good me rushing,' I emphasised. 'I can only do this if I take at least one and a half days and bivouac for one night.'

'We will see what happens,' he said evasively.

I weighed up the situation. It was possible that we could reach the top in a day and Treas could descend to the Eiger Glacier station while the other guide and I bivouacked. The two of us could then descend the next day. I wanted to pin down Treas and the other guide to more definite arrangements, but it turned out that there would be no opportunity to meet the other guide until an hour or two before beginning to climb. The plans were not satisfactory because they were indefinite, but they were not sufficiently vague to cause me to cancel the arrangements. We planned to start climbing shortly after midnight on Wednesday, 25th August.

On Tuesday I packed my equipment and went down by train to the Eiger Glacier Station Hotel. It turned misty during the afternoon and I doubted that we would climb. Another delay looked likely so I didn't feel very excited. Still, I went to bed very early in the evening in case the weather improved.

Treas woke me at two a.m. The sky was clear and starlit.

'We can go,' he said.

I hurriedly put on my legs, hoisted my rucksack and went to join Treas and the other guide, Robert, for breakfast. Robert was about the same age as Treas, in his mid-twenties. He was bearded, softly spoken and smaller than Treas. He didn't speak much English, but anyway at that time of the morning we were mostly silent. Who wants to talk at two in the morning, when sober?

We sat around a coffee table in their hotel room and drank tea. Knowing that later I would be glad I had eaten, I forced down a few slices of bread and jam, for energy. Ugh! Fifteen or twenty minutes went by before we pulled on warm outer clothing, slipped our rucksacks on and tramped to the front door of the hotel. The air outside didn't feel very cold. There was no wind and hardly any cloud.

'We put the rope on here in the light,' Treas instructed, and we tied on to the rope, me in the middle and Robert at the rear, with three or four yards of rope between Treas and me. He lit a candle lantern and Robert produced an electric torch.

'Ready?' Treas asked me.

'Yes.'

So, here at least was a chance to see if I could get up the third of that great trio. It was nearing three o'clock. He led off up the rocky track which ran for a few yards beside the railway, then it went to the right of the tunnel. I found once more that walking in dark surroundings was difficult. People with feet can keep their balance in the dark partly because of leg and foot muscles telling them which way the ground is sloping. My dead feet told me nothing, so the eyes became more important for giving information about any alteration in the slope and nature of the land. My eyes could glimpse the stars, a few clouds and the dark, looming outline of the Eiger, but mostly they had to remain on the mobile patches of light cast on the uneven track by the candle lantern and the torch. In an hour or so it would get lighter and as the mountain steepened I would be able to use my hands as well – then there would be no balance problem.

The track continued along a moraine, the broken rubble which collects on the edge of a glacier. An avalanche crashed and rumbled down the mountain to our right, a long way away. We came to natural steps of black rock which was wet and slippery. There were easy ways to choose through this section but it was not simple to pick the route in the dark; straying to the left or the right would have made the going much harder. Robert and Treas engaged in much discussion about the route as we picked our line up the rock, and now and then we retraced our steps to find an easier way. In daylight there would have been a fairly obvious route to follow.

Slowly the mountain silhouettes took form, to become three dimensional as light fell on faces, snowfields, ridges. Eyes, fixed on rock, on snow, on anything still, were like a long visual arm stretched out to help balance. Wherever possible I kept both hands on the rock, for steadiness and power. Sometimes when Treas and Robert walked upright it was better for me to scramble on all fours, like a chimpanzee, especially on loose plates of rock which clinked like chunks of cast-iron as we walked over them. Within an hour of leaving the Eiger Glacier station, Treas extinguished the candle. The sky was light in the east, still dark in the west. The rock was just discernible, sloping on average at about forty degrees. There were a few steep steps of six to eight feet but the climbing was easy.

Half past four. The absence of cloud was encouraging. Thick mist masked the valleys, but that was nothing to worry about. We carried on over a long slope of small stones to the base of a snowfield which looked as if it had a gradient of about thirty degrees. Here was crampon territory, so we sat to strap the spikes on our boots. Treas, being in the lead on the rope, cut steps in the snow and ice to make it easier and safer. The ice was very hard in parts and required several stokes of the ice-axe to make a reasonable step, big enough to take nearly half a boot. Chop, chop, chop, chop. This was a restful period for me because there were a few seconds between each pace upwards. Plates and chips of ice slithered down as Treas chopped.

A beautiful pink glow spread over the white snows of the Jungfrau, backed by a sky of light blue. It was one of those superb moments that may suddenly strike the mountaineer as soon as he has a chance to take notice of his surroundings, when he reaches a summit and relaxes, or strolls on an easy path, or stops to put on an extra sweater. When there is time to look around, the mountains can in a moment remind you that just being among them is part of the fun.

The snowfield was several hundred feet long and it took half an hour to climb. We continued up more rock as soon as our crampons were off. The limestone here was fairly steep and we traversed to left and to right along ledges to choose the best route, rather than taking a direct line up the tiers. We climbed two or three hundred feet up and took another short rest. As we moved on we came upon verglas, a thin coating of ice making the rock look as if someone had attempted to preserve it under a layer of glass. There was no way to avoid the verglas so caution was needed with every move, whether when walking along a ledge or climbing upwards.

How would I regard the climb if I had legs? My viewpoint of any route was coloured very much by disability. I had embarked on a serious expedition and was four hours away from civilisation; the trip was not undertaken lightly. Yet a fit mountaineer could trot up to where I was in an hour and a half. He could have set out at the same time as me, climbed to the same height, returned to the Eiger Glacier Station Hotel and been in bed for an hour or more. For him, a bit of exercise before breakfast; for me, a journey which was exploring my limits. Anyone who is blasé about the danger on even the easiest of high mountain routes is either foolish or inexperienced, but the fact remains that the able-bodied man does not need to approach a route with quite the same serious consideration – he would not take two guides on the Eiger west flank, for instance. (Nor would I, now.)

We arrived at the Frühstückplatze (Breakfast Place), a level area of rock where climbers often stop to rest and eat, about two thousand five hundred feet about the Eiger Glacier station. Less than three thousand feet of height to be gained. I felt fine. We sat down and looked across at the precipitous North Wall.

'I think you should not bivouac,' Treas said. He pointed to the summit of the Jungfrau. 'See how the snow is blowing. The wind is too strong.'

I had noticed the plume of wind-blown snow which streamed from the head of the Jungfrau. Obviously the wind was quite strong high up, even though the sun shone in a clear sky and we were in only a light wind.

'I have been on this mountain before and there is nowhere up there to bivouac,' Treas added. Either he was lying, or he required a palatial place to bivouac.

'People bivouac quite often on the west flank,' I said. Especially the English, I thought ruefully, many of whom were slow, once a year alpinists, laughed at by the experienced French, Swiss, Germans and Austrians, who could visit the Alps for weekends.

'It is not good with this wind. On the ridge up there we could be blown away,' Treas countered, changing tack.

'We will not be on the summit ridge today.'

Robert sat in silence. I wasn't sure that he understood what was going on. I had climbed slowly but even so at the rate I was going we had a good chance of getting two-thirds of the way up the mountain in another two hours. Even though the climbing might be a little more difficult, I could keep up the same speed. In daylight and with plenty of time we could find a good bivouac site, I felt sure, and from two-thirds of the way up the mountain I should reach the summit the next day.

'We must not waste our lives,' Treas remarked. 'You have no feet and you don't want to lose your hands as well.'

Cheeky monkey, I thought.

For several seconds I said nothing and stared at the rock at my feet. I was angry and extremely disappointed, and I considered going on alone, but that would have been stupid. There was no alternative but to follow Treas's advice. Without companions the climb would have been too dangerous, and it was obvious that it was useless to argue with Treas. He had been reluctant from the start to talk about bivouacking.

'We can go a bit higher so you can take some photographs of the North Wall,' Treas said. 'There is a good view from a bit farther up. Then we must go down.'

Thanks for nothing, turd. He had little or no idea what this climb meant to me. I was merely a source of income.

How about going up farther and then saying I was too tired to descend? No, they would start to talk about a rescue party, or Robert could flatly refuse to go any higher the next day.

'Damn it! Damn it! Damn it!' I said in a murmur to myself. Disappointment tempered my anger, leaving only a slight feeling of annoyance. There was no point in making a fuss.

'If we're not going up to the top we might as well go down now,' I said.

Treas took a radio from his rucksack and spoke into it to let someone at Kleine Scheidegg know that we were returning. A few words in acknowledgement came back.

We started down at once. All the way I was wondering if the next year I could find two companions who would be prepared to bivouac on the Eiger. Also, I was thinking about the Matterhorn. The normal route is about the same length as the Eiger west flank. Part way up the Matterhorn is an emergency hut which could be used on the way up and down, so could it be that the local Zermatt guides would go with me? They wouldn't have to bivouac. It seemed preferable to try the Matterhorn rather than attempt to find two guides who would promise to bivouac on the Eiger. I could think of no other mountain with a hut so conveniently placed from my point of view; there are many, but I did not know about them then.

As we approached the Eiger Galcier station Treas said, 'It was good today. You are a strong man.'

In the circumstances such a statement gave me no pleasure. I felt drained of energy, not because of the effort but through disappointment.

From the hotel I rang Judy and promised to head for home so we could go on holiday together. We talked about going to Scotland to walk and climb. I felt that I was at a turning point where I could accept that the lengthy routes were too much for me, then I could spend my time on short and less exhausting routes. This feeling stayed with me for less than a day, until I was on the way back to England. Then I knew that I would continue to pursue other mountains because failure was a bitter food. I would not be satisfied until I had climbed a few long routes or proved to myself that I could not manage them. If able-bodied mountaineers could tackle extremely hazardous routes involving several bivouacs then there was no reason why I should not bivouac on routes which were within my limits.

Within minutes of arriving home I was persuading Judy that she would enjoy a mountain walking holiday in Switzerland. She liked the idea.

'Then I can try the Matterhorn,' I explained. 'There's a hut part way up so I wouldn't have to bivouac. Ueli thought it might suit me for that reason.'

A week later we were in Switzerland. As soon as we reached Zermatt I went to the guides' office. The man in charge refused to find me a guide because he considered the climb to be too much for me.

Judy was waiting outside the office.

'Laughing boy in there says I might find a guide at the Hörnli hut, but I'm not very optimistic about finding one up there if he can't or won't find one in Zermatt.'

Next I rang Felix Julen, the President of the guides, who was at the Hörnli hut at the time. It was from this hut that the Matterhorn was usually climbed.

'Well, come up to the Hörnli hut so a guide can give you a test to see how you can manage. If you can climb all right two guides could go with you on the Matterhorn at the weekend or early next week.'

The idea of a climbing test was sensible, and the suggestion meant that Felix Julen was at least prepared to give me a chance to show what I could do, rather than turn me down right away.

We took a cable car to Schwarzee, 8,480 feet (2,582 m), and then there was a rough trail to walk for a couple of hours to the Hörnli hut at 10,700 feet (3,260 m). At first, the stony trail weaved up like any well-used path on a British moor or mountain. The final bit of track zig-zagged up the Hörnli Buttress to the hut. It was cold enough for small patches of ice and snow to remain there in the shadows. How many times we zigged and zagged, I don't know. Thirty, thirty-five, forty? The sharp turns to left and right went on and on, bringing us at last to the hut.

When I met Felix Julen he had changed his mind and suggested I should go to the guides' office again.

'The man there said he would not find a guide,' I explained. 'You will remember, that is why I rang you. But there is plenty of rock around here for the test.'

'Well, I think the weather may turn bad,' Herr Julen said.

It did not, but it is not always easy to tell. However, impending bad weather was no reason for going down to the valley. There was rock to be climbed within a couple of hundred yards, and a hut and hotel to retreat to if the weather did turn bad. It was obvious that the embarrassed Felix Julen had had second thoughts, perhaps after talking with other guides. That a guide was cautious about climbing with me was understandable because I was an unfamiliar type of problem, but I was far from pleased that I had been invited up to the Hörnli hut for a test which did not take place. Yet I knew so little in those early days, and did not have a basis on which to press my case.

'Poor thing. You haven't had much luck,' Judy remarked later. 'And it was his suggestion that you should come up here.'

'If I met some other guides perhaps they would go. I don't know.'

Felix Julen was well respected in the valley and on the mountains. Without his backing it was unlikely that I would find a guide. I felt like some kind of mountain leper, but I was not going to leave it at that.

'What will you do now, Norm?' Judy asked.

'Do you remember I told you about Eric Beard, the man who was killed while I was walking to Land's End?'

'The man the police thought was you?'

'Yes. Well, he wanted to climb Mont Blanc with me. He thought that as I couldn't go far in a day it would be a good idea to go hut to hut, doing a little bit at a time. There are three huts I can use on the way up. Might even miss one out on the way down.'

'Fine. It's worth a try.'

So we caught a train to Chamonix-Mont Blanc. The hyphenated name, linking the famous mountain with the town that thrives because of it, is officially used nowadays. Altitude: 3,400 feet. Population: about 8,000 people. A clean French mountain valley resort where dozens of hotels and restaurants await the tourist.

We booked in at a cheap dormitory and I went to the guides' office as soon as possible. There's just a chance, I told myself, that they'll help. Just a chance. I explained my circumstances and somewhat to my surprise the woman behind the counter said she would find me a guide, and asked me to return the following day. I'll believe it when I see it, I thought.

An hour later Judy and I were having a meal in a café when two young Americans, a man and a woman, came in to eat. We got into conversation and they, Kevin and Barbara, said they hoped to climb Mont Blanc too. They were experienced rock climbers, and Kevin had some mountaineering experience, including having climbed Mont Blanc once before.

At the guides' office the next day the woman didn't duck behind the counter or put on a false beard and glasses. She smiled and beckoned to a middle-aged man.

'Francis Bozon, Monsieur Croucher,' she said.

The man and I shook hands. He was about five feet seven inches tall and strongly built. His dark hair, trimmed short, was turning grey at the back and the temples. He was serious looking, and obviously a quiet man. Chris Bonington has skied with him and once described him as a 'good-tempered sheep dog'. Even as we shook hands he was weighing me up. He spoke hardly any English so we struggled along in French.

'The lady has explained?' I asked.

'Yes.'

'It may take me six days.'

'I understand. You have climbed with crampons before?'

'Yes. Quite often.'

'Where have you climbed?'

'Mönch, Jungfrau, some snow climbs in Britain, a little way up the Eiger west flank, rock climbing in many places for ten years. I've acclimatised for a month at 11,000 feet.'

'Have you a stove?'

'No.'

'I have one. Gloves and something to cover the face?'

'Yes.'

I didn't want to assume prematurely that he had made up his mind to go, but judging from his questions about equipment I was almost certain he had.

'When you buy the food, I would like plenty of soup and when you get the cheese, ask for "*fromage de la montagne*". I like dried fruit too,' Francis said.

No doubt at all. He would go.

'What's the weather like?' I asked.

'I think it will be all right tomorrow.'

'I have bivouac equipment for the Vallot hut.'

'There is an old observatory near the Vallot hut. I will get the key and we can stay there. It will be more comfortable.'

We wrote down a food list.

'I can't carry much weight,' I explained. (Nowadays I would carry my share.)

'I will take all the food.'

'That's good. It will help a lot.'

'Have you a car?'

'No.'

'We can use mine. We go along the valley and board a train at Le Fayet to Nid d'Aigle. Normally we would go from Les Houches but at this time of year the cable railway is closed. Tomorrow we'll walk from Nid d'Aigle to the Tête Rousse hut.'

Judy could tell from the look on my face when I left the office that the arrangements had been made. She was waiting with Barbara and Kevin.

'We go tomorrow,' I said.

'Great!' Kevin said, and Judy beamed.

'I'd better go home. I've had twelve days of my holiday already and I want to save a few days so we can go climbing in Wales and Scotland,' Judy said.

We all went for a meal. On the way Kevin explained that he was interested in my climbing because his father had an artificial leg. He and Barbara decided that they would not take the train up to Nid d'Aigle but would make the three-hour journey on foot from Chamonix, a trip which hardly any climbers bother with nowadays.

The sky was overcast when Judy and I got up the next day. We headed for the Co-op, which was open by half past seven. We were hunting through the shelves for light food when Francis Bozon appeared and helped to fill the wire basket to the top with provisions before disappearing in a hurry. He had selected enough food for at least six days.

'He really does intend getting to the summit,' Judy remarked. 'I'm not judging just from the food, but from the way he behaves as well.'

Judy and I had breakfast together, and after that things happened quickly. Francis Bozon arrived at the guides' office with his son, a cheerful young man who was training to be a pilot. Francis managed to pack all the food into his rucksack, Judy and I hastily made our farewells, and the trainee pilot attempted to get his car airborne on the road to Le Fayet. From Le Fayet the Tramway du Mont Blanc trundled up to the terminus at Nid d'Aigle (7,800 feet) where we arrived at eleven thirty a.m. The sky was clear and the sun quite hot. We stepped from the train. Ahead of us, two thousand five hundred feet to rise over an easy trail to the Tête Rousse hut.

I slipped my arms through the shoulder straps of my rucksack and fastened the waist strap to prevent it swinging around.

'I prefer that you walk in front,' Francis said, indicating the rough path we would take southwards. I began to walk and could picture Francis watching each step, weighing up whether we should go on or not. With an ice-axe to steady me on boulders, I moved slowly and all the time watched where I was placing my boots. It became unpleasantly hot after a few minutes of exercise, but at least I didn't stumble. A bad performance at that stage could have meant the end of the whole trip.

Our route took us through rocky country, devoid of pretty colours but starkly impressive, where vegetation begins to give up the struggle to live. Not far above was the line where the snow remained all year round, and only a few species of hardy plants survived. We stepped over tough grass and small plants clinging where they could in the shelter of boulders and stones. No trees or bushes could live at that altitude. The view was far from exotically beautiful or lush, but was imposing and rugged. Here beauty was represented by wildness in simple form and limited colours.

A few minutes walk brought us to a typical weaving mountain track, often turning sharply to the left and right, left and right, to gain height up a slope. The path was well used and the rocks faintly whitened and polished by countless boots.

Ahead, thirty French soldiers who had come up on the train drew away and in half an hour were out of sight. They were probably aiming to stay that night at the Aiguille du Goûter hut, which I wouldn't reach until the next day.

Words passed infrequently. Language difficulties restricted us and I was concentrating too much on walking to have time to chatter or take much notice of the scenery. On a popular hiking trail to Mont Blanc I was having to work hard where an able-bodied person could amble along.

My stumps felt slightly painful in much the same way as your feet may feel uncomfortable if you walk ten miles on a hot day. This unpleasant sensation would worsen until I stopped walking and climbing, but it would be a long time before it became distressing. There was cool mist only a few hundred feet higher.

Odd patches of snow lay in dips in the ground and in the shade. We approached a huge rib of rock, part of the Aiguille du Goûter. The trail zig-zagged up in an easy gradient over gritty mud at first, then over fractured brown rocks. The only noises were those we made, the sound of breathing, the scrape of an ice-axe, the crunch of a boot. Thin mist came down around us and the air cooled. Turning now this way, now that, we followed the track. About an hour was enough to take us to the top of the rib, where we sat by the edge of the Tête Rousse glacier. From there on only steep rock would be free of snow and ice.

I knew we had to cross the glacier but I had no idea how far it was to the Tête Rousse hut. We had taken just under two and a half hours. The guide-book mentioned that two and a half hours to three hours was a normal time from Nid d'Aigle to the Tête Rousse hut. It seemed reasonable to reckon that it would take me another hour to reach it.

'Five minutes to the hut,' Francis said.

'Ah, good.'

It was a surprise. Time spent at the Hörnli hut had helped me to acclimatise well enough not to suffer from lack of oxygen. We were over 10,000 feet high and although the lower level of oxygen is not very serious at that height, one can rapidly become tired with exercise before acclimatisation.

There remained only two or three hundred yards to go, slightly upward across the glacier. The mist rose, and there was the wooden hut at 10,390 feet (3,167 m). The snow covering the glacial ice was firm and no crevasses could be seen near us. We followed footprints which went towards the hut. A guide with a young lady client came down the glacier in our direction and stopped; they had come up on the same train. We shook hands all round and the guide explained that the young lady was suffering from altitude sickness. The guide chatted with Francis for a while before leading his client back towards the valley.

The Tête Rousse hut was not unlike a wooden army barrack hut, with room for sixty people. The climbing season was drawing to a close, so the summertime guardian had departed. During the winter the hut would remain unlocked and there would be plenty of blankets for the few people who arrived.

Francis went outside to fetch a can of clean snow to melt, and he soon had some onion soup bubbling over a gas stove. He served it up and I made appreciative noises as I ate. Then I went outside and was sick. This was not unexpected as I had moved on all fours for quite a while, causing my stomach to be compressed. The altitude may have been affecting me too, but I didn't think so because I experience similar trouble when climbing stooped over at low altitude.

Kevin and Barbara arrived. They were tired after the trek from the valley. It was cold in the hut as there was no heating. We sat on benches with our elbows on wooden tables and talked as we sank mug after mug of tea, until the light began to fail. By then there were four other climbers in the hut. Everyone pottered about with torches, packing kit for an early start in the morning, and we all turned in by eight o'clock. The weather was good and Francis thought it would be fine the next day. Because of the cold we all wore plenty of clothes as we slept on the long, communal mattresses.

Under a blanket, I took my legs off, switched on a torch and examined my stumps. There was no damage on the left but the skin was rubbed away in two small patches on the right. If the slight injuries got worse they could prevent me climbing far, for when the flesh was badly damaged the stumps would swell and make movement very difficult. This had happened a few times on long walks; on the road it was possible (although unwise) to carry on walking until the muscles swelled and seized up. Going to such limits while climbing was not wise because of the lack of concentration brought about by prolonged pain. Already there was a very real threat to success. I washed the stumps in icy water, put antiseptic ointment on the injured spots, and went to sleep. I slept deeply at first but later in the night awoke for brief periods, to lie wondering if my stumps would manage the journey. Through a small gap between the window shutters the sky remained clear and starlit.

During one waking spell an alarm clock clattered unpleasantly. I looked at my watch – nearly half past five. It was still dark, and very cold. Francis stirred from the mattress a few feet away in the dark. He groped for his boots, put them on and clumped into the dining-room. The click of his cigarette lighter was followed instantly by the hiss of the gas stove.

The cold, rather than tiredness, kept the rest of us where we were, cocooned in blankets. After five minutes I sat up and punched the air to get warm. On with my legs, and I joined Francis in the dining-room, which was faintly illuminated by the blue gas flame. He was making tea.

'The weather is good now,' he said. 'But the barometer has fallen a little.' He knew this because he carried a small altimeter. If the altimeter reading crept up when we weren't climbing, the barometer was falling.

We drank tea and ate in silence. I finished a couple of slices of bread and butter. My stomach was settled and the stumps were not sore.

More people drifted in from the dormitory. Polythene bags rustled, buckles jingled, boots shuffled, karabiners (snaplinks) clacked together, crampons clinked as they were picked up. The sounds of preparation for a climb stood out starkly against the silence of the climbers. No one hurried. Gradually the sky lightened.

Francis finished eating and packed away the last of his equipment.

'You must take your time. Go at your own pace,' he said.

'I hope I don't go too fast for you.'

He laughed, appreciating the joke. He was not bad tempered, but didn't laugh often.

We carried our rucksacks outside and sat on the front step of the hut to strap on crampons. The light grey sky gave no hint of the way the weather would turn. The wind was light.

Francis passed me an end of the climbing rope and I tied it around my waist. Although it was not a dangerous glacier route, it was comforting to have the rope as a security measure while we crossed the edge of the Tête Rousse glacier.

A glacier grows in much the same way as an ordinary river, from precipitation which flows downhill. In the case of a glacier the snow which feeds it slides down slowly, almost imperceptibly; for instance, a large piece of rock borne by the Aletsch glacier in Switzerland took thirty-three years to move about four miles. There is another, more widely known example of how slowly a glacier moves: the body of an Englishman who disappeared on Mont Blanc after an accident was disgorged from the end of a glacier about four and a half miles from the scene of the tragedy, thirty-one years later.

Francis stepped forward, ahead by a few yards. There were indistinct bootprints from the day before and we followed their line. The snow was firm but not icy, and sometimes under our boots it let out a squeal like a distinct flock of geese, or creaked with the noise of an old wooden chair. These sounds are so much a part of the scene that you might not notice that each of the many forms of snow has its own slight but definite sound under a boot, the geese sound resulting from the fracture of tiny snow crystals.

The trail curved a little to the left, then to the right, in a steady pull upward over snow inclined at twenty degrees or less. We went up the left bank of the glacier; the words left and right are applied to a glacier as if you were looking at it from the source. We soon left the glacier behind and began to scale the Aiguille du Goûter, at the top of which was visible our next proposed stopping point, the Aiguille du Goûter hut. The hut stood 12,520 feet (3,817 m) high at the top of a cliff. We had two thousand feet to climb up that cliff, via an easy rock rib. The angle of the rib, varying between thirty-five and fifty degrees, suited me because I could use my hands most of the time. The place is notorious for stonefall and several people have been killed or injured there. I was concentrating too much on where I was putting my boots to think much about falling stones, although my ears did pick up the sound of a few rocks clattering down in the distance. The guide-book suggested up to three hours for this section from the Tête Rousse hut to the hut above, so I expected to take four hours or more.

The rock was quite broken but offered plenty of safe holds. Parts to be taken with extra care were the many snow- and ice-covered rocks. We kept our crampons on all the time and alternately grated over rock or crunched across ice and snow. There were cracks which gave good holds, plus little natural steps of rock and small slabs so chipped and rough that hands or boots would grip anywhere.

'Wait here,' Francis said at one point early on. He went ahead to a spot from which he could belay me across twenty feet of fairly steep snow and rock. He watched closely as I crossed; I was still being auditioned for the part.

The right stump hurt a little but the cold helped. The cliff faced west so was shaded from the early morning sun when it broke through the cloud.

The risk of stonefall would have been greater if there had been people above us to dislodge them, but apart from four figures descending far above there was no one to be seen. Francis kept a few paces ahead. I could see that he was picking the best places to stand in case I slipped. He remained silent and vigilant, always expecting the unexpected. At times he could walk up steps of rock where I had to climb, but it was pointless to envy him his powerful legs. If I had legs I would have to climb much more difficult routes to gain the same satisfaction as I would if I reached this summit . . . if, if, if.

About half way up the rib we met the four descending climbers, two German and two English. We exchanged greetings and they told us that conditions above the Aiguille du Goûter hut were good the day before. The men carried on down. I looked around at the sky, seeing that it was clear apart from a few slow-moving clouds high up. Not much wind, and that from the north. The signs were not bad, although the weather could change quickly; it could make the climb too dangerous for days on end and force us to turn back. We were insignificant in the face of mountains and mountain weather.

At eight o'clock we stopped for a rest.

'This is a bad place to be after a storm,' Francis remarked. 'Ice covers the rocks. If the weather turned bad we would have to go down. But it looks good. Perhaps we can go as far as the Vallot observatory today if you feel all right. We must take advantage of the weather.'

'Perhaps.'

I didn't sound enthusiastic because the prospect of going from the Tête Rousse hut to the Vallot observatory (14,307 feet) in one day, missing out the Aiguille du Goûter hut, had seemed out of the question. The guidebook suggested it would take an able-bodied mountaineer six hours in reasonable conditions so it would take me at least eight hours, and possibly as many as ten hours. That was too long for the stumps if I wanted to continue to climb to the summit the next day. No, better to be prudent than too eager. Four hours to the Aiguille du Goûter hut would be a comfortable amount of climbing for one day. Caution could prevent me getting to the summit, but it would keep me out of trouble. After all, I was a learner.

I did not miss the significance of the proposal Francis had made: it meant that after watching me like a hawk he was satisfied that it was all right to aim for the summit.

We pressed on again. My boots gripped well on rough rock but it was the handholds which gave most reassurance. Below, we caught glimpses of two ascending climbers, probably Barbara and Kevin, who left the Tête Rousse hut a few minutes after our departure.

By nine a.m. the hut perched on a ledge above us looked strangely close. If I needed four hours to get from the Tête Rousse hut to the Aiguille du Goûter hut, it would take an hour and a half to reach that ledge. Distances can be deceptive on mountains, but I was almost certain that the hut was only half an hour's climb away. Our pace remained constant and soon there was no doubt that the hut was close. In half an hour we were there. It was a wooden building, covered in sheet metal outside. Some of the windows were round, like port-holes, and the long, low building looked like the hull of a stranded ship.

'Good. Three hours,' Francis, grinning. 'Now you can rest and this afternoon we go on to the Vallot.'

'I think so.'

This was not what I had planned. What I had had in mind was to leave the Aiguille du Goûter hut only if the weather forecast was favourable. I didn't mind being caught in that hut in bad weather, but the Vallot observatory was rather high to be stranded in. However, we had plenty of food and could stay warm in the observatory, so if the weather turned bad we could sit it out and descend at the first opportunity.

Outside the hut we sat down to unstrap our crampons. In this hut, as in many alpine huts, it was usual to remove boots and stack them in racks in the entrance, and people wore rubber shoes provided by the hut guardian. Francis soon had his boots off and went in to order tea for us. I sat on a step and unlaced a boot, but when I came to slide it off it wouldn't budge. It was frozen to my wooden foot. After a good deal of time spent banging the foot on the ground, tapping the boot with my ice-axe and levering up the leather, I got one boot off. I was hard at work on the second one, thumping it with my ice-axe, when I looked up. A climber, walking past, was staring at me. I smiled at him and carried on with the job in hand. He moved away, open-mouthed. When I went into the hut I sat near him at a table. Giving me a funny look, he got up and went to a table at the far end of the hut. When you think about it, I don't suppose many people would want to sit close to someone who belts his feet with an ice-axe!

Inside the hut was room for about seventy people on the mattresses. The dining-room was large, like a village hall, and there were half a dozen other climbers there. Delicate Jack Frost leaves decorated the windows but it was warm inside the building. We sat at a table and drank tea from large bowls, and our talk centred at first around the weather.

'It may change soon,' Francis explained. 'The barometer is still falling.'

'The wind looks strong above here now.'

This was clear from the streamers of snow being blown from crests.

'It is, but not too strong for us to go on. I have spoken to the guardian and we can rest here now.'

'That's good.'

'And at midday we start for the Vallot?'

It was a question, not a statement.

'Yes.'

'We will rest then, for two hours,' Francis said.

We made our way to a dormitory where I took my legs off. The right stump was bleeding from the end, where the bone finished. The wound was no bigger than a 2p piece but the small area of damage was surrounded by swollen flesh. I was tempted to stay at the hut until the next day.

Two hours of dozing sped by. Back in the dining-room we had a bowl of soup each. Kevin and Barbara were there, having arrived about an hour after us. They decided that their four-hour stint up to the Aiguille du Goûter hut was enough for a day

'See you tomorrow at the summit,' Kevin said, as Francis and I prepared to leave.

Boots on, crampons strapped under boots, glacier cream and lip salve smeared over skin, goggles on, rope tied, gloves on. Without goggles, the dazzling sunlight reflected from the snow could be unpleasantly bright and could even cause snow blindness. Crevasse danger was small the way we were going. The hut guardian provided a spare ice-axe to help me along. It would be snow and ice all the way from the Aiguille du Goûter hut at 12,520 feet (3,817 m) to the Vallot observatory at 14,307 feet (4,362 m) and from there to the summit.

It was one o'clock when we started. The sun beat down as we mounted a fairly steep snow slope, which rose for a hundred feet behind the Aiguille du Goûter hut. We turned to follow the ridge at the top of the slope towards the south, trending soon south-eastwards. On the right side the rocks of the Aiguille du Goûter fell away steeply – two thousand feet of cliff is quite a sight when you walk along the top. A well-trodden trail led across the ridge, which was an extended mound of snow like a huge long-barrow curving along the clifftop. It was a spectacular, yet not dangerous, place to be.

Our boots sank perhaps five or six inches in the snow. I walked in Francis's footprints because his weight had compacted the snow there. While sorting out equipment and rejecting all but the essential articles, I had decided against taking ski-baskets for the ends of the ice-axes, and I soon regretted leaving them behind, for the ungainly craft needed outriggers on soft snow. With great effort, muscles were forced to correct balance; two ice-axes with ski-baskets could have done the same job with almost no effort, like ski sticks.

An hour passed and I began to find it hard going. The right stump hurt a lot. I struggled to inhale sufficient oxygen to fuel a straining body. The gradual incline, fifteen to twenty degrees, dragged on and on up the snow; a hundred yards, two hundred yards, three hundred yards, five hundred, eight hundred. My ice-axes sank alternately in the snow to the left and right and provided hardly any support. Our boots, after being raised clear of the snow, would be thrust forward to sink six inches, six inches through which they had to be raised at the next step.

Two hours after leaving the hut I was very tired.

'I must rest,' I called out to Francis.

'All right.'

Dropping slowly to my knees, I stayed where I was, kneeling. It was as relaxed a position as any other in the circumstances.

'We are going slowly,' Francis remarked.

'Yes, but Vallot today,' I said between gasps, 'and perhaps the summit tomorrow.'

'Perhaps.'

By three o'clock the sun was much less hot than when we left the hut. The biting wind precluded an extended rest and in two or three minutes we toiled on. The gradient lessened, for we were nearing the top of a huge dome of snow, the Dôme du Goûter, a hump with a width of about 700 yards. Gradually, almost imperceptibly, the snow levelled out and became firmer. Though bathed in sunlight, the snow was frozen by the wind racing across it. We trudged over the top of the Dôme. It had taken over two and a half hours from the hut by the time we reached the top of the Dôme. I wondered if twenty-four hours later I would look on the summit with contentment and satisfaction, or with disappointment. Hope was so strong it was uncomfortable.

The Vallot hut and observatory, half a mile away, came into sight. To reach the observatory it was plain to see that we had to descend from the top of the Dôme du Goûter to a saddle called the Col du Dôme, and from there climb a slope of snow and ice at about thirty-five degrees. Had I been fresh it would have been easy, but I was struggling to keep going.

On the descent of the Dôme the sun no longer shone. Whether this was because it was behind the Dôme du Goûter or clouded over I did not notice, but the air turned bitterly cold. Without the warming rays of the sun the wind could have chilled the body and sapped the strength to a dangerous extreme in a short time. I was glad there was not far to go. It was like being forced to run for hours on end: I would have been relieved to have stopped at any moment. There was no chance of any more than a brief halt, though, until we reached the hut, because it would have been unwise to have lingered for long in that wind.

Icicles formed on my beard and my gloves froze stiff. The cold affected me more than usual because of the fatigue brought on by between six and seven hours of climbing. Despite the freezing wind, I had to stop to catch my breath when we reached the Col du Dôme.

The wind buffeted from the left side in gusts which made it difficult to keep balance. It was like walking in a crowd with people shoving you around. I felt close to exhaustion as we began the two or three hundred yard climb up to the observatory. Normally it would have taken about ten minutes but I was stopping every fifty yards to catch my breath. Each time we halted Francis stood a few feet above me and now and then I thought he looked a bit concerned. I hoped he was not deciding that we should go down the next day.

At last we reached the observatory, a wooden hut built in 1890 on a tiny isolated outcrop of rock. The hut was about twenty-five feet long and ten feet wide, and the windows overlooked the Dôme du Goüter. A few yards away was the Vallot emergency hut, a life-saver in bad weather. We were using the observatory because there was a big stove and wood there, and it was more comfortable. I wondered how many scores of wearying treks had been made to take the hut timbers there piece by piece.

Francis produced a key and unlocked the door. We took off our crampons and went in. There were a couple of tables and two chairs, rows of shelves along the walls and two beds with blankets piled on them. The shelves were crammed with pots, pans and crockery. A small stove stood near the door. The place had an atmosphere of passing time: enamel pans stacked by plastic bowls, candles and new electric torches, polaroid sunglasses on a shelf near some seaside postcards which were forty or more years old, and Francis's portable gas stove on a table above a box of firewood.

'How tired are you now?' Francis asked.

'Tired and a bit ill, but happy.'

'You have climbed for seven hours today. That is quite a lot at this altitude.'

'Yes. I don't like soft snow. I made a mistake not bringing ski-baskets to fix on the ice-axes.'

'Four hours is a long time from the Aiguille du Goûter hut to here.'
'Much too long,' I agreed.

Francis soon had the stove going and we drank soup and tea. Icicles from my beard plopped into the tea as I sipped. The sky grew dim and we lit a candle. The hut groaned and shook with the force of the wind which roared outside. Even with the fire blazing it was quite cold, so we sat close to the stove.

'The wind is bad,' Francis remarked. 'If it stays like this we will not be able to go up. We may have to go down.'

We turned in early, each wrapped in a huge pile of blankets. My right stump was swollen and bruised and blood had caked at the end. If we continued to climb the next day it would get worse. The normal time from the observatory to the summit was about two hours. If the weather was good the next day the only thing to do would be to carry on. It wasn't working out at all like the reasonably easy, injury-free trip I had had in mind. I was learning about my limits the hard way.

The wind howled and tugged at the hut all night, causing it to creak and shudder. By four a.m. it had not eased, nor at six o'clock, nor seven. Francis got up and lit the fire. He stood for a while at the window. From my heap of blankets I called out; I knew the answer already.

'Can we climb?'

'No. The wind is too strong.'

I settled back and fell asleep again, to be woken a few minutes later by Francis, with a cup of tea. I drank the tea, then with a feeling of dread reached for my legs and put them on. It would be obvious right away if the overnight rest had been enough, I told myself, as I stood up. My heart sank. The stump was still very swollen and tender, in which case further movement would increase the damage. If the weather cleared up, which was unlikely, there would be a painful journey ahead. Outside, the sun was shining but white whirlwinds of snow scurrying across the Col du Dôme were further evidence of the raging wind.

We drank soup and ate ham and bread. Francis hated being inactive and wandered around like a caged animal. On the other hand I sat as much as I could. I hoped he didn't realise that this was because I found it painful to stand. He made no complaint when left to do all the odd jobs.

At about half-past five that same morning Kevin and Barbara set out to try to get to the summit from the Aiguille du Goûter hut. Six more people left the hut at the same time. The wind was so strong that two people soon headed back. Before long, two more returned to the hut. Kevin and Barbara kept going as far as the Vallot hut and observatory, where they came to the conclusion that it would be silly to go any farther. A short distance ahead of them two German brothers had a disagreement about whether they should continue. One detached himself from the rope and walked towards the top. The way to the summit was clearly visible, as were the huge streamers of snow being torn from the summit ridge by the wind. The other brother, and Kevin and Barbara when they arrived at the hut, watched and waited. The longer they sheltered in the hut, the more they became convinced that Francis and I had headed for the summit and come to grief. What they didn't know was that they were in the emergency hut while we were safe close by in the observatory.

The lone German eventually reached the summit, began the descent, and rejoined his brother. Together they started back to the Aiguille du Goûter hut, followed closely by the two Americans.

At about half-past ten Francis noticed someone descending the slope near the observatory and we went out to watch them. Barbara and Kevin waved excitedly when they saw us.

'We thought you were dead!' Kevin bawled above the noise of the wind.

'No. Not by a long way,' I called back.

'You going to try tomorrow?' he wanted to know.

'If the weather's all right. You be coming back tomorrow?'

'No. We've had enough today. We're frozen. But good luck to you.'

Kevin and Barbara carefully cramponed down the icy slope. For some reason the German who reached the summit had taken off his crampons, so it was not surprising that he slipped, dragging his brother behind him down the slope. They slithered, gaining speed, until they were able to halt their slide with ice-axes. Kevin told me later that the one who had reached the summit was not very alert on the way back to the Aiguille du Goûter, and he almost stepped into a crevasse. The climb had drained him to the stage where he could not think or act properly.

The wind blustered all day, hustling up flurries of snow. We drank tea and kept the fire going, read a two-week-old French newspaper from end to end, and talked within the limits of my French about Francis's teaching job with the National School of Ski and Alpinism at Chamonix. He had won many ski competitions when he was younger.

Francis stood looking out of the window for long periods, or paced the room. At three o'clock he was standing at the window when he said, 'I think it is finished for you.'

Probably true, I thought, but I hated to hear the words.

'It's in the hands of God now,' I said. I couldn't decide whether God would be interested in getting anyone up a mountain. Despite the misery I felt, I tried to remain outwardly optimistic so we would not make definite plans to descend the next day.

'It would be bad to be caught here in a storm,' Francis said. 'We could be stranded for days. Tomorrow, probably we should go down.'

'How's the altimeter?'

'It's dropping.'

'That's good.'

'Perhaps.'

Success hung by a thread, a thin, thin thread. The chance of reaching the summit could fall away and be lost. Even the descent could be difficult if snow conditions were bad.

In the afternoon the sun began to sink into a hummocked sea of clouds above which only a few of the highest mountains, including the one we were on, peeked out. The red sun, big and round, slid from a sky of gold and yellow into the cloud in a display which in itself might have made the journey to the observatory worthwhile for a mountaineer who had no summit ambitions.

'The sun was watery when it went down,' Francis said. 'It's a pity.'

We lit a candle and had more soup, tea, cheese, bread, ham and dried fruit. The wind hammered away at the observatory. There was none of the usual excitement and preparation in anticipation of a day's climbing; we just went to bed and fell asleep.

A number of times during the night I woke up. The wind continued unabated. Forlorn thoughts seem worse at night and I was glad to spend most of the time in sleep rather than thought.

I didn't see the dawn break. In the early daylight I looked at my watch. Half-past six. It was cold and quiet in the building. There was no noise. No noise at all. Then I realised why: no wind! The wind had died down!

Francis started to shuffle about. He looked at his watch too, then sprang out of bed. Hurriedly pulling on his boots, he called out to me at the same time.

'The wind has gone! We can climb!'

It was evident as soon as I stood that thirty-six hours of rest had reduced the swelling on the right stump. The pain was slight.

We gulped down tea and gobbled bread and ham before packing a minimum of equipment into our rucksacks.

Outside the observatory we put on our crampons. Francis locked the hut. It took only seconds to rope up. It was about seven o'clock. The sun was bright in a clear sky. There was hardly any wind. Two hours to the summit, the guide-book said. In two-and-a-half hours, I thought, I could be on that summit. What if the weather turned bad, forcing us to retreat? That would be extremely unlikely in such a short time. Stonefall? No danger. Avalanches and crevasses? Hardly any risk at all. Mechanical failure of legs? A bare possibility.

He led the way. The wind had stripped the slope beind the observatory of much of its snow. We cramponed upwards across ice and hard snow for a few yards, then swung along, left, right, left, right, at a smart pace up a gradually rising snowfield. Four people, in two parties, were ahead of us by two or three hundred yards. They had started out early from the Aiguille du Goûter hut. We could see no one below.

The slope narrowed, became steeper and joined the Bosses ridge. Apart from the difference in colour it looked like a desert sand-dune. We charged along the crest. I breathed like a stag pursued by hounds, and Francis coughed frequently.

The pace didn't slacken across two snow humps, the Grande Bosse and the Petite Bosse. The top of the Petite Bosse is less than a thousand feet below the summit. A few feet to the right was the border with Italy; we may have walked right on the border in some places.

The route descended into a slight dip after the Petite Bosse. Two of the other climbers were only twenty or thirty yards ahead, and the other pair were not far in front of them. We were not racing, but it was clear that two nights spend above 14,000 feet had aided acclimatisation.

'Rest for a minute, please, Francis.'

'All right.'

The observatory was already an hour's march behind us. Time had flown. The weather showed no sign of changing.

I caught my breath and we began the trudge up snow past some rocks, called the Rochers de la Tournette. That left four hundred feet to rise. The ridge to the summit stood out unmistakably. From a broad slope it grew up at an easy angle to the top of the mountain. This was the most exposed place above the observatory: the top of the ridge narrowed until it was about as wide as two bootprints, side by side.

On the broader section of the ridge, low down, we kept up a good speed. The two men in front decided to belay right away; whenever one of them moved forward the other stood still with the rope passed around an ice-axe which was rammed deep into the snow. The theory is that if someone falls the ice-axe will remain in the snow as an anchor; snow conditions are rarely suitable for holding more than a very short fall. Francis considered that we did not need to belay on the lower part of the ridge so we tramped past the two men by walking below them on the slope to our left.

'The suffering is almost over,' the leader of the pair said to us in French.

Soon after, Francis went seventy or eighty feet ahead while I remained stationary. As soon as he had his ice-axe firmly planted in the snow and the rope around it, he called for me to advance. When I reached him he moved ahead again on his own. Four or five times he belayed in this way. The pair a few yards in front, two Italians, were belaying as well. They belayed several times, then they just walked on because the ridge broadened. We followed them, a few yards behind. They stopped, took off their rucksacks and started taking photographs. They were at the summit. Within seconds we were beside them, 15,781 (4,807 m) high on the top of Mont Blanc, western Europe's highest mountain.

Francis and I shook hands.

'Thank you,' I said. 'You have been a patient guide.'

Weeks and months of tensions simply disappeared, as if washed away. I was ecstatic just to be there, without fully knowing why I had gone. But wow, I was there! There was a sensation of such excitement, as if I felt good music without hearing any. Sometimes a glimmer of that summit feeling comes back at an odd moment and I know again why I went. The ascent, once over, never dies.

The date, 18th September 1971, was exactly two years after I walked out of John o' Groats.

The settled weather allowed a good view across the Pennine Alps, to the Matterhorn and Monte Rosa. Between them and Mont Blanc stood mile after mile of snowy peaks, a gigantic mountaineers' playground. I hoped to explore it all one day.

We had taken an hour and three-quarters from the observatory to the summit. After about fifteen minutes we were on the way down. Back at the observatory, Francis started to peer at the sky again.

'Now we can rest, but we ought to go down to the Aiguille du Goûter hut this afternoon. This would not be a good place to be stranded.'

We continued slowly down over the soft snow. My right stump became swollen and painful again. If only I had stopped at the Aiguille du Goûter hut on the way up, instead of pressing on to the observatory, the stump would have been all right. But if I had stopped at that hut Francis might have decided against heading for the observatory in high winds the next day. We might not have reached the summit at all. No, the discomfort was a small price to pay.

The descent was not easy for Francis as my snail's pace prevented him taking rhythmic strides. For the first time he became impatient and his voice was sharp.

'No, move to your right! The snow is firmer there!' he barked. Even a good-tempered sheep dog may snap now and then. Few people could have remained patient when fatigue made my movements progressively more slow and sloppy. On top of that, he had risked his reputation as a guide by accompanying me. If any mishap had occurred on the mountain he would have been criticised heavily. He was entitled to be a bit tense.

We took three and a half hours to struggle from the Vallot observatory to the Aiguille du Goûter hut. An able-bodied party could have managed in half the time, or less. The slushy snow yielded underfoot and occasionally we sank almost up to our knees. Once more I learned that it was all I could do to keep going in such warm conditions on snow.

At the Aiguille du Goûter hut I went straight to the dormitory and flopped on a bunk. As soon as I lay down I was seized with violent coughing fits. My overworked back muscles felt as if I'd been carrying a cow around all day, nausea came on, the right stump was in very poor shape, my head ached with a pulsing pain, I shivered and my nose started to bleed. Did I still feel it had been worth it? Without a doubt.

I slept deeply and the next day we flew down from the hut by helicopter. Really I wanted to climb down but one stump needed a day's rest, a day which Francis did not wish to waste in inactivity. He was afraid that the weather would turn bad and leave us stranded in the hut for days and cause him to lose lucrative guiding time. I suggested that if he wanted to go down I would find someone to descend with the next day, or whenever the weather allowed, but he would not hear of this. In fact we argued for some time for I felt that while it was stupid to damage the stump further, flying was taking too easy a course. It was appropriate to my circumstances to make good use of the hut. It seems strange, looking back, because the stumps would take three times as much punishment nowadays. But these were early days and I was still finding out how the leg amputee could best manage in the mountains. With mixed feelings I agreed to fly, rather than to climb, but there was one temptation: the chance of my first helicopter ride was difficult to resist.

The Aiguille du Goûter hut was frequently visited by helicopter taxis and there was a landing pad nearby. On a sharp snow ridge the pad had been levelled out at the top, at the apex of the sloping sides. The helicopter had to alight on a flat snow area about the size of the floor of a large room.

We sat on the edge of the landing pad with our heads down. The Alouette III helicopter hovered over and dropped with a screaming racket and tremendous downdraft. We had read in the old newspaper at the Vallot observatory that a helicopter had crashed in the same place two weeks before. Crouched low as we were, the big rotor blades were high above, but the tail rotor looked close and menacing, able to turn us to mincemeat in an instant. The aircraft settled gently and we scrambled in. In front, the cliff of the Aiguille du Goûter dropped 2,000 feet. The helicopter lifted a little, tilted forward and plunged down the cliff. For a couple of seconds I couldn't be sure whether we would crash or not, then we were floating forward and down, away from the cliff. The pilot made a gradual descent so our ears had time to get accustomed to the change in altitude. We hung over the sunny valley which, from 10,000 feet, appeared like a pretty relief map of itself. Tiny houses lay clustered along thin, twisting ribbon roads; fields were irregular patches of green fitted into a carpet for the valley floor; it might have been green baize stretched up the valley walls except that as you got closer the individual trees could be picked out; the rock formations above the tree line might have been moulded in plaster and painted brown, and the snow on top had been left unpainted.

The helicopter passed low over Chamonix, went farther up the valley, skimmed over some trees and landed on a tarmac area amongst them. There was an ambulance waiting. I don't know what message had reached the driver, but it had gone wrong somewhere. As Francis and I alighted from the aircraft the ambulance driver ran his eyes over us and a rather sickly smile crossed his lips as if to say, 'Someone's got it wrong again'.

The next morning the guides presented me with a certificate, signed by the chief guide and Francis. A few reporters came to the guides' office and I made a radio recording in hesitant, inaccurate French. Francis was recorded too, and although I didn't understand all that he said I was pleased to hear some of his comments.

'We took about four hours from the Vallot to the summit and back. That is a good time,' he said. 'And he walks better on crampons than many normal people.'

A short celebration with some guides was followed by lunch with a press photographer, his girlfriend and two young guides who had completed an extremely hard ascent. The same day I flew home from Geneva. Perhaps it was really September but I was a little boy, it was Christmas and Mont Blanc was mine.

# 3

## *Back to the Eiger*

Life was busy after Mont Blanc. Following a few television and radio broadcasts I was picked as one of the thirteen 'Men of the Year' who attended a luncheon at the Savoy Hotel in London. It was interesting to meet the other 'Men of the Year': the world motor-racing champion, Jackie Stewart; the English cricket captain, Ray Illingworth; John Dawes, who captained the British Lions rugby team; Sir Geoffrey Jackson, the former British Ambassador in Montevideo who spent months as a prisoner of guerrillas; Chay Blyth, the solo round-the-world yachtsman; Jack Bodell, the boxer. As well as these famous personalities a soldier, a policeman, an RAF pilot, a lifeboat coxswain, a fireman and a submarine captain were presented with certificates for bravery or achievement. It was sobering to meet men who accepted danger as a part of jobs they felt they ought to do. The sportsmen may have looked more dashing but we were humbled by the presence of men who risked their lives for others.

The Eiger was on my mind so I kept in training by climbing and walking. All the time I hoped to meet two or three good climbers who would leap at the chance of going up the west flank of the Eiger, but no one turned up.

In September 1971, Georges Nominé, one of France's top climbers, offered to do the route with me in the summer of 1972. I appreciated his offer but hoped that I would not need to hire a professional like Georges. I had served my apprenticeship with a few guides and felt it was time to branch out. Sadly, in March 1972 Georges was killed in a mountain accident when he fell a long way from the top of a very difficult climb.

At the annual dinner of the South Wales Mountaineering Club, in February 1972, I made a point of outlining my intention to climb the west flank. A few people showed interest, and most of them were amongst the best dozen mountaineers in the club. They all asked for time to think about the climb before deciding whether or not to accompany me.

The tedious wait for good conditions on the west flank in 1971 was engrained in my mind; for this reason I made sure I would be free to climb for several weeks in the summer. Mountaineering dictated my life pattern, and I took a temporary job. The job lasted until midsummer, which meant I would be free to spend as long as I could afford in the Alps then. It may seem irresponsible to count mountaineering before a career, but I was not going to lose out on the wonders of the mountains because I chose regular pay or job security instead. Age, family responsibilities, a minor permanent injury to hip or back, lack of money or short holidays – each could rob me of the mountains if I delayed too long. Thirty-one is not old for a mountaineer, but as the years creep by opportunity can suddenly or slowly disappear if you don't take it when the time is ripe.

At the Roehampton limb centre my prosthetist (formerly known more simply as a limb-fitter), Brian Campbell, suggested strengthening the artificial legs and the work was soon carried out. This reduced the possibility of mechanical failure from the stresses of mountaineering.

Shortly after the annual dinner of the South Wales Mountaineering Club I met some of the members again, at a party. One of them, Dave Parsons, was keen on the Eiger west flank plan. He grasped the full implications of climbing within my personal limits; he realised that to force myself up a mountain and all the way back to a valley as quickly as possible would often be more dangerous than going at a comparatively leisurely pace. Right away, Dave understood how the climb had to be conducted.

'I definitely want to go,' he told me. 'Some of the other lads are interested too. Bloody fools!'

It was too early to count chickens. People could change their minds.

In March 1972, Dave rang me from South Wales.

'We're getting a mini-bus for the summer. Thirteen people again, counting you and Judy, going to the Bernese Oberland.'

'It's on then?'

'Yes. We haven't decided yet who will be on the rope with you and me, but it may be Len Dacey. He's a good man on the mountains. We'll have to meet up and talk about equipment sometime.'

For a few weeks details of equipment and travelling arangements sped by post and telephone between Cardiff and London. At the limb centre Brian Campbell checked my legs to ensure that they were mechanically sound. Time dragged. There was no way to make summer come early, and just wanting that to happen seemed to make it take longer. Then it was time to go.

Judy and I were picked up from home one Friday evening near the end of July. We collected three more people from Victoria Station and the party was complete.

We reached Grindelwald after one night's camping in France. Six tents were quickly erected on a camp-site overlooked by the Eiger. The camp served as a base from which groups of climbers could go off to huts for a day or two at a time. It was pleasant there, at the top of a grassy meadow, near two big chalets and a wooden barn, and close to a stream which spilled steeply between trees. Huge mountains, just a few miles away, rose ten thousand feet above us.

Several of the others climbed the Mönch and the Jungfrau, then went down to the valley, while Judy and I caught a train to the Eiger Glacier Station Hotel. Dave rang from the valley two days later.

'The weather's bad and Helen's got a face like a football. She was in the sun too long a few days ago,' he said. Helen was his wife.

Judy and I settled down to wait. The daily telephone call from the valley and dinner at six-thirty p.m. became the foci of our lives. Mist hung over the mountains and cleared only infrequently to give a view of the west flank, at whose foot the hotel stood. We gazed at the misty mountains and strolled around the alpine pastures below the hotel.

Friday, Saturday, Sunday and Monday crept by. I met Frau Sommer.

'If the weather is bad for a long time, can I wash glasses at Jungfraujoch again?' I asked her.

'Of course. We would be pleased to have you back. You can stay in one of the staff rooms like you did last year.'

I hoped I would not have to wait long for good weather but it was good to know that there would be work to occupy me if the weather remained unsuitable. There was no harm in planning ahead.

A phone call came at midday on 2nd August.

'We're coming up,' Dave said. 'We should be there at four o'clock.'

They arrived on time and Judy caught the train to the valley. We expected the climb to last two days and Judy preferred to wait at the camp site with Helen and Len's wife, Robbie. There was no doubt that Judy was apprehensive. In the office where she worked was the widow of a man who was killed on the Eiger, and this had brought the dangers home to Judy.

Dave was bearded, bespectacled and jovial, and had the Welshman's tendency to talk in a high-pitched voice when excited. At the time he weighed a bit more than twelve stones, which looked heavy for a man of five feet eight inches. This was his sixth visit to the Alps and he had wide climbing experience in Britain. He was twenty-eight years old and had just abandoned the career into which his degree in ceramic technology had led him. He was a life-and-soul-of-the-party sort of person, occasionally too much so first thing in the morning. Having once made up his mind on any topic he stuck firmly to his point of view. The year before he had had a spectacular fall of over a hundred feet in the Alps, but this had not dimmed his enthusiasm. He had fallen over a cliff, pulled the second man off, and Dave's wife was about to disappear over the edge on the end of the rope. With two men already falling she could not possibly have held them without a belay, and she had no belay. Then someone on another rope caught her around the waist and held everyone! The friction of the rope over the edge of the cliff must have contributed a great deal towards making such a dramatic saving of life possible. No one had more than minor injuries.

Len Dacey was about thirty years old, quite slim and around five and a half feet tall. He, like Dave, was bearded. His eyes were the features you noticed most about him: brown, and at times fiery, they seemed to explain immediately what the man was all about, showing him at a glance to be sensitive, moody, intelligent and restless. On the mountains he could move with great speed when he wished, and he had climbed in the Alps five times. He worked as a design engineer.

Excitement gripped us all and over a huge dinner and a few beers we speculated on our chances, and were optimistic. It was nearly ten o'clock when we went to bed, with the intention of sleeping five or six hours. There was no need to start very early because we planned to climb for only six or seven hours before halting to bivouac. A light snow shower had begun but if it stopped soon we could still climb.

I woke up at half-past three that morning. It was still snowing and two or three inches of snow lay on the ground. We couldn't go. There would be too many avalanches and too much powdery snow.

It was not until nine in the morning that we got up and strolled out to look at the west flank. Light snow still fluttered down. What could be seen of the route was whitened all the way. We stood around sighing and swearing for a while, then went back to the hotel.

During the day Kurt, a mountain guide who lived near the hotel, expressed interest in our climb. Birgit, one of the staff, acted as interpreter and told us that if I had no one to climb with Kurt would be prepared to go when the conditions were right. Looking ahead again, that was good news; Len and Dave could wait only a few days before going home.

For three days the sun worked on the west flank to reduce the avalanche-prone snow. Time was short. The mini-bus would leave for England in five days. The west flank was not in good condition because there was far too much ice around. A year before Ueli Sommer had gone on two rescues in the same day on the west flank. Ice had put eight people in danger on that day and one of them had fallen and died. We had no intention of going in conditions which were as bad as on that occasion, but we decided to climb as soon as the weather forecast was favourable. Even if there was quite a lot of ice about it was possible that we could proceed slowly to the summit.

The television weather forecast was good and the sunset turned the mountains pink. With the kit packed, we went to bed.

Stars showed that the weather was clear at four a.m. Herby, chef de service at the hotel, and Birgit had prepared a tray of flasks of coffee, bread, butter and jam the night before. Dave ate sparingly while Len and I made do with sugary coffee.

Five o'clock was not many minutes away when we left. Daylight had come by then. It was warm enough with a shirt and a thin sweater on.

The rock rose in steps which varied between a few inches and six or eight feet. We would rise up a rock step to a platform, up another step to a platform and so on. Some of the broad platforms sloped and were littered with small stones. We moved unroped, with Dave leading and Len last. Apart from discussions about which way over the rock looked best, conversation ceased.

The sky graduated from bright blue in the east to dark blue in the west. It took an hour and a half to reach the bottom of the first snowfield that we had to climb. A year before I had estimated it sloped at thirty degrees but looking at it again I reckoned the angle was a little less. We roped up with me last. Len had a cigarette while we put on crampons. He was a heavy smoker.

The firm snow was just right for Dave to kick steps to stand in, and we followed in his footprints. The snowfield presented no problems and in forty minutes we were on rock again. To our right was a wide gully, or couloir. Frozen streams snaked down the mountain; between them there was no ice. Occasionally we would spot a cairn which marked the way but we would be unable to reach it easily: thick ice coated the rock on the way. The normal route weaved up, traversing frequently to the left and right to avoid the hardest or most dangerous, broken rock. Time and time again we had to abandon what would have been an easy way if there had been less ice.

As we would on a rock climb in Britain, we belayed frequently. The usual way of tackling a route like the west flank, with everyone moving at the same time while roped together, did not seem appropriate in such conditions.

We kept to rock as far as possible, following little ribs, surmounting small, easy cliffs and scrambling up slabs of loose rock which fractured under our boots. Mostly it was not steep or difficult, but in places we felt uncomfortable.

'This is the sort of place where you get the chop if you're clumsy,' Dave said.

It was plain to see that in good conditions the climbing was not hard, but the ice made a tremendous difference. However, like the vast majority of climbing parties on the west flank we carried on without incident.

In every direction were ferns of frost, displayed over rock like the most delicate of silver jewellery. Snow lay in cracks and places shielded from the sun, and occasionally we climbed for a few feet in a narrow gully filled with snow. Wherever possible it was better to avoid the snow because it had become soft. Avalanches thundered down neighbouring mountains but we were not threatened.

The route took us up and to the left, towards the north face. It became a plod, up easy angled rock and along wide ledges which had collected small stones. Suddenly we were on the edge of the north face: vertical rock sections and steep icefields. We stared for a long time.

The place where we stood was familiar. It was there that we had turned back on my first attempt on the west flank. Treas had called this Frühstückplatze, but another guide told me later that Frühstückplatze was the name given to an area lower on the mountain. The first time it had taken four and a half hours to get that far; this time we had climbed for six and a half hours. Heavy rucksacks had slowed us, but most of all the ice had been the enemy, forcing us several times to leave the route.

Len sat and had a cigarette. Dave and I ate a little chocolate.

'We must be over half way now,' one of them remarked.

'No. Not yet,' I said. 'This is where we turned back last year.'

When we talked of half way we were trying to judge the height. Some mountains rise irregularly and the difficulties may be concentrated in one short section, not necessarily near the top. The Eiger west flank rises fairly regularly and the climbing is roughly consistent throughout, so height gained was a guide to our progress.

'How are your stumps, Norm?' Dave asked.

'They feel fine.'

'We could keep on for an hour or two, then?'

It was Len who asked.

'Certainly,' I told him.

'It's not been easy going,' David said. 'I don't mind admitting I was gripped a couple of times.'

'Gripped' means 'scared' to a climber. Some would say 'terrified' is nearer the mark.

We climbed for two more hours. In hindsight, I can see that a better knowledge of the route would have helped us over this section; the steep rock we climbed could have been avoided. Belaying as much as possible, we headed slowly upwards until at half past one we reached a broad, snow-covered ledge.

'Great bivi spot,' Dave said. 'And it's about two-thirds of the way up.'

Len thought we were near two-thirds of the way up too.

'I don't think we're much above half way,' I said. It was meant as a comment but it sounded like a moan.

'We've been climbing for nearly nine hours,' Dave said. 'If you're going to climb for long tomorrow you'll have to stop now.'

'That's true,' I agreed. 'I didn't intend moving for longer than six or seven hours. What do you think, Len?'

'We'll be lucky to find as good a bivi site if we carry on. I think we should stop. We can dump most of our gear here and climb light tomorrow.'

'All right,' I said. I was tired and glad to stop. I estimated that we were 10,500 feet up.

The ledge was about ten feet wide and twenty feet long. At one end the north face fell away vertically. We were pleased to find such a big step in the ridge because there was room to put up our bivouac tent. With ice-axes we chopped a level space in the snow and erected the shelter. Six feet eight inches long, three feet ten inches wide and two feet eight inches at its highest, it was made for two people but we planned to fit three in. In case the wind increased we hammered pitons into the rock and attached several guy-lines to our blue nylon 'dog kennel'.

Kleine Scheidegg stood nearly four thousand feet below and Grindelwald was over seven thousand feet lower than us. It was warm, clear and sunny, and peak after peak showed itself as far as the horizon. If you were told to make something beautiful from grey, brown and black rock and some snow you might think the task impossible, yet nature has succeeded countless times in the mountains.

We drank tea and admired the view. Some pretty butterflies (red and brown and yellow, I think) skimmed by. The sun warmed us and we idled the afternoon away. I got some more tea going at four o'clock and a couple of hours later we cooked beef stew and drank mugs of hot beef extract.

Dave puffed on his pipe and Len smoked cigarettes. The sound of huskies whining reached us from the Eiger Glacier station and the doleful notes of an alpenhorn drifted up from Kleine Scheidegg. Brightly painted small planes buzzed between the peaks. The gradual darkening of the deep, green valleys towards sunset heightened the glorious pink glow of the snowy mountains. Close by, a clear stream splashed and sprayed its course down. It was an enchanted evening.

'We should make good speed tomorrow,' Dave forecasted.

'We can leave the tent up and stop here again when we get back from the top,' Len said.

It grew cold. We put on down jackets and prepared to go to bed. The rucksacks were tied to a piton outside the tent. It was a tight squeeze but we all managed to find a fairly comfortable position to lie in. By eight o'clock the light was fading quickly. Fine weather tempted us to believe that we would reach the summit the next day. The night was not cold.

Cough, cough, cough, cough. The morning sounds of Len and Dave getting up were as unpleasant as an alarm clock. Five o'clock. Clear sky.

Dave sat on a rock outside the tent and made some tea.

'Anything wrong with your legs, Norm?' he asked.

'No.'

'Pity. We could have used it as an excuse to go down.'

He was not serious. There was nothing but ourselves to stop us going up.

I mentioned that if I could not make it they could go to the top while I waited, but they refused to consider the idea.

'We're doing this as a team,' Dave said.

At six o'clock we moved off. Frozen streams hung down the mountain and restricted our choice of route once more. We were soon on rock which we thought would be graded as Difficult. It was harder than we should have encountered on that part of the route. Some days later I discovered that the rock was much easier to climb on our right, on the far side of a broad, frozen stream.

On tiny holds we picked our way up the rock. The angle was probably less than fifty degrees but we were uncomfortable again. Sometimes, strung out at the full 150 feet of the rope, we couldn't find one good belay anchor between us. Thin splinters of rock scraped and crackled underfoot.

'I'm not coming down this bit,' Len remarked definitely.

Dave led with great care. He was silent when he concentrated and chatted when he relaxed.

'This is like climbing in the Avon Gorge,' he said. 'I like it! I like it!'

In an hour we had risen only three or four hundred feet. Icicle beards hung from the rock, to tinkle down if we brushed past. Two Englishmen passed us, going well. Two more climbers reached our tent at about half-past eight and turned back, probably because they found they were slowed by the ice.

Weaving through snow-cloaked boulders, we arrived at the bottom of a snowfield. In three and a half hours we had not risen more than six or seven hundred feet. We sat to put on gloves and crampons, and two German-speaking climbers caught up with us. They waited for us to climb.

Len took the lead because he had more snow and ice experience. There was a step of nearly vertical ice, ten or twelve feet high, in front. I suggested we should look around for a better way on to the snowfield but we could not see one.

Len chipped out a couple of footholds with his ice hammer, a tool with a long pick for cutting into ice. His crampons bit in the holds he had made. He moved up a short way and embedded his ice hammer in the ice as a handhold, then found an icy hold for his left hand and used the front points of his right crampon. The ice hammer dug in higher up and his left crampon came up and bit home. With one or two more movements he was standing on the snowfield.

Dave followed and I got up with less effort than I expected.

The German-speaking pair watched us and wandered off below the snowfield, presumably hoping to find an easier way on to it, or around it.

'Must be quite close to the top now,' Dave said.

'Yes. Not far now,' Len agreed.

I could not share their optimism but did not voice my opinion. The Eiger is a deceptive mountain, like many; viewed from Kleine Scheidegg, prominent features which are two thousand feet below the summit appear to be within five hundred feet of the top.

Estimating the angle of a snowfield is not easy but I think this one was about forty degrees. I suppose it was four hundred feet from top to bottom. The snow was a bit on the soft side and rather likely to avalanche, I felt. We plodded steadily up. Part way up the snowfield we could probably have moved to the rock on our right, but we were not sure. We kept to the snow. For safety I would have preferred the rock. Above the snowfield was a cliff. To avoid it we went to the right. I knew Dave and Len thought we were quite close to the summit. It looked as if we would soon see how close when we skirted around the cliff and gained a little height.

We rounded a corner and our hearts must have sunk at the same time. We were not even as high as the ridge which ran between the Mönch and the Eiger. At the lowest point that ridge was more than a thousand feet below the Eiger. At a rough guess I put us one thousand five hundred feet below the summit of the Eiger.

'Oh, hell!' Dave said.

For a minute or two we stood and looked around before tramping up a forty-five degree slope of snow. The slope had been exposed to the sun for several hours and had lost its firmness. Each minute seemed long as we struggled on.

Midday was near. Dave stopped.

'It's time we talked about what we're going to do,' he said. 'I'm not saying we should turn back but we ought to take stock now.'

The snow stretched up for several hundred feet and at the top of the snow was steep rock. I couldn't pick out the summit. A thousand feet to go? More, I thought.

'What do you think, Len?' Dave asked.

'We can't stop now.'

'How about you, Norm?' Dave asked.

I slipped my rucksack off and sat on it.

'I think we should let Norm make the decision,' Dave added.

'O.K.' Len agreed. 'He knows how he's feeling.'

'Hold on then,' I said. 'Give me a couple of minutes. I want to be sure that if we do turn back I won't find myself regretting the decision tomorrow.'

Did we have to abandon all hope of success? The snow was soft and would become softer; there would be an increasing danger of avalanche, particularly on the descent. Even the snow we stood on could have slipped away. The final snow to the summit would be hazardous, too. Descent on soft snow was my weak point. Wishing the facts to be different did not alter them.

'We should go down,' I said. I had had my doubts about reaching the summit so I was not suddenly disappointed. For Dave and Len it was worse.

The snow was noticeably worse as we descended but the ice was quickly melting to make the rocks easy to climb. If we had been able to start two days later the rock would have been almost free of ice. Taking our time, we were back at the tent in four hours.

'Let's have a brew,' Len said, starting to make tea.

I sat on a rock and nodded off to sleep for a few minutes. Len woke me when the tea was ready. I think we had all pictured what it would be like when we returned from a successful ascent. As we sipped our tea, the reality made a sad contrast.

'I'm pissed off,' Dave announced. 'But we made the right decision.'

'You going to try again?' Len asked me.

'I think so. It's a pity you two can't stay for a few more days.'

'I'm tempted,' Len said. 'I can't stay, though. Will you look for a guide?'

'Yes. Kurt wants to go.'

I had hoped to climb the Eiger with friends rather than guides, and whether I went with friends or guides the mechanical effort required of me would be the same. However, there was one advantage of taking a guide: we would not be slowed by route-finding problems.

We sat quietly and stared at the valley. Our wives had come up to the Eiger Glacier station and were watching through a telescope as we arrived back at the bivouac site. From their viewpoint it looked as if we had bivouacked two-thirds of the way up the route so they believed all had gone according to plan. Judy started writing joyful postcards to friends and relations but fortunately she decided not to post them until she had confirmed the good news.

'There's beer down there,' Len said at last. 'When I'm in the valley all I want to do is get up here, and when I'm up here I want to get down there. It's crazy.'

'We haven't seen the women for five days,' Dave remarked.

We thought of the things we were missing. Ours was a dismal group. The snow platform under the tent had melted away, leaving us on a lumpy stone mattress.

The tent and other equipment was packed up by half-past seven the next day.

'How are your stumps?' Dave asked.

'A bit sore, but not too bad.'

Much to our annoyance we found that the ice had melted away to leave a route which we could have climbed in half the time. Higher up it was probably still quite icy but not as bad as when we were there. Time and time again we recognised places that were so slippery on the ascent that we could climb them only with great difficulty. Now we could saunter down; if it were today, I would have said, 'Back up we go,' but this was a long time ago.

We were descending an easy section of rock where we could scramble, facing outwards. Occasionally we needed to put our hands to the rock for balance. I was leading the way with Len at the rear. Suddenly we heard a cry, almost a scream.

'Aagh!'

Out of the corner of my eye I saw Dave shoot forward and down. We had the rope tight and I threw myself back on the rock, waiting for the strain. He was quite heavy, and we had no belays.

Dave stayed where he was.

'It's all right,' he said. 'I wasn't falling. I sat on the pick of my ice hammer.'

Going down the lowest snowfield was enjoyable because I slid while Len and Dave held the rope to make sure I didn't get out of control.

Below the snowfield we sat around for a while and the two German-speaking climbers we saw the day before caught up with us. They had reached the summit and been forced to bivouac high up. They had run out of fuel for their stove and spent a very uncomfortable night during which one of them sat for hours with frozen socks. We gave them a cylinder of gas and they went to make a hot drink in their tent, which they had left near the bottom of the snowfield.

After unroping, we ambled down. It took about four hours to make the descent from the bivi site. Helen, Robbie and Judy met us near the Eiger Glacier station. They were surprised and sorry to hear our news.

Back at the camp-site that evening I discovered that my right foot was loose. The movement was not great but it was too much for me to attempt the Eiger again without having it corrected. Three choices faced me: I could try to find someone in Switzerland who could correct my foot, I could go back to England for my other right leg and then return to Switzerland, or I could give up. If I chose the last course I had an easy excuse, that my artificial legs would not stand up to the work. However, I didn't believe that. The looseness of the foot was so slight that I could possibly have climbed for days without trouble, but I didn't want to risk having a foot falling off when I was half way up the mountain.

A local doctor gave me the address of a firm which repaired artificial limbs but the information proved to be out of date. After much hunting I found, listed in the telephone directory as orthopaedic appliance manufacturers, the address of Botta and Sons at Biel. When I rang them they agreed to take a look at the limb.

Bad weather had prevented most of the group from climbing more than one or two peaks in the whole holiday and they were pleased to pack up and go home. The homeward route passed close to Biel so we made a small detour and found Botta's premises. A man there examined the limb and put it right in a few minutes, much to my relief.

At Biel station we made our farewells before I caught a train back to Grindelwald.

'Pity you have to go home,' I said to Len and Dave.

They were both tempted to stay but had to go back to work.

Judy looked as if I were about to play football in a minefield. She was not usually so anxious when I climbed.

'You could be home in five or six days,' she said. 'All you need is good weather and a couple of guides.'

* * *

Good weather and a couple of guides. It started to rain just after I reached Grindelwald. I rang Birgit at the Eiger Glacier Station Hotel to ask if she knew where Kurt, the guide, was.

'He has to go into the army for three weeks,' she said.

'That's a pity.'

'You should go to the guides' office in Grindelwald, and see if they can find someone.'

At the guides' office I explained to the woman in charge about hiring two guides who would bivouac for at least one night. On a postcard, I showed her where Len, Dave and I turned back. The woman asked me to telephone her in two days.

From the dormitory where I stayed, over the station buffet at Kleine Scheidegg, I could see the Eiger. A hundred times I climbed the west flank with my eyes. Experience had taught me to be patient about the things I could not change, but that did not mean I enjoyed waiting. I wanted this ambition behind me so I could climb without such urgency, for sheer pleasure.

The time came to ring the guides' office and the woman asked me to contact a guide, Hans Kaufmann, by telephone.

It took several calls that afternoon before I caught Herr Kaufmann at home in Grindelwald. In slow and clear English he began to question me.

'You are the man who wants to climb the west flank?' he asked.

'Yes.'

'Is it right that you have no legs?'

'Yes. Below the knees.'

'How did you get on before on the west flank?'

'Very slowly. There was too much ice. I was with two friends who had to go back to England. We started a day or two too early.'

'What is hardest for you?'

'Going down on soft snow.'

He asked how long the various stages had taken me on Mont Blanc and I told him.

'How long can you climb?'

'Last time I climbed for nine hours on one day and ten hours the next day. I could go on for longer but I think that would be unwise in normal circumstances.'

'We could take bivouac equipment with us and if you are going well on the first day we can leave that equipment part way up the mountain and go on to the summit.'

'Maybe. But we'll have to bivouac once.'

I did not want him to think I could manage without bivouacking. He was silent for a few seconds. Had I put him off by insisting that we would bivouac?

'I will find another guide for when the weather is very good,' he said.

'Thank you. I'm pleased.'

That was an understatement!

The weather was bad at the time so I decided to go to the hotel at the Jungfraujoch to wash glasses and acclimatise. If it were not for that job I would have been unable to have afforded to wait for long.

Four weeks after leaving England I was waiting for good weather while a blizzard raged outside. That meant the west flank would take a few more days to come into condition. The news was not all bad: Herr Kaufmann had found another guide to accompany us.

I met Hans Kaufmann one day at Jungfraujoch. He was thirty-five years old, younger than I had judged from his voice on the telephone. He was broad, ruddy-complexioned and heavy featured, a farmer, I was told, who guided during the summer. He seemed like someone who made up his own mind and went his own way.

'We could go in three or four days if the weather is good,' he told me. But it did not improve, except for short periods.

September came. Six weeks had elapsed since I left home. Six weeks and still I hadn't got up one mountain! Sunday, 3rd September, was not a happy day. In the morning I saw that it had been snowing quite heavily. I had to face it – my chances of making another attempt on the Eiger in 1972 were small. The season was drawing to a close. The Eiger Glacier Station Hotel was due to shut down in a few days until the ski season. And it would take several days for the recent snow to clear.

One Sunday evening the television weather forecast was good. Within ten minutes Hans Kaufmann rang.

'The forecast is good,' I told him.

'I know. I will ring the other guide. We need two or three days of good weather. If it is all right we can go to the Eiger Glacier Station Hotel on Wednesday and climb on Thursday.'

Monday was hot and the fresh snow melted quickly from rocks in front of the hotel. Tuesday was hot as well.

The station master at Jungfraujoch was always a helpful man. When I asked him if he had any insulation tape he contacted an electrician who gave me some. I wound the tape and long strands of nylon string around my feet and legs to strengthen them.

Early on Wednesday morning it was snowing lightly but the shower was brief. Once more I rang Hans Kaufmann, who suggested we should wait until noon to see how the weather turned out. If it was fine we could go to the Eiger Glacier Station Hotel the same day.

The glass washing machine droned away in the little room where I worked. At a quarter past twelve the phone rang. It was Hans Balmer, the second guide.

'What do you think about the weather, Hans?'

'Well, I think the weather will be good. We can start at two o'clock tomorrow morning.'

The train ride down through the tunnel felt like the beginning of an adventure. The tension of waiting subsided. I found it difficult to believe that the weather could get worse again in a few hours.

In the early evening someone said the last train had come up from Kleine Scheidegg. The guides had not arrived. Anxious minutes dragged by. Much to my relief, there was another train and they were on it.

Hans Balmer was twenty-six years old and looked more like a fit, blond German than a Swiss of the Bernese Oberland. He was often silent, unlike his older friend, Hans Kaufmann. They were both strong farmers and had more sense of humour than most of their neighbours.

Birgit asked if I thought I could manage the climb without a bivouac and I told her I was certain I could not. Within twelve hours I would learn the significance of her question.

The guides and I went up to our room to sort out equipment. I kept an eye open for articles of bivouac equipment and they had plenty. They brought torches, stoves, matches, fuel, food and ample warm clothing. We each had a nylon bivi-bag.

I went to bed and fell asleep before the guides turned in.

The light flashed on in the room shortly after one a.m.

'Time to get up!' Birgit called to the three of us.

We all dressed quickly and, taking our rucksacks, went downstairs to the restaurant. The usual breakfast was a flask or two of coffee with bread, butter and jam, but we were in for a surprise. Birgit was serving bacon and eggs. Soon the unexpected breakfast party grew to a dozen people, including several of the railway workers, a two-man television team and two journalists. The railway staff had been drinking until then and were in high spirits, in contrast to my mood of quiet nervousness.

'The weather looks all right,' Hans Kaufmann remarked.

While we ate, people laughed, talked loudly in German, and tottered about. No one was tired and this was the noisiest early morning start I could remember.

With the last of the bacon and eggs and tea finished, the guides and I hoisted up our rucksacks and went outside. It was not very cold.

'It is a bit too warm,' Hans Kaufmann said. The snow, particularly as we went higher, would not be in the best condition.

Torches were switched on and several people accompanied us over the first two or three hundred yards of track. The TV crew set up some powerful lights and a journalist took still photographs before recording a short interview.

'We will make another interview when you come down,' he said. It crossed my mind that I would not look forward to the interview if I failed once more to reach the summit. What a miserable occasion such an interview would be!

After the special breakfast and the recording, we did not set off until nearly three o'clock. Hans Kaufmann led the way and Hans Balmer followed me. Like a pair of cinema usherettes they shone their torches where I put my boots. They did that job well.

'Do you want the rope?' Hans Kaufmann asked me when we reached steps of rock.

'I'm happy to go unroped for a while. The rock is dry and easy to climb.'

My two companions conversed in German.

'I hope you don't mind us talking in German,' Hans Kaufmann said. 'We are deciding which way to go. It is not easy to find in the dark.'

'No, that's fine. I don't chat much when I'm climbing anyway.'

I suspected that as well as discussing the route they were weighing up my chances of reaching the summit. If they were not it was surprising, because they had not seen me climb before.

Breathing was no problem because I had acclimatised. Outlines of mountains could just be discerned against the sky, but without torches we could not have seen the grey rock where we climbed. Snow and ice avalanches and rockfalls that we heard were all a long way off. A stream gushed down to our right. The night was full of the noises of rock, snow, ice and water heading relentlessly downhill.

The rock steps were familiar: up five feet, almost level for ten feet, up three feet, straight ahead for seven feet, up eight feet, level for twenty feet, and so on. Even though near vertical in places, each step had sufficient holds to give easy climbing. We neared the top of the steps when Hans Balmer stopped to pass me one end of a five-yard piece of rope.

'It is better if you put a rope on now,' he said. 'In the dark it is not easy.'

He went ahead, trailing a few feet of rope behind him, and watched every move I made on the next short, steep sections.

Ten minutes past four. We were strapping on crampons at the bottom of the snowfield. We roped up with me in the middle. The snow was reasonably firm and Hans Kaufmann kicked steps with ease.

I tried to keep my thoughts on the climbing of the moment, rather than thinking ahead to the summit. Somehow the time would pass and in four or five hours I would have a good idea of the chances of success; by then we could be aiming to reach the summit the same day. Or would we have decided to turn back because I moved too slowly? I concentrated on going at a reasonably fast pace in the hope that we would be in a good position in a few hours. Contrary to my expectations I did not bring up the egg and bacon. Because of the extreme effort of climbing, a feeling of nausea was often with me.

The light was not strong enough for us to start over the snow without torches but the sky began to grow brighter as we approached the top of the snowfield. The torches were switched off. We crunched ahead, crossing an icy, ten-feet-wide channel left by an avalanche slipping down, probably days earlier. The avalanche chute presented no danger and we found an easy place to step over the gap between the top of the snowfield and the rock. The two hours we had taken was twenty minutes less than on the previous attempt.

In a minute or two our crampons were off and we were scrambling upwards to the left of a wide and deep gully. Daylight strengthened rapidly. We walked with little effort along ledges which had given trouble to Dave, Len and me. Now we stepped over little streams which trickled quietly and spread themselves to a width of a foot or two. A month before they had been yards wide and frozen in the morning.

In an hour and a quarter we climbed from the top of the snowfield to the place Treas Schluneggar had called Frühstückplatze. The same section had taken over four hours with Len and Dave. What had been quite hard climbing turned out to be an easy scramble when there was no ice.

'Frühstückplatze,' I said.

'This is not Frühstückplatze,' Hans Kaufmann said. He pointed the way we had come. 'Frühstückplatze is down there. Can you keep going like you have done?'

'I think so, or nearly as fast.'

'That is good.'

With a remarkable view across the north face, this was a natural place to rest. We then took no more than half an hour to reach the spot where I bivouacked with Len and Dave. In three and three-quarter hours from the Eiger Glacier Station we covered the section of the route which had taken eight hours and forty minutes the time before. The difference was due mostly to ice.

'This is about half way,' Hans Kaufmann said soon after we passed the former bivi site. That meant we were about 10,500 feet high.

A little later he said, 'We will leave your rucksack. We can reach the top today and come down here to bivouac. If you do not want to get down this far Hans and I will come and carry your rucksack up to you.'

'Sounds all right. I may not be able to descend as far as this today if we do get to the summit. All the way up and half way down in one day is pushing it for me.'

I lodged the rucksack under a big boulder. Several other boulders in the vicinity were large enough to provide weather protection if we chose to bivouac under them.

'How are you feeling?' Hans Kaufmann asked.

'I feel in great form.'

'And your legs?'

'The stumps seem to be undamaged.'

Hans Balmer grinned and made a remark in German. The only word I understood was 'champagne'.

Having left the rucksack behind I could keep up a good pace. We scrambled between boulders where Len, Dave and I chose to climb a snowfield; it was possible to pick an easy route over rock beside the snow.

'Many people say we are crazy to climb with you, but they say we are crazy anyway,' Hans Kaufmann said.

'What did the other guides say?'

'Mostly they say you cannot climb the Eiger. They say it is not possible.'

'Why did you and Hans think it was possible?'

'Well, I talked to you about what you have done before so I thought you could do it. We have even bet a bottle of champagne that you will go up and down in one day.'

'With Birgit?'

'Yes.'

She's won, I thought, and it disturbed me a little to think that after all my explanations the two guides still believed I could manage the Eiger without bivouacking once. It was a long way to the summit, let alone back to the hotel.

'I think I will have to bivouac on the way down,' I stressed.

'We will see.'

It was not many minutes past eight o'clock. Hans Balmer climbed until he was out of sight behind a hump of a snowfield, then he called out for me to follow. I faced the slope, grasped an ice-axe in my right hand and punched handholds in the firm snow with the left hand. After a few steps I found it easier to use two ice-axes. Hans Kaufmann had a good rock belay and Hans Balmer had an ice-axe belay. It was a safe way to cross the snow.

Hans Kaufmann followed after I crossed and we were soon on rock again. Much of the snow that had been around a month before had melted away.

We passed the place at which Len, Dave and I turned back. My final estimate of the height there was thirteen hundred feet below the summit; with no prominent landmarks to use as reference points, this was a very rough estimate.

The sun beat down but a gentle breeze kept us cool. Once or twice an hour we stopped for a minute while one or other of the guides took photographs.

'It is not possible,' Hans Kaufmann said in German. Then he said in English, 'He cannot climb the Eiger,' and laughed.

'It is not possible,' I echoed, in German.

'Champagne!' Hans Balmer called out.

'Champagne!' the other Hans shouted.

It crossed my mind that it was a bit early for such confidence, but it must have been a relief for them to see we were progressing as fast as I had said we might. I reminded myself that there was quite a long way to go and slackened the pace a little.

At the Eiger Glacier station some of the railway and hotel staff were taking turns to watch through a big telescope. Clear weather allowed them a perfect view. Almost the whole route could be seen.

White scratch marks showed us where people had climbed the rock with crampons when it was icy. The angle varied a few degrees above and below forty. It was easy as there was hardly any ice. The rock rose monotonously for a hundred feet, two hundred, three hundred, five hundred.

'It is not possible,' we all said many times, in German.

The route wended again towards the north face. We climbed on the very edge of a mile of rock which approached the vertical. On our left the drop was exciting and awesome at the same time.

Hans Balmer went ahead in a small, steep gully. As he ascended, stones clattered around him every second or two, but fortunately none of them was large. He climbed thirty feet up the right bank of the gully as we looked at it.

The summit was in sight, separated from us by a few hundred feet of rock ridge and then a ridge of snow. An hour to go, I thought.

Surely we could not fail? The weather was right, and I was not tired. What could stop us? Dangerously soft conditions on the final snowfield, stonefall, or injury from a fall. The risks from stonefall or a fall were remote. So, it depended on the snowfield. 'It's a bit too warm,' Hans Kaufmann had said on leaving the hotel. Yes, it depended on the snowfield.

'It is not possible!' Hans Kaufmann sang.

'Champagne!' his friend yelled. 'Champagne!'

We followed the rock ridge. No ice. Easy climbing. Plenty of holds. Ledges and steps of a few feet and rock sloping gently. Brittle stones crunched under our boots.

Soon all the rock was behind, apart from a small mound visible at the summit. We put on crampons. Ahead, a snow ridge at forty degrees or less. It looked about a hundred yards long. We started to climb. Hans Balmer took the lead. I kept my eyes down on the snow, watching every step. Right axe, left leg, left axe, right leg, right axe. The snow was far from firm.

'It will be dangerous here in an hour or two,' Hans Kaufmann said. 'The snow is getting soft. If you fell you would be finished. You could not stop.'

Right leg, right axe, left leg, left axe. Minutes went by. I took a peep at the summit. It seemed as far away as it had five minutes before. A trail of bootprints behind proved we had risen a long way, but the summit seemed to argue with that.

Left leg, left axe, right, right, left, left, right, right. I drew deep breaths easily. We moved fast, eagerly. I kept my head down. The angle of the slope was constant, then it lessened quite suddenly. I noticed there were some rocks at the same height as us on the right, ten feet away, and then I saw that we could not go any farther. We were on the summit. In front, the south-east face plunged. From the right and left, sharp ridges of rock and snow met at the summit, 13,026 feet (3,970 m) high. Was I dreaming or was I really there? For a moment it was difficult to appreciate the reality.

The guides shook hands with me.

'Thank you both,' I said. 'I'm delighted to be here.'

They deserved more thanks than I put into words.

It was half past eleven. A number of guides had told me they reckoned to take six or six and a half hours with a client, so I was not dissatisfied at reaching the summit in eight and a half hours.

There was great excitement amongst the onlookers at the Eiger Glacier station. I was glad they could witness the event because some of them had given me a great deal of encouragement. It was a pity that Len and Dave were not on the top too.

The guides took photographs and I picked up a few small stones for Judy. The rock was black and brittle.

The deteriorating snow dictated that we should descend quickly so we rested only briefly. To the south and east, fluffy white clouds added soft lines to a mountain wilderness, and I would have liked more time to sit and stare.

'How do you feel?' Hans Kaufmann enquired.

'Not bad. A bit tired but in three or four hours we can stop where we will bivouac.'

'I think you will get back to the hotel today.'

'We'll see. It will be more sensible for me to bivouac, I expect.'

My stumps were sore but felt as if they were not bleeding.

'We must leave here now,' Hans Kaufmann said.

I hoped that after an easy descent of four hours we could bivouac at least half way down the route. I felt sure that until then I could maintain reasonable concentration. However, things did not work out as I thought.

The sun had been relentlessly at work; the snow towards the bottom of the ridge was noticeably softer less than an hour after we had passed over it on the ascent. It was dangerous and I was not at ease until we left the snowfield behind.

There was no need to hurry. Hans Kaufmann led the way down the rock. Heat made the descent tedious but I was too contented to take much notice of physical discomfort.

'It is not possible,' we joked. 'Champagne!'

We drew level with two ascending climbers. From their speech I took them to be English. They asked where the summit was and Hans Kaufmann pointed it out. As they plodded on I wondered how they would manage on that final snow ridge, which they would reach nearly two hours later than us.

Quite soon we passed the place where Dave, Len and I turned back. I was sure we had made the right decision in not carrying on to the summit on that occasion.

As we continued a rock crunched down the mountain a hundred feet from us. Like an under-inflated football it bounced in shallow arcs, and was soon out of sight. For several seconds we heard it thudding on. Now that we were descending, gravity was more in our favour, but could still cause a fall, or send down an avalanche, or rocks.

A few minutes later Hans Balmer shouted from behind.

*'Achtung!'*

I turned to see something flying through the air towards me. I ducked behind a rock and was showered by small particles of ice. The ice had smashed on the rock and the pieces were too small to do any harm. For an instant as they fell they had looked menacing.

We carried on.

'When we reach your rucksack we will rest and have something to eat. Then we can go down to the hotel,' Hans Kaufmann said.

'That will not be wise,' I told him. 'I think I should not climb much more today.'

'We should not bivouac up here if we can get back to the hotel.'

The last hour before we arrived at the boulder where we had left my rucksack was a wearying trudge. In the heat my stumps began to feel very painful. It was four o'clock so we had climbed for thirteen hours. That was the longest I had climbed and I could not expect the stumps to take much more punishment without serious damage. I estimated that it would take four to six hours to reach the hotel. To climb for such a length of time would far exceed my reasonable limits.

When we had rested for a few minutes Hans Kaufmann said, 'Now we must go down.'

'I think we should stay here,' I objected.

'If it snows we could be in trouble,' he added.

'It's a bit late to remember that it sometimes snows up here.'

Hans Balmer picked up my rucksack and was busy tying it on the top of his own. The extra few pounds would not make much difference to him.

Certainly, if we went well below half way we would be safer in the event of a storm. The weather was fine but it was possible it would change.

'I'll go on for an hour or two and see how I feel,' I said.

Needless to say, I moved slowly. Fatigue was partly responsible and I could not put my heart into a descent which I regarded as unnecessary. From experience I knew that once the stumps had had enough their condition would deteriorate rapidly.

The fourteenth hour of climbing went by. I moved as an unwilling slave. I could keep going, but wondered if I should.

'How heavy are you?' Hans Kaufmann asked.

I told him.

'If you become very tired we could carry you when it is dark,' he said.

'No you bloody well won't!'

'No one would know.'

'I would know.'

Hans Balmer joined in, saying, 'You are very hard-headed. Just because you have no legs you don't want to be carried, but sometimes men who have whole legs have to be carried. Some people like to say they have bivouacked on many mountains.'

'It doesn't take much sense to see that this is a special case. We knew I would need to bivouac.'

'You have climbed down all right so far,' Hans Kaufmann said.

There was no rhythm to my climbing; each movement had become a separate mental and physical effort in a disjointed labour.

The fifteenth hour passed – a whole, long hour of great exertion and failing concentration. We took a rest. Lying back on a rock, I tried to muster my thoughts. I had climbed to the summit and descended to a safe height to bivouac and it was not sensible to go on. I was worried about causing serious physical damage to my stumps. I vomited, through sheer overwork.

'Come on,' Hans Balmer said after three or four minutes.

Hans Kaufmann tugged at the rope to get me to stand.

'Hang on a minute!' I said. 'I want time to think.'

Thoughts came slowly and were hard to grasp. Feelings flooded my mind: exhaustion, pain, elation, indecision, anxiety about my physical limits. I could have sat down at any time and refused to move, so why didn't I? But assertiveness was not quite so fashionable then, and the truth was that although I believed it was stupid to continue, half of me wanted to complete the climb in a day. It felt so wrong to go on for more than fifteen hours; I battled with my own better judgment. I would have liked half an hour in which to sort out my jumbled thoughts.

'Come on!' Hans Balmer said. 'You can do it.'

I stood and began to climb down again. The sixteenth hour crept by. By half past seven it was getting dark. We were at the top of the lowest snowfield. The two English mountaineers we had seen earlier passed by. Poor snow had forced them to give up not far from the summit, on the final snowfield, and I realised how lucky we had been. In the whole day they were the only climbers we saw.

'You can sleep in a good bed when you get to the hotel,' Hans Kaufmann remarked to me.

'I could sleep in a good sleeping bag now if you bandits would stop,' I said. 'Anyway, I want some of that champagne if we get down tonight.'

'Of course,' he said. He smiled. 'You know, you will be happy if you can climb the Eiger in one day.'

'I hoped to climb the Eiger but I did not want to be a stupid sort of mountaineer. I would never have set out to climb it in one day.'

On the descent of the snowfield my knee joints ached and the flesh at the back of the knees was tender. That worried me because knees do not put up well with bad treatment. I wondered how long I could go on without suffering serious effects from exhaustion and excessive exercise. One thought frequently entered my mind, that I was not cold. It was a good sign.

The seventeenth hour passed. After the first six hours of climbing I was, understandably, quite tired. Six more hours had taken me to what I considered to be the extreme of my reasonable limits. Five hours of discomfort and fatigue had followed and we still had to descend a long way over rock. We needed torches on the lower part of the snowfield and I did not relish descending the rock by torchlight. But I did not stage a sit-down strike. I knew if I insisted on bivouacking the guides would stay with me; they could not risk abandoning me on the mountain. I wondered why they were so keen to reach the hotel. Was the attraction the thought of proving the other guides wrong? All the time I wondered why I did not stop, and the only reason I could find was that I wanted to complete the route in one day. My cautious self had to be content that we were approaching safety. Obviously, determination and sense were not to be completely and simultaneously satisfied on this occasion.

I appreciated that it was a big mental strain for guides to undertake the responsibility of leading a disabled client on a long route. The pair with me were among the very small number of Grindelwald guides prepared to take the job on, and I was grateful to them.

Our torches probed through the darkness, seeking the way. It was not easy to find. Hans Balmer went ahead, searching for a route down the rock steps. He wandered to the left and right, finding the route and losing it every few minutes. I took advantage of every delay to rest. We meandered down for an hour, the eighteenth hour. I had passed through hardship into joy, then back deeper and deeper into hardship; but the joy was still complete.

Someone with a powerful torch left the hotel and came towards us. From a few hundred feet above them we could see that they were waving the torch around. It was Birgit and Barry, the English chef, swinging the torch about in greeting and encouragement. They signalled for several minutes before returning to the hotel. It was nice to know someone was thinking of us.

Every step down, every reach for a handhold, was like the movement of someone who has just woken in the middle of the night. My feet might have been made of lead, not wood.

The nineteenth hour came to an end. Slowly, we neared the lights of the Eiger Glacier station. At last we reached the track through the glacial moraine. Nearly there. We passed by the railway lines and overhead cables, the houses and huts. We were a few yards from the hotel when I saw a table supporting glasses and bottles of champagne. A dozen or fifteen people waited to welcome us. As we reached the hotel entrance the television crew started to film. Suddenly it came to me that I was feeling cold. It was a strange sort of feeling which I could not understand. It was like nothing I had felt before. Then I put my hand down and found that there was no seat at all left in my trousers! From then on I made sure I was facing the camera.

The time was half-past ten and the climb had lasted nineteen and a half hours.

'You look well for someone who's been up there all day,' said Bruno, the manager of the Jungfraujoch self-service restaurant.

'Well done,' one of the journalists said with great enthusiasm. 'We wish we had been with you.'

Everyone seemed thrilled. Someone started pouring champagne, the journalist conducted another interview, then we had a celebration meal and wine. While several people drank, laughed and talked loudly in the restaurant I fell asleep sitting upright. The guest of honour, asleep at his celebration party!

The next day I heard that Hans Kaufmann had said in advance that he had no intention of bivouacking unless it was absolutely necessary. I was angry about that, but the guides had carried out the job and I liked the pair of rogues. And I could have insisted on stopping. By carrying on I had been taught something new about my limits: sense was likely to stop me long before fatigue.

Frau Sommer arranged a champagne breakfast for the morning after the climb. She, the guides, Barry and I sat on the hotel balcony for a meal of eggs and bacon, assorted meats and pickles, tea and champagne. The next day I went to Berne for a radio recording, and a Scotsman at the studio provided more champagne. I flew home the same day and at our local pub there was more champagne as soon as Judy and I walked through the doorway. 'Congratulations on your feat,' someone said, and from somebody else came, 'He hasn't got any'. For a few days life revolved around newspapers, radio and television broadcasts, and celebrations with friends. Then it all went back to normal.

# 4

# *The Matterhorn*

'You must miss your legs when you climb,' Dave Parsons said one day.

'I was very attached to them.'

'Your jokes get worse.'

'How about doing the Matterhorn in the summer?' he asked.

'I've thought about it. I'm not too sure. The normal route is crowded. I like quieter routes. But I'm tempted.'

'It'll be a great summer anyway,' he said. 'It's nice to look forward.'

We arrived in ones and twos at the Zermatt camp-site, about 5,000 feet (1,600 m) above sea level. Dave was bleary-eyed after an all-night journey standing in the crowded corridor of a train from Austria. Len and two other club members, Don Hillman and John Hodgkins, turned up soon after, and finally came Adrian and Alan. Mountains of 12,000 and 13,000 feet contained both sides of the valley, close to the camp-site.

'Out of all these peaks it's always the Thing that stands out,' Dave said. The Thing was the Matterhorn. Steep on all sides and wildly beautiful, the remarkable pyramid demanded attention, and it was easy to see why it tempted climbers to the top. It stood there, seemingly aloof, yet accessible at the same time.

Five of us decided to go up to the Rothorn hut and climb a peak or two from there. The hut, at 10,500 feet (3,177 m) is about five hours walk from Zermatt along a well-beaten trail. As it would be the first alpine trek of the season I reckoned it would take me near eight hours. In the heat of the day this would not be at all pleasant so I set out ahead of the others in the cool of the early evening. Up the steep Trift Gorge, over a sturdy wooden bridge, through a forest, never far from the stream which found its way noisily down the middle of the gorge. As shadows lengthened and the gorge grew cool, hikers thinned out; still in any stretch of half a mile at least a dozen people would pass, heading down the trail to their dinners in Zermatt. The track left the forest, and trees were replaced by short vegetation which clung close to the ground.

Two men called from a hundred yards farther along the trail and pointed up the steep mountainside to my right. Leaping up with graceful strides were two chamois, moving with bounds which looked as near to effortless as you could imagine. I've read that they can jump more than a dozen feet in the air.

Two and a half hours out of the valley, the abandoned Trift Hotel loomed on the right of the track. There was no one in sight on the trail, above or below, and the decaying building had an eerie look about it in its lonely mountain setting at 7,500 feet (2,337 m). Deserted, neglected, disused, unwanted, the building had been robbed of any significance to mountaineers by the more recently built and higher Rothorn hut.

Darkness was less than an hour away. Rotting floorboards and stinking debris left by tourists made it preferable to sleep outside the hotel. In a sleeping bag I slept heavily under the brilliant stars.

Morning started in bright sunshine with a slow walk along grassy moraines to a stony plateau. A cold stream fed by melting ice farther up the mountainside broadened to form a small, shallow lake cupped in an undulation of the plateau.

I had been walking for an hour when a sudden, piercing whistle startled me. On a rock a few yards away stood a marmot, a stocky, short-legged, squirrel-like inhabitant of the Alps. They grow up to two feet long, but this one was shorter. It remained on all fours for several seconds, then darted away behind the rock. The whistle I had heard was the marmot's alarm signal, a signal which has saved many a chamois from an approaching hunter.

The long haul began up the crest of a lateral moraine; this type of moraine is a pile of rubble forced up along the edge of a glacier by the tremendous force of that glacier. In this case the Trift Glacier had done the work with its gigantic ice tongue.

Eight thousand feet, nine thousand, ten thousand. The altitude had a considerable effect. There was no point in rushing so I strolled on for six hours and sat beside a stream near a small snowfield to wait for the others. The Rothorn hut was only ten minutes' walk away. I dozed in the sun, and felt rather pleased with myself because I had for the first time made a long hut walk from the valley instead of using mechanical transport.

I went on to the hut and my four friends straggled up the trail an hour later. They decided to climb the Trifthorn the next day. A peak of a little over 12,000 feet (3,728 m), it was a fairly easy training climb. I stuck to the usual rule of not doing too much too soon and opted out, though I was not sure whether this was through sense or sloth.

The others got up early, at half-past three, and spent a few pleasant hours going up and down the Trifthorn, without incident.

Four o'clock the next day saw us all, apart from Len, tramping over crusty snow, up the Trift Glacier. John and Don were ahead by a few minutes. For a while Dave wore a head-torch, but it was soon daylight.

'Crevasse there,' he warned as he stepped over a gaping split in the glacier. 'And another.'

The target was the Wellenkuppe, 12,800 feet high (3,903 m). The route was quite easy and relatively short.

We picked our way across an ice slope of twenty degrees or less. The sun rose to shed pink light on the mountains.

'Look at that panorama!' Dave said every few minutes. Neither he nor I could resist the temptation to stop many times and absorb the scenery with our eyes.

We curved to the left up the glacier, across more crevasses, and the snow steepened – time for crampons. Mounting a broad, glistening shoulder of snow, from which the route swept sharply to the right, we kept close to but a little below a sharp rock ridge. This was the sort of place where helmets were a wise precaution. And sure enough, a few minutes after we had put on our helmets, down came a nasty shower of stones. They bounced past a few yards away.

Rock gave way to snow, and snow to rock. With crampons removed, we climbed over easy rock which in most places was sound and rarely steeper than forty-five degrees. One short exception, a few degrees from the vertical, was loose and unpleasant. An impressive slab section was climbed for two hundred feet on firm, dry rock with abundant holds.

'Can't be far now,' Dave remarked as we neared the top of the slab. He was right. The rock finished and stretching up to the summit was a gently rising snow crest, and in fifteen minutes we joined Don and John on the broad snow top. They had been waiting a long time for us, and were cold, so they started back down. In a few minutes we followed down the snow, down the slab in two pitches of a hundred feet or so. On the second pitch I was facing outwards with my hands, bottom and boots on the rock. This was the quickest and easiest way to descend in the circumstances. A crack running parallel to our direction of travel was just wide enough to jam a boot in to give a firm hold. Unfortunately it proved to be too firm and the boot stuck fast. Pulling was no good. I thought about having to leave behind a boot, complete with foot and leg, to puzzle future generations of alpinists. But no, if tugging failed I could unlace the boot and pull the foot out, then the leather would not be jammed tight. I pulled the leg with both hands to no avail, so began to kick the wedged boot with the other. In a few seconds it was free. Have to watch that in future, I thought.

When we reached the glacier I again encountered the old adversary, soft snow. Dave strode along with relative ease while I floundered. My boots sank deep, seeming unwilling to go on. In similar circumstances Geoffrey Winthrop Young, a one-legged mountaineer, thought, 'The Trift glacier would at this hour be for me impassable, and exceedingly dangerous, with snow-covered crevasses under broiling sunshine'.

Each time I passed over a crevasse I warned Dave to look out for it. The icy, green depths looked menacing, but the real danger lay in the depths we could not see as we trod the soft mantle. The afternoon sun beat down with unpleasant fierceness.

'This is murder,' I told Dave.

'Looks like the only solution will be skis or snow-shoes. Best to stick to rock until you have some.'

'I've been avoiding them because it will mean humping around extra gear, but it looks like the only way.'

Every so often I went on a climb which led to the solution of a problem. The ski basket on the end of an ice-axe, knee pads, snow-shoes: these and other aids made a great difference, and it was worth going on the Wellenkuppe just to reach the decision in favour of using snow-shoes.

Bootprints of previous parties showed the route, but there was no way of knowing that snow which had held an hour before would now support the weight of a man. Hardness had deserted the snow and would only return with the night. Progress was slow, but eventually we reached the comfort of firm rock near the hut. It had taken nearly five hours to climb up and almost as long to descend. Slow going.

'That was a grand day,' Dave said. 'No epics, time to look around. Very pleasant.'

By the time I arrived back at the camp-site the next day, the greater part of a week had elapsed since arriving in Zermatt. Including treks to and from huts, an occasional rest day, and allowing for the weather, my lack of mobility at that time meant that I could expect to climb only three or four peaks in a holiday of three weeks. The descent from the Rothorn hut which my companions had tacked on to the end of a day's climbing had been for me four and a half very hot hours, and it was preferable to take yet another unwanted day of idleness to help some small abrasions on my stumps to heal. Once more I paid for an ascent with pain. I knew the lesson so well: when the stumps became damaged, a day or more of relaxation prevented them from deteriorating.

We witnessed a very sad scene. Next to ours stood two tiny tents, temporary homes for four young Japanese men. We didn't see much of them because they spent most of their time climbing. One afternoon word filtered down to the valley that two Japanese had fallen to their deaths on the normal route on the Matterhorn. It did not occur to us that it might be two of the men from the neighbouring tents because there were hordes of Japanese climbers in the Alps. But on the morning following the announcement of the accident two of the men turned up, obviously shocked, to pack up both tents and all the equipment. They did so quietly and one sight really brought home the sadness of the occasion – when the two small men left the camp site each was burdened with two large rucksacks, one tied on top of the other.

Most of our group chose to climb the Breithorn next. This is very easy by the normal route but it is snow all the way. The snow was in poor condition and had been so for many days because of high temperatures;

some people reported that the snow on that route was soft even early in the morning.

'You coming, Norm?' someone asked.

'No thanks. I'll stick to the rock until the temperature goes down a bit.'

'Wish I had legs like yours,' Dave said. 'I wouldn't have to climb so much with an excuse like that.'

Adrian, Alan and I headed up the Ober Rothorn, which is just over 11,200 feet (3,415 m). It was a walk, during which Adrian repeatedly popped up on boulders, like the marmot on the way to the Rothorn hut. Unlike the marmot he kept yodelling, 'And your old lady too.'

Close to the top we passed a lady who had stopped for a rest. As I went by she said, helpfully, 'You should put your feet like this,' and demonstrated how to place them.

'I'd like to if I had any,' was all I could think of saying at the time, and then I spent a while chatting to assure her that there was no need to be embarrassed.

It reminded me of something which happened at Jungfraujoch a couple of years earlier. Close to the hotel was a small, snowy plateau which was reached by a gently sloping snow path. One day I was walking up the path when I heard an American man say to two women with him, 'That guy must know what he's doing because he's wearing the right boots and clothes. See how he walks on his toes? Now that's the way to do it. Come on, let's go!'

Within seconds there was a tremendous smack as he hit the snow and the last I saw of him he was being helped back to the hotel by his companions.

Back at the camp-site Dave was preparing a chicken curry. He was pleased at having been able to purchase very cheaply a bag full of bits of chicken. When he came to tip the bits in a pan they turned out to be mostly from the back ends of the birds. Considering that his surname is Parsons, it was appropriate.

Later on he told me about the Breithorn.

'You were right not to go up with us. It's dead easy but the snow's soft. Like walking on porridge. Don and I went up Monte Rosa and it was the same.'

'I'll stick mostly to rock then.'

'How about the Thing? That's mostly rock. Better than festering down here.'

'I think I'd like to go.'

'It's a fantastic shape. Pity to miss the chance while you're here. We could climb part way and see how it goes.'

'As far as the Solvay hut, perhaps.'

Len, John and Don went off to the Weisshorn, while Adrian and Alan picked the Allalinhorn.

The Belevedere Hotel on the Hörnli ridge of the Matterhorn was much improved since my previous visit and the kitchen, particularly, was no longer filthy. We stayed in the hut next door and were away by half past three the next morning, along with about sixty other alpinists; yes, sixty.

The moon was just bright enough to manage without a torch, although most people wore head torches. We followed a long line of lights up a rocky path. A fixed rope of twenty feet hung down the first bit of climbable rock and everyone went up quickly, hand over hand, with feet walking up. Without that rope there would have been a bottleneck close to the hut.

An easy track climbed and dipped, and several lights in front veered a little to the right into dark shadow. The track steepened. Everyone else continued to walk upright but I found it easier to scramble than to walk in some places.

'Not like that!'

The voice from behind me spoke in German. The leader of a party of three was talking to me. My knowledge of German was poor, but I did my best to explain my unconventional technique.

'I must. I have no legs,' I said. At least, that's what I thought I said.

The man made no reply and headed away up the mountain with great speed. No wonder! A friend explained to me later that what I had actually said was, 'I must. I have no bees.'

We followed the lights up a crumbly rock face, nearly vertical in places but very easy. At the top a party of three seemed to be having trouble. We had to wait quite a long time while the leader descended into darkness over a cliff. In a minute there was a sound of clattering rock from his direction, a sound which recurred several times in the next few minutes. The leader called up; he sounded anxious. The man feeding the rope down to him found a spike of rock and passed the rope around it.

'I don't remember this bit,' Dave remarked. He had been on the route before, once when he climbed up and down that way and once when descending after climbing the Zmutt ridge of the mountain.

Time crept by and the leader's rope was fed out slowly.

'Wrong way,' Dave said. 'Must be. There's nothing difficult around this part of the route.'

'Might as well go down the bit we've come up then.'

'Yes.'

We retraced our way down the rock face. As the light improved we saw that we had been on the top of a rock tower which stuck up on the ridge. In all we must have wasted a large part of an hour by following the wrong people. They passed us again an hour later. We pressed on over slopes of broken rock.

'What a heap of rubbish,' Dave remarked. At close quarters the mountain lost much of its beauty.

People above were dislodging lots of stones and in the half light it was not easy to see them coming. We were worried, with good reason as it happened. As one shower of Mother Nature's cannonballs bounced down we froze, ready to duck or dodge. The stones thudded down to our right and stopped not far below as they hit a large ledge. A minute or two later another rock barrage began to fall from three hundred feet above. They came nearer and nearer but we could not see them. Judging from the noise it gradually became more and more evident that they were coming our way. We pressed ourselves against the rock. Clunk, clunk, clunk. Fist-sized stones sped by and there was a loud thump on my helmet. It was probably a glancing blow because the helmet was not split.

'Christ!' my companion muttered.

'You all right, Dave?'

He was about four yards away.

'Yes. They missed me. You all right?'

'Yes. Got a smack on the helmet. I think one hit my ice-axe too.'

The axe was passed through a shoulder strap of my rucksack, between the rucksack and my back. On this occasion the axe had a wooden shaft, and when I came to examine it in daylight there was a chip of wood missing. I was lucky not to have been struck on the back of the neck.

'What a heap of rubbish!' Dave said again.

Snow patches were only a few square yards in area. The rock was poor in many places. Difficulty in route-finding slowed us. It was not that we went the wrong way often, but time was lost as we talked over which way looked best. We lacked the confidence of being sure we were on the route. Instead of thrusting ahead, as one can on some obvious routes, we had to pick the way, to fret at it.

Other parties had route-finding problems and after four hours' climbing several people were only a few minutes ahead. A man with a bandaged head descended with two companions.

Nowhere was the rock climbing above Moderate standard. In six hours we were at the Solvay hut, 13,120 feet (4,000 m). That was a very long time – four hours would have been satisfactory for me.

The hut was perched right on the sharp ridge. Five or six disconsolate people hung around, waiting for friends who had carried on. Most were tired, probably because of the altitude, and one had injured his knee in a fall. He felt that he would be unable to descend so a message was taken to the Hörnli hut to summon a helicopter.

'What shall we do tomorrow?' Dave asked me. 'To tell the truth, I'm not too happy to go on when there are only two of us.'

'I was thinking about that. We usually would have someone else on a route like this.'

'So we'd better go down tomorrow?'

'I think so. Anyway, this has been a good reconnaissance.'

'Yes. You wouldn't have any trouble with the rest of the route.'

At six a.m. the next day we abseiled down a couple of steep pitches and climbed down the mountain. (In simple terms, abseiling means sliding down a rope.)

Len, Don and John had turned back on the Weisshorn for a number of reasons, including lack of sleep the night before, so Len's greatest ambition was unrealised. I failed to climb the Thing and as it was a rubbishy route I was not disappointed. Or was I? It was strange. I had felt little ambition to stand on the summit, but it was as if the mountain had control and could make me want to climb. Where was my former indifference about that peak? It was gone for sure, for ever; the lure of that lovely peak was just too strong now I had seen it. The Siren song of the mountains is irresistible.

Of our small group Len and John, neither having reached their mid-forties, died soon after; Len of alcoholism and John of a heart attack. Their deaths reinforced in me the desire to live life to the full, among the mountains, without delay.

The mountains had given me much pleasure and I wondered how many other disabled people took part in outdoor pursuits. There was a lack of information available, and after a talk with Lady Hamilton, Chairman of the Disabled Living Foundation, I was given the job of compiling a guide on outdoor pursuits for disabled people.

Although I was in favour of competitive sports for disabled people, I felt that the emphasis had been so much on that side that non-competitive activities had been neglected, partly because of the often unfounded assumptions on the part of some organisers of sports for disabled people that such activities were beyond the abilities of the people they dealt with. There was a tendency to expect disabled people to take part only in a limited number of sports and mostly in a segregated situation. Total integration within the community was clearly not always possible but it did seem desirable to lean towards integration wherever this was realistic. With very few exceptions, only the more obvious and easiest sports had been tackled on a large scale; the most notable exception was the Riding for the Disabled Association, which brought riding to thousands of disabled young people and adults.

Since becoming involved in compiling *Outdoor Pursuits for Disabled People* I have noticed an increase in concern for the subject in the media and within interested organisations, and I was pleased to be involved in various ways in several of these developments. The Spastics Society decided to build an adventure and field studies centre in Cornwall; many outdoor pursuits centres ran courses for disabled people; the Sports Council set up a steering committee concerned with water sports for disabled adults and children, and that committee published a book on angling, rowing, sailing, canoeing, sub-aqua diving and water-skiing; increasingly, mentally handicapped people were accepted at outdoor centres; an organisation for disabled skiers was formed; sailing schools took more disabled pupils; a course was run especially to investigate the safe limits in sub-aqua diving for paraplegics and amputees; experiments were carried out in what types of life jackets, buoyancy aids and protective clothing best suited physically handicapped sailors and canoeists; a guide was compiled to access for those in wheelchairs or with walking difficulties, in about fifty nature reserves; and the outdoor pursuits guide was published. As months went by it was encouraging to see a move towards the ideal of as many sports as possible being made available to people with all handicaps. Always there was the proviso that the activity should be suitable from a medical and safety point of view, although most outdoor pursuits could never be completely free of risk. But at least the debate on safety and medical aspects was begun, rather than faint-heartedly avoided, as in the past.

The presence of a handicap meant that for each individual the circumstances in which he or she took part had to be carefully chosen. Experienced, able-bodied canoeists might go down a fast, cold river while a handicapped person might never progress beyond paddling around a still lake in summer. As a hard climber scales a big north face, a spastic girl may be scrambling over easy rock, with a rope, or hill-walking. The important common factor is that each person can find enjoyment and fulfilment within their limitations. I believe that anyone with a physical handicap needs to avoid injury more carefully than an able-bodied counterpart, because an additional handicap, even temporary, may affect him or her more. But, on the other hand, there is a danger that over-protection may condemn that person to a life which they feel is hardly worth living. Somewhere between these extremes a balance must be struck, and the balance must depend a great deal on the choice of the adult individual.

At the limb centre my artificial legs, which had had a very hard life for many years, were condemned and I received two new pairs. I kept one of the old pairs for some tests on the effects of falling in water. The results were definite: even with a waterwing blown up inside each leg, I sank.

'You've got three pairs of legs now,' someone remarked. 'That makes you a wingless insect.'

The old legs had been made rather short, leaving a disproportionate shortness from the knees down. Being one-and-a-half inches longer, the new legs made walking seem easier because the swing of the limbs felt more natural than with shorter legs. I strutted about on the new legs and waited for friends to notice the new, taller Norm. Three successive people stared and said, 'Have you changed your hair style?'

Summer approached and I put my thoughts to the coming alpine season. On arriving home from work one day Judy found me walking about with a bath tray strapped to each foot.

'What on earth are you doing?'

'Snow-shoes. Lighter than the ones you can buy. But I think plastic may be a bit slippery on snow.'

'You look pretty silly like that.'

In any case it took just a few minutes of walking to split the bath trays, and in the long run it turned out better to buy a ready-made pair.

The Matterhorn had been on my mind all year. After climbing to the Solvay hut I had asked at the Zermatt guides' office if a guide could be found for the following year and the man there said it would be all right. However, when I wrote to the office to confirm this I received no reply.

The London editor of a Swiss news agency contacted me to see what I had planned for the summer.

'The Matterhorn. But I don't know if any guides will go; and even if they do I can't afford to pay them. And none of my friends are going to Zermatt this year.'

Because of a way of life which left enough time to do two things I very much wanted to do, climb and write the outdoor pursuits guide, my annual earnings were only £500.

A couple of years before I had written half a dozen letters to large business organisations to request funds for a climbing trip. I was always rather uncertain about writing these letters because I couldn't really believe that anyone would be prepared to take the responsibility of being associated with one of my climbs, and I couldn't see why someone else should pay for my excitement and pleasure. The response from the firms was three dozen cans of beer and the offer of a free tin of antiseptic ointment.

The Swiss editor of the agency was sufficiently interested in the proposed climb to be prepared to pay the guide fees. Unfortunately the President of the Zermatt guides then decided that the ascent was too dangerous for me. True, like anyone else attempting the Matterhorn I could be killed or injured, but I did not consider the risk to be any greater for me.

Eventually contact was made with Hans Kaufmann, with whom I had climbed the Eiger; he would go.

Brian Campbell gave my legs the usual, thorough, pre-alpine check at the limb centre, and less than twenty-four hours after leaving Victoria Station I was nearly 10,000 feet above sea level at the Gandegg hut, reached easily in twenty minutes' walk from a cable car out of Zermatt. August was not quite half way through.

Training at altitude was essential and the next day I sat on the moraine at the edge of the Theodul glacier and waited to hitch a lift across with anyone who would let me join their rope. The glacier is not especially dangerous to cross but on rare occasions people do fall in crevasses there. No more than five minutes went by and two Germans and their wives came along. They knew what I was waiting for.

'You vant to go to zee Theodul hut?'

'Yes, please.'

'You can come vis us.'

We rose slowly through a thousand feet in a gradual pull up the snow and crevassed ice. Skiers hissed downhill making us look out of place, like snails caught in the snow. In one and a half hours we crossed the high frontier as the mountaineer smugglers used to, into Italy.

There was no opportunity get to know my companions, who took a look around the hut, said something like, 'Filthy Italians!' and marched back down the glacier. For a mountain hut the place seemed acceptable and another group of German people soon included me in their company.

'You are going up the Breithorn tomorrow?'

The question came from Gunter, a serious yet cheerful man of forty who worked as a judge. The Breithorn, 13,660 feet (4,165 m), was close.

'No. I am alone.'

'Come with us then,' Hans said. He was a priest.

'I am slow, particularly on a snow route.'

Although I explained why and they appeared to have understood, it turned out that they had not.

'You can come with us,' Hans reaffirmed.

So at half past five the next day I roped up with Gunter and his friend, Franz. On another rope were Hans, two young ladies and Bernhard, an apprentice railway worker.

There must have been forty or more people trudging the same way. For my sake, I believed, Gunter set a very slow pace – too slow for me because I found it impossible to get into a good rhythm.

A short, steep, icy slope, a gentle gradient, a stretch of moderately steep snow, a couple of crevasses to step over, a plateau of softening snow: an easy route, yet for me quite hard. Much of the way was just a walk over gentle white undulations, and there was always a good view of the surrounding peaks if we lifted our eyes. Hours went quickly.

'You can go faster if you like,' I explained to Gunter, but we kept the same pace, and by the time we had pulled ourselves up the final steepish snow to the summit five hours had gone by. It was certainly one of the easiest to reach of alpine summits over the 4,000 metre mark. Franz produced a tin of delicious raspberries for us to share on the top, and then we had a tin of pineapple chunks which Bernhard had brought.

On the descent Gunter stayed with me while the others hurried to catch the cable car to the valley. The climb was a useful training exercise and was valuable in one more important respect: as we headed back to the hut I tried out the snow-shoes. They were ideal, and would see a lot of snow over the next few years. If I had had them on Mont Blanc or on the glaciers beneath the Jungfrau and the Wellenkuppe those ascents and descents would have been transformed into the easiest of climbs.

'Is one of your legs hurt?' Gunter enquired.

I explained again.

'Now I understand,' he said. Obviously they had all misunderstood what I had told them the night before. 'And still you love to go to the mountains.'

'Oh yes. As much as anyone. More than most, I believe.'

'I understand.'

On the dawdle back across the plateau Gunter called a halt a couple of times so we could just sit and look. I had never met such a man for taking his time and stopping to savour every moment. Even when a fifteen minute hailstorm thrashed at us he plodded on at his unhurrying pace. In fact we took so long that we were out for ten hours that day.

Back in Zermatt I booked in at a dormitory at the top of the Bahnhof Hotel, and rang Herr Perll, the Swiss editor of the news agency. He was a mountaineer and intended taking pictures on the climb. He was away for three days, I learned.

I mooched around Zermatt. The weather stayed fine and the climbing boomed. For three or four days the Matterhorn was thronged with mountaineers, and then the weather turned nasty. I had missed my chance. Damn, damn, damn.

On ringing Herr Perll again I was told he was still away on holiday, so I moved to a dormitory in a mountain hotel at Gornergrat and spent three days walking about at around the 10,000 feet contour.

Down to Zermatt again. On the telephone to Herr Perll.

'I will come to Zermatt on Wednesday,' he said.

Three more days to wait, to wander about.

In the basement of the hotel was a kitchen where you could cook for yourself, and it was there that one day a very distinguished visitor appeared: Lord Hunt. In company with his wife and a friend he was planning to travel over to Chamonix across the mountains. As a result of our meeting there Lord Hunt later came to the press launch of the outdoor pursuits guide. Sir Roger Bannister, at that time Chairman of the Sports Council, was at the launch too, so with the leader of the successful British Everest expedition and the first man to run a mile in four minutes at the same event we were not short of famous personalities. And it was very appropriate that the foreword to the guide was written by Sir Jack Longland, who used to climb with one-legged Geoffrey Winthrop Young.

It was tempting to go and do some more high peaks, but I had to stay around to be ready to climb the Matterhorn. I could not risk doing too much in training for fear of damage to the stumps. Instead of going up the high peaks I made do with easy ascents in the area: twice I went up the Ober Rothorn, 11,250 feet (3,415 m), and twice up the Unter Rothorn, 10,200 feet (3,103 m). Mostly I went alone because these were safe, busy trails, and once with Jon Ryder, an exceptionally fit American who became so fond of Zermatt that he stayed on to work on the Gornergrat railway for the winter.

Days crept by. In the brief spells when the weather was fine Hans Kaufmann considered that conditions on the Matterhorn were not good enough for me. The weather was never stable for long, and then there was another setback: Hans Kaufmann said he was busy for several days so could not go even if the weather was suitable. The Zermatt guide who would have gone with him was busy too. Whether they were really busy or had had second thoughts I could not say, but I had to start looking for guides again. I'm not superstitious but the day on which this news came was Friday, 13th September.

I had been in Switzerland five weeks and was still waiting. I was always bloody well waiting, it seemed.

A few phone calls led me to get in touch with Eddy Petrig, a guide. He had heard that I was in the village so there was no need for long explanations.

'When do you want to go?' he asked.

'As soon as possible.'

'We will meet tomorrow and talk. I cannot say yet that I will go.'

We met next day and sat on a low wall outside the Bahnhof Hotel to talk about the climbing I had done.

'How long do you think you will need to get to the summit?'

'Seven and a half or eight hours. Perhaps more.' Geoffrey Winthrop Young took nine and a half hours to the summit, eighteen hours for the return trip in conditions better than had been seen for many years. Was my estimate to optimistic? And one guide who knew Geoffrey told me that the ascent had been very difficult for him and caused many problems for his guides.

'I would like to go,' Eddy said at last. 'I will contact another guide to be with us.'

'That's fine.'

'And I will ring you when it is time to go.'

Eddy was influenced, I believe, by the fact that he felt that the guides had not behaved properly in failing to reply to my letter.

Frau Biner, who usually ran the Bahnhof Hotel, was convalescing after breaking a thigh, so two of her relations, Kathy and Miriam, looked after the place. Being among the longest staying guests that year, Jon and I were treated with special kindness, and the friendliness of many people is one of the things I remember most about the trip to Zermatt.

'If you climb the Matterhorn you will be very happy,' Miriam said one day. 'And if you cannot it will make me very sad.'

The weather forecast gave no cause for optimism for a couple of days. 17th September arrived and my sixth week in Switzerland began.

'What's the matter with you?' Eddy's wife asked him with irritation. 'You're out looking at the weather every fifteen minutes!'

He admitted to me later that he had been very anxious while waiting. I was under a strain too.

'I feel like my stomach's connected to the barometer,' I told Jon. 'Every time I see it go up or down my guts do too.'

'You'll do it if the weather gives you a chance,' Jon insisted.

Still the weather would not let me go, and waiting was getting me down. A feeling of utter desolation gripped me. Anyone who has set his heart on a dear goal and has been frustrated day after day, week after week, will understand what I mean. I lay on my bunk and tried to convince myself that to climb the Matterhorn was insignificant, but, selfishly, the one thing I really wanted in life at the time was to stand on the top of the Matterhorn.

'Hallo! Telephone!'

It was the Spanish housekeeper, a large, friendly lady, calling me. Eddy was on the line.

'The weather is not really settled but we should go,' he said. 'You should ring Herr Perll and get him to come to Zermatt now. Otherwise you may not get a chance this year.'

Götz Perll arrived the same day. Bearded, dark, of average build, thirty-four years old. Gradually scraps of information built up a picture of the man: independent, determined, married five years with one baby of nine months, originally from Germany, fond of skiing.

The next day was 20th September. At eight a.m. thick mist cut off the sky. By half past nine the same morning it was raining lightly. Eddy rang at ten a.m.

'We will wait until the forecast at half past twelve. There has been some snow at the Hörnli hut.'

'If not this year, then next year,' I said. Like the grains of sand in an egg-timer, minutes were running out. If they ran out completely it would be next year before the timer could be turned over to start again.

Eddy was definite: 'I want you to do it this year now you are trained.'

The barometer fell a little. Oh dear! And by noon it was raining again. At one o'clock the phone rang and Götz picked it up. He talked seriously for a minute or two, and as he talked he raised one thumb in the air.

'We go to the Belvedere Hotel this afternoon,' he said. 'Eddy is very confident that you can do it but it depends on the weather.'

In haste we bought food for the trip, had a good meal and hurried off to the cable car, where Eddy waited with Richard Biner, an aspirant guide who was to climb with Götz. Richard did not speak much English and was a quiet man.

Eddy stared at my boots. They were light, ideal for me but too light for a mountaineer with real feet.

'Don't your feet get cold with those boots?'

'I suppose so. But it doesn't matter.'

'Of course. I am stupid.'

He was an amazingly young-looking man. At first I thought he was in his mid-forties but in fact he was fifty-seven years old. He was not the type who bulged with muscle; this lean, agile person moved in a deliberate, cat-like way and it was difficult to believe that in most societies he would be only a few years from retirement. Eddy had travelled to several countries and had lived some years in Canada. He had been married a few years, and perhaps his young children helped him to remain as young in mind as he looked in body. He seemed to belong more to my generation than to his own.

The cable car whisked us up through light rain, up more than three thousand feet in minutes to Schwarzee, at about 8,500 feet (2,582 m). A thick mist blanket hung greyly over the area.

'It is no good. We must go down,' Eddy said, but he was not serious and led the way up the trail.

'You can go in front and make the pace if you like, Norman. Go as slowly as you like,' he suggested, and within five minutes said, 'Don't go so fast. I don't want you pooped for tomorrow.'

'Going too slowly makes it more difficult. It's like doing press-ups: the slow ones are harder.'

'All right. You know what is best for you.'

Down in Zermatt a chimney sweep called at the Bahnhof Hotel.

'That is good luck,' Miriam told Jon. 'Now I know Norman will succeed. The chimney sweep is always a sign of good luck.'

For an hour we tramped on in single file. The mist thinned. It was wonderfully cool for walking. Snow and ice lay on the zig-zags of the Hörnli buttress.

'The wind is from the north,' Eddy announced. 'The weather will be good tomorrow. That is because you are an angel without wings. You are lucky. And you did not say you could do more than you can when I talked to you. Now I am excited. As long as the weather is all right you will do it.'

The weather. Always the weather. If one heavy snow shower came the route would probably not be in condition again that year.

We were at the Belvedere Hotel in one and a half hours. The manager and his wife had kindly promised to keep the hotel open for an extra night the following day, the day on which, if all went well, we should either get back or be staying in the Solvay hut. This brought home to me just how close we were to the end of the season.

A man arrived at the hotel.

'Norman, this is Leo Imesch,' Eddy said. 'He will be going with us.'

Leo was broad, tall, fair, about twenty-five years old, a kind and cheerful man with a big moustache. He hoped to qualify as a guide the next year. So there we were: Eddy, Götz, who had made the event possible, the cheerful and enthusiastic Leo, quiet Richard, and me. The hotel manager kept offering me wine but I drank tea instead. His wife prepared a very substantial meal. Suitably fed, we went to look at the weather again. Stars stood out sharply over mist-filled valleys.

'It will be good,' Eddy said once more.

I turned in early, and while I slept Eddy and the hotel manager argued violently about my chances. Eddy was confident, the manager was not, but still gave Leo a bottle of strong spirit for us to share in celebration if we reached the summit. We would learn the irony of that argument the next day.

The sound of someone laughing quietly awoke me in the morning; my legs, still wearing trousers, leaned against the bottom of my bunk as if resting too, and caused much amusement.

Yesterday's trail walk had lifted us through more than two thousand feet. Now the real climbing would begin, four thousand feet up the jagged Hörnli ridge, keeping mostly to the left side, at other times moving on the very crest of the ridge. This was roughly the route of the first ascent more than a hundred years before, when four of the party of seven fell to their deaths on the way down.

Five a.m. Not light, but not black. Eddy led, with me and then Leo behind. Richard led Götz. The weather refused to let us know for sure that it would remain good, but the signs were reasonably favourable.

Three people left the hotel in front of us: the manager and two friends.

Thick snow had accumulated on the normal way near the hotel. Throughout the usual climbing season the rock there would have been clear but now we crunched over a firm, white covering.

'Numerous short pitches of 2', the guide-book said. Two is equivalent to something between Moderate and Difficult, and we started up the first of those pitches. I saw little of the surroundings apart from the rock, ice and snow under my boots and hands, and I remember the mountain only in bits and pieces. There was a vertical pitch, short and not hard, there was a bit of track through broken rock, there were stretches of snow-covered, sloping rock and more steep rock with good holds.

Eddy had climbed one ridge of the Matterhorn, the Zmutt, fifty-two times, and had often used the Hörnli ridge for descent. With one companion he made the first winter ascent of the Zmutt ridge in 1948.

Head torches were soon extinguished. Unlike on my previous trek that way there had been no long line of lights ahead of us, and the absence of other climbers meant there was little need to wear helmets as a protection against stonefall.

I had to push myself to keep up a reasonable pace. After half an hour, an hour, an hour and a half, two hours, it would have been too easy to drop back to a more comfortable pace, but it was essential to press on so we would be as high as possible as quickly as was sensible.

'Go as you like,' Eddy emphasised. 'You know what you are able to do,' and soon after he said, 'I think you should go a little more slowly. It is a long way.'

'You are doing well,' Leo added in encouragement.

Götz did not request any hesitation for photographs, but took them as we went. We climbed and scrambled without interruption and that made it easier to keep going. Sometimes Götz and Richard were ahead and sometimes they were behind.

Another pitch of Moderate rock, and another, until we were directly below the Solvay hut. The three men who had been ahead turned back because the hotel manager was feeling unwell. He looked very sheepish, as well as sick.

Ahead was the Moseley Slab, at the top of which, the route description said, was a near-vertical corner to climb. Here, or on the slab above, one of Geoffrey Winthrop Young's guides had fallen and was saved on the rope by another guide. On an earlier occasion a guide accompanying one of Geoffrey's friends, Sir Arnold Lunn, fell at the same spot. Sir Arnold and the guide were saved by another guide on the same rope. The slab was named after an American doctor who was killed there. All went well for us and we were soon seated inside the wooden Solvay hut, 13,120 feet (4,000 m) high. Three and a half hours from the bottom of the ridge. Not bad.

We sipped hot tea from flasks and ate little bits: cheese, dried fruit, meat.

Götz asked, 'How do you feel?'

'Fine. This sort of route really suits me.'

'Do you think we'll make it?' I asked Leo.

'If the weather is all right.'

There was mist higher up. For the time being, at least, the weather was satisfactory.

How lucky we were that there were no other climbers around: no stonefall, and we had the peak to ourselves, without delays on the harder sections. It felt right. My major disappointment with the route, that it was crowded, did not apply that day.

In a few minutes we were on our way again, up the Upper Moseley Slab, fifty feet, steep and graded Moderate. Then there was one of the few exposed, narrow rock ridges to walk and scramble over. More scrambling and easy climbing brought us in half an hour to the Shoulder, a large snow and ice slope at forty-five degrees. Time for crampons. At intervals of a hundred feet or more large metal stanchions had been driven in as belay anchors. Eddy went ahead from stanchion to stanchion and I followed only when he had the rope around one of them.

Down in Zermatt, nine thousand feet below, Miriam was watching through a telescope. She picked us out against the white backcloth of the Shoulder, and was even able to see that the second man on the first rope was hunched over and moving quite slowly. She knew who that was.

On the Shoulder a familiar feeling of nausea began to bother me. I think this was caused by physical effort because six hours of any exertion which really makes you puff is quite a strain. So there was the nausea barrier to be faced again. In one way it would have been easy to have stopped but ambition drove me on. At the same time it was as if the decision had been taken away from me; the Matterhorn would not let me rest. It was silly to believe that the mountain was in charge, because the ambition was within me, but it felt as if the Matterhorn would not release me until I reached the top.

Firm snow held reassuringly at each step. It took several minutes to get up the Shoulder. More climbing on rock brought us abruptly to the edge of the north face, plunging down on our right, but we hardly hesitated to look.

Leo and Eddy were talking to each other cheerfully in German; obviously they were optimistic. Now I was confident too.

Next to overcome was a section with fixed ropes. I knew that afterwards there was only a steep rock and snow slope to the summit. The ropes hung permanently down the steep rock and were ice-coated in places. Without crampons it would have been difficult to have kept our feet firmly on the icy rock as we hauled ourselves up hand over hand. I felt that the route would have been more enjoyable without those ropes, although in icy conditions I was pleased to use them. Without the ropes it would have been for me a very serious expedition.

'My mother worries when I am here,' Leo remarked. 'My uncle was killed on the Matterhorn when a fixed rope broke. On the Italian side.'

Up a rope, heave, heave, heave with gloved hands, up another and another. There was a last vertical pitch to pull up at the top of that section, and then we were on the slope known as the Roof.

Only the Roof to go. I would make it! I would make it!

From then on it was a scramble over rock and snow. Loose rock and snow moved under our feet.

'It's not far now,' Leo said, pointing upwards. 'That's the summit.'

Four or five minutes to the top, it appeared.

'Can't go on!' I joked.

We were moving quickly. My ambition was almost at rest, but not quite. Another glance up at the top, a rapid, triumphant scramble and there we were, on the summit of the Matterhorn, 14,690 feet (4,477 m). The sharp summit ridge was almost horizontal and approached a hundred yards in length, with flanks falling away steeply for thousands of feet on either side. Seven-and-a-quarter hours from the hotel was slightly less than I had expected in those conditions.

Everyone was grinning.

'I know this sounds silly but I don't know whether to laugh or cry,' I said.

'You do what you like. We understand. It is a very happy day for us too,' Eddy told me.

Leo added, 'This is one of the best days I have ever had in the mountains.'

Götz looked thrilled and declared that this was one of the happiest days of his life. It was his first time on the Matterhorn.

I laughed quietly, frequently, like someone with a secret. I was released and had no need to return next year.

As we shook hands all round Götz clicked away with his camera. Moving a few feet below the summit to escape the bitter wind we sat on rock to nibble at food and drink tea. The bottle of spirit supplied by the hotel manager was forgotten.

No one else reached the summit that day. We had met three men who turned back and later saw two more who got to the Shoulder before going down again.

Cloud blocked our view of Zermatt but we could see Mont Blanc. A red helicopter chattered by, quite close, and people inside waved. We waved back and I thought how pleasant it would have been to tell them how contented we were. The aircraft flew down and was soon out of sight behind cloud. Before long we followed the same general direction, downwards.

'Can you get back to the hotel today and miss the Solvay hut?' Eddy wanted to know. And clearly he wanted a positive reply.

'I think so.'

Our elation was understandable but we had done only half of the job. Now we had to get down safely. We descended the Roof and the fixed ropes with reasonable speed. On narrow ridges we tried a new method: Leo would walk while I lightly rested a hand on his rucksack to help balance. In this way we moved quite rapidly on airy ridges.

We passed the two climbers who had reached the Shoulder. Difficulties in route finding had slowed this pair, and they failed to get back to the hotel that night.

Eddy and Leo remained patient, vigilant, good-humoured. The Solvay hut was reached in what for me was a sprint time, two hours. We sat there having a snack and sipping at the hotel manager's spirit. There was no question of spending the night in the hut; we felt we could reach the hotel before dark, and in any case we had torches.

The steepness of the mountain suited me as I found it easy to descend by lowering myself with my arms. After ten hours of climbing I was beginning to tire and Eddy twice called a halt for a rest.

'There is no hurry,' he advised. 'Just concentrate.'

While we sat and admired the view he said, 'You should not push yourself so hard. You enjoy the mountains and perhaps ten hours is enough for you in a day.'

Down again, down, down, steady, down, steady, concentrate. Down a hundred feet, two hundred, four hundred, seven hundred, a thousand. We drew close to the hotel, where a small group of climbers waited to congratulate our party. Night did not overtake us: we were back in the hotel at six-thirty p.m., twenty minutes before darkness. The round trip had taken thirteen and a half hours.

Soon only a dim outline of the mountain remained. I watched it for a long time. Had I really climbed up that shadow?

I felt very guilty at not being able to touch the special meal which the manager's wife cooked for us, but I could not keep anything down. I must be one of the few people in the world to have celebrated a climb with a glass of hot water. There I sat, quite tired, rather sick, and above all, delighted. Of the manager, there was no sign.

Miriam, Frau Biner and Jon rang to congratulate us all. Before long I went to bed. The only damage to my stumps was one abrasion about the size of the nail of my small finger.

By half past six the next day we were up and breakfasting. The two men who had been caught out by darkness had bivouacked above the hotel and descended safely at dawn.

Richard and Leo hurried down to the valley while Eddy, Götz and I went more slowly. What followed then? A welcome bath at the Bahnhof Hotel, half a dozen cups of tea with Miriam and Jon in the kitchen, the warmth of their sincere congratulations, some wine with Eddy and Jon, plenty of big meals, a telephone call to Judy, who was delighted. Now I could go home.

Miriam and Jon saw me off at Zermatt station. It was growing dark as the train trundled down the valley but I could still see the fresh snow which lay in a continuous carpet down to 7,000 feet. The following day I would be thirty-four years old, and I felt more like eighteen. I was overwhelmed with feeling, with the wonderful taste of success. The ambitions were behind and I could go and climb without such single-mindedness. Trail walks, glacier treks, beautiful mountains: all were waiting. Yet despite feeling so young it was as if I had already lived one life, in a hurry. Any more would be a bonus.

The Wellenkuppe, the Mönch, the Jungfrau, the Breithorn, Mont Blanc, the Eiger, the Matterhorn: they are my dear friends who have let me taste life at its sweetest. I have memories which cannot be taken away, and what better treasures could I hope for? I am indeed a rich man.

# 5

# *Plans for Peru*

On lush Swiss mountain pastures and silvery glaciers we wandered contentedly above Saas Fee, a delightful village of timber chalets and bright flower boxes and jingling, clip-clopping horse-drawn carriages, all sheltered in a broad valley. In every direction, fields and forests and pastures lifted from the valley floor, gently at first, then more and more steeply until they met the white hems of peaks where the snows always lay. A fat glacier snout poked down the head of the valley and in some lights threatened to thrust its way right into the village and crush it all. Judy found complete enjoyment in walking but I burned to climb, so I talked with a mountain guide, a local man, who agreed to do the south-south-west ridge of the Egginer. Though short, the ridge was supposedly quite hard, and it was wise to be with an expert. Camillo, big-limbed, heavy-featured, ruddy-faced, about six feet tall, could get along quite well in English so it was easy to explain what was on my mind. His pleasure at learning this prospective client was a fairly experienced climber was in no way diminished when a shortage of legs was mentioned, so I began to wonder if his command of my language was as good as we had mutually and tacitly accepted from the start. It seemed better not to labour the point too far. He would find out soon enough and perhaps by then it would not matter.

'I'll take the cable car with you when you go tomorrow and wait at the bottom of the mountain,' Judy announced. Hopes of training my wife as a climber had never borne fruit, though for a while she had tied the rope on and I had dragged her around, an unwilling puppy on a lead. She managed a thin semblance of enthusiasm over some years but there was no point in trying to fool ourselves. It's simple enough to understand what was wrong: she carried the burden of reluctance all the time. She wanted to climb because she did not want to be left behind but she had no love for the sport itself. There's no shame in that; maybe she had too much sense. Sometimes we walked together on the easier slopes, so mountains were half bond, half wedge between us, though not strongly so in either sense.

She was not so fast uphill, but on the way down and headed for home she moved like a camel that has smelt water.

From the way he bubbled full of cheer on the fine, fresh morning of our climb, and chatted amiably to total strangers on the path to the cable car, it was clear the prospect of a shortish climb with a mountaineer of some experience appealed to Camillo. Poor Camillo. While we sat to wait for the first car of the day, the unusual outline of my trouser legs caught is eye; straps and metal created unnatural bulges at the knees. His brow folded into two vertical furrows about his nose and a finger pointed.

'Vat is this?'

So he had not understood. What on earth had he thought I was saying as he nodded and said, 'Yes, yes,' the day before?

'The leg is artificial, Camillo.'

From Camillo there came a long, uncomfortable pause, then he made a statement just to end the awful silence.

'You must be very careful.'

'That took the bounce out of him,' was Judy's observation afterwards. Camillo's bounce had deserted him right enough, and his already long face seemed stretched another two inches by jaw-drooping misery. Battling with indecision, he teetered uneasily on the very brink of changing his mind about going until, like a delivering angel's chariot from my point of view, a hearse in Camillo's eyes, the cable-car drifted quietly down and I got in, fast. Camillo followed, leaden-footed.

Fifteen awkward minutes of silent ascent crawled by and from the isolated upper cable-car terminus we headed for the mountain. I could have done with a straightforward walk on even, compacted snow, but nature had decided shortly before that it was time to have an avalanche there, so we had to pick a way through a jumble of ice chunks up to tea-chest size sprawled in our path. A long ice axe helped me balance in a walking stick manner, but this was tough going and Camillo saw me waddling along at my worst even before we had reached the ridge. Once at the ridge's bouldery foot I squatted on a rock to tuck my trouser legs out of the way in socks, and in order that Camillo should realise properly what he was taking on, and to give him some encouragement, I bared one beige-painted metal leg, hairless of course, with an ankle sufficiently slim to be coveted by the ladies.

'Strong enough for climbing,' I said, hammering the limb, clunk, clunk, with a fist. Camillo brightened a little and I deceived myself into believing, because I wanted to, that I had won his confidence, until his next question arrived.

'But zee other one is all right?'

It had the ring of a prayer.

'No. It is the same.'

'Ah.'

Poor devil. I felt for the miserable man who stood before me, but found myself unable to generate sufficient compassion to let him off the hook.

'They're off below the knees so it's not so bad. I climb a lot,' came out in a rush. Might just as well have said, 'I don't fall off *every* day.'

'I've done much longer routes, Camillo.'

That was better. Despite his grey gloom a retreat was not suggested. For a while Camillo seemed prepared to accept me rather like an iron ball on a chain that would follow him everywhere if it could and pay the fee at the end of the day. It's not quite the relationship you expect between guide and client, but it would do.

So we got on with it. The south-south-west ridge rose at first as an intimidating jut of cliff several hundred feet high, though one could assume from its grade (3, 1 being easiest and 6 hardest) that it could not be as hard as appearances suggested.

Having roped ourselves together we called goodbye to Judy and set off through higgledy piggledy boulders strewn about the base of the ridge. Judging from the look on Camillo's face we might never meet her again; he possessed a kind of 'We're going to die with our boots on' expression and held his head high.

First the ridge presented a short chimney as high as a two-storey house; a chimney is simply a crack wide enough to get your body in. This was an easy one. Subsequent rock sections had helpful holds just where I would have asked: sharp ledges an inch wide for the toes, or large as window sills, prows of rock big as a fist to grasp or stand on, cracks that would take fingers or a hand, a deep hole which admitted the toe of a boot, and a thin flake with a tombstone resemblance over which a hand could be hooked.

So good and so numerous were the cracks and protrusions that we could move quickly, and quite soon we passed the only others out to enjoy the route that day, three in all. It was rare for me to pass anyone. My word yes, rare. Camillo's face was easily read, and radiated growing surprise and relief. Was he relieved! Misery had evaporated with the humpy white morning mist of the valleys below. Camillo smiled again; some of the bounce had come back. Perhaps the Englishman was not mad after all.

'I am happy now I have seen how you can climb,' he informed me.

He would go ahead and find a ledge to stand on so he could hold me on the rope if I fell, and from eighty feet or so above he would call, 'Coming now', and when I caught up he would say, 'Stopping now'. Ahead again, he would order, 'Coming now', once more.

'Always we must make the safe,' he repeated many times as he flicked the rope behind a rounded spike of rock, a bollard against which the rope would run and buzz if I tumbled.

On that day, on the Egginer's firm rock, rust-red and lichenous, even the steepest parts felt safe, though very occasionally with a tentative touch, like a cat pawing its way carefully around a strange room, I found a loose hold and rejected it. So, steadily we gained hundreds of feet up the cliff and within an hour and a half were ploughing ankle deep across a clean, level, fresh snow plateau, a distinct step in the sharp angle of the ridge. Camillo's happy yodels darted and echoed around. His bounce was definitely back to normal and he said, 'We will make all the difficult pieces on the way. There are some steep pieces we can go around but we will go over. There is more snow than sometimes and that makes it harder but we will make them.'

A thin cloak of snow masked the holds here and there and had to be brushed away with a hand, but mostly the climbing was agreeably straightforward. Camillo bellowed down to three people far off on the easy route to tell them the way, but for some reason we could not fathom they retreated when no great distance from the top. I basked in the warm pleasure of being for once on a harder way up, though we had not reached the top yet.

The summit came in sight sooner than I expected. A couple of pitches on rock, a short scramble, and there we were, after three hours on the go. The climbers behind conferred sincere congratulations when they arrived, for Camillo explained my circumstances.

'We have done everything, all the hard pieces, and I am happy,' he told them.

The descent of the easy way, a monotonous clamber down loose stones, was tolerated rather than enjoyed. At the bottom where Judy waited, Camillo stopped hikers on the trail to tell them proudly of his unusual client. Each would listen for a while, nodding Germanically, seriously, very slowly, and saying something like, 'Is that so?' and then they would ask the whereabouts of this man. The image they had could not have matched the real thing, for each time Camillo pointed me out I was leaning limply against a boulder and retching noisily, like an unhappy donkey braying. It lasted three hours or more; sometimes I could not eat for twenty-four hours. The nausea barrier, I called it, and on some alpine climbs I felt as if I had volunteered for a bad dose of flu; continuing to climb while in this condition could be a terrible hardship. What I did not realise in those early days was just how much each climb was taking out of me.

A grade 3 ascent. A quiet pleasure came over me later in the day, but that feeling was soon rudely dismissed for in a Saas Fee bookshop I came across an up-to-date guide-book in English, and, picking it up to read the route description and gloat a bit, I learned that the route had been demoted to the grade below. Some rat had downgraded my route! Grades of alpine routes are not subject to much alteration but I had managed to pick one which was. Tucked away was one more package of mountain memories to look back on and enjoy, and at least I had begun to break away from the easiest routes, but I was deeply dissatisfied that this short route, no more than a trainer for most alpinists, was not grade 3. Perhaps I was too concerned about grades at the time, but it's a stage most of us go through and some never get through. Having wrung as much joy from the mountains as anyone I knew, I greedily wanted more, and somehow it seemed right to attempt harder routes. Not very enlightening that, but it is the only way I can express it: it *felt* right to climb harder. Having got thus far it seemed proper to stand on the shoulders of experience and reach higher; I would try again on another mountain.

With unreliable weather skulking around and dangerous snow conditions high up, it would have to be one of the lower peaks. The Jagihorn above Saas Grund village fitted the bill: 3,206 metres, or about 10,500 feet. The South Rib was grade 3; a sneaky look at the guide-book in the bookshop confirmed that. And the route was short. Jon Ryder needed hardly any persuasion to go, and on foot we followed a meandering trail climbing steeply through a forest towards our objective.

Our journey was broken conveniently for the night at the Weissmies hut at 8,900 feet (2,720 m). After three hours on the mule trail at my plodding pace we drew near the wood-shuttered building and there was the mule itself, chewing at short grass. A doleful St Bernard lay outside, then padded up to be patted. Not far away the pale terracotta Jagihorn, a cathedral arch in outline, rose sharply to a humpy summit. It was only slightly snowy, where isolated specks of white had survived the sun.

On a short, sound and snowless route there was no need for the usual sleepy zombie-walk into the biting cold at three or four o'clock in the morning, so we waited until seven o'clock before emerging from the hut. A faint scratch of rarely trodden path took a direct way across moraine and two shallow streams towards our mountain. The steep pull up the lower grass and earth flank took perhaps twenty puffy minutes before we scrambled over broken rock to the foot of the South Rib.

'Looks like where we join the rib and the real climbing starts,' Jon remarked.

'The rib must be very short. Takes about an hour and a half to the summit. Still, I reckon I'll be pushed to get up so we could take a long time.'

On rock lying back a little from vertical, a horizontal ledge, at its narrowest half the width of a boot sole, invited us along a wall without difficulty on to the rib. Jon muscled up the steep first pitch. He had left his home in America and slogged all winter clearing snow on a Swiss mountain railway, saving his pay and reserving the whole summer for a climbing holiday. His age I put at about twenty-five years and his muscular physique and short-cropped fair hair gave him the appearance of a typical fit and strong American sportsman. Apart from climbing, fanatically keeping fit and playing chess, he would explain with a mock Noel Coward accent he 'took a certain interest in the popsies, too.' With the same accent English friends were addressed as 'You bloody rotter.'

The mood was right and I threw myself at the rock, savouring each sight, smell, sound and touch. There was a delightful pitch of 3 (about Very Difficult in the most common British grading system) and we moved together rather than one at a time; only rarely did either of us feel the need to stop alternately to belay. We relied instead on slipping the rope behind natural gateposts or spikes of rock as we went, 'making the safe', as Camillo would say. The mountain gave us more rock of about grade 3: a short wall rising almost straight up but with an abundance of holds. My lack of leg muscles resulted in staccato movements: jerk, jerk, jerk, too much jerk, so after moving one boot I often had to look down to make quite sure its partner was behaving itself, staying on the hold where it was supposed to be. Compared with the usual climber, power came more from the arms, and I resorted to using rubber knee pads to gain any extra holds I could. Progress was hard, a sweaty business, spasmodic, punctuated by animal grunts and pauses to work out what move would come next. Whenever I put a boot in a narrow vertical crack on the Jagihorn I had to be careful not to put too much weight on it; the boot would go in all right but it didn't always want to come out again, so quite often I had to miss out a hold other climbers would use. Another useful method of climbing, by jamming a leg or a knee in a vertical crack, does not always work for me because a metal leg just slips out; but I cannot emphasise too much that the biggest problem stems from those rigid feet.

A steep corner, like two walls meeting in the corner of a big room, bulged where we would have preferred not on the right and forced me to hug the rock close like someone scared, to press past the bulge. I had to be extremely cautious and avoid that dreaded fall which, even if of only six or seven feet, was too dangerous to risk, almost too frightening to contemplate, for someone who would land on metal legs. What would the impact do to spine or hips? And, my mind kept asking, if I landed from a great height, would my knee caps be torn away as I sank into the metal legs? Falling and not striking the rock below was a different matter; I'd had one or two falls of ten feet or so in circumstances where the stretch of the rope merely cushioned the fall and prevented me hitting the ground. In reality the thin red rope offered great security against death, and serious permanent injury was improbable as long as we took the trouble to climb as we should. However, I could never forget that one bad fall could mean the end of climbing, perhaps of walking too. Buckled legs could be hammered back into shape but real bones might not mend so easily. Perhaps I was over-concerned and over-cautious, but I remembered an acquaintance of mine who fell from a horse, landing on her one artificial leg; she had severe long-term problems through damage to the stump.

The route followed the crest of the rib more or less, with air on either side.

'Want to keep goin' fairly fast so we don't get stormed on. Would be tricky if it got wet,' Jon said as he moved on.

There was angry weather headed our way but we expected to be up and down well before it caught us. Where Jon skipped nimbly across like a competent tightrope walker, I straddled a short, sharp horizontal ridge and worked across in little bumps. *A cheval* the French say: on horseback.

On either side the rib fell away, precipitous and exciting, inducing the enjoyable state of mind in which alertness was not spoiled by too much fear.

Jon started up a vertical wall. Soon the rope hung straight down from his waist, clear of the rock for twenty feet, and I wondered why I wanted to follow. Why did I enjoy all this? No answer came but I realised what an important place climbing had seized in my life. The restless urge to be in the mountains surged through me with increasing strength as years went by.

'Mountains are dangerous. You could waste your life if you go on climbing,' a friend once advised, but I could not agree with that. Life could be wasted by climbing *carelessly* and it could be wasted in another sense by not climbing at all.

The rib gave almost continuous climbing connected by short bits of scrambling, and gradually and surely we gained hundreds of feet. An hour and a half winged by.

'Wait until you see what's ahead,' Jon shouted down.

'What is it?'

'I don't like to tell you, you bloody rotter.'

'What?'

'I think it's the summit.'

'There must be more.'

'No, there's a big stone man here.'

I'd never heard that expression for a cairn. But he was right, and in a couple of minutes we ambled over the last bit of easy scramble to the jagged summit, where twenty people could have stood at once. We were the only ones there.

'We should have looked for some harder bits to do on the way. It was too easy,' Jon said.

'Speak for yourself, buddy. But it did all go surprisingly easily.'

It had been easier than expected. Formerly I had had extreme trouble walking on soft snow. On that same holiday I had started practising on snowshoes; it required care to avoid stepping with the giant feet on the rope to the man ahead and the resemblance of my gait to that of an elderly cowboy was remarked upon, but hours of snow-muffled steps confirmed that my old mountain enemy, soft snow, could be defeated with these ancient weapons. Once more the mists of confusion rolled back and the way ahead was clear: where necessary I could avoid floundering in soft snow by wearing snowshoes but, provided they were not too long, some harder rock routes were more attractive than easy snow routes. Though there was still much to be learned the harsh days of mountain initiation were at an end. Now I was on the right track. And if I could go on some slightly harder routes, how about some really big mountains, with a few bivouacs? It was worth thinking about.

We wandered down the easy way and Jon headed straight back to the valley. I took some time off at the hut because I liked it there, and the afternoon was whiled away in dozy contemplation of the peaks.

That evening, dim gaslamps left dark shadows untouched in corners of the warm hut and under tables and benches. Hammering rain, with us at last, made the building more cosy. I ate a meal which had the fantastic flavour only a hard-earned appetite can impart, and dreamed of future climbs. That was the nice thing about climbing: there was always something to look forward to as well as something to look back on.

The weather throughout Switzerland deteriorated and it was time to head for home. In a way I had accomplished little in two weeks: a few walks, one peak of 11,000 feet and another of 10,500. Yet I felt profound satisfaction; admittedly it was short, but there was one grade 3 behind me, and I had learned a lot besides. Now I could just get on with enjoying climbing without bothering too much about grades.

Frequent visits to the Roehampton limb centre were necessary when I climbed, and this was one of many reasons which pushed me towards being self-employed, so I could go as often as was required. Everyone at the centre was helpful, particularly my doctors, Doctors Tiwari and Fletcher, and my fitter, Brian Campbell. We often discussed possible adaptations to my legs for climbing, and for a while we even contemplated using some form of cloven foot; mountain goats manage well enough, was the basis of our argument. However, Judy was not impressed.

'I know you're a bit of a devil but that's going too far.'

From a practical point of view, as yearnings turned more and more towards mountaineering rather than rock climbing, the idea was not so good because it would mean carrying yet more weight in the form of a pair of feet and a spanner or two, but I did regret a little the lost opportunity of leaving a very interesting set of tracks in the snow. Or getting on a bus to go climbing would have been amusing.

Climbing at home never brought such delectable thrills as the Alps, but was still good in its own way and was, additionally, essential training for the big peaks to come. I should therefore tell you something about climbing in Britain – just a few pages to give you a better idea of what climbing is like for me.

My friend Des Turner bought a car, hand-painted bright lilac and for that reason christened Lilac. We often took her for weekends to climbing areas. I had the advantage that if we arrived late at night and slept in Lilac, with my legs off I fitted comfortably along a seat. Des had given up his mathematics degree course several years before and turned to taxi driving because he felt he did not fit in at college, which is not surprising because he summed up the course as 'a waste of time'. He was something of a cynic and the sort of son mothers worry about. I met his; she did. On his best behaviour he was very helpful and good-natured, though there lurked in him a moody character who was seen less often.

In the summer of 1977 I began to feel increasingly tired and exceedingly bad tempered. Soon afterwards the cause became apparent: I had shingles. If you've not suffered from shingles you probably won't know how painful and tiring the ailment can be. A shooting pain jerked frequently down the left side of my chest and down the left arm, for about two weeks. And I felt awful for some weeks afterwards.

The illness did bring with it one bonus: for many years previously I had experienced a pain in the left side of my chest whenever I became very tired, and though this pain increased a great deal during the outbreak of shingles, it disappeared at the end of the attack. Naturally enough a pain in that region had caused me some concern, and though some tests had not revealed anything amiss, I did wonder for many years if I was negligent in ignoring it. But, though the symptom had seemed worthy of attention, I was reluctant to fuss about it.

When I got back to climbing, Des and I discussed whether I would ever manage a Very Severe (VS) route. That's no great thing if you have legs, but for anyone like me it was an ambitious prospect. Five days later Des and Colin, a gypsy-looking man with a mop of dark hair, stood with me below Pharaoh's Wall, high up on the north side of Llanberis Pass.

For twenty feet the climb runs direct and easy so we all went that far, to a ledge as big as two car roofs at the base of the steep wall. Colin belayed while Des climbed and slotted in three runners. For a while he rested, twenty feet above, allowing the top runner to bear his weight; it occurred to me that I would have to be very, very spent to put trust in such a tiny runner.

Light drizzle started to drift down and with that disappeared any slender chance there might have been of my getting up. The rock was too slippery, and now Des had to choose to go up or down. My vote was for down, taking everything, including his ability, into account.

'You can always use the excuse that I wouldn't be able to follow,' I offered, because he was wavering. 'I'd have no chance in the wet.'

He rejected the way out and inched above the top runner. He tried tentatively to get higher and backed down, tried again and backed down once more. That was his style, yoyo-ing nervously up and down in cautious little forays until he did it. Or didn't. Suddenly, as he stretched for a handhold, he gasped a short, 'Ah!' and his feet slipped off. Hands alone could not keep him up and he fell. Colin held on to the tightening, stretching rope from below but the top runner was plucked out by the force of the fall. From Des's lips crept a quiet, strangled cry which continued as he fell.

'Aaaaaaaaaaaa!'

We all knew the bottom runners were too low to save him from striking the ledge where Colin and I stood, and he would accelerate in a fall of twenty feet before he hit rock. In an upright position Des flew down, a dummy with arms flapping pathetically, and all the time he plaintively uttered his quiet wail. He shot past, so far out from the wall that he missed our ledge. Now the low runners and rope might cushion him. As he dropped from sight there came a nasty sound, a stomach-tightening slap and a crack as some part of his body struck the lip of the ledge. His jaw or head, I thought. Or perhaps an arm. Colin was pulled tight on his belays as Des went ten feet below us, and then the rope buzzed by no more. He had gone as far as he would go. Thirty feet in all.

Silence. We would not be able to see him until we unclipped from our belays. I freed myself while Colin stayed where he was to hold the rope. He called:

'You all right, Des?'

Two or three tortoise seconds went by and a reply drifted back on a croaking voice.

'My arm's broken. Think my leg's busted too.'

So a stretcher was fetched and he was ferried down sliding scree to the road and an ambulance took him to hospital. When we visited Des in hospital the score was one broken arm and a broken bone in his foot. Prior to being trundled away to the plaster-room, true to form he insisted he would not stay in hospital overnight, though the doctor advised this.

'Want to go down the pub,' he said, cussed to the end. We thwarted him by stranding him without transport.

Des feared his mother would hear about his accident but managed to keep it from her.

'She rang to ask if I was going home to the Lake District for the weekend,' he said a few days later. 'I told her I couldn't because I was broke. It was true, in a way.'

A few weeks went by before I had a try at another VS route. This time my partner was Gordon Stainforth, whom I had met through the South Wales Mountaineering Club. From Pen y Pass, at the top of the long uphill haul out of Llanberis, we ambled in half an hour through lovely Cwm Dyli, past little Llyn Teyrn to the Teyrn bluffs. Yes, this was the slab we sought, where Via Media ran up the centre. Without clumps of purple heather, a gorse bush dotted here and there, and thick moss, the grey and brown rock mass might have looked dull, but it was a colourful display. Rock and adornments, and pleasing.

'Magnificent slab!' Gordon praised with great enthusiasm as he got a runner on twenty-five feet up. 'Beautiful rock.'

By the time he stopped almost all of the 150 feet of rope had run out.

'When you're ready, Norman.'

The first few finger holds turned out to be small, enough only for the tips; with knee pads to help it was possible. In short bursts ten feet were grabbed, then ten more, twenty more, thirty. Sometimes the rock had little more than slight ripples on its surface, but that was enough. Pad, pad, pad, on the knees.

'Superb!' Gordon shouted. 'You're going very fast.'

Fast for me, that was. Using knees, or boots where the configuration of the rock permitted, I pulled up on any tiny knob or ripple, on any edge of thin crack, or dent. Every fifteen feet or so there was something big enough to stand on comfortably, for a rest.

'Now look down,' my companion called a couple of times. 'Nice, isn't it?'

In twenty minutes the hard one hundred and thirty feet were behind and I led the last easy bit. You can argue about grades, but I had seconded either a VS or a good Severe. Whichever it was, another memory had been collected, another day spent well, another itch satisfactorily scratched.

VS aspirations stirred again, in the Lake District, two weeks later. My partner was Jim Morgan, a local man and a member of Cockermouth Mountain Rescue team. At Shepherd's Crag in Borrowdale, a cliff peeping out of the trees close by the road three miles south of Keswick, someone was struggling up a route near the one we were on.

'What's that one, Jim?'

'Brown Slabs Crack. VS.'

'Any chance I could get up?'

How was he to know?

'Don't think it's a good one for you, lad. It's savage. But if you want to give it a try . . .'

I did. The third of a party of three hauled himself up the crux with considerable difficulty, then Jim went ahead. With every subtle movement of his feet the route seemed to confirm itself to be too hard. I was short on leg strength but most of all it was foot mobility which was lacking.

Lashed securely to a tree ninety feet above, Jim called, 'Made me sweat a bit. Now, you.'

The first thirty-five feet held no difficulty. The job in hand then was a smooth slab no steeper than a climb we had done earlier, close by, but much harder on account of a lack of holds. It was angled at seventy degrees, and on the right the slab was bounded by a slightly overhanging wall. For several feet where the wall met the slab there was a crack, big enough for a hand. Apart from that crack neither the wall nor the slab offered much to grip or get a toe on.

The right hand slid into the crack and arched to wedge fingertips, ball of thumb, bottom of palm on one side and the back of the hand on the other, tightly against the rock like a crab wedged in. As I heaved up a little and tried to work out what to do next, sweat made the hand slippery and less secure.

What now? Knee pads helped upward progress inches at a time and I got into a position where my knees, hands and boots were on the slab and my back was pressed hard against the overhanging wall. Now it was the whole body imitating a crab. With hands low down I pushed upwards to gain half a dozen sweet inches for the right boot to come to rest on a toehold the size of a small Brazil nut. For minutes at a time, with knees and hands forced exhaustingly in opposition to my back, I pretended to push the overhanging wall back, to separate it from the slab, and that action squeezed enough friction from the rock to keep me up. Another hand jam and a frantic burst won ten more inches. It was so smooth! Every inch was fought for and I made more racket than a bag of grumpy baboons. Despite all the noise some moves gained no more than two or three inches.

How high am I now? Fifty feet? Is that all? Only half way up and the hard part is to come. The other climbers had to turn their feet this way and that.

My mind tried to squeeze out sufficient will to move again. For a minute, reluctance to plunge once more into an area almost devoid of holds made me freeze, but in the end I tore myself free. The crack was climbed by laybacking, that is, by gripping an edge of the crack and leaning back, taking much of the weight on the arms. Laybacking was the only way and for a few feet I managed with the knee pads rather than boots on the slab. Breath hammered in and out, loud as any runner's, and my arms didn't like it. The crack faded to almost nothing and died muddily away. No more laybacking. From the bottom this had looked like the end of the hardest bit, but when he reached there Jim had shouted, 'It's not over yet by a long way.'

He advised, 'Now you have to get your left foot out on that hold.'

Whether it was a small shallow scoop or a bit of a bump I cannot remember, but it was tiny. To get a boot on there would require a wide bridging movement; in other words, I had to do the splits.

I took stock. The right boot rested rather awkwardly in the main crack, poised ready to slip out if I moved jerkily; even if I made no movement it looked as if it might go. The hands could not find anything to hold but could be rested flat against the slab for balance. The left knee pad helped prevent me sliding down and was also keeping me in balance, and it was this leg which had to be moved. While the leg moved, only the unreliable right foothold in the crack would prevent gravity having its way. So with nothing to hang on to, and with one dodgy foothold, I had to stretch a leg out leftwards and finish up doing the splits on two dodgy footholds!

High up on the wall on the right I discovered a hold. Not a good hold, but better than just pressing a hand to the rock.

'Well, Jim, I'd better make the move.'

I stretched the left foot out ever so carefully, stretched, stretched as far as I could go, and the boot came to rest on the hold.

'Great!' from Jim. A nervous giggle from me.

The slab allowed something small for the hands and Jim was only a few feet away. I slithered and grovelled up to the tree as fast as possible and we went up the last comparatively easy thirty feet to the left of an easier groove.

'Well, you did it lad!'

Very glad to have finished, even more pleased to have succeeded. An agreeable tingle spread through the belly region, chasing out the slightly sick sensation of nervousness. Hadn't led it, didn't do it in good style, took nearly an hour for a hundred feet, but I did a real VS – nothing by the standards of today, but satisfying at the time. I looked at my world through the rose tint of success and liked what I saw, and ambition lay for a while as calm as Derwentwater below. We quit the crag as it faded in the dark.

'To tell the truth, I wouldn't have put any money on your getting up that,' Jim said.

'Nor would I.'

I did not deceive myself. As VS's go, this was not an impressive one, and it would be only on rare occasions that I could find in myself what it took to get up that grade of climb. And relative novices have seconded VS climbs with no trouble. Leading can be even more frustrating; I had led up to Severe but there are a great many easier climbs which I would be able to lead only by taking a very great risk.

Yet climbing would for me be blighted if ever I became infected with a feeling that grades were everything. There has been many a memorable day on easier climbs, like one I remember with Dave Parsons, who patiently taught me over several years. One weekend we were in North Wales when hurricane force winds tore up trees, ripped off roofs and blew over vehicles; it was a fiend that hunted for weaknesses and found many. All over the country storms caused the deaths of over twenty unfortunate people in the worst winds recorded for three decades. The wind and rain eased somewhat and we grabbed a climb. With a 'Hee! Hee! Hee!' every so often, like a wheezy accordion, Dave headed up. Far below in a lake we could see a battered lorry trailer that had been blown into the water being hauled out by crane. Dave had made a hundred and fifty feet up the rockface when he yelled happily, 'The wind's colossal up here.' While he hesitated, hunched up for a few seconds, the wind gusted as if deliberately, devilishly trying to tug him from the rough, grey rock.

'Beautiful,' he roared, and made another move in defiance of the wind. 'Beautiful!'

Dave's friend Huw took second place and I third up a crack big enough to squeeze a leg in, which we all did to make progress, then up another steep crack and left along an exposed wall we went, beneath a bulge as big as an elephant. Where the bulge met the wall below it, a horizontal crack, like a letterbox ten feet across, let us hook in fingers and hang on to the lower lip whilst stepping leftwards along the wall for several moves on tiny, tiny footholds. The longer the fingers clutched, the more they were robbed of warmth and though they ached with cold inside they were numb outside.

'Felt a bit sick on that traverse,' Huw said. 'Couldn't feel my fingers very well.'

For me, getting from the end of the traverse to the belay a few feet away was a long stretch and a frantic, strenuous struggle above a big drop.

In the end I managed. With that climb over the chill started to eat at our resolve to do another route and finally gobbled it all up, so we squelched a way ever so carefully down a mucky wet gully and back to the little roadside refreshment shack near the lake for a warming cuppa. The climb, the descent and the tea were all that much more enjoyable with the elements against us.

My first easy climb in Wales using pitons (the metal pegs which are hammered into cracks) was memorable too; it was as high as a four-storey building and overhung steeply for the first fifteen feet, relenting for a few more feet to a little less than vertical before bulging and then overhanging again.

'Keep your head to one side if a peg pulls out,' my companion, Gordon Stainforth advised. 'When your weight is on them they come out with a hell of a force if they go.'

One piton, which had been taking all my weight seconds before (you hang from them as if you are dangling in a parachute harness), I was able to tug from the crack. It had moved out a little while I was clipped to it; I had seen it move, and I was twenty feet above the ground. My, oh my! An uncomfortable scarey sensation flowed like liquid through my stomach.

'Look at the ground. Savour it!' Gordon, safe at the top, told me, as he moved about taking photographs.

'Pay more attention to the rope, Gordon.'

'Stop wittering.'

It was a fine experience, once it was over. Perhaps I was fortunate that my legs introduced a greater element of the unknown, of exploration, because I could not always imitate the movements of others.

No two climbs are the same and one relatively easy one sticks in my mind because of its character: it is called the White Edge, in Mewslade Bay in South Wales. This steep 200-foot pillar rears sharply up from a beach, more like a mini Dolomite peak than a British sea stack. I remembered it because it looks so impressive but when you get half way up it turns out to be a splintered horror of loose limestone which almost attains verticality at the top. If you could glue everything in place it would be all right, but those who had climbed it described it as 'a rotting pile', 'a tottering heap' and ''orrible'.

'It *is* loose!' Dave Parsons said as he led, and, 'The block I'm standing on is loose so watch out below!'

When I followed him rain came on as I neared the final steep section, and limestone becomes slippery when wet. It was awful in a way, yet when I looked back I was glad to have climbed it, because it looked so good.

The practice on rock went on but more and more I began to see success in terms of climbing mountain after mountain and never risking the whole mountain future just to get up one short bit of rock.

'I'm taking Lilac to Chamonix this summer,' Des announced one day. 'Want to go?'

'Yes please.'

'Right.'

'Dave Parsons and some of the other South Wales Club people will be there in July too.'

To my usual equipment I added a pair of items not used for fifteen years: crutches. Frequently the long, hot walks to and from mountains were more responsible than actual climbing for skin being rubbed from my stumps. With the assistance of crutches I hoped to move more quickly and with less harm to the stumps on trails in the heat of the day. To my way of thinking they would be the right tools for the job if they increased range and stability and at the same time reduced stump injury. Only misplaced pride could influence me against taking them. Another advantage of crutches was that if an artifical leg broke I could still move over rough ground on one leg and crutches. (They are not special legs in any way, I should point out.) Crutches would provide safety because they would allow me to rescue myself independently in certain circumstances. If there was a target it was to try another grade 3 route (how tame that ambition seems in retrospect!), and the one that appealed most was the Arête des Cosmiques (see 'Arête' in Glossary) on the Aiguille du Midi in the French Alps; but foremost in my mind was testing the crutches.

At the tail end of July we left, Des, his friend Alan and I, for Chamonix. We tracked down a ten-strong brotherhood from the South Wales Mountaineering Club, camped near the town. Four of them led by Dave Parsons had already agreed they would head for the Cosmiques hut; that suited me because from there the Arête des Cosmiques could be climbed. Des and Alan had no plans, so we tagged along, up in a cable-car, then a half-hour mist and snow trudge to the wooden hut, perched on a little brown rock island in the snow. The guardian and his wife served soup, drinks and meals to the twenty or so people who turned up, while their Alsatian dog wore goggles in the bright sunlight and chased snowballs for anyone who would throw them from the porch. He could never find them when they landed, of course!

Dave Parsons' group had their own plans and we went our separate ways. A sluggish pair trailed behind me amidst the strange, sharp early morning sounds of a cold place, to the foot of the Arête des Cosmiques of the Aiguille du Midi; the Midi is distinguished as the highest of the Chamonix Aiguilles, reaching about 12,500 feet (3,842 m).

'I don't feel like doing it. Got a stinking headache,' Des said, and Alan's only comment was in the same vein: 'I don't mind if we don't.'

But this was a day made for climbing so I tramped on hoping they would follow, and they did.

The easy bit of the arête is at the bottom so it was not long before we had only six hundred feet to go on a ridge of pinnacles separated by deep cleavages, up, down, up, down, up. Des and Alan still followed, conscripts, but more willing than before. We could expect short problems of up to Very Difficult or Severe. Considering the ascent normally needed only three hours or so it was ideal for early in the holiday.

We had reached the feeling better stage and went on, until after a step around a corner the mountain plunged into its first cleavage where the rock overhung. That was the way we had to go, down under the overhanging rock, sixty-five feet by abseil (sliding down a rope). But first there was a delay while climbers ahead slid down. There were so many people we had to hang around for over half an hour. This was not the way to climb; seeking quiet places took on an even greater priority from that day. Not long after came another abseil of fifty feet down a steep, polished ice gully, a narrowing ridge, and then the mountain steepened suddenly into a blunt buttress, blocking the way. A near vertical wall faced us at the buttress's base. There was one vertical crack though, and that weakness alone would be enough by the look of it. Des led, I went next, fifteen feet up the crack, to shuffle horizontally left for several feet on a ten-inch-wide ledge to a tight vertical chimney of only nine or ten feet. Poor Alan suddenly turned pale and looked awfully sick, and fell without injury a few feet to the bottom of the wall. The sudden illness was a mystery.

He rested for a few minutes and then Des and I gave him a nice tight rope and up he came. I lessened his load by taking the abseil rope and went ahead while he rested limply. Morning had run out and heat left the ensuing gully snow soft. There was no enjoyment in climbing the untrustworthy porridge, which collapsed at every step.

An advantage came of having waited for a little while: the other climbers had gone ahead. Alan soon seemed back to normal and in any case we could see there was not far to go. After the last enjoyable couple of pitches on dry slabs we approached the luxury which waited: we could go down to the valley by cable-car from the summit.

Alan felt better but was too tired to have enjoyed himslf and a grumpy Des moaned about having to pull people up on the rope. In contrast, I was delighted with the day; I appreciated the experience even though it was rather frayed at the edges. We had taken more than twice as long as we should have, and I had not managed as well as I might have, but to do a grade 3 route on the second day was far harder and more rewarding than my companions could appreciate.

For the greater part of the next day we washed, ate, drank and lounged around, until Des and Alan started to walk to Montenvers and I took the train; this privilege was granted me without too many hints that it was a shameful thing to do, on condition I carried up a bottle of wine. Montenvers, where the railway ends its steep and winding way up the mountainside, overlooks the famous Mer de Glace, the sea-of-ice glacier which at the time presented a grubby face; a fresh snow fall would have prettied it. Des and Alan arrived at dusk looking like they had been up Everest, having missed the trail at some point and floundered through a forest.

The following day was not planned as anything special (but turned out as a special day in an undramatic yet important way). To see the Montenvers area for the first time and to try out the crutches was enough for me, and no one else had any plans. At first light we took a rising wooded footpath; Alan had to turn back after an hour and a half with a nasty blister on his heel. For me there was no turning back because those crutches gave me wings! For the first time since losing my legs I felt as if I could run. In reality, on level or downhill stretches the pace was no better than a fast walk, but what a joy that was! No longer did I have to take every step with care on the rough path, for with two sturdy outriggers it was possible to make long strides or short, to pick and choose where my boots landed, to drop lightly on movable stones and pass by so quickly that it did not matter if they rolled over. Now I had become a four-legged animal, there was no need to concentrate on keeping in balance all the time or to use back and stomach muscles to correct a lean this way or that. A slight stumble of one leg or crutch was of no consequence because there were always three other legs around to keep me under control. Immediately, and delightfully, it was apparent that approaching mountains would be not only less tiring but safer because I was steadier. The walk from John o' Groats to Land's End toughened the stumps a good deal but still they were vulnerable in the heat. Hiking from a valley for five or six hours to a high alpine hut could be a terrible slog when the sun was up; now, with the new-found freedom, the magic carpet, those walks could become another part of the fun. Crutches could even help on snow sometimes, I felt sure. Snow had always been my worst foe when the sun turned it soft, and to battle along in mid-day heat, sinking up to the knees or further, made me hate snow. But sometimes bad snow had to be tolerated. In an attempt to keep the stumps cool and less sweaty at one time I used to wear long socks and fill them up with snow when the sun grew hot. The theory was that by keeping the metal legs cold the stumps would stay cooler. While sitting on my rucksack and scooping handfuls of snow into the socks you can imagine I was the object of many a questioning glance, and people who came my way chose a wider than necessary detour to get past! If the method had any effect it was slight, and I had soggy socks all the time. Now with crutches adapted like ski poles the snow problems could be reduced. There was another advantage which I did not realise at the time: crutches took so much of the effort out of balancing that the 'nausea barrier' had to be broken through less often.

The wretched random rubble of a glacial moraine gave a lot of trouble and I floundered there almost as badly as I always had, but everywhere else easy movement and the freedom to gaze all around were mine. I saw the forests and pastures as never before; the need to watch every step like a head-down man looking for mushrooms was gone. We were out for twelve hours that day, and though the balls of my thumbs looked red as ripe tomatoes through taking the weight, I was overjoyed to have discovered the best way to get about on the lower mountain slopes. The trails seemed suddenly to have become prettier and to have shrunk to a third of their former length, so without even trying to reach a summit a great feeling of satisfaction was mine. And I started to think more seriously about longer ascents on bigger mountains. That was how much difference the crutches made.

Soon after, with Des and Alan, I climbed the easy Tête Blanche at a bit over 11,000 feet (3,429 m) and had an enjoyable jaunt with Harry Curtis from the South Wales Club on the Index. The short south-east ridge of this mountain is a safe grade 3 climb on sound rock. I followed Harry up a hard groove to a congenial slab, then to a brown arête decorated with yellow lichen, and on to a knife-edge section and a wall, and in one and a half hours we were there, at 8,500 feet (2,595 m). A long and impressive abseil down to scrambly rocks and a loose, clattering scree couloir put me once more in a place where the crutches were a tremendous boon.

Two days later, with Des, a two hour walk from a cable-car station under an angry evening sky. The cairned track disappeared and re-appeared capriciously in moraine gravel, boulders and ice. At somewhere around the 8,500-foot contour (2,500 m) we settled down for the night under a boulder. Dark night came insistently, to be torn apart by brilliant flashes and hollow crashes of a ferocious lightning storm. Like miserable trogolodytes we watched from under our rock as rain streamed down and blew in and found other ways to get at us through gaps and cracks. Even so, the boulder gave a feeling of security in the midst of a hostile environment; comfort is relative.

'Mummy! Mummy!' Des shouted every so often while we huddled in big polythene bags and laughed a little nervously and polished off a small bottle of rum, while the thunder and lightning drifted away to frighten people elsewhere. We lay in darkness in a contrasting silence broken only by the crisp-packet crackle of polythene bags, and the drip and trickle left behind by the storm.

Cheerless morning crept towards us very slowly, with grey sky and wetness, and we reluctantly accepted it to be folly for me to do any but the easiest of routes. A feeling of 'let's do anything rather than nothing' just triumphed over the option of going down. The only suitable candidate

John o' Groat's to Land's End, 1969

Early rock climb in South Wales

Judy at eighteen

Judy Croucher

Norman aged about six

Judy aged five

Norman Croucher on Tocllaraju

Tocllaraju, Peru, with bergschrund visible at the bottom

Tour Ronde north face

The White Edge, South Wales. Dave Parsons at the top, Norman Croucher climbing

The Matterhorn

On the east summit of Ameghino

Difficult terrain on Ameghino

Julie Tullis and Huascaran, Peru

Huascaran, Peru

Nun (*left*) and White Needle

Aconcagua (*left*) and Ameghino

was the Aiguille de l'M (called M for its profile when seen from Chamonix), about 9,300 feet (2,844 m) high.

A slow start over glacier ice and a slog up a foul couloir of loose stones took us to the col we had reached on the day when first the crutches were tried out. A final twenty minutes of climbing to the summit on good and easy rock left no feeling of satisfaction with our efforts, but as we descended the rotten couloir the weather threw rain and then hail in our faces to remind us why we were cautious. People above dislodged stones and it became like a children's game, make yourself as small as you can, while stones clunked and jumped by.

Des walked down to Chamonix and I went to get the cable-car; the mental approach of the pre-crutch days was still there.

Time had run out. The young woman who ran the camp site hoped we would 'Ev a god treep 'om', which we translated eventually, and off we went. Stopping at Boulogne for a meal in a café with a resident terrier, Alan ordered steak tartare and the waiter flatly refused to serve it, saying in good English, 'It is no good for you.' He seemed to know what he was talking about for the food turned out to be awful. We didn't eat much but the dog kept coming up to beg. It seemed an unfitting end to the holiday, for now I was not just picking a poor or single item from the mountain menu as I had so often in the past. From now on there would be a feast of mountains.

Mooching about in the Lake District beneath a crag to pick a route I slipped on a stone and twisted one leg. A purple swelling, half a hen's egg, rose up immediately on one stump and a large area was bruised.

'Your stump's like a giant plum,' Judy said. 'Moby Plum.'

After all the time spent climbing without much in the way of injury it seemed incongruous to be hurt on a path. Walking was very painful and the crutches came to my aid. The stump swelled so much I could not get the artificial leg back on, but with one leg and crutches it was possible to get about. So I had learned something more, that if a leg failed mechanically or if a stump was injured crutches really would enable me to move over rough country. Practice bore out theory, and greater independence was a proven fact. So how about those bigger peaks?

All at once in me was a real yearning to go to the Andes. The Andes. The Andes. The name conjures up a feeling of excitement, of greatness, of seriousness, of adventure, of challenge, of peaks around 20,000 feet. But where, in the huge Andes?

Little bits of information, whether correct or not, coupled with impressions and assumptions, nudged me this way, then that. A couple of visits to the Alpine Club in London to browse through books and journals led further towards the Peruvian Andes and gradually I homed in on one region: the pretty Cordillera Blanca.

Invitations to go on other people's expeditions do not pour in when you lack the lower parts of your legs so it soon became clear that if I wanted to go there I would have to do the organising myself, and in all probability lead the expedition as well.

It must be emphasised that if it were not for the greater independence which resulted from using crutches, I would not seriously have considered going. After experiments in different types of terrain it was obvious that metal spikes on the ends would be an advantage sometimes, and I had some made.

To get an expedition going several hurdles had to be cleared, not the least of these being the fact that I did not know anyone else who wanted to go. An expedition of one. It was hard to decide where to start, except that it was clear other expedition members had to be found. I had less time than most to seek out a team; usually it takes a year or so to organise a first venture of this nature, but because of the shingles I had shelved the plans for a while and when they were taken down from the shelf again we had less than seven months to go. Nowadays I could organise an expedition much more quickly, but those were my dilettante days, and I had no expedition track record.

Early on I contacted Julie and Terry Tullis, climbing instructors who also ran a climbing equipment shop. They said they would go and suggested that a globetrotting friend of theirs, Dennis Kemp, might like to as well. He soon wrote from New Zealand to say yes. As well as having built up wide experience in the Alps, Himalayas, USA and Antipodes, he had climbed in Peru. His appearance was that of an ageing hippy, and he was tougher than first impressions might suggest. Another member, Harry Curtis, was invited as much for his good nature as for anything else. He wrote back saying he was excited by the prospect and was getting himself fit 'doing three push-ups a day and jogging the hundred yards to the pub.' Then someone who was prepared to help with the organisation of the expedition, and put in some funds too, turned up. His name was Mike Welham and he worked as a diver. Mike's experience included alpine climbing and an expedition to Arctic Norway in winter. Most of the work of an expedition goes by unseen and this was where Mike's help with the organisation was extremely valuable. His wife, Jackie, enthusiastically joined in the work too, and few expedition organisers can have been as fortunate as I in coming across so much assistance. One of Mike Welham's friends, Mike O'Shea, was taken on more to look after base camp than as a climber; he was so keen to go he even gave up his draughtsman's job and became self-employed so he could have time off. So when Terry and Julie finally sold their shop and committed themselves to the venture, we had seven members: the two Mikes, Harry, Julie, Terry, Dennis and me.

Raising sponsorship was hard work. Write to this one, write to that one, everyone suggested helpfully, but the problem of approaching the

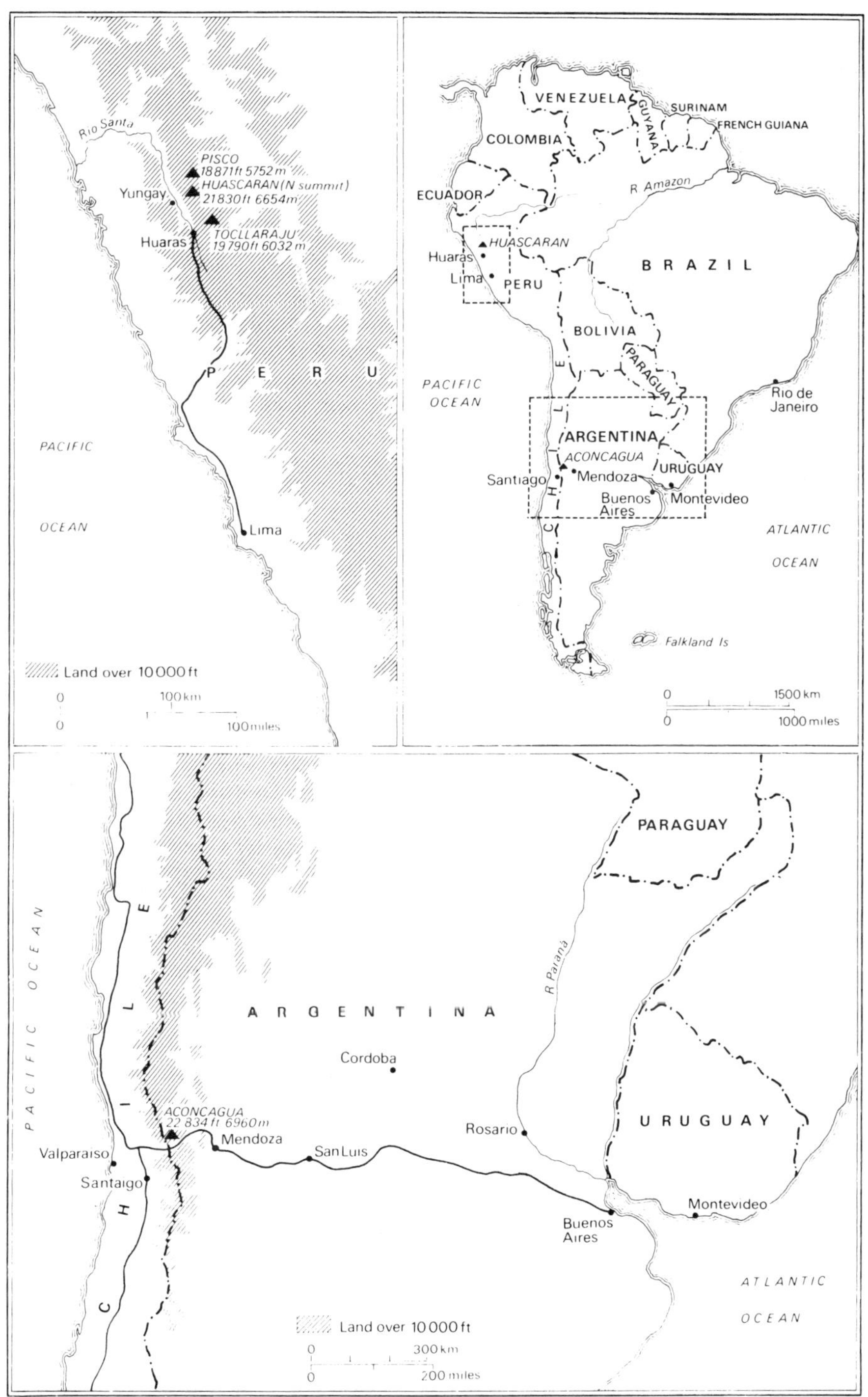
Rio Santa
PISCO
18871ft 5752m
HUASCARAN (N summit)
21830ft 6654m
Yungay
TOCLLARAJU
19790ft 6032m
Huaras
P E R U
PACIFIC
OCEAN
Lima
Land over 10000ft
0 100km
0 100miles
VENEZUELA
GUYANA
SURINAM
FRENCH GUIANA
COLOMBIA
R Amazon
ECUADOR
HUASCARAN
Huaras
Lima
PERU
BRAZIL
BOLIVIA
PARAGUAY
PACIFIC
OCEAN
Rio de Janeiro
ARGENTINA
ACONCAGUA
Santiago
Mendoza
URUGUAY
Buenos Aires
Montevideo
CHILE
ATLANTIC
OCEAN
Falkland Is
0 1500km
0 1000miles
PARAGUAY
PACIFIC OCEAN
CHILE
R Parana
ARGENTINA
Cordoba
ACONCAGUA
22834ft 6960m
Mendoza
San Luis
Rosario
URUGUAY
Valparaiso
Santaigo
Buenos Aires
Montevideo
ATLANTIC
OCEAN
Land over 10000ft
0 300km
0 200miles

apparently most likely sources was that lots of other people thought the same way. The result of fifty letters to various large commercial and industrial organisations, appeals through newspapers, radio and television, was many expressions of good will but hardly anything to reduce expenses.

I applied for a Winston Churchill Travelling Fellowship and got to the stage of being short-listed for an interview. In the year before, 1976, over three thousand applications were received and just over a hundred awards made, so I did not overestimate my chances. However, shortly after the interview by a very distinguished panel I was awarded a generous grant of £1,400. Considering that mountaineering can be a risky activity, I felt their decision to back me was very enlightened.

Jackie sent off two dozen more letters seeking sponsorship, like casting two dozen hooks at once into the sea. Until then the bait had been taken by very few fish, and they were small ones. This time we caught forty pounds and some offers of free food and medical items.

Then we were offered film at trade price, a welcome gesture as we had several photographers in the party, and good news began to come in from several quarters. Terry and Julie, having been in the climbing equipment business, had the task of procuring equipment, and despite their reluctance about approaching suppliers whom they regarded as friends, the response was good. Polar jackets and tents were the most valuable items, and they obtained many less expensive but equally essential gifts. Soon after, Hangers, the firm who make my legs, put up £500 through their parent body, Intermed, and another Intermed company supplied some very good aluminium trunks for baggage. That £500 was the biggest single donation apart from the Churchill Fellowship.

A host of details required attention: injections, travel arrangements, visas, equipment, currency, elusive sponsors still to be found. With expedition members living in Wolverhampton, Norwich, North Wales, Kent and London, communication was not always easy, particularly as two people were not on the telephone. But slowly, detail by detail, things came together.

Denny Moorhouse, founder and managing director of Clogwyn climbing equipment manufacturers, readily promised us a lot of equipment, and some weeks later he showed an interest in going himself. I said yes, and that made us eight.

Up to a few weeks prior to departure, air fares were still the biggest problem. In the end we were booked on flights with Viasa, the Venezuelan airline. Paperwork went on and on, as important as physical effort if we were to succeed.

All eight expedition members were invited to the official opening of the Calvert Trust Adventure Centre for Disabled People in April 1978. The expedition team all seemed very favourably impressed with the place. We knew the expedition would attract a certain amount of publicity so we decided early on to use that publicity to promote the Calvert Trust, of which I was a trustee.

We gathered from our separate directions on a wet Sunday in early July at Heathrow's Terminal 3. All the people and all the equipment arrived in good time. Ten rucksacks, three kitbags, four metal trunks and one cardboard box containing a pair of legs were stacked outside. Soon, Senor Gonzales-Mata, London Sales Manager of Viasa, personally supervised the acceptance of our baggage into the system.

A small and rather forlorn group bade us farewell when the flight was called: Mike O'Shea's daughter, Jackie Welham and Judy.

The DC10 trundled fast, faster, very fast, roaring, lifted its nose and jumped into the sky at 2.20 p.m. It stopped briefly at Lisbon, and delivered us to Caracas, Venezuela, that evening. An overnight stop was required, and Twickenham Travel had arranged hotel accommodation. We wanted to leave our equipment at the airport but Viasa's storage space was full; they were in the process of building more, we gathered. A conversation with a local architect who started talking to us while he awaited his wife's arrival led to an introduction to Venezuela's Minister for Youth, who happened to be at the airport. A few words from him and some previously unco-operative customs men became co-operative, and locked away our heaviest baggage for the night.

A day was enough; we wanted to be on our way. The customs men had other ideas, however, for they had moved all our equipment to another airport a few miles away and had no intention of releasing it in time for our flight to Lima. A form they had issued and stamped, confirming that the equipment was in transit, carried no weight with them at all. Consequently, we had to leave two people behind in Caracas to retrieve our equipment; Mike Welham was one of them because he could be noisy and pushy, and Harry was the other because he was intelligent and could also get on the pushy side when roused; young men from Liverpool are not famous for shyness.

The rest of us flew with our rucksacks to Lima airport, where a representative of Lima Tours saw us without a problem through customs and escorted us in one of their buses to our hotel. Mike and Harry turned up there at about 7 p.m. the next day having suffered a tiring battle with customs officials. A female employee of Viasa proved to be our saviour; she got them a driver and vehicle to travel to the other airport and ferry the baggage, and she bullied the customs skunks relentlessly. Mike and Harry had lived through a complicated series of ups and downs of fortune, eventually repossessing our equipment. If they did nothing else they had earned their places on the expedition. With that and the work he and Jackie had put in Mike had earned his place three times over.

The following morning Denny and Dennis went ahead by bus to find accommodation in Huaras, the mountain town which was to be the civilisation centre of our activities. There was no rush for the rest of us to go because we wanted to talk to Senor Morales Arnao, the Andean expert of the official government sport body.

'Would you like to met Walter Bonatti?' he asked when we met.

WOULD WE LIKE TO MEET WALTER BONATTI?

For those who do not know, the Italian Walter Bonatti is a remarkable hard climber whose triumphs include a solo first ascent of the south-west pillar of the Dru and an ascent of the north face of the Matterhorn in winter. Through reading one of his books, *On the Heights*, Harry started climbing; Harry was our truest disciple. We trooped in reverent manner to his hotel and spent half an hour talking to the small, grey-haired, alert and charming man who commanded so much of our respect. The audience was a significant and delightful start to our adventure. With customs problems behind us, we had all our equipment and ourselves in Peru; hopes nourished over a long period might flower now.

While the bus to Huaras was being loaded we had a moment to enjoy the Mike Welham Street Theatre, for he had discovered that his *very* expensive new camera was not functioning for the second time in two days; he was our chief photographer, on his own recommendation. Crimson-faced and swearing, he threatened to smash the camera against a wall.

'This is all going down in my book!' he shouted, referring to a document which he hoped to write but never did, as far as I know. The book was an often-used threat and he had a habit of jotting down notes about anything or anyone, including us, that displeased him.

'I see Chaucer's at it again,' Mike O'Shea remarked as his friend scribbled away furiously.

The bus, with every seat filled by a local or a foreign visitor, droned out of early morning Lima, past plush hotels and big statues and monuments, past single-storey hovels half-hidden behind bamboo fences, past buildings with crumbling faces. Over all there was a greyness which came partly from thick fog, the 'garua' sitting on the city for months each year. The city has a population of almost three million people, many of whom live in slums, or in shanty towns hung on dry dust hills or planted on dismal flat land.

By no means everyone is poor; in some parts of Lima the grand Spanish-style houses and squares are well kept. In ten minutes you could leave a slum and be drinking tea in a bit of old England, out of time, out of place, in the Lima Cricket Club, or eating in an expensive restaurant in the Miraflores district. Towards the city's outskirts the road verges deteriorated into dust and rubbish tips, and the smell of rotting matter took over.

In simple terms we had to head north and a bit westwards on a road hugging the desert coast, with the sea on our left. The steep plunge of two or three hundred feet down red sand to the sea was a constant danger; some time later twenty-six people were killed forty miles along that road from Lima when a bus collided with another vehicle and went over the edge. At about the half-way point a hundred miles up the coast we turned right to zig-zag roughly north-east through rapidly rising country, and then left to go a bit west of north again. Houses and shacks thinned out as we went further up the desert road, until there were no dwellings and hardly a speck of growth to break up the sandy monotony.

We slipped gradually into the sort of Peru that was to fascinate us all for the next six weeks. Flashing by like a quick taster of a way of life we would get a little closer to, went cacti of highly individual species, barefoot children, women with babies in colourful blankets slung on their backs, bright home-woven clothing, dark skins of smiling Indian faces, small scavenging dogs, roadside cafés, and drinks stalls, dirt roads and donkeys, and hairy little pigs wandering free and quite tame. Nearly everyone wore a hat of straw or a trilby or a bowler, against the sun.

We had followed our right-hand turn and the road was soon a real mountain twister, taking its time to get up to the high country. Now almost always on one side or the other was a gigantic drop but the driver hammered on. In Peru, driving seemed to involve faith as much as it required petrol; some taxis had on their dashboards little shrines in which bulbs lit up each time the brakes were applied.

Ladies spinning wool while they walked along, cows, pigs, goats, horses, lambs, potato and maize crops and thatched adobe houses sped by the bus windows, and as we topped a hill a surge of excitement ran through the gringos, for there ahead were the fantastic sharp peaks with their gleaming white coverings of snow. Between us and the mountains light browny yellow, almost golden, plains intervened and the sky above was bright blue and clear. It was unbelievably beautiful.

A screech of brakes blasted the mood away and the bus jerked to a stop.

'What's happened?'

Slowly the facts came together from bits and pieces of accounts which travelled down the bus to us near the back. A boy on a bicycle pulled out, overtaking a slow lorry on the lonely road. He had been coming downhill towards us, fast. He hit the bus. We peer out of the windows to the left. There's a bike lying there with a crazily buckled front wheel, and a small group of people has gathered near it. Where is he? At first most of us did not spot him. Then we did. A lad of abour fourteen, tears on his cheeks and one limp forearm cradled protectively in the other, is the centre of attention. He stands there with his arm hurting and his bike busted, and now someone is shouting at him and most likely telling him what a fool he is. He knows that already, or doesn't want to know, so why try to tell the poor young man? Now is not the time; he's hurt, and his prized bike is a distorted mess. People leave the bus to even out the score a bit; he may have made a mistake but we all feel sympathy for him. We take him in the bus to his home further along the road. A tearful scene with his family outside their adobe home ends when a woman, probably his mother, comes with him on the bus to the hospital in Huaras. So it was that we made our first acquaintance with that hospital.

I saw the woman with him later. His fingers on one hand were splinted and he looked all right.

Huaras. We had arrived. There around us was the town, population 50,000 people, 10,000 feet (3,050 m) high. Only a slight shortage of breath told us we were that far above sea level.

Denny and Dennis had found us a dormitory in the Hotel Barcelona, and a couple of tricycle baggage transporters were quickly bargained for to carry our equipment there. On the fifth floor of the square concrete hotel we dumped our rucksacks on some of the mattresses and hurried upstairs to the flat roof just above. Being the tallest building around, the hotel made a fine viewpoint; the countryside rolled away and away in humps to a superb array of peaks dominating the skyline.

How can Huaras be captured in words? Any attempt must be inadequate but, first, think of straight concreted streets, some of them recently built after earthquake and alluvion damage; an alluvion is a rapidly-moving mixture of rock, sand, mud and water spilled by collapse of a lake's morainal dam, or by massive ice avalanches falling into a lake and displacing the water. Earthquake hazard influences the height of buildings, which mostly have no more than two or three floors. Away from the main streets the majority are single-storey, while larger structures of reinforced concrete have been put up in the centre. Roofs are made of red tiles or corrugaged iron. Some of the living creatures that crowd into the town centre I have already mentioned: barefoot children, women carrying babies in blankets, donkeys, little pigs and street traders. Shoeshine boys and newspaper boys wander everywhere, and ice-cream or drinks vendors pedal their three-wheeled barrows slowly around. In all of the several markets, squatting women sell vegetables, eggs, and fruit spread out for display on blankets, and there are stalls, too, for meat, ironmongery, clothes, wool and herbs. Higher up the scale are bookshops, shoeshops, chemists, dress shops, like anywhere else. So it is a spectrum, from the lady squatted beside a single cake sold slice by slice, through small tattered stalls, through big and well-kept and well-stocked stalls, through small shops, to some large ones. Eating out is characterised by a similar spectrum of style and price. You can buy a slice of that cake or some bread from a barrowboy or a stallholder, then there are scruffy cafés and better ones, and a few good restaurants. Wide-eyed adults and children stare in through restaurant windows like they were watching TV. Grubby stalls, grubby feet, grubby children, grubby streets. Banknotes are tatty, begging by children is commonplace, buses are crammed full, fares are cheap, the police are armed, there are lots of rickety, ramshackle cars and gaily-painted trucks coming and going. The air is more of activity than bustle, with people going about their business but not rushing. The hills and mountains stand all around but not too close; Huaras does not feel closed in. And usually the sky is clear and bright blue. As you leave the centre you come across adobe huts and shacks on rough and dusty stone roads, amongst cacti and glossy eucalyptus and other trees. Patchwork farming, corn and other crops and grazing for cows and pigs, creeps into the edges of town. By day the parp, parp, parp of horns on the tricycles of ice-cream vendors, and tinny South American music from cassette and record stalls, and the traffic noise, are constant. At night the streetlighting is good because the surrounding mountains give the town hydro-electricity.

We soon made the acquaintance of Pepe, the young man who with his family looked after the Hotel Barcelona and its guests. Dark, smooth-haired, demonstrative in a Spanish way, friendly, shrewd-eyed, Pepe had the never-still nature of a small bird. It was to him that we turned if anything needed arranging.

'Ees possible,' and, 'Ees no problem,' were his usual responses. First, he fixed up a storage space for our food and equipment, and then when we wanted to transport it to our first base camp he got his truck out and drove us up an exceptional track bulldozed out of steep mountain flanks.

Denny and Dennis had ridden up the day before, to spend a headachy and nauseous night at 14,500 feet (c. 4,400 m), and this was the fate of some of the new arrivals, who wandered around like sick ghosts next day. One reason for selecting a camp with a road quite close was that anyone who had trouble acclimatising could descend for a while, and this is just what Denny and Mike Welham did, at different times. Trees, grass and flowers flourished in the steep-sided valley all around the tents and a small stream conveniently supplied fresh water.

While the rest of us lazed around for a day, waiting for acclimatisation to put a bit more life in our steps, Dennis scouted ahead up the valley. At fifty-six years of age he was our senior member by far, a most experienced expeditioner, and somewhat intolerant of our inexperience.

All at once one of my legs began to rattle loudly with each movement. My heart sank; this was even before the climbing had started! Julie and Harry were about to descend on foot to Huaras to replace two defective paraffin stoves, and they volunteered to run a spare leg delivery service at the same time by collecting the reserve limb from storage at Pepe's. A feeling of guilt crept over me as I watched them hurry down the hill and out of sight because as soon as they disappeared the rattling stopped. They arrived back in darkness the next evening, having had a difficult time because Harry had twisted a knee. To ease the pain on the way up that afternoon he had taken to bathing the poorly joint in streams, and in order to do this he had to slip his climbing breeches down to his ankles. As they passed close to a village Julie decided nothing was to be lost by trying to hire a donkey and she succeeded in persuading a teenage girl with such an animal to come to a stream and pick up Harry. The intention was that Harry would be transported a considerable way up the hill, but Harry had chosen that moment to cool his knee. The girl arrived to find him kneeling in a stream with his trousers down, and she may have noticed a leg lying on the bank, too. Whether she did or not, the scene can have done nothing to convince her that gringos are civilised or sensible, so she turned her donkey around immediately and went straight back to the village! Harry shouldered my leg and soldiered on to arrive at camp just after dark. My rattling noise had not returned, its cause remains unknown, and the replacement limb was not required; but thank you Harry, all the same.

Among other things, acclimatisation to the altitude we were at resulted in a sixty per cent increase in red corpuscles. After a couple of days at base camp three people emerged as getting on best with the altitude: Julie, Dennis and me. Dennis set off and took a tent up to about 16,000 feet and returned to base camp, and then Julie, Terry and I set out carrying quite heavy loads. Terry intended going part way to help with the weight.

The hiking was easy on grassy slopes made prettier by lupins and a yellow flower looking like a cross between a big daisy and a marigold, but possessing little or no stem; it seemed to hug the ground to survive.

After a rise of 600 feet we escaped leftwards from the confines of the valley up easy grey slabs, and Terry turned back as planned. Julie and I took on board the things he had carried for us.

The weather had been deteriorating and, after two hours on the go, hail started to patter down through coiling mist. This was followed by a clap of thunder which shook the ground, and made my stomach go tight. Taking shelter in a cave beneath a boulder, we considered bivouacking, but an improvement in the weather allowed us to go on to a tent left by Dennis. He had left a note, suggesting a peak we should try. The right skyline ridge, though nearly vertical in places, did not look too hard, and the summit was only a thousand feet above us, so it was a suitable choice for an acclimatisation climb.

Next day brought steep walking for a short way, then a scramble over boulders to the foot of the ridge. I led a short pitch up a steep step, and was amazed at how I puffed on the relatively easy rock. Fresh snow during the night had made it harder, but to an extent you could not grade technically; here and there it was slippery, and you could not say much more than that. We alternated the lead, with Julie doing the hardest bits first: a short, vertical crack and a rather unstable snow slope to the summit, reached two and a half hours after leaving the tent.

Within just over a week of arriving in Peru the expedition was successful, though not wildly so. This 16,800 feet (5,120 m) mountain was modest by Andean standards. It had been a cautious and gentle introduction. We were overjoyed, for this was the highest either of us had been.

Descent to the tent took only an hour and a half so we were back in the early afternoon. Dennis, Terry and Harry arrived soon after, flushed under heavy loads. Terry and Harry looked awful, just how we must have looked the day before. We all sat and stared at the mountains, prettier for their fresh coats of snow but at the same time dangerous in consequence, and it was amicably agreed that it was not the time to attempt other peaks in the area. The loads were taken down again. The slabs had iced over and were none too easy in a couple of places.

The night of the following day was spent by several of us in a hut below our base camp. We cooked a meal and shared it with the guardian of a nearby dam, guardian in the sense of keeping an eye on the water level. Language was a problem because our Spanish was thin and the guardian had no English. One of the few things Terry could say in Spanish was 'a dog with fleas', which was best left unsaid as the guardian had a dog and gave Terry a dirty look when the phrase was used. Then Terry got into a real tangle trying to extract the Spanish for 'aristocrat'. Things like doors, windows and tables we could get by pointing, but try explaining 'aristocrat' in sign language. Egg; that was another word we needed, so I demonstrated with an orange which, after due clucking noises, was laid on the floor. We pointed at the orange and asked its name.

'Orange,' the guardian said in Spanish, and gave me a look which seemed to say, 'Stupid gringo. Everyone knows oranges grow on trees.'

Eating good food and drinking rum and honey by candlelight was only the first of many celebrations we would enjoy.

We slept on the floor that night. In the faint dawn light Harry was woken by a movement and a found a rat nuzzling his arm, so for half an hour he played smash the rat with a ski stick whenever the persistent little creature returned. The rat did not lose, but retired when good light came.

The next two days were spent returning to Huaras, bathing in a natural spring bath, eating, drinking, wandering about the town, writing postcards, talking to anyone and everyone who liked to chat to gringos, dancing in a disco and having an interview with a reporter who wanted to know if I had been carried up. Some of the newspaper reports were hilariously inaccurate: they had us up the wrong mountain, with a mother called Julia Turbiens (Julie Tullis) and I had broken two legs on the way.

We shopped for food in the colourful local markets, where tiny potatoes came in so many bright hues you could have strung them like beads for a pretty necklace. Because the next camp could be approached from a reasonably close track up which a truck could be driven, we were able to take fresh fruit and vegetables. With the food bought, it was off for thirty miles (fifty km) along the beautiful Rio Santa valley, a deep river cleft of rich green and yellow plenty growing on red earth, topped higher up the sides by the more mellow colours of drier country. Our truck took us to Yungay, the tragic scene of the worst alluvion in history. In 1970 earthquake tremors set off the alluvion which became airborne and smothered the town, killing an estimated 17,000 people. The total of deaths in Huaras at the same time was put at 16,000.

Pepe had arranged the transport and came with us as far as Yungay, a new town rebuilt a few miles from the former site, and he took us to one of his favourite restaurants. The waitress, Patti, was as much an attraction as the excellent cuisine, and our amorous Peruvian friend chose to stay in Yungay. We continued by truck up a bulldozed track. Eucalyptus trees, bulbous cacti, yellowing grain crops and adobe houses blended and pleased the eye. Exchanging waves with colourfully dressed people, particularly with the children, was like giving gifts equally; they appreciated having notice taken and shouted 'Gringo' in a friendly way as we went past.

Delays occurred in a couple of places where bulldozers cleared rocks and earth which had tumbled on to the track; on the running board was a man whose job it was to leap off every so often and trundle boulders aside. The road wiggled back and forth, back and forth, an embankment on one side and the usual frightening drop on the other. Around sharp bends and across little wooden bridges we hurried. In a straight line it was only ten miles (sixteen km) but the road was forced to twist and turn all the way. We climbed for an hour and more, up through a gorge whose steep walls were staggering to see.

'Heads!' someone cried every so often as we drove under low branches of gnarled and twisted papery-barked trees into the broad Llanganuco valley, and past two beautiful copper sulphate blue-green lakes. After unloading our gear a mile or more above the lakes we transported it on our backs to a pretty, flat-bottomed, grassy valley. There we set up base camp on the edge of trees beside a river washing quickly over smooth white stones like huge eggs.

Next morning was cold and we huddled in our sleeping bags, waiting for the sun to let us have its warmth. At 8.45 a.m. the rays touched us and suddenly it was a different, warm world.

Everyone was asked if they wanted to attempt the next mountain, Pisco, and of seven of us Terry and Mike Welham opted just to carry loads part way, which was a great help. Mike O'Shea stayed behind in the vital post of camp guard.

By crossing the river on a rough wooden bridge of three thin logs, we could begin to rise up nice walking country. Starting from base camp at 12,500 feet (3,800 m) we tramped in silent single file on a self-imposed treadmill: Denny, Mike Welham, Harry, Julie, Terry and me. Dennis, as usual, was somewhere above, having come up two days earlier to scout.

At first only the white tip of Pisco's head was visible, but gradually our target unfolded and grew. About 2,000 feet above base camp, Camp 1 was set up on a broad plain.

'If I had brought my equipment I could have stayed here and gone higher tomorrow,' Mike Welham moaned, and went down to fetch it.

The next stage for the remaining four of us was a sharp gradient up a stony moraine. From the top of the moraine we faced a steep descent of forty feet on dry, loose dust and grit into a mass of precariously perched boulders and rubble, half a mile wide. It was our misfortune to follow a line of cairns which went too far to the right.

'This is a cow,' Julie said as we clambered about in the burning heat, rucksacks pressing down like they were full of rocks.

We got there in the end, to a tent Dennis had left at about 16,000 feet. Though we had met him as he descended he seemed mostly to float ahead as a phantom, rarely if ever glimpsed. His work in the planning stages had not amounted to much, but he had picked out how he could best help the expedition in his own way and he served us well in his solo role. Denny and Harry turned back to the camp we had just left to bring up a tent and more supplies next day.

Next day, for Julie and me it was a leisurely time, carrying the tent and equipment a few hundred feet higher in two journeys. We pitched the tent by a little blue-green lake at the snout of a big glacier, up which we would have to climb. Washing and basking in the sun, we waited for the others. An extra day would give Mike Welham time to make up his mind and come with us if he wanted.

They arrived in the early afternoon, Harry, Dennis, Denny and Mike Welham, a slow-march crocodile which at sea level would have looked comical, but we were at over 16,000 feet (4,900 m).

That evening I went a short way up the glacier snout to see which would be the best way for the next day, and found the steep ice to be stepped conveniently.

Pisco's top was nearly three thousand feet higher. To reach a summit close to 19,000 feet high would indeed be success, but luck did not come our way for during the night snow fell quite heavily. That would mean deep, fresh powder snow higher up, and powder was one of my worst enemies, a pet hate. But still, at 4 a.m. I quit the tent to rouse the others.

Mugs of tea, and away at 5.20 a.m. in faint moonlight, up steep ice. Some of us wore head torches, some managed without. With no more than a hundred yards of the glacier slope behind us one of my crampons came off. We stopped while I put it back on, heaving on the straps hard enough to stop the circulation in a normal foot. Twenty more yards and the damned thing jumped off again. It was difficult to understand how a crampon could escape from a rigid foot, but there it lay in the snow. A previous set of crampons had given no trouble in years. The third time a crampon dropped off a few minutes later, Denny suggested managing without. That made it harder, but was better than fiddling about with straps all day.

We tramped on for an hour in our brightening crystal world, watching out closely for crevasses but still taking the time to look around as the sun turned the high peaks pink, then gilded them splendidly.

There was a big crevasse in the way, one with the far lip higher than the near one, a blue-green grotto of a hundred feet depth. From a few feet width at the surface it widened to ten feet half way down, and then the walls came slowly together. Fall down there, and the likelihood was that the victim would hang free and have trouble getting out, or be wedged in the narrowing bottom, injured by the hard ice walls. In the past I might not have got across but the crutches allowed a kind of double pole vault and the gaping hole was left behind. We weaved a way through hummocks of snow, giving a wide berth to more lurking crevasses, nothing unless you fell in, awful if you did.

Crossing a white plateau we took on an ice slope with a few inches of hard snow cover. It would have been easier with crampons, but Denny cut some good steps, quite close together, and now and then Julie shoved the shaft of her ice axe under my boot if she thought it might slip. At forty degrees at the steepest the slope was not really hard but high up to the right was an ice cliff draped with gigantic icicles; if any of them broke off several hundred pounds of clear ice would torpedo our way. We might just as well be walloped by a telegraph pole. There was an additional hazard: at the bottom of the slope in the line a sliding body would take was a broad snow chute which would channel everything, everyone, over the top of a huge ice cliff.

Mike Welham began to lag behind, but kept going. The slope lessened and the snow got more powdery; we sank to our ankles, then to our knees, and Denny and Dennis found their alternated work as trail-breakers growing harder. At the worst we were up to mid-thigh as we ploughed along in a line. The altitude had an effect and though there was little or no conversation a curse burst out from one or other of us every so often. The route was technically easy but powder snow at 18,000 feet is no joke. That's a feature of big mountains: a slog may be technically easy but exhausting all the same. Already I was planning that if we did not get there this time we would try again next day when the sun had chased some of the fluff from the snow.

Particularly in view of the recent snowfall, there was some danger of avalanche. To have eliminated the hazard completely would have meant staying off the mountain; the small risk just had to be accepted if we wanted to climb. Experience can help, but you can still get killed. We had to like the mountains enough to put up with the risk.

The wind picked up, whipping snow into our faces, and we pulled across face masks stitched to our fibre-pile jackets. Inside the masks, breath roared in and out.

'Much harder than when I did it before,' Dennis said. 'Much harder.'

The weather remained good, as it did much of the time in the Cordillera Blanca. We toiled up a massive snow mound to the relief of a steadily easing gradient. Denny and Dennis continued to break trail, then stood aside for Julie and me; we were close to the summit and they were letting us get there first. The order in which we arrived was of no concern to me, but it was thoughtful of them. Julie and I were on the summit at eleven o'clock, then Denny and Dennis, with Harry approaching soon after, swearing at himself to keep going, and then dropping to his knees every forty paces. He drove himself on competitively.

'Every time I looked up there was some rat on crutches still going so I had to do it,' he said of the easy but long final stretch. He lay down on the snow and hit it repeatedly with his ice axe, all the time shouting, 'I hate you! You're going to melt! I hate you! You're going to melt!' Climbing was never dull with Harry around.

Like a man with lead legs, Mike got there eventually. He was on fairly safe ground so was not roped to anyone. After that day he went quieter.

Feasting on Christmas pudding and oranges, we stayed on the summit for three-quarters of an hour or so. With the ascent of the first peak nine days earlier we had no reason to go home feeling we had made fools of ourselves; and now, at 5,760 m, or a hundred and thirty feet short of 19,000 feet, we had even less reason to be ashamed. The expedition was a success and the faith of a great many people had been rewarded.

When we packed up camp next day, with Dennis leading we found a better way through the moraine mess. As we passed the flat area where we had put up our first camp above base, two porters looking after someone else's camp called us over for some tea, which was taken gratefully. Their names were Manuel and Pedro; some of us were to meet Manuel again and share some important days with him.

Within three weeks of arriving in Peru, and in two weeks of climbing, we had done what we came to do. And we had over three weeks left. From the start I had planned that the team would split up once we had achieved our rather vague objective because it seemed wrong that people should be held back by me all the time on what might be their only visit to Peru. Not only that, if we had to stay together for the full expedition period I would have been more fussy about the composition of the team. For three or four weeks our little idiosyncracies were not serious as long as we were achieving our objective, but over a longer period they might have created problems. There were bound to be a few differences of opinion and complaints, but disagreements all stayed within reasonable bounds, and everyone made a predominantly positive contribution. I was more than a little fortunate in having a team which functioned so well.

Over two days we rested in Huaras, ate, cleaned ourselves in the warm natural spring water at the Hotel Monterrey near the town, and danced and drank in the local disco. We sampled the local fire-water, a brandy called pisco as it happens; it is said the mountain got that name because after a French ascent in 1951 two porters consumed two litres of the stuff.

During this period we shaped our plans, or our plans shaped themselves, partly based on who got on well with whom, partly on how people had been managing at high altitude, partly on how ambitious each individual was, and partly on many other threads of this and that. To start with, Dennis met a Swiss climber and they were keen to climb together, so they headed off to their chosen peak. As Mike O'Shea was more of a walker than a climber he was quite content to be left out of further climbing plans. Chaucer was his friend so they stuck together and went touring. Harry, Julie and I liked climbing together, but Terry did not want to because he worried about Julie. Denny did not think the weather would be good enough for the route we had in mind so he went off sightseeing. 'The route we had in mind.' Not *we*, really, but Julie. Unlike most expeditions, we had not selected definite objectives before arriving in Peru because my performance at high altitude was an unknown; we had to plan as we went along. One thing we had decided before leaving England, though, was that the real big ones of the Andes, 20,000 feet and more, were too much for me. The others might do one or two like that, but not me, so Peru's highest mountain, Huascaran (pronounced Wasca-ran) was out because it was about 22,000 feet high. However, Julie changed all that.

'Why don't we do Huascaran?' she asked.

'Too big,' I said.

'But you're getting on very well. Let's do Huascaran. Harry, you'd like to wouldn't you?'

'Yes.'

'Come on, Norman,' Julie coaxed. 'Please.'

I knew someone who was not going to take no for my answer when I met her, but I wanted a while to think first. Trying Huascaran could be biting off more than I could chew even though things had gone far better than they might have on two preceding ascents. Now Julie had brought Huascaran, formerly filed away in the mind under 'Forget It', back into circulation, and it had to be reconsidered. We heard that the higher of the mountain's twin summits, the south, was out of condition, but the north was all right.

Early next day I was up and looking out of a dormitory window of the Hotel Barcelona. From the dormitory we could see Huascaran, or rather, on that day we couldn't see Huascaran but could see the gigantic, fluffy stormcloud mass that wrapped itself around the mountain. Aha! An excuse for not going. Excuse, yes, but bad weather could not be ranked as a real reason. The sun was lighting up the cloud, turning it reddish. I watched for a while and then the realisation came that my mind was made up already. I could not resist this one. The spell was cast. And if we were going we might as well go right away.

Julie and Harry were delighted, but not Denny, who thought we were mad to go when the weather was, to say the least, inclement. But the bad weather was higher up, and it would take us a couple of days to reach it. If we did not leave Huaras until the weather on Huascaran was favourable we would waste part of the fine period. It was a simple view, not something founded on any special knowledge of meteorology, and it had a great bearing on subsequent events.

We bumped into Manuel on the street. Yes, he had been to Huascaran before. Yes, it would be wise to take a porter to help carry lower down, and to look after base camp; we could hardly have expected him to say otherwise. Yes, he was free and could go tomorrow. He jumped at the chance. Back at the hotel Pepe refereed as a deal was struck: Manuel would receive 1,000 soles a day and his food. At 300 soles to the pound it would not cost us a fortune and by local standards Manuel Fabian Oropeza, married, aged thirty-two, would be earning well.

Two days had passed since our return from Pisco, so we had not wasted much time in relaxing after one climb and getting ready for the next. We selected and packed our equipment, bought fresh food and ate a lot, and waited for the next day.

'Pepe, can you get us a pick-up to Musho tomorrow, please?'

'Ees no problem, my friends.'

We climbed into the back of the pick-up belonging to Pepe, who had found five girls to share the cab with him. Terry was coming along for the first part of the walk to base camp.

Pepe roared his vehicle up the road which followed the river valley northwards and a little to the west until five miles (eight km) short of Yungay we came into the little village of Mancos. Within three minutes he had bargained for another truck for the last leg of the journey on wheels to Musho. Quite a few vehicles stood around in most villages and you just went up and asked how much, beat the driver down a bit because it was expected, and there you were. Equipment was soon transferred and away we went up a road which was hardly horrifying at all. Rough, bumpy, dusty, yes, but not much of a horror. Straight ahead lay our destination, less than 180 feet short of 22,000 feet above sea level. Already the unwanted weather had slipped away and we could see it all gleaming, bright as silver.

The tree-lined village of Musho, where lived the poor local farmers, was about 9,900 feet (3,000 m) high. There the truck driver pulled up in front of a little café and we unloaded. Harry paid for the truck hire; he was keeper-of-the-purse for communal expenses like that and he handled the job very well. The top left pocket of his jacket was known as 'the bank'. There always seemed to be someone who was behind with his contribution, but Harry kept it all straight with great patience. Meanwhile, Manuel was bargaining with someone in the café for two donkeys; the café seemed to be the centre for such deals. Within minutes two donkeys and a tiny girl, about ten years old, appeared, and Manuel loaded the beasts. With four rucksacks and two kitbags as well as two tents we had more than was necessary, but we had allowed for the fact that the weather could keep us waiting at base camp or the next one, and we could get extra food to those camps with little trouble. In other words, extra time could be bought with food. I had played the waiting game with many a mountain, and won sometimes more through patience than great effort. It's not that I am by nature especially patient, but I can wait when there is no other way.

The two donkeys may have been in excellent health but to us they looked like the sort of creature for which old ladies set up sanctuaries in this country. The laden beasts, looking ready to buckle at the knees at any moment, moved slowly foward, breaking wind, sounding like wrestlers who had been at the beans.

For half an hour Terry was with us under a boiling sun, then he shook Harry and me by the hand, kissed his wife, and turned back down the trail with a quiet, 'G'luck.'

At one point on the trail a large group of very well-dressed Austrian climbers looked aghast at Harry's untidy appearance, which included trailing bootlaces and a face smeared white, clownlike, with ointment because of sunburn. Blobs of white toothpaste on his clothing, from a tube which had burst in his rucksack, did not help. They looked even more aghast when Julie appeared in view. A woman! 'We do not climb with women!' one of them had announced. Imagine their reaction when around a corner appeared the third member of this small band, with his crutches quietly clicking at each movement.

'That's our leader,' Harry said.

'But where is your expedition?' they asked me.

'This is my expedition,' I said, and they stared in amazement at our tiny group.

The biggest part of an afternoon disappeared in a nice walk between stone-walled fields, over open grazing land, up through a giant honeysuckle forest, and finally amongst twisted trees to a flat area with a cascading stream nearby. We had gained about three thousand five hundred feet. Already in place were two tents belonging to a large American expedition whose members were higher up the mountain. Two porters and a doctor sat around. The latter was conducting research into cerebral oedema, a fairly common sickness at high altitude, when fluid collects on the brain.

'What are the symptoms?' Harry asked him.

'One of them is simply swearing.'

'Bloody 'ell,' said Harry. 'Is that so?'

Tents up, brew on, food, another brew, more food. Lovely sunset.

We nearly started very early next morning. I woke Julie.

'Wha's up?' she asked.

'Time to go.'

'Go where?'

'Up this mountain. What's it called?'

'Huascaran.'

She looked at her watch, one which lit up.

'It's one o'clock.'

'Oh.'

I saw the dawn come but couldn't really pick just when; it was so slowed down by waiting. We had a fifty-foot rock step to start, then steep walking up a moraine. Taking a gamble, we carried everything to an advance base camp only 1,500 feet higher, rather than taking less and going on to a higher camp. I was glad of another day for us all to acclimatise instead of rushing at it, and I favoured increasing our chances of success from a higher base even though it meant we did not make full use of a good weather day.

Fifteen thousand feet. Several crestfallen Americans passed by in small groups on the way down. Two were descending because of breathing problems, three had not reached the summit because of high winds, and another four failed for the same reason. Quite a few people climbed Huascaran in any year, and quite a few failed. Three died on the route while we were in Peru. So were we biting off more than we could chew? Perhaps not; we would take it nibble by nibble.

When the time came we all put on crampons and roped up to begin threading a way up a huge glacier, between high ice blocks here, up ten feet of steep ice there, along a narrow ice bridge between deep, open crevasses, stepping over gaps, mostly up, occasionally down, on slopes of all angles. Anything steeper than seventy degrees was only a matter of feet high. Once a way had been found through the worst jumbled area of ice, in about half an hour, it was uphill snow all the way, for hours. Manuel went better than any of us, dumped the load he had been carrying at the next camp, and went back down to base camp with another porter descending from that high camp. Packing, snailing up the glacier and pitching the tent took about seven hours that day. It may not seem long, but we felt it was enough at that altitude, 17,500 feet.

At high altitude the need for liquid increases; serious dehydration is a risk. So we guzzled tea, soup, meat extract, hot chocolate and orange drinks, all made from melted snow. Porridge, a rice meal cooked in a pressure cooker at base camp and reheated, fruity Christmas pudding, egg powder and some very good dehydrated meals made up our solid food.

We seemed to have picked the busy season. Sharing the level snow patch were three Americans and about nine Austrians. Some of the Austrians had reached the summit that day and the Americans were aiming for it the next day. One of them, Eric Perlmann, a twenty-eight-year-old, freckle-faced, red-haired adventure journalist traded some of our matches for a length of strong rubber cord, which solved my crampon binding problems.

The sunset was the best of many in the Andes. The breast-shaped sugar bun that was our target blushed salmon pink while golden clouds surrounded a sun as red as a ripe Peruvian tomato. Gradually, wide black-berry juice stains spread through as the clouds turned to pale custard.

Sunday morning came and the fine weather held. The Americans had a problem: three porters they had engaged to carry skis part way were late, or had not set out at all. The longer they delayed the less chance they had of making it, and even if they set out as early as possible they would not arrive back before dark, after a long day. Though we did not need them we said we would take the porters off their hands, which was twenty per cent co-operative international gesture and eighty per cent laziness, and Eric, Rick and Bruce set off. We could afford to go later as we intended establishing yet another camp higher up; most did, some didn't. It was just one of many equations to be balanced: carry more weight and go slower or carry less and go fast. Our way was safer, and perhaps less certain of success; we aimed to have something in reserve at all times on this one. This one?

'What's this mountain called, Harry?'

'You forgotten again?'

'Yes.'

'Huascaran.'

For some reason the name would not stick in my mind; this mountain did not seem like one of mine somehow, and that bothered me a little. I wondered if I might finish up hating its very name.

The porters straggled up, unladen, late, and most of the morning had gone before we were away. Perhaps it was silly to take them on but we were glad that we had for they took weight from our backs. There was no rush. We knew four hours or so would be enough for the next stage, a rise of two thousand five hundred feet. The porters soon pulled a short way ahead; living in a high village conferred an obvious advantage and I envied them. Snow slopes of only forty degrees were a hard pull at that altitude and then came a snow step of thirty feet which was at about eighty degrees. At that altitude even short stretches of steep climbing really take it out of you. That particular step had a yellow fixed rope hanging down. Harry went first, relying a lot on the rope lower down and less and less as he gained height in case it gave way. A bulbous lip at the top soon hid him from view.

'It's attached to an aluminium stake,' he shouted. 'Bit wonky but it seems all right. OK Norm.'

Half way up was a ledge as wide as a chair seat. Hanging on to the rope I waited for my panting to subside before resuming the movements which won a foot at a time to join Harry. Julie came up; no problem.

We found ourselves on a narrow horizontal ice spine with the wall we had climbed falling away on the left and a big crevasse on the right. It was not hard but 'For God's sake be careful' country. And careful we were as we balanced across for forty feet.

Soon we were heaving ourselves up another fixed rope of a hundred feet, and another, on steep and very tiring slopes of snow. We belayed quite frequently in other places and then the hardest ground for that day was left behind. The porters dumped their loads, Harry dipped into 'the bank' and paid them, and they descended. Downhill and without loads they would be back at base camp quite soon.

The sun's heat hit not only from above but also by reflection from the snowfield we were on. We were about 19,000 feet up and heavily laden; the altitude punished Harry most.

'You'd better go on. I'm going to take hours,' he said.

The gradient was not too bad and, though there were a few crevasses around, the area held no special dangers. However, Julie and I preferred us to stick together. Every few minutes as we ploughed through the soft crystals Harry flopped down for a rest, then forced himself up to march on, grunting and swearing at his pack, the snow or the ski stick he carried. Blame did not lie with them, of course, but under stress Harry had a habit of grumbling at himself or some innocent, inanimate object close at hand. He never blamed anyone else unfairly, a trait which helped make him a very good climbing companion. It was probably his well-tuned power of self-criticism which made him such a pleasant man; he sought no scapegoat when the blame was his.

A massive ice avalanche had crushed down a slope which we had to traverse, leaving in its wake ice chunks, some as big as cars, over a width of three hundred yards. The biggest chunks were avoidable so the way was not so bad as it might have been, but the ice cliff which had spawned the avalanche looked ready to send down others, large and small. One day it would send down ton upon ton of grinding, charging, concrete-hard ice.

'We had to give up on Huascaran because three or four large avalanches wiped out the route just above Camp I,' a friend wrote to me the next year.

Having crossed quickly beneath the hanging menace, Julie was moving best and went ahead up a stiff snow ramp. At the foot of the ramp was a flat area surrounded on three of its four sides by high mounds of snow.

'Julie, this would do as a camp,' I called when I got there.

'Don't like it,' she shouted back. 'I'll look ahead a bit.'

Harry soon puffed up.

'Camp here, Harry?'

'Yes. Not going any further.'

'Julie, we think here's all right. It's high enough.'

'Think I can see a tent further up,' she insisted. 'Come and have a look, Norman.'

'Not going any further,' Harry croaked again. He slumped to his knees and rolled over to lie with his rucksack on the snow. I felt like he did. I dropped my pack and started up the ramp to join Julie. With Harry and two rucksacks at the bottom of the ramp I could appeal to her better nature.

In front there was a very large crevasse.

'See up there. Looks like a tent,' she said. It *could* have been a green tent. We were not sure.

'Don't fancy crossing this crevassed area after the sun's been on it, and with heavy packs. And it doesn't look so sheltered up there as in the hollow below.'

'Suppose not.'

'We may cross the crevasses and find it better to come back here again.

We won't know until tomorrow whether it's the right decision but I'm prepared to accept the consequences of that.'

'All right.'

The minority joined the majority. No argument. I came to feel increasingly that I was fortunate to be with Julie and Harry. We were three individuals, different from each other in many ways, but at the same time very similar because what mattered now was that we were three vulnerable human bodies 20,000 feet up on a mountain. Differing philosophies, faiths, political beliefs, incomes, professions, cultural backgrounds, were irrelevant now; all that mattered to us was taking place in a tiny segment of the world of mountaineering, and we were dependent on each other. Shelter, food and drink were foremost in our minds, along with some thoughts about how the next day might go. The tent was soon up, and snow was heaped on a pan to melt over the stove. I was obnoxiously cheerful, the others were quieter; I'd have to watch it or I'd get on their nerves.

The three Americans passed by at dusk, having made a successful ascent, and a fast descent mostly on skis.

We had taken much trouble lashing my crampons on and we did not want to go through the same performance early next day, so I left them on and parked my legs, trousers, socks, boots, crampons, bindings and gaiters in a polythene bag under the flysheet. Then we zipped up the tent and got into our sleeping bags; night time temperatures above the snow-line could drop to minus 20°C.

It nearly always seemed something needed doing, some little job, a piece of equipment to be checked, adjusted, sometimes just fiddled with for the reassurance this brought; there was food to be sorted, clothing to be chosen, a hundred and one tasks to increase our safety and our chances of success, not only in reality when the time came but also in our minds. Though sleep might occupy eight or nine hours and climbing only seven hours or so in a day, in the remaining hours there was surprisingly little time to take things easy. Now and then, when we had ceased ferreting about, we would be still in our sleeping bags, in warm flickering light from a candle carefully placed in a pan, and we would talk. This night we had time and it was revealed that my partners, both teachers, by the way, had been expelled from school. Julie's final crimes were falling off a rocking horse and breaking her wrist, and pushing a button up her nose. The latter sin was considered to be grave because a doctor had to be called in to retrieve the button. She had felt herself to be a victim of extreme injustice; after all, it was *her* wrist, *her* nose, *her* button. Harry's offence was more obviously defiant, the deliberate plan of a fertile young mind: he threw a lot of paints at a teacher and when a senior girl was deputed to supervise him he cleared up the mess and threw it all over the girl. Harry was rapidly expelled from school and put in another where his brother was a pupil; that was where he had intended going all along.

Doziness came over in pleasant, deepening waves.

'Tomorrow, if the weather's right, we'll be on top of . . . what's its name?'

'Huascaran', they reminded me.

The wind worsened in the night and I went out to fix extra guylines on the tent. Julie woke as I got back in.

'Wind sounds bad, Norm.'

'Yes.'

'Hope it drops tomorrow.'

'Expect it will.'

There was no point in saying anything different to someone who had just woken up, who was 20,000 feet above sea level, and who knew that at that altitude bad weather could be very serious even if you were only trying to retreat.

Six o'clock in cold morning daylight. I had been awake and lying still on my back for a while. At first the hammering wind had made getting up seem pointless. Now it had fallen a bit so I took a look outside.

'How is it?' came from one or other of my companions, with just the tops of heads and faces peeping from their sleeping bags and looking like shy tortoises.

'It's all right. We should go.'

The words sunk in and as if someone had thrown the switches on two robots they suddenly got into action. All at once the tent felt very cramped with three moving bodies in it. Thick breeches and fibre-pile jackets were donned hastily in the cold. We had slept in thermal underwear. I left breeches, legs and boots till later because they had crampons on; when I did come to put them on a lot of time and effort was saved doing it all in one go. So I did have some advantages.

Breakfast went down because we knew it should. The porridge seemed more like a medicine we had to take than a meal we wanted to eat, but the tea was enjoyed. Ah, liquid!

Harry had trouble putting on his gaiters.

'Take mine instead,' I offered. 'I don't really need them.' I wore them to reduce the likelihood of a crampon point catching in a sock but I could manage without, so it was no real sacrifice.

'No, it's all right thanks, Norm,' he said, continuing the struggle with his own. I thought no more about it; later I would wish I had.

The wind had almost died away. Balaclavas, mitts, windproofs on. Rucksacks hoisted. Glacier cream and lip salve smeared on. Rope on. We were ready and it had taken nearly two hours; much of that time had elapsed while we melted snow.

Leaving the tent and all but essentials behind, we crawled out into the sharp bite of the cold. Julie led off up the snow ramp we had been up the day before. A right turn at the top took us along a crest above the huge crevasse we had seen. Trying to find a way around either end would have involved going into very badly crevassed areas. So instead, we had to descend a steep slope of forty feet, drop straight down seven feet of vertical hard snow directly on to a little platform, and step or jump from there across the horrible hole. The top of the vertical bit was in fact one lip of the crevasse, that much higher than its partner. It was only a few feet, a wide stretching step, to the other side. One by one we made the step, each time hoping that the snow on the far side would not collapse. Julie, me, Harry. Nothing went wrong. Getting back was going to be a bigger problem.

Crossing that crevasse put us in a long, wide snow trough. Turning left, we walked the length of the trough, parallel with the crevasse, then took a level ridge with gaping holes running its 100-foot length on either side. Another giant crevasse barred the way; no, it was spanned by a snow bridge. We would have preferred a more substantial one but there was no choice. We crossed.

The tent we thought we had seen several hours earlier turned out to be a triangular ice face. Ours was the best spot to camp, after all.

At first the slope remained at a few degrees above or below thirty-five. Julie kept up a steady pace but every so often I was brought to a halt as the rope pulled tight behind; Harry was having trouble with the altitude.

'The pace on Pisco was all right,' he said.

After an hour of stop, start, stop, start I remarked to Julie, 'We're not going to make it at this rate. I'll be slow on the descent so I must get up there reasonably early in the afternoon. We're stopping too often, for too long, and going too slowly in between. The longer we take the softer the snow is so the longer we take, and so on.'

Going slower than the pace which feels right can be very tiring. We had to face it: one or all of us would have to turn back. We could try again tomorrow, I thought, not liking the idea. Nothing more was said for a while because I hoped Harry would feel better. Half a minute after we had restarted following a rest the rope went tight, dragging me to a halt again. I tried, only partly successfully, to suppress pointless anger by reminding myself that Harry was a friend who was prepared to attempt a big mountain with me, and he had always been patient with me.

'My crampon's come off,' he shouted from a kneeling position. Then he called, 'I think you'd better go on without me.'

It was natural enough to feel disappointment for him because he had put in as much work as anyone to get us that far, but I must admit that the predominant feeling was one of relief.

'What a shame,' Julie said, as Harry untied from the rope. 'But I think he ought to go down.'

We had spotted two men descending from Huascaran's south summit after a bivouac. They would have to cross the worst crevasses so Harry could join them to get back to the tent.

The two of us started uphill again, swinging along at a good pace. I lost track of time but probably an hour had passed before I noticed how frequently we were stopping to rest.

'You'd better take the lead,' Julie said. 'You're going so well.'

In good snow, leading was only marginally harder. The firm south-west slope of the north summit was getting steeper. For *very* short stretches of a few feet at a time the angle may have gone over fifty degrees but that was not common.

'Just a minute,' Julie called a couple of times, but I tried to anticipate her halts so she would not have to. It was better that she should not; better that the rat ahead should stop first.

Another hour elapsed. Julie had been standing catching her breath for a while when she said, 'I think I may not make it. My leg's hurting.'

She would not have mentioned it unless it was really troubling her.

A lot of time had been wasted already and it really would have been sticking our necks out to hit the summit in the late afternoon. I couldn't skip back down nearly as fast as other people. The weather was good but the thought of moving in the dark amongst the crevasses, in a strong wind and with tiredness upon us, seemed too big a risk to take.

An idea crept into my head: if I soloed on quickly that would give us a reasonable chance of one person reaching the top and the expedition would be an enormous success. But I could not leave Julie on her own, especially with a bad leg. We were finished for this day, and I was not optimistic about the weather for the next.

Below us, far, far below, a lone figure climbed up slowly. It looked like Harry. It was Harry! He would not reach where we were for a long time but he was on the way up again and here was a solution: Julie could join Harry.

'Be good for the Calvert Trust if I get up this one,' I said, avoiding a direct proposal that I should solo.

'Oh yes. Superb.'

I never had to worry about climbing being futile because mountaineering often had beneficial effects on my work. Always there seemed an added sense of purpose which could not be divorced even if I had wanted it so. But was that really me being swayed by a non-mountaineering reason? To some extent, yes; but I wanted this one for me too. The ambition dragon was back again, big and fiery. And with only eight hundred feet to go I did not want to let down all those people who had helped put us that high. Every reason pushed me up. There might be a small risk from crevasses but the angle of the snow was going to ease before long. Solo was the only way. Unless we turned back. I would have to put it directly; try it and see what she says.

'One of us has got to get there, Julie.'

'Yes.'

'Better unrope, then. I'll solo.'

'Yes.'

It would not have come as any surprise if she had said no. When you earn your living through climbing instruction your work might well be affected if you did nothing to discourage a double leg amputee from soloing a big mountain, particularly if he got hurt or killed. People would not understand if anything went wrong; a few might, but most would condemn. What they would fail to understand is that those who have climbed with me, or helped me in other ways to go climbing, have led me along a path to the finest experiences of a lifetime. The mountains have already given more joy than a man could expect in three lifetimes. Sometimes I am troubled by what may be said of companions who may one day survive on a mountain when I do not. In some ways, more than those who would try to overprotect, they have given me life; if they are in at my death they should not be censured. They deserve no blame, only praise for their understanding, for not backing away when they could so easily have done that. Perhaps I might live longer if I did not climb, but that is arguable, and life must be measured more by quality than by length alone. Certainly, a long hollow life has no appeal to me.

Julie coiled the rope.

'See you on the top,' I said tritely; who the hell stops to make up a good speech at a time like that anyway?

Almost immediately I was faced with a wall of hard snow, eight or nine feet high. A mere garden wall, when you think about it, but running along the bottom was a body-width crevasse. Stepping across and climbing up made me sweat a bit.

I have already said that Huascaran's north summit resembled a white breast, and it even had a snow cone nipple at the top. It was a deceiver, though, for behind the nipple the mountain still rose for quite a long way; I had been warned that this was the case. The gradient eased, eased, eased back to thirty degrees, then less, getting more pleasant all the time, and I topped the false summit, slightly on its right side. Behind the phoney nipple summit, which looked so like the real one from lower down, the mountain stretched back and back for a distance I could not judge. Now steepness was not a problem, though it was slightly, tiringly uphill all the way; distance and soft snow were all that stood between me and the summit. I wondered how many people had turned back through disappointment and fatigue at that point. My body wanted to go up, but at the same time did not. It was such hard work, such an awful, awful slog, like climbing in a suit of armour on a hot day.

Though distance was difficult to estimate, shortly after passing the false summit I thought forty minutes would see me up this soft, lumpy mattress laid thick on the mountain. Many times I stopped to catch breath; I did not want to stop, but had to. Before long I was down to a hundred paces between unwilling halts for gasps of thin air. On a slightly steeper slope only fifty paces separated the stops, then it was back to eighty or a hundred. At each stop I would wait a few seconds before saying to myself, 'Stopped isn't going,' and it was strange how much that sea level silly sentence helped me keep moving up there. Another helped even more: I kept approaching mounds which I hoped would be the summit but they never were and each time I avoided disappointment by saying, 'It is what it is.' What I meant was that these things were essential, for I needed the mounds one after another as a steady stairway to the final one, so there was no sense getting angry and wasting energy. They were there to be accepted as elements of a game I had chosen to play and wanted very much to play. Over mound after mound I went, looking for a summit which seemed to be running away and hiding. But I knew it could not hide for ever, and gradually I leaned less and less on my sentences as a different strength which required no willpower took over; almost nothing could stop me now, even if I had to crawl, and a feverish elation began to fuel me for the finish. Shouts and giggles and laughs came from my mouth like it was someone else making them.

'Hey! Hey! Hey! You're going to do it! You're going to do it! You're going to do it!'

Now we were on a big mountain and not a British rock climb the fact that part of my legs were artificial was creeping more and more into the background. I had found where fulfilment lay.

I shouted loudly, happily, mad with joy, and turned to look back at the ground which had been covered. And there, twenty minutes or so away, was the tiny figure of Julie, still going.

'Hey! Hey! Hey! *We're* going to make it!'

She was too far away to hear.

Five more minutes pushing on and I turned again to see how she was getting along. There was another figure close behind Julie. Harry! The more distant figure fell down in the snow, got up a minute later, slumped again within another minute and lay there. He rose again, managing no more than fifteen or twenty paces between halts.

'Hey! We're *all* going to do it! Two of us at least and probably three!'

Where was the nausea barrier? Dismissed because of the crutches. Formerly I had been ill purely through trying too hard; I had vomited long and often through effort alone.

Every muscle was tired but eager. And then I spotted it, the fairly level area of slightly ruffled snow that was the top. A rush of emotion came over me, a weepy feeling that is not uncommon in such circumstances, and my eyes were wet out of sheer euphoria. I didn't mind; Bonatti cried a lot, anyway, when things went well.

Could it be done in fifty paces, in one go? No. After fifty it was still a long way away. Snow seems to stretch like elastic as soon as you set foot on it, and so often slopes turn out to be twice as long as first impressions convey. Another forty paces and a pause was inevitable. But now it was within reach. The summit had one last steepish bit, a mere twenty-five degrees but exhausting all the same. Then I was there. In front the mountain plunged away.

'You've done it,' I said to myself.

I had indeed! It was 2.15 p.m. so it had taken six hours. Twenty-one thousand, eight hundred and thirty feet (6,654 m). Over four miles up. Nineteen years of effort had led here by stages and it was fantastic! Ten years of rock climbing, John o' Groats to Land's End, eight summers in the Alps, finding out all the while, the toil of expedition organisation, and now this. Through my blood surged that wonderful sensation which no words can properly describe – sweet as love, warm as friendship, and overwhelming. All the effort was repaid.

Julie arrived fifteen minutes later, bright-eyed with the thrill of success.

'Well, we've done it, Julie.'

'Yep!'

The people who made the first ascent could not have been happier than us. It was a moving moment, particularly as Harry was still on the way up, half an hour behind Julie. Eventually his head and shoulders approached the final steepish bit.

'It's here, Harry. We're standing on it,' we called.

The head and shoulders dropped instantly from sight as Harry crumpled in the snow, down for a count of sixty. He was up again, to stumble-step nearer before buckling knees let him down again. Flop. He dragged himself up once more, managing twenty paces before going down. But he was on the summit this time. His determination had received a just reward, and I had learned a lot about Harry: next time he stopped on an ascent I would be more inclined to spend time encouraging him to go on.

To discover something you burn to do, and to do it, is one of life's greatest rewards, and a privilege which does not come often. The discovery can be as elusive as the success; we had been lucky on both counts.

'Seems daft though,' I said.

'What?'

'Our most important ascent is the only one we said we wouldn't do.'

We nibbled at chocolate and took photographs, some of them with Harry's camera, which, along with the film, was stolen later. Of our seven cameras three more went wrong and Mike Welham, the main expedition photographer, made only one ascent. So the pictures were rather disappointing.

There was little time for Harry to rest before we started back, but he moved downhill with no trouble. About half way back to the false summit we met the first of five Austrians (whom we had seen on the march) who toiled to the top the same day. Now gravity was in our favour their laborious movements looked strange by contrast.

Where the snow was steep we belayed; a slip was more likely on the way down. At one place where I went down first I hammered an aluminium tube, the lower piece of a crutch, into the snow, and wound the rope around it a couple of turns as a belay. Julie descended towards me. She came near and then level with me on my left, when something frightening happened in an instant. Suddenly she cried out and her body sank in the snow.

'I'm in a crevasse!'

I held on to the rope and prayed the crutch tube would not pull out. She dropped up to the top of her thighs into the snow-covered hole and went no further.

'I've got you.'

It is impossible to say whether she might have fallen far. Perhaps she would have, perhaps she would not. Such minor falls without serious consequences are not uncommon. Some crevasses widen as you go deeper and it can be a real problem to get someone out, but we didn't go poking around to see what shape this one was, I can assure you.

'That's all I need,' was Julie's only comment after she had climbed out, and then she carried on with the job. Her leg was hurting still, so she took a pain-killer.

My stumps started to get very sore after ten hours out and I had to push myself quite hard. Now we were in the most dangerous part of the day, with sun-softened snow bridges and tiredness against us. Another hour, and we approached the big crevasses in near darkness. Three of the Austrians were just ahead, having overtaken us an hour before because of my slowness in descent. Crossing a snow bridge to join them, we found that one of them was preparing to bivouac because he felt unwell.

'Our tent is nearer than yours,' we explained. 'You are welcome to come in.'

The other two Austrians favoured the idea and persuaded him to join us, and they crossed the last big crevasse ahead of us without preparing any belays. We could not treat it that way. An ice axe and a crutch were arranged as belays and Harry stepped across from rather soft snow to the other, higher side where he hooked in his ice axe and got himself tight up against the seven foot wall. He stood on a small bulge of ice with Lord knows what sort of hole below and behind him. We heard bits of dislodged hard snow clump clumping down the crevasse and suddenly Harry let out a sharp squeal of fright and said, 'Oh, God! Oh, God!' Whether he felt he was toppling back into the black hole or thought his feet were going to give way I do not know, but for a couple of seconds he whimpered, a very frightened man; most of us get like that now and then. Reaching rapidly over the top lip of the wall he got his ice axe deeply and comfortingly into the hard snow, and pulled up, while his crampons ran up the wall. A relieved man stood at the top and moved back many feet to set up a belay. Me next.

'Keep your belay on too, Julie,' I said. 'Please.'

After a quick step across I whammed my hammer into the wall. Now I knew something of what Harry had felt. I didn't like it. Though not hard there was an indefinite, unreliable characer to the problem. What I stood on could have broken off, and the top of the wall arched gradually in a soft and untrustworthy snow hump to join the slope above, rather than providing a distinct and firm junction. I moved up far enough to hammer my ice axe into the slope, and pulled up. A mere three feet of height was gained but the danger of falling into the crevasse was over. Julie followed with no bother.

The poorly Austrian had not waited. That was fortunate in a way because we had been out twelve hours and were ready to flop down and get the stove going; it would have been very cramped in the tiny refuge.

The gas stove's hissing purr and faint blue light said welcome home. This was a wonderfully secure and warm shelter to us now. Harry had assumed the role of fetching snow for melting, without anyone asking. Jobs were done, with no more than an occasional suggestion by one or other of us that they needed doing. And when the food or drink was ready the light aluminium plates or plastic mugs were handed out almost reverently, with utmost care; food and drink were comfort, fuel, and life in the end.

'Let's have something else,' one of us would say, and another pan of snow would be stuck on the burner. The white cone would sink slowly and shrink, we'd pile more snow on, that would go down, and we would make up our minds what to have next. We spooned down tasty oxtail soup, and sipped tangy hot orange, meaty Oxo and good old tea, and had some more tea and orange.

Harry had trouble getting his boots off but managed in the end. He felt his feet for a while and was quiet. Then he said, 'Frostbite.'

We both turned towards him.

'I think my toes are a bit frostbitten,' he said, and Julie softly said, 'Oh, Harry.'

'My own fault,' he murmured. 'Should have put my gaiters on. The snow got between the inner and the outer boot.'

Everyone but me on the expedition wore a pair of double boots, a soft leather inner like a plush red slipper that laced high up the ankle, and an outer like any big brown mountain boot.

On Harry's toes white patches and angry red blisters had formed. He wrapped his feet in his sleeping bag. Julie's leg was sore, and my stumps were a bit hurt, but she and I had not paid dearly for what we had had. What it would cost Harry in the end we could only guess. In a period of six months I heard of three climbers who lost their feet through frostbite. So it was a rather subdued trio that settled down for another night at 20,000 feet. Our down sleeping bags smelled familiar and gave us some reassurance.

During the night the wind started. Harry slept almost without a break, but many, many times Julie and I woke up, took a few sips of cold orange juice and lay there listening to the devil wind blasting at our tent. The fabric flapped fiercely with a noise like someone hammering an iron roof.

At eight o'clock we still cuddled our sleeping bags and downed hot tea, while the tent shook just as badly as during the night. At nine o'clock it was as unrelenting as ever.

'I think we'd better go anyway,' I said. 'We should be sheltered lower down. Don't want to get caught up here in a storm.'

We had all been approaching the same conclusion. The contents of three rucksacks do not take long to pack, and when this had been done we crawled out to get the tent down. After kneeling and sitting on the writhing brown monster to prevent it flying away once it was down, we finished up with a lumpy bundle.

The sun shone in an almost cloudless sky, yet after quitting our hollow we entered an even worse wind, which picked up white crystals and blasted them at us; it was choking to breathe. Face-masks on our fibre-pile jackets solved the problem. Thin clouds of snow were drawn up and chased hither and thither, now in a curve, now a whirling vortex, as the wind left a clue to its path, marking its way as in a fog. It buffeted unevenly from different directions. Julie moved up a slope on to a sharp horizontal snow ridge, with crevasses on either side. The bully wind blew even worse and Julie dropped to one knee, head down, her body rocked by violent gusts. She moved forward a short way on one knee and both hands, stopped on both knees, moved a little further and halted once more. We had to watch it here because of the crevasses. If the wind had been from a constant direction we could have crossed the ridge on the sheltered side, but it kept changing and pushing us all ways. I crawled for a short way behind Julie.

One thing was certain: a day later, and we would not have reached the summit.

Descent into a downhill snow trough brought some relief from the wind, and I felt a little more relaxed. However, a sudden cry from behind soon changed that: Harry was sliding down the snow towards a crevasse. Face down and feet first, he gathered speed very rapidly, then stopped himself with his ice axe.

The wind still pushed us around as we crossed the big avalanche track.

'That fixed rope's gone,' Julie said as we reached the first steep snow slope. 'But we don't really need it. Just have to go down carefully.'

It was worth belaying, which we did. The next fixed rope had been removed as well, but that did not matter too much either. We would really miss having a fixed rope on the near vertical section, though. We approached the top of that step. A glimpse of yellow, yes, it was still there, and it helped us down in turn. In that small height loss the shelter turned the wind to a mere whisper; even the thin white fringes of blown snow swirling from the heights could not convey the force of the monster still roaming up there. The sun's warmth forced us to take off our windproofs right away.

Only the glacier trudge to go.

'Sod!' Harry said to a rucksack shoulder strap which had worked loose. He had been uncomplaining about his feet but grunted a lot as he walked. 'You'll have to go on. I'll be ages.'

For a while the rope was not essential so Julie and I moved ahead, but with no intention of leaving him; we knew him better now and expected that he would not lag far behind. This was so and in a few minutes he joined us again, muttering quietly to himself. We stuck together and weaved in and out of ice humps, between crevasses, over ice bridges and around small pools. There rarely seemed to be a right way, a best way; it was just a matter of picking a route every few minutes out of many options. Time and time again two, three, four or five possible ways lay before us.

Julie was a constant optimist, always seeing a 'right' way, whether it was there or not.

'To the left a bit I think, Harry,' Julie would say.

'*Where?*'

In his voice now was a faint edge, a barely perceptible trace of sharpness, but he was well-controlled. Everyone was a bit edgy because as the afternoon wore on it began to look as if night's rapid approach would catch us out on the glacier. Harry's feet, Julie's leg and my stumps were all giving pain, our packs were heavy, and we were tired. I have climbed with people who in those circumstances would have been at each other's throats, but we had no rows. Temperamentally, these were two of the best climbing companions I have come across.

As we lolloped down the glacier we had no way of knowing that there was a scarey bit to come. We had been just that little bit too slow to escape from the glacier before night. In failing light we tried to find a way between high ice towers and perched blocks, and watched the darkness creeping up from the valley to get us. Up steep slopes, down steep slopes, across gaps, through gullies, we pressed on. By torchlight we could not see far enough ahead to pick a way which did not soon become a dead end. Half the dark holes turned out to be non-holes while some real holes thinly covered by ice and snow were difficult to recognise. We came upon a huge crevasse, twenty feet across. A retreat and detour were called for. I began to wonder if we should start to face the prospect of a bivouac.

'I think we should bivouac,' Julie said, beating me by ten seconds. Harry was in agreement. We back-tracked to an ice block with a level top as big as a dining table and removed our rucksacks. Sleeping bags and spare clothing were coming out when suddenly we all jumped. *Bang!* The block shook as the ice beneath cracked through the enormous pressure it was under. Hell's bells! We scattered, pointlessly.

Next we settled on an ice sofa; an insulating closed-cell foam mat on the seat, another on the backrest, made it comfortable enough. With extra clothing on, good sleeping bags, and the tent laid over us and tucked in, we were warm as kittens in hay.

In good weather a night out 15,000 feet up was not serious in the Andes, though by temperate sea level standards it was as if we had gone from summer to winter in an hour.

What was serious, though, was that we were near the end of the glacier tongue, where it cracked and broke up continually. Around and under us the ice was moving, mostly at an infinitesimally slow speed, but every so often big blocks reached a point at which their equilibrium was disturbed and they tumbled over with a fearsome noise. Tremendous pressures forced cracking and movement, and the resultant sounds, like slamming doors, pinging bedsprings and creaking floorboards could have been caused by human beings in a block of flats.

'The people are in downstairs,' Julie remarked as she handed out our rations: chocolate, sardines and peanuts. I had the stove hissing beneath a pan of snow, to make a drop of tea for our parched bodies.

'This is one of the hardest mountain trips I've ever been on,' Harry commented in a resigned way.

The glacier emitted from its bowels a groan, a bang or a high-pitched crack once or twice a minute. We lay back, silently promising to lead better lives if we came through a night in this awful place. The unsought and unwelcome was with us and would not go away for hours. However, it was not as bad as it might have been because the weather was dry and not too cold. In fact I was so warm I had to remove some clothing; it is one advantage of being an amputee, that body heat is retained better, and one day that could mean the difference between survival or death.

For a long time I watched the flit of brilliant shooting stars sowing sparkling trails across the sky, and made a wish on each one: wish morning would come. The others fell asleep long before I finally nodded off.

I awoke suddenly. Something was wrong! At first I could not register what it was until I noticed in the faint light that though Julie was beside me Harry had gone! Then I saw him; he had slipped down an ice slope while asleep. He was still asleep a few feet below us, with his feet just inches from a crevasse. I called out some sleepy stupid words.

'Harry, Harry, should you be down there?'

He woke and, still in his sleeping bag, wriggled back up to us.

Who woke first in the morning I don't know, but it was not until long after light had reached us. With daylight on our side it took only fifteen minutes before we had our boots on the crunchy little stones of the moraine. Had we tried the night before we might have made it in twenty minutes or an hour, or we might have wandered around much longer in a dangerous area.

'Congratulations, Norm,' Harry said. 'I didn't want to say it before, but we've finished it now.'

As we approached base Manuel rushed up easily.

'Cumbre?' he asked. ('Summit?')

'Si, Manuel.'

The mountain was left behind, the snows and intricate ice patterns constantly changing shape through sun-melt and wind-blow and gravity's downhill tug. It remained for others to enjoy, if they were lucky. We left nothing there, and took away nothing but happiness; and now the cloud of gloom which had hung over us and dulled that happiness was dispersed. 'Leave nothing but footprints, take nothing but pictures,' is an old saying which almost sums it up, but I would add 'and happy memories' to what we should take. Our hearts were free of anxiety and we began to feel the lightness which came with the realisation of a dream. Even our concern about Harry's feet was reduced, and I don't think any of us expected him to suffer permanent damage.

Now base camp had a different atmosphere. The excitement of the way up was replaced by the contentment of success, and the place seemed different because we were changed in mood. We ate and drank and mid-day drew near. They had been a hard few days and a rest was inviting.

'How about waiting so we can get you a donkey or a horse, Harry?' I suggested. 'You could ride at least part way.'

'No. We couldn't get one until tomorrow. I want to go down and see a doctor today.' His mind was made up firmly.

Julie bandaged his feet and very gently rolled one sock on. She had the second one almost on when she said in a voice full of concern, 'Oh, Harry.' Two words, quietly spoken, but they rang out.

What now? I thought.

'Harry, there's a big lump on your heel. We'll have to get the sock off again and see what it is.'

Poor Harry. The sock, so carefully put on, was peeled off with great gentleness.

'Well?' I asked. 'What is it?'

Julie examined the heel, and frowned, then looked in the sock. She turned to me and said, 'Knickers.'

'Pardon?'

'Knickers. A pair of mine.'

Apparently, not wishing Manuel to stumble across her underwear, she had hidden various items in her socks and other places.

'Those are not *my* socks,' Harry burst out defensively.

We laughed and laughed and laughed. The elation of our small triumph was beginning to sweep over us even more.

'Fantastic expedition!' Harry said. 'And what happened was my own fault. I *think* it's mostly blisters anyway. Will this be worth a *foot*note in your book, Norm?'

'It may be worth pointing out that you can expect trouble if you will go around with those old-fashioned legs.' His laughter crawled out with the deep hump, hump, hump of a distant pump.

Soon after, our casualty shambled out of sight through the trees in short, wincing steps. Within a few hours he was back in the Hotel Barcelona.

At eight the next morning the donkey arrived in the charge of a sixteen-year-old called Nelson. In response to his curiosity about my crutches, I showed him one of my legs on the way down. We had been descending for two hours when a slender man in ragged pants and shirt appeared through the bushes. In one hand he carried an enamel dish with a lid, in the other a bottle. It turned out he was Nelson's father, and the family were working on a small field on a steep hill opposite the trail. They had seen us coming and dad had run over with Nelson's breakfast of boiled potatoes, which the latter tucked into right away. Before long dad had been told about my legs and he came up to where I sat on the trailside bank; with a finger pointed at himself he made a gesture with the other hand which meant, 'Can I touch?' Si. He felt the metal in the region of the knees, grinned, took a hasty step leftwards to where Julie sat, and felt her knees too!

As far as we could discover, the only transport leaving Musho village to go down the valley was a pick-up, rumoured to be heading for Mancos at two o'clock. Julie went on a successful beer hunt, and we sat in the shade with a bottle each. Children streamed out of a school and a hundred curious brown eyes surrounded us. A score of dark hands reached out to touch my legs when Nelson explained about the gringos who had been up mighty Huascaran. For twenty minutes all, whether five or fifteen years old, stood and stared and smiled and chattered around us. We told them her name was Pedro and mine Maria, that a scar on her arm had been made by a lion which Pedro had killed with her bare hands. It wasn't the beer, well, hardly at all, it was just joy and relief made us talk that way. We did wonder what happened when they went back to school, fifty children insisting to the teacher they had met a woman called Pedro who had killed a lion, and a man with metal legs had climbed Huascaran and his name was Maria.

With the return of the children to school the village resumed a quiet afternoon air; most adults would have been out working in the collectively-owned fields and looking after their animals. Compared with the poor of Lima, village life conferred upon them great richness and security. The pick-up driver turned up and readily gave us a lift. After an hour's dusty drive, there was Terry walking up the road. He was taken on board and he seemed even more pleased than we were that the ascent had been made. From the Datsun we transferred to another pick-up with several members of a family in it. The papers had already put the story of our ascent around so as soon as they realised who we were they traded a twenty-five mile lift for some autographs.

Terry had been thoughtful enough to bring towels and soap, and we stopped off at the baths to soak away a week's grime. My stumps found such relief in the warm water; it was almost worth doing another climb just to repeat such pleasure. Most important of all, they were not rubbed raw in a single patch. That was unusual, and was the result of training, of taking the climb by reasonable stages, and of using the crutches.

The Hotel Barcelona, 6,000 miles from England, felt like home. Harry was limping but thought his feet would be all right; the blisters seemed to be the main problem. Terry, Julie and I went with him to Huaras hospital. Rest, the doctor said, so he and I stayed at the Hotel Barcelona. Everyone else went touring various parts of Peru. We were due to meet one week later in Lima.

'I think I'll fly home for treatment, to be on the safe side,' Harry said. 'Get close to some nurses, the little darlings.'

Two seats to Lima were soon booked on a colectivo, which is a cheap communal taxi. For about £5 each five passengers travelled 200 miles (330 km).

'If ever you come here again this is your home,' Pepe said.

We rode to Lima and somewhere along the way Harry's camera and the film taken on Huascaran went missing. After a couple of beers and a bit of thinking we came to the conclusion that the colectivo driver might know where they were so we headed for his office. He could keep the camera, all we wanted was the film, we intended saying, but once we had the film we had it in mind to cause him a certain amount of physical discomfort. So on a pair of sore feet and a pair of artificial legs we took purposeful steps towards a showdown; it was all very Gary Cooper and High Noonish. Harry grunted with pain and muttered, 'Four foot six of Peruvian crap! I'll blow 'em all over.' We turned right off a main street into the side street we sought. Harry wanted me to take his wallet and watch, for safekeeping. No, we're in this together, Harry. One hundred yards to go. Fifty. Twenty. The office was closed.

As we swore our way back up the street the thought did cross my mind that the short colectivo driver had a fair amount of muscle under his shirt, and there never seemed to be less than eight other drivers hanging around the office. We tried to comfort ourselves with the notion that it was better to have climbed Huascaran and lost the film than to have nice pictures but have been denied the ascent. There was little comfort in the argument that night though; it mattered a lot at the time but, as these things do, it faded in our minds with the passing of months. We decided against reporting the camera's loss to the police in case the colectivo driver was innocent after all. When we came to book into a cheap hotel for the night we had to enter through a lion's cage door, and spend the night in a room with windows barred like a prison cell to keep thieves out (or us in if the place caught fire).

Lima Tours responded very quickly to arrange an immediate flight home for Harry. A representative picked him up in a huge, black, hearse-like car, and that was the last I saw of him for a long time.

Meanwhile, Dennis climbed two more peaks, Chopikalki and Ishinca, before being laid low by the Peruvian runs. Terry and Julie visited Cuzco: Mike and Mike and Denny travelled to tourist spots. I had time to take it easy and reflect. After sending off fifty postcards to sponsors and others who had helped, I visited a disco where one leg, after surviving two weeks' training in Italy, and the expedition, finally gave up and broke under the strain of some very energetic dancing.

Seven of us gathered together and boarded a Viasa plane for London in mid-august. As we descended the steps from the aircraft at our destination a dozen photographers and reporters waited.

'Tell them you were first on Huascaran,' Julie said.

'I wasn't going to. They'll exaggerate it all as usual.'

'It will help the Calvert Trust and Harry would want you to.' It was like the sort of thing you say when someone has died.

A large number of people had helped us, so the story was not one to be hoarded. Terry, Dennis, Mike, Mike and Denny, all of whom had contributed a great deal to the success, melted away in the crowd. Julie and I faced the cameras but it all felt incomplete because Harry was not there.

Harry. What happened to Harry? Well, in the end he suffered the loss of just two toenails, removed because of an infection underneath. It was a tremendous relief to learn that success had not cost him more, and we were amused at his account of his visit to hospital. Picture him, an untidy man who has no need of the fripperies of fashion to prop up his confidence, scruffy after two days of flying and considerable delays, and tired through pain. Of all the hospitals Harry could pick in London he chose one which sees a large number of vagrants and alcoholics. On a hot day in August he wandered into the casualty department and announced, 'I've got frostbite!' As you might imagine, there was a certain amount of scepticism on the part of the nursing staff.

A radio broadcast centred partly around the expedition brought in several thousand pounds for the Calvert Trust, so from that point of view, too, the trip was a success.

We had to go back home and 'settle down'. Many people expected, suggested and advised the same thing: settling down. Damned settling down. Awful settling down. Horrible settling down. Maybe they were right, but I could not believe it. The settling down could only be temporary; there would be other mountains, other adventures. I had found a slice of life as good as any I had ever tasted, I had the recipe and I wanted to make it again.

There is a sad sequel to this story. Julie was so enchanted by her first exciting relationship with big mountains that in order to climb frequently she became a sound recordist working on documentary films of high altitude expeditions. In 1986, having climbed higher than any British woman, to the summit of K 2, the world's second highest mountain, she died peacefully, trapped in bad weather on the descent. She had had many fulfilling years on the mountains, and perhaps one should not ask for more. Though many might think she had sacrificed her life pointlessly at the age of forty-eight, she had always said she would not mind dying upon a mountain; I'm sure she meant it.

# 6

## *A Broken Leg in Argentina*

I can offer a partial explanation as to why I climb. Though I am rather lazy about any work which does not interest me, it was evident in my teens at grammar school that I was capable of great effort when I chose. Being keen to 'get on', whatever that meant, I blindly studied hard at all subjects. In examinations I was always in the top three overall for my year, and while in the end my academic achievements were not outstanding, I came top each year in the whole school for 'effort marks'. Under this system teachers subjectively rated each pupil according to how hard they thought he was trying, and I was rammed down the throats of peers as the goody who was 'an example to you all.' I redeemed myself in their eyes by turning down the role of head boy and being demoted from prefect twice for 'crimes' I had not committed (throwing a snowball indoors and talking in class). I did not protest my innocence too strongly because, as is common under these circumstances, there were other undiscovered misdemeanours, really bad things, like not wearing a school cap and breaking a window. But my point is that I did put great effort into what I was doing; unfortunately what was lacking was enthusiasm.

Concerning sport I was more enthusiastic, and I put a lot of effort into cross-country running, rugby, gymnastics and gliding. Though I ran in the school cross-country team and captained the gymnastics team, my efforts in sport were not rewarded with shining success; no matter how hard I tried, I did not seem to have what it took physically to excel. The one exception was when I started climbing, and everything fell into place. If I tried hard, I succeeded. Lack of enthusiasm for the subjects held me back academically, and in most sports enthusiasm and effort did not seem enough on their own, but for climbing I was both physically and temperamentally suited; I was fit and strong and climbers come in all shapes and sizes, for the sport does not demand a certain ideal physique.

Promoting outdoor pursuits for disabled people was another challenge which came my way more by chance than by intention. And, since climbing was crucial to my being a spokesman, this campaign gave an added and respectable incentive to enjoy the mountains. In any case, the challenge, adventure, excitement and emotional rewards I sought were found in greater depth in climbing than in any other sport I had experienced, and in greater depth the more effort was put in. When I resumed climbing after the loss of my legs, in essence nothing had changed; trying hard brought rewards, and enthusiasm produced the necessary effort.

Naturally enough, work allowed too little time to enjoy the special life of the mountains, for my days were filled with varied and interesting work. As time went by I wrote two editions of a guide on outdoor pursuits for disabled people and I gave talks on my climbing experiences and on outdoor pursuits for disabled people; a considerable amount of time was consumed in writing articles and booklets on these and allied subjects. Though formerly I had not been one for sitting on committees, from 1970 onwards I selectively accepted membership of several which did produce good results. I had a great many other casual voluntary commitments, so was very busy, and earning a living was not easy to accomplish simultaneously. It was an insecure way of life but there was no realistic alternative but to take whatever work was going or adopt a more 'responsible' lifestyle; ironically, that 'responsible' way of living would have entailed less climbing, less voluntary work with disabled people and, in my view, an abandonment of what I was supposed to do in life.

From all this you might assume me to be a man dedicated without any reservation to the service of disabled people, but this was not so; it is only honest to admit that I did not always enjoy such a heavy involvement with disability, disability, disability. I grew tired of hearing patronising talk of how wonderful a disabled person was because he or she sailed or fished (there's no reason why most should not). And I was weary, too, of hearing some disabled people adopting the negative line that no one cared – that was taking rather a lot for granted. I was driven as much by a pragmatic sense of what I ought to do, as by a feeling that I wanted to do it; I felt I should do all I could to help on positive aspects such as access, mobility, sporting and leisure provision and, above all, integration of disabled people into our society.

It became evident I would be asked to be even more committed to voluntary work when the United Nations designated 1981 as the International Year of Disabled People. More demands were inevitable and the first came well in advance in the form of an invitation to join a national committee co-ordinating the efforts of 'The Year'. Oh, how I struggled to make up my mind whether to take on yet more work; in the end I joined the committee.

Throughout this and many preceding years Judy maintained an indifference to things material. We managed in a cheap rented bedsitter, did not run a car, and spent little on clothes or meals out. Much of the time my earnings were about one third of the national average. We were not complaining, for life was interesting and rewarding, and by the standards of two-thirds of the world we were well off. We believed that many people were too concerned with material possessions and too mean to have adventures.

In January 1979, in Scotland, with an instructor from the Loch Eil Outward Bound Centre near Fort William, Alan Kimber, I tested out some crampon bindings which kept the spikes in position with wire cable. In my case they were like Cinderella's slipper on the foot of the rightful owner and that was a big problem solved for ever. Next we tried out an ice axe pick clamped to a crutch to see if it would stop me in a fall on ice or hard snow. I slid down head first, feet first, on my front and on my back, and found that it worked quite well as a brake. The extra second which it took to apply, by comparison with an ice axe, meant there were some limitations to the method, but the pick and the bindings increased my safety on the mountains.

Alan suggested Achintee Gully, a narrow icy gash up a steep mountain-side. One rope length of snow gave way to forty-five degree ice. I led a bit, swinging two short axes in turn to dig into the here clear and brittle, there translucent white and firm ice. An ice bulge at seventy degrees was Alan's task; I was glad not to be leading, but soon it was obvious that in some ways ice would give me less trouble than rock because ice always allowed options. The hands and feet could be placed more or less where desired, in moves which were as short or as long as I wished, so if I wanted I could make a dozen reasonably smooth moves where someone else might gain the same height in six or seven moves. This made ice climbing a good deal less strenuous than rock climbing, for me, and I suspected that if ever the urge came to tackle some more serious mountain routes the way should lie mostly on ice and snow. Until then I had tackled only short ice sections, believing the longer and steeper stuff to be beyond my abilities.

From a vague guide-book description we expected four hundred feet or thereabouts of climbing, but after a break for a sandwich the peering up ahead started and simultaneously we arrived at the conclusion that this winter there was much further to go than the book estimate. One hundred and thirty feet of rope ran out as Alan climbed pure ice. We hurried on for another rope length, another, and the afternoon wore on. One more rope length, and we escaped from the shadowy top of the gully on crisp snow, and into winter sunshine. We were back at the road just before dark.

'Eleven hundred feet. Grade 3 at the top,' Alan said. 'Not bad for your first Scottish snow and ice climb.' (There are five grades in Scottish snow and ice climbing.)

The next one was even better. With Allan Roberts I walked one grey morning on three-inch white sheet ice, up Glen Nevis towards six hundred frozen feet of white and gentlest turquoise, the Steall waterfall. The ice mass descended in several humpy steps, spilling like melted sugar poured and instantly turned solid in the cold. It bulged and humped and hung in thick beards and shrouds and portcullises, vertical walls, columnar organ-pipe icicles, bulbous scollops and shining, slippery slopes.

'Good grade 3,' Allan said, as he set off, chip, chip, chip, half an inch in with ice axes and crampons. Occasionally we could move rightwards to the waterfall's edge, where trees were put to work as secure belays. We needed them, for it was steep as the sides of an 'A' in places.

Three hundred feet up. A lost axe or a crampon off and the waterfall might just as well expand to five times its size; we were dependent on our equipment, and no mistake. Allan led, then I, then he took over again. Chunks of ice levered out by his axes bounced past all the way to the bottom. Two-thirds of the way up he started to yodel and sing, and we climbed on great arches of pure ice curved clear of the rock wall, with water thrashing beneath. Already it was melting, a playground disappearing to find its way down Glen Nevis and to the sea.

The finish was up easy snow, the descent safe and easy, down more snow.

It was bound to happen: ice climbing and the splendid experiences in the Andes were themes which reinforced each other and set me dreaming about the Himalayas. In 1979 I started planning an expedition to Nepal for the spring of 1981. Four people were invited and all accepted the invitation, and I started on the work of organisation. After some months we had promises to cover fifty per cent of the costs in one form of sponsorship or another, permission to do the climb had been granted, and work on other aspects was going ahead satisfactorily. But then the blows came. Firstly, a newspaper which had offered to cover about twenty per cent of our costs was threatened with closure because of union problems, so we lost their support; then because of budgeting problems an airline withdrew the largest part of the assistance provisionally offered, resulting in a further loss of fifteen per cent or more; and then three of the four prospective expedition members said they could not come up with their share of costs. They all made a living through climbing in one way or another and were hard hit by the recession of the time. These setbacks came fast one upon the other; in a period of about three weeks, over half of the promised money and three out of four members disappeared, and 1981 was only a few weeks away.

I came to understand more and more that organisational setbacks were just part of expeditions, as much a part as soft snow or loose rock or porters going on strike. Eventual success could come only to those who overcame these obstacles before starting on the real climbing. The preparatory stages sorted out who was sufficiently committed to the venture; this was how you qualified for a try at the big prize, in this tiresome form of eliminating heat. You had to take knocks, but as long as you knew that, it was possible to plod on; those who did not expect the knocks might stagger at their impact, and perhaps not recover. As in many sports, the winner must overcome the extraneous difficulties which have repulsed those of equal sporting ability but less commitment.

Perhaps the setbacks were a blessing in diguise, for I soon decided against trying to shore up the planned expedition. One reason for this was that I was already extremely busy, and organising an expedition in a hurry did not have any appeal; another was that as 1981 was the International Year of Disabled People and success would help the campaign, it might be as well to increase the chances of success and go on two expeditions. The latter reason sounds rather virtuous, but the former was really the one which mattered, and even if it had not been the International Year I needed no urging to go on two expeditions in one year! Flexibility is an important element of problem-solving and by changing the objectives I wiped out most of the problems and greatly increased the chances of having a successful year. The choice of peaks was out of my hands this time; I had to accept what was available and go on any expeditions which would have me. In twenty hectic days I found myself places on two.

Before the expeditions, September 1980 brought three quiet and unambitious weeks based at Arolla in Switzerland. I went alone, largely because I felt the need to fend for myself completely. In an emergency it could be an advantage to have had the right mental preparation, in case a companion was ill or injured, for it might be necessary to go for help alone. I made an ascent of L'Eveque, described in the guide-book as 'steep and elegant', with an English climber I met there. We dawdled, and enjoyed the day. Then I undertook two safe and easy solo climbs of peaks of 11,000 feet (La Luette and Pointe Kurz). Unsensational as it may seem, that predominantly solo holiday was as much a part of my mountaineering life as any of the more dramatic climbs. It involved no more nor any less hazards than harder routes done with companions, because the routes were carefully chosen, and I could find within myself no sound argument against soloing easier and safer routes under the right circumstances. It required experience to pick the right circumstances, of course, and I would be opposed, particularly, to soloing by relative novices. My nature is gregarious and for that reason I would rarely, if ever, solo mountains by choice. The important words here are 'by choice', because I was heading towards a set of circumstances in which choice would be very limited and my solo preparation would make a lot of difference.

It was time to grab some living again; it waited there to be taken, I only had to go out and get it. There was ambrosia for the asking, trees to be plucked of their magic fruit, call it what you will, if you knew how to find them. In my case climbing was the way to reach the ambrosia and the fruit. If life became drab that would be my fault, for I had found my path and the initiative lay with me. I felt privileged to have found the way, which was now to take me to the Andes of Argentina as a member of an American expedition. Our objective was Aconcagua, 22,834 feet, the highest point of South America's Andean spine, by the Polish glacier route. I had telephoned one of the organisers and been in touch by letter, and being accepted had been a relatively trouble-free process, but last minute hitches, or apparent hitches, were almost inevitable.

The Argentinian authorities laid down certain medical requirements which included having an electro-cardiogram and running a kilometre at high altitude. If they insisted on the latter I would be making a wasted journey to South America. There are reliable reports of a very experienced climber being refused permission (by a non-mountaineer) to attempt Aconcagua because it was thought his trousers were too thin. Another tells of an Englishman who was given a psychological examination in Spanish, a language he did not speak; it is hardly surprising that he was turned down.

At Miami airport I met five of the team with whom I would share a month, unless I were refused permission. We flew off immediately to Mendoza, Argentina, to join the leader and deputy leader, Bruce Klepinger and Dr Peter Cummings respectively.

Argentina. Plenty of open space. Scrub patches around us, vineyards, orchards, farms and ranches, with pampas a long way to the east. Ten times the area of the British Isles. By appearances, a fairly affluent country compared with Peru, though I was told there were quite a few poor people there and unemployment was fairly high. Inflation, inflation, worrying everyone.

Mendoza. Almost one million population. Spanish influence in the architecture. Tree-lined, wide, straight boulevards. Frequent and inexpensive buses running like good blood through the city's veins, reducing the relative underprivilege of the poorer classes. Busy with traffic, bad parking problems in the centre. A clean place where people take a pride in their dress; European and American fashions. A high proportion eating out at pavement restaurants after 8 p.m. Orderly.

Concerning the medical requirements there was news of great significance. We sat in a hotel lounge for a briefing.

'The regulations have been scrapped. Everyone can climb,' Bruce announced.

There was no explanation from those who formerly enforced the regulations, but we speculated that they had reached the conclusion there was no point in applying the rule because Aconcagua still killed a lot of people.

Things got moving. Equipment was sorted and packed, and the local press came to interview us; I kept out of their way to avoid attracting attention from the authorities. In two hired trucks we drove 100 miles and passed without incident through a military checkpoint, where our passports were retained until our return from the mountain. Aconcagua, being close to the border with Chile, is in a sensitive military zone. Four Americans whom I met had made the mistake of checking in at the wrong army post, and at 1 a.m. were taken at gunpoint from their tents by soldiers who came from the post at which they should have checked in. It was all sorted out in the end, but cocked weapons left the Americans in no doubt that the formalities were to be treated seriously.

Unloading the trucks a little further on at the end of a dirt road, we pitched camp for the night in Punta de Vaca, a valley entrance at 7,500 feet (2,285 m), close to tall poplar. Now it really felt that the adventure could begin; there had been a greater possibility than I had admitted to anyone that I might have been refused permission to climb.

The first day on foot towards base camp was hot; someone recorded it to be 31°C (88°F) in the shade at 4 p.m. Under packs of forty to fifty pounds (eighteen to twenty-three kilograms) the fairly gentle gradient was enough. Two valleys, carved by the Rio de Vacas and then the Rio Relincho, would allow us gradually to cover thirty miles up something over 6,000 feet (c. 2,000 m) in three days. We walked with our water supply, a big river, on our right, up the steep-sided canyon, through shrubs and yellow flowers and grass and thistles, all the time close to smooth, buttocky boulders. At the end of day one, approaching a high valley plain known as Pama de las Lenas at about 9,500 feet (2,900 m), one of our party who had been ahead dashed back through the scrub towards me. Born in Germany, brought up in Australia, resident now in the USA, Mike Skreiner was one of our comedians.

'Hey, limey, there's an army officer up ahead with a dozen men. They're staying in a hut up here.'

The army. Blast. Would they try to stop someone on crutches? I might get away with saying I was only going to base camp. Or was Mike joking?

'I'll carry your pack,' he offered. 'You can manage better without the crutches then. They've got a big wood fire going so just carry a few sticks.'

Collapsing the crutches, I put them in my rucksack, which Mike shouldered. With a few sticks under one arm I followed him a hundred yards, past a large green tent to a stone hut. No, Mike was not joking.

Outside the hut I first made the acquaintance of Lieutenant José Alberto Guglielmone and his men; it would not be the last time I met them. The green uniformed soldiers were busy handing out bread and cheese to everyone, a kind gesture followed by the even more friendly gift of large chunks of delicious freshly cooked meat, then prunes. The lieutenant handed around whisky, and the soldiers plied us continually with mate (rhymes with paté), a strong local tea drunk through a metal straw.

Under the orders of the lieutenant, the soldiers had cheese and ham rolls and warm, sweetened milk ready for us in the morning. We were fairly sure the lieutenant would not make any attempt to persuade me not to climb, but to avoid any possibility of controversy I headed out of their encampment first and put some bushes and boulders between us before resorting to crutches again.

Two-inch lizards basked in the sunshine, to dart off at our approach. A condor wheeled and soared three thousand feet above, taking advantage of the up-draughts from a cliff to our left. A low flank of that cliff forced us

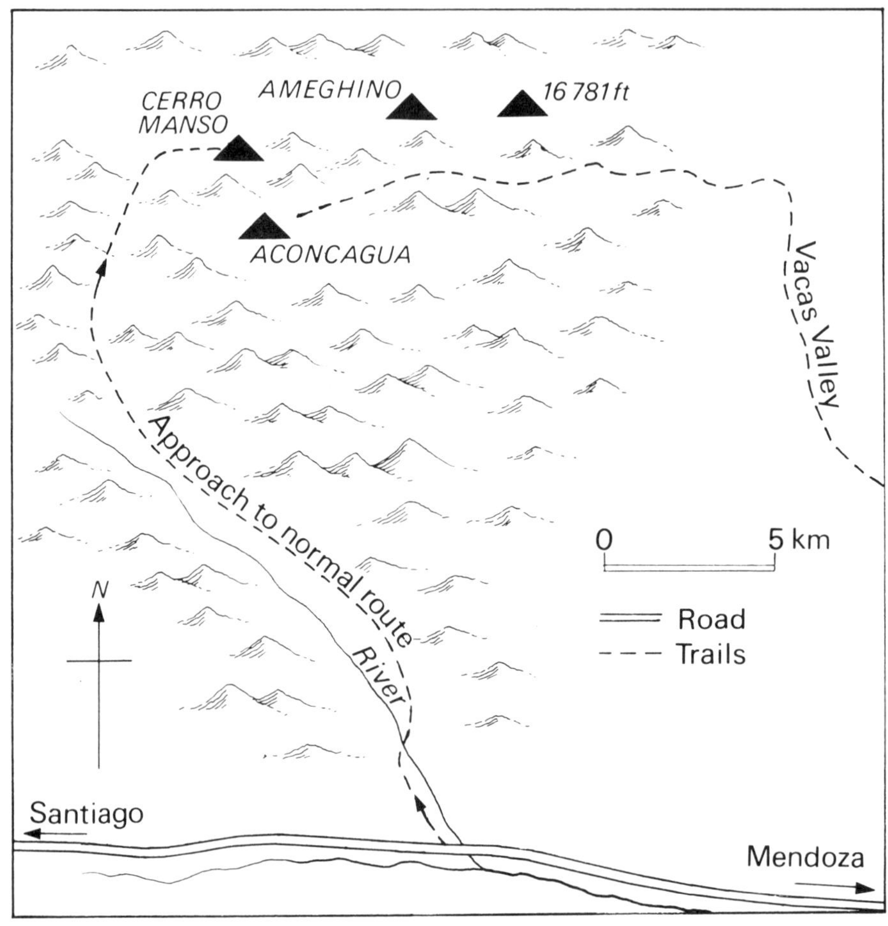


*Aconcagua Region*

to scramble along the steep left rock bank of the river, and soon after we had to climb ten feet of a seventy-five degree slab on tiny toeholds to insecure earth, then unstable scree. Bruce stayed with me, helpful, attentive and reassuring, and practical at the same time.

'Take care now,' he said in one spot two hundred feet above the river. 'If you slide you'll go over the edge into the river.' The vertical part of the earth bank dropped fifty feet straight into the river, which was thirty feet wide, and fast and deep. With metal legs on I had no chance of swimming or floating.

Two hundred feet of loose traversing later he pointed out: 'Still have to be careful. You'd drop fifty feet on to the shingle bank.' A hundred feet of that and we were safe.

'Thanks, Bruce.'

'No problem.'

Steep, loose earth and stone banks just above the river were neither particularly dangerous nor to be taken for granted. Towards late afternoon the terrain turned more sandy and gently angled, in a broad valley bottom.

Tents, some equipment and food were travelling up separately on the backs of mules driven by two gauchos. We met up each evening but, being able to ford deeper and faster water than us, they often followed a different route. At eight o'clock that evening we had our first sight of Aconcagua's tip peeping down a steep V-shaped valley. Everyone was very tired, and though we camped in sight of our goal and this raised our spirits, we could see too little to get very excited.

The third day's march on a loose stone bank above the river was scarey, less so for the others because they could manage better. Expedition marches like this would be quite dangerous for me, it was clear, with river crossings and loose banks. A short jump from one big boulder to another in the middle of twenty feet of fast river was nothing to the others, a time for a tiny bit of courage on my part. Bruce sat on the far rock ready to grab me. It was soon done.

'Thanks again for your help, Bruce.'

'No problem.'

He had accepted me. As far as I could assess, the degree to which the others accepted me was proportionate to the extent of their climbing experience, with the least experienced, though friendly enough on the surface, being the most uneasy. The experienced ones were better able to judge from my track record.

After one steep pull up a sandy vegetated slope for five hundred feet, we got a proper look at Aconcagua, and what a beauty she looked, as did her sister peak, Ameghino, standing to the right.

The land turned to grey and red desert, sandy, dusty, parched. Valley walls rose in dry scree slopes to typical weather-sculpted desert rock towers. Of a few hardy plants surviving, the most common was a spiky green species growing like giant macaroons a yard across and known as cushion plant. A gently sloping plateau of red earth and stones took us almost to base camp; we then turned right into a boulder field, and that was it. In a wilderness of cracked rocks we found sufficient clear, dusty space to stand the tents. Though in fine mountain country this was a desolate place.

Henry Bergner had trailed into camp last, just behind our only lawyer,

Tony Battelle, and both looked ill from the altitude, which was about 13,800 feet. Tony ate nothing that night, and Henry managed only a morsel of tuna.

We turned in around dark, two to a tent except Bruce, who was on his own. I was fortunate to finish up sharing with Tom Vaughan, an even-tempered doctor with a wife and three children in California. At the age of forty-three he reckoned he had better get some of his high altitude ambitions behind him before it was too late, so had borrowed the money from his bank to go to Argentina. I wanted him more than anyone else on the expedition (except me) to succeed.

Just about everyone was asleep when someone clattered downhill through the rocks into camp. It was a lone Argentinian who had been in a party of four on the Polish Glacier route. One had fallen and been badly injured, he told Bruce. My knowledge of Spanish is not good, but I believe Bruce asked if there was anything we could do and the reply was negative, and did we have a cigarette? No one did, and the man continued down in near darkness.

A day of odd jobs and rest followed. At 8.30 p.m. Pete and Tom diagnosed pulmonary oedema (fluid in the lungs) in Henry, and he was put on emergency oxygen immediately.

Next day at dawn, with over thirty hours of rest behind us, we were eager to get moving, so with thirty-five pound packs all of us bar Pete and Henry set out to carry gear three thousand feet up. The plan was to dump it there, return, and make two more carries on subsequent days from base camp.

'We're going to go at what may seem like a ridiculously slow speed, but you all know why,' Bruce said. Yes. Altitude. It had stopped Henry already.

We were no more than twenty minutes above base when I heard a faint crack that made my heart sink; as my left leg lifted at the next step it felt strange and confirmed what was wrong. My left leg was broken. And I had no spare.

Bruce was just ahead.

'Bruce, I've got to stop. My leg's broken.'

Sitting on the stones, I lowered my trousers as the others gathered round. Just by the knee a steel bar had snapped.

'Metal fatigue,' Jan Balut said. It was his subject and he knew. Jan was fifty-six years old, a metal fatigue expert with Boeing Aircraft Corporation. He had settled in the USA after making an escape from Poland in the early fifties.

Someone suggested trying the mountain with the leg splinted and without a pack on my back.

'No. I'd only be a passenger then. It would slow everyone.'

Our two engineers, Jan and Mike, began a short discussion on whether the leg could be splinted or otherwise repaired. They thought not, and as their conversation approached this conclusion I felt increasingly dejected, and said, 'I think it's finished for me.'

'How will you get down?' was the anxious question of John Pratt, an English physics lecturer who was prone to worrying.

'No sweat,' Mike said. 'There's always the mules.'

Two or three people stooped and patted me on the back in genuine and touching sympathy, and said things like, 'What a bitch,' and, 'Aw, hell, Norm.'

'Well, you can't win them all,' I said, at a loss for anything else to say. 'Anyway, you lot had better get going.'

Pete came to meet me and took my pack down. I followed on crutches.

'Tough luck, Norm.'

'I'm going to do *something* though,' I said, partly to conceal the disappointment I did not want to talk about, and partly because I did think it might be possible to get up a small peak on one leg.

Pete decided to take Henry to a lower altitude to assist his recovery; he was not getting worse but he was not getting better, either.

'At one point last night I thought he might die,' Pete told me.

They left base camp at 1 p.m., walking extremely slowly, and I was left alone in my disappointment. If only I had brought a spare pair of legs! But the reliability of the limbs over many years had led to complacency beyond reason; intermittent breakages were to be expected, taking into account the severe treatment to which the legs were subjected.

Disappointment. Following shortly on the relief of finding the medical requirements scrapped, this was a particularly savage blow. Yet disappointment is something which anyone operating near his or her limits must face and come to terms with. By sticking to the Alps I could expect to get up most mountains eventually if I chose routes which were not too hard and if I was prepared to wait out the weather. But the Andes and Himalayas are different, and failure is a large inherent risk on the high peaks.

What to do? Various vague plans for one-legged ascents sprang to mind but I could see no reasonable options; the stony peaks all around would lack water. Vainly, I hoped those who had climbed higher might have spotted something for me to do. When the group descended that afternoon they looked tired.

'D'you think there's any reasonable alternative around here for me Bruce?'

'No, don't think so, Norm.'

It looked as if I would be sitting alone in the desolate base camp for a couple of weeks or more before trekking out on one leg, or taking a mule.

A few crumbs of comfort for the future came from Jan, when I asked him if I should give up expeditions because of the possibility of leg breakages.

'No. Just replace the broken bit with a new one, don't let them get too old and fatigued, and take a spare pair.'

Pete arrived quite early the next morning, got the stove going and admonished everyone in an authoritarian and rather self righteous manner for not being up. Being deputy leader and expedition doctor he had a lot of responsibility, which he took seriously. Early on he showed himself to be hard-working and efficient. I would apply the same description, efficient, hard-working, to Bruce, but he was more paternal than authoritarian. Henry's condition had improved so Pete planned to make the carry to Camp 1 and return to base camp, then descend around a thousand feet to Henry. It occurred to me that it would be preferable for Pete to be with the main party if Henry was well enough to be left, so without giving it much thought I volunteered to look after Henry. Pete jumped at the offer, saying he would descend with me to check Henry out after the loads had been carried.

At the same base camp were four members of a Canadian expedition bound for Everest in 1982. Though described as the 'Canadians' three of them were in fact English expatriates. They were short of a plastic funnel for filling their stove and also lacked Valium tablets; I possessed both commodities and did not want either, so traded them for half a bottle of cognac and a khaki kit-bag which had burst when one of their mules fell from the trail. The latter item could be converted into some knee pads if I found it necessary to crawl, and a tough mini skirt so I could slide on my bottom with greater comfort from the extra padding.

The sun was within a few degrees of overhead when Pete descended, eager and well ahead of the others, to base camp. Together we went down easy dust, earth and small stones to the tent where Henry waited. Pete examined him, pronounced him much improved, said, 'I owe you a million dollars, Norm,' and returned to base camp. As he left I was aware that his departure reduced to little or nothing my chances of making an ascent because Henry would require care for several days. He had quite bad headaches, coughed a lot, was bringing up a little blood, and had more fluid in his left lung than his right, though this was reducing. My responsibilities were to cook and fetch water, make sure he took his drugs, and see that he did not do too much.

At 6 p.m. Lieutenant Guglielmone and a soldier arrived on mules. When I explained our circumstances he kindly offered us a ride down. Henry did not want to go, and I did not try to persuade him because his sense of balance was poor, two mules between four would mean two to a mule or a lot of walking for someone, and it would take at least seven hours, much of it in darkness, to reach the military camp. If Henry had not been getting better descent would have been advisable, but his condition was improving, and in any case the lieutenant had come up to look for and help one or more Argentinians; it could be a matter of life or death for them, whereas our emergency was over. The lieutenant gave us bread and some cooked guanaco meat (from an animal related to the llama; it was with great regret that I learned later that guanaco are not as common as I had thought) and departed uphill. Within a few hours he passed by again, taking two Argentinians down. What had happened to their companion we would not learn for several days.

I was four nights and three days with Henry. At times he joked.

'Anybody can climb a mountain but it takes a real man to get pulmonary oedema,' and, 'Why do climbers rope together? To stop the sane ones going home.'

At times he was depressed.

'Worst thing about this is when you go home and everybody says, "Hey, show us your slides!" and, "Three thousand bucks I've wasted on this trip," and, "It's all screwed up."'

He ate well all the time, and drank plenty, and mostly seemed content lying back being looked after. If he was morose or apathetic it was easy to make allowances because he was not well, and because of his disappointment.

One mountain was framed by the tent doorway and in between trying to improve my Spanish with the aid of a book, or being housemaid to Henry, there was plenty of time to study that peak and wonder if the patient would recover so I could attempt it. I judged it to be almost certainly possible to get within eight hundred feet of the summit, but the final cliffs or steep ice would quite likely be too much for anyone on one leg. The river stood in the way and each day I spent two hours searching up and down the bank for a crossing. The explorations were fruitless, and the roar and hiss of the river were inescapable, day and night, reminding me all the while that the river was in the way.

By the third day Henry was greatly improved, taking long walks, and getting restless.

'I'm getting antsy. Approaching the limit,' he said.

So on 5th February 1981, nearly two weeks after landing in Argentina, it looked as if another little adventure might come my way, and I started to make preparations. The ripped kit bag made two knee pads for crawling, and a mini skirt. The stove and most food had to be left with Henry, so the choice of provisions was very limited: a small tin of tuna (7 oz) and another of corned beef, some stale bread, and nuts, mostly peanuts and walnuts.

During the night I was unsure whether I could make myself go. If I had not climbed alone in the Alps the previous summer I would not have considered the prospect at all.

Shortly before 8 a.m. I woke, and packed: sleeping bag, insulating mat, bivouac bag, torch, jacket, waterproof jacket and trousers, mittens, crawling pads, two water bottles, spikes and an ice axe pick for my crutches, small first-aid kit, knife, camera, film, a mug for soaking the hard bread, and food.

‘Henry, I’ll either be back in a couple of hours because I can’t get across the river or I’ll be gone several days.’

‘Have a nice time,’ he mumbled from his sleeping bag.

I had already pointed out where I was going; he could see almost the whole route from the tent. Heading westwards and uphill towards base camp, I kept close to the ravine cut by the river. In half an hour there was below me a spot where the river divided between four shingle banks. Sliding a hundred feet down the stony bank I had a closer look, and felt reasonably confident that if I could just bring myself to make a few jumps with the crutches I would be across the twenty feet of noisy white water. After a short hop on to the first bank I had to put my left stump on a rock submerged two or three inches beneath the water, and make another jump, thrusting with the right leg and crutches to roll forward on to the next bank. From there it was easy and by 9.15 a.m. I was across on the far bank, a loose earth and stone slope of no more than thirty degrees. I began to realise what I was taking on when it took fifteen minutes to crawl a mere hundred feet.

Gently sloping ground permitted the use of crutches again. Perhaps only five per cent of the dusty earth was covered by the giant green spiky macaroons, so when it was necessary to resume crawling I could go between them. For three hours, crawling alternated with crutching; I gained height mostly through arm strength, in little jumps on the crutches. This soon brought on a very unpleasant ache in my wrists, and sore palms, and a sharp muscle pain developed in the left shoulder. So, soon it was a relief to crawl, even though this was extremely slow.

At the time I did not know that the mountain towards whose east summit I was headed was called Ameghino, but I had a vague recollection from a map that its height was 5,116 m or 16,800 feet; this was correct. The route to the summit of a mountain whose name I did not know was influenced by the availability of water. There was a more direct route, it seemed, but it was devoid of water. At that altitude, where the body dehydrates rapidly, I could not risk three or more days without finding water, because I had no stove to melt snow, and lacked sufficient containers to carry all that would be required. It was a relief and pleasure, therefore, to discover there was a stream where I had estimated there would be one.

Below a very steep scree slope of four hundred feet I picked out what I called my three o’clock boulder and reached it by 2.45 p.m., after an hour and a half on my knees. I felt good, and crawled on with head down. Shortly afterwards I passed close by the first snow penitentes, an unusual formation of snow like shark fins sticking out of the sea of scree, or like six-foot axe blades, or arrowheads, or dagger blades. They varied in shape and size, up to six feet or so, but all were brilliant white and thin, and clustered close. How snow could stand up in sunshine in blades so thin – perhaps a foot thick at the base, tapering fairly evenly to the top – was a mystery to me.

By 5 p.m. I had had enough for that day. On thirty degree scree I settled down for the night on a body-sized level platform beneath a big, stable boulder. The precious tin of corned beef was opened, and half was consumed with bread made soft and soggy with water. The other half was saved for the next day, wrapped in an empty soup packet brought specially for the purpose. Every spare morsel of food had to be saved for the diet was not only dull but frugal.

Perhaps by then I had reached a little more than 13,500 feet, having gained not much over a thousand feet in a day. It was indeed slow going, but I fooled myself into believing I might be as high as 14,000 feet.

The next day was much the same as the day before, except that as well as crutching and crawling there was rock climbing too. I followed a brown rib, at sixty degrees to start, and rapidly easing back to thirty. It would have been bad enough with both legs on because of the looseness, which meant not only were most holds likely to break away but also what holds there were had a layer of grit and small stones covering them. Cleaning the stones away and testing each hold was very time consuming, and the padded left stump was cumbersone because it would not fit on anything small. However, I gained seventy feet more quickly than I would have on the very steep scree to the left and right. Though at the most I could not have fallen more than forty feet from the rib, climbing minus one leg gave a deep sense of vulnerability.

Soon the rib was too broken to be of use so it was back to the scree, where each knee gained only eight or nine inches at a step and more often than not slipped back half that distance. Sometimes I crawled on all fours, sometimes I was on my knees in an upright position, digging in the spiked crutches. At 11 a.m. I took a gully crammed with snow penitentes; using a boot and a crutch spike on the right, on the strange snow formations, and the left knee on the gully's left wall, I moved more rapidly than anywhere else. After two hundred feet the gully petered out. Scree again.

Lunch was bread and nuts. Then the scree got worse. Some of it was too steep for me to gain any ground at all; at each movement of a knee I slid back further than I had climbed. By aiming upwards and to the left I actually went downwards, but gained the bottom of some slabby rocks. These, too, were hard to climb because of loose stones and grit, but they gave me another twenty-five feet. On sore knees I struggled up more scree, scree, scree, barely rising at all; it must have taken an hour to get my body a hundred feet higher. When I chose to stop for the night at 6 p.m. I was close to 15,000 feet high, but based on the over-optimistic estimate of the previous day I thought 16,000 to be nearer the mark.

In a few minutes I had arranged some stones around a level space to prevent me rolling off. That night's treat was the reminder of the corned beef. The hard bread had to be chipped with my knife from the round loaf, but was eatable after a couple of minutes soaking in water in my mug.

At 9 p.m., far away to the south-east a thunderstorm lit up the clouds almost every second, turning them into giant, translucent, internally illuminated mushrooms. The storm was too distant for thunder to be heard, but I awoke intermittently over hours and it was still going on. The weather had been kind to me so far.

Having over-estimated my altitude, I began the third day believing this might soon see me on the summit. Once more it took ages to clear the debris to climb on loose rock, and I had to lose a hundred feet to avoid a rock spur which was beyond my capabilities while on one leg. An unpleasant slope of fractured, sharp edged boulders went on for three hundred feet and led to more loose rock climbing, then to a scree traverse and another scree slope as long as the boulder slope that went before. By mid-afternoon it was clear the summit would not be mine that day, if at all.

How I looked forward each day to ceasing the fight and sliding into my sleeping bag, and eating. I want to stop, my mind said most of the day. Keep going, another part said. Why? You will know why, if you succeed; you have found out why in the past.

By now I was drawing close to the snow and ice field which might be the key to getting through the final steep cliffs, but from a few hundred feet away it looked too steep and dangerous. Beneath an overhang of three hundred or four hundred feet of cliff I chose a spot for the night, but before turning in explored along the cliff base to the right; it ended in a chasm and offered no way up.

Being at the bottom of the cliff allowed a more accurate assessment of altitude; at around 16,000 feet I was only as high as I had believed myself to be on the previous night.

Though freezing temperatures made the streams quiet every night, I was never cold. The hours of darkness passed in fitful sleep punctuated by vivid dreams and brief awakenings. That night I had eaten tuna mixed with wet breadcrumbs, but I thought and dreamed of meat and two veg, meat and three veg, pork, lamb, beef, chicken, mutton and gravy. The vividness of high altitude dreams usually stayed with me when I descended to sea level, diminishing in intensity over a week or two. At times, whether at high altitude or at home afterwards, it was impossible to distinguish the dreams from reality. This was the case when I dozily got out of my sleeping bag and sat on the edge of the flat platform to relieve myself down the icy gully to the left. It seemed real, in a dreamy way, but I could not be sure whether I was awake or dreaming. I remember wondering if I was dreaming, and realised that indeed I had been when I woke up properly to find myself at home, where I had returned two days earlier from Argentina; what had appeared to be the platform was the bed, the icy gully was moonlit floor, and I was sitting on the edge of the bed and piddling on the floor!

Nuts and soggy bread started the next day, as soon as the sun struck me at 8 a.m. It may have been reluctance to face failure which made me unwilling to start, and I sat quietly until 9.30 a.m. Yet I was fortunate, for I was free of any fear.

Crossing between snow penitentes and up a slope for an hour, to the bottom of the way I hoped to go, I left most of my equipment beneath a rock wall. Food, waterproof clothing, camera, water bottle, jacket, mittens and crutches were chosen to go up.

The way I hoped to go. At close quarters the impression of the previous day returned, that this was too serious. The mixed snow and ice slope reached sixty or sixty-five degrees in places, and was composed of hard, unstable snow penitentes weighing up to 400 pounds (180 kg) each.

An alternative route up an ice-crammed gully to the right looked more attractive, so, traversing the lower part of thirty-five degree ice, I headed that way. The transparent gully ice went up in steps, six feet up, four feet flat, five feet up, three feet flat, and so on. A higher section looked dangerous and added to that there was frequent stonefall. Uneasiness increased, and determination waned, after thirty minutes. One o'clock approached and, feeling very low, I turned back.

Sliding down the scree towards my equipment at the bottom of the snow and ice which had at first appeared to be the way, I found myself saying, 'Thy will be done,' over and over again. I think I did this merely for comfort but as the words came out I looked again at the snow and ice I had originally thought might be the way, and I knew I should try it.

It is impossible to think of any other configuration of snow and ice reaching sixty or seventy degrees which might be climbed on one leg and one knee. The shark fins lay in rows across the slope, and a lot were only five or six feet high. Some of the highest must have reached fourteen feet or so. Where it was impossible to climb between the fins because they were closely packed I had to get over them. This was done by knocking the top from one with the crutches to form a little platform the size of a narrow tea tray, on to which I dragged myself to stand or kneel and reach across to knock off the top of the next up the slope. The crutches were long enough for the job but I had a limited stride through having only one leg. Sometimes it was too far, so I had to slither down from one snow penitente and haul myself up the next. Movements had to be made with great care to avoid toppling several hundred pounds of ice on to myself.

The ice went on for five hundred feet and at 3 p.m. it had all been climbed. I was on a wide stone ridge like a huge whaleback, leading me to the left. There could be no more than three hundred feet to rise in the summit. On the broad back of the rounded ridge stood vertical rock towers of between two and three hundred feet and I knew I could not climb them on one leg. To the left, the whaleback fell away in vertical cliffs, so that way was barred also. With the left side and the crest blocked, everything depended now on whether the ridge would let me through on its right flank, or whether that too fell away in impossible cliffs.

Though the ridge was angled gently I lacked the strength to use the crutches, so was forced on to all fours again. To the right of the towers I crawled slowly, and the slope unfolded gradually. At first I was fairly optimistic that the slope would let me through to the right of the towers and then all the way to the summit. I skirted the first big tower and could see the slope continuing a hundred feet ahead, and the further I crawled along beside succeeding towers the more the slope opened out, revealing itself to be gradual, and it became evident there was nothing in the way. The stone slope went right to the summit.

At 3.35 p.m. I crawled on to the east summit of Ameghino at 16,800 feet. I could not have been more pleased with an ascent of Aconcagua itself. Ahead I looked down the cliffs all the way to our lone tent, though I could only just pick it out. I waved in case Henry happened to be looking through his telephoto lens.

By 6.10 p.m. I had picked up the belongings left below the field of penitentes. What had been hard on the way up was easy on the way down, and I slid on my bottom down the scree with my one boot dug in ahead like a plough, and spiked crutches forward and ready as brakes. A couple of times I had to arrest the rapid descent for fear of tobogganing on a mass of sliding scree over a cliff, but mostly it was exhilarating and fast. The khaki mini skirt helped prevent ripped clothing to some extent, though the legs of my waterproof trousers took a battering.

In only two and a half hours from the summit I was back at the height I had been at a day and a half earlier; by 8 p.m. I was bivouacked where I wanted to be. The last of the tuna was delicious and a cresent moon came up over my peak. Excitement drove away sleep throughout almost all the night, and it didn't matter a bit.

The scree slide next day lasted until mid-day and it took an hour to find somewhere to cross the river. The last crawl up an earth bank was over in twenty minutes, and I crutched to our tent. Within half an hour the weather turned bad.

Henry had left a note saying he had gone up to base camp or higher, so I was alone for the fifth day. I did not mind, and started in on the food. He had left a stove, and first I cooked cream of asparagus soup, because it required the least time to cook. Vegetable soup and bread was the next choice, followed by hot chocolate. I must confess to feeling very pleased at having prompted Pete into pronouncing that Henry should not drink any alcohol, for otherwise there would have been none left; half an inch of cognac remained, and I settled back with a drink, to savour the contentment of a climber who has made it. I had had my mountain; I had proved to myself that if a leg broke I could rescue myself.

Three inches of snow fell during the night. Though I would have preferred a rest day, it seemed right to go up to see where Henry was. Simultaneously, I started to heat up some soup and to stitch my badly torn waterproof trousers. In twenty minutes I had burnt cream of chicken soup and the ugliest trousers in Argentina.

I was almost at base camp when along came Lieutenant José Guglielmone and half a dozen men, on mules. He was going up to base camp and offered to take a note from me for Bruce, and leave it at the camp if no one was there. It transpired that Henry had gone higher looking for the others, so I descended with the lieutenant. He shared a mule, giving up his own well-behaved animal to me; if he had not offered the ride down I would have had to have started down immediately.

At first the ride was easy, down firm red desert, but it was a different matter when we were on boot-width tracks traversing forty-five degree dirt slopes five hundred feet above the thrashing river. The big mules (as large as horses) plodded up steep scree, across steep scree, down steep, sliding scree on a trail I had hardly noticed on the way up. I noticed now; perched high on the animal, with only the right foot in a stirrup, I was scared. The animals waded, feeling all the while for a firm footing, hesitating, belly deep in the fast river, and walked precipitous slopes just inches from the edge of high river banks. I was aware that with a metal leg on I had no hope of floating or swimming, even with a water wing blown up inside – a method I had tried once. When the mules coped with steep dirt and boulders I had to work at balancing to stay on, and succeeded, except once; using only the right stirrup, eventually I tipped the saddle in that direction as we turned a corner on a steep zig-zag track. For several seconds my brain was not clear as a dull pain registered, and I realised only slowly that I had fallen off and landed right on the stump of my leg. My mule stood absolutely still beside me. For the rest of the ride I was scared quite often, and suffered an awful pain in the stump which had taken the knock.

In the early evening we reached the army refuge, where large portions of meat, salad and mate were consumed and I was made very welcome. Clearly Lieutenant José had assumed I would stay until the others descended from Aconcagua, and I was pleased to fall in with his plans.

'This is your home,' he told me. 'If there is anything you want you say me.'

For four nights home was a stone-walled, iron-roofed refuge ten feet by ten feet, in which five of us and José's Alsatian dog, Neger, slept on the floor. These were the quarters of the officers and NCOs; the men had a tent.

Twenty-four years old, dapper José wanted to improve his English, something he did with great persistence, and in only four days his conversation was much better. In return I learned a little Spanish, was fed generously on meat, tomato salad, cheese, onions, bread and apricots, and was plied with mate, sweetened milk and wine.

'You are the adopted son of the Argentinian army,' they said to me. 'We will shave off your beard and put you in a green uniform.' (Beards are not permitted in the army.) Unbeknown to me, of course, they were soon to be our enemies, but there was no hint of forthcoming trouble in early 1981.

Three of the 'Canadians' arrived first. They had reached Aconcagua's summit on the same day as I had climbed my mountain, 9 February. On the way they had come across the body of the Argentinian who had fallen, sustaining head injuries. Not far from his body was the wreckage of a search helicopter which had crashed while attempting his rescue, with the death of the pilot and serious injury to the co-pilot. The 'Canadians' had moved the body down a thousand feet to a flat area from which it could be lifted off by helicopter. On the descent one of the 'Canadians', Dave Reed, had been snowblind for a while and walked through a cornice, but got himself out of the predicament. Everyone but Henry and Tony had made the summit. Tony just seemed to have run out of steam, having failed to eat or drink much after seeing the helicopter wreckage. He, Henry and Pete had been at Camp 3, ready to make a try (Pete's second) for the summit, when an avalanche ran over their tent at 1 a.m. There were no casualties but after three hours digging themselves out and re-siting the tent they were in no shape to go up. John Pratt had been affected on the descent by cerebral oedema (fluid on the brain). He fell quite often and at base camp sat wild-eyed on a rock saying, 'I am proud to have won the race to Camp one,' before falling over sideways. His sense of balance was gone, temporarily. Physically he had been strong and fast, until the descent. Because of the cerebral oedema poor John had undergone a dream experience which sounds amusing superficially: he thought he had found a cure for scurvy and believed he wandered the world trying without success to convince people that he had an answer to the disease. He suffered terrible nightmares about it and cried a lot in consequence at night. The 'Canadians' described him as 'a gibbering idiot' but felt the improvement would not last as he came lower.

The team arrived in ones and twos on the day after the 'Canadians', and were fed generously by the soldiers.

The time came for me to descend from the army camp. José presented me with the wooden cup from which we had drunk many a mate, and a set of bolas, the three weights strung together and thrown to catch animals by entangling their legs. Not long before we quit camp I was informed that an unladen mule had fallen from the trail lower down the day before, and was dead. However, this ten-mile section was not nearly so horrifying as the twenty which had gone before. We headed for a roadside bar, where several of us congregated to thank José for his kindness.

A truck took us back to Mendoza where we had a rest day and a huge meal in celebration. I had to get home on one leg, but as my luggage could be carried in a rucksack on my back this was no great hardship. Within three days we had scattered to Barbados, Peru, Chile, Canada, the USA and England, taking with us our disappointment or our joy, according to what we had done. I was full of joy.

# 7

# *Kashmir*

When distant mountains called again I joined an expedition not as a candidate for reaching the summit, but as one of several working towards putting even one climber on that summit. The mountain in question, Nun (23,410 feet, 7135 m), had had several ascents but only one success and three failures by the east ridge. Even the successful Japanese team who achieved the ascent put only two of fourteen members on the top. So, when I joined the team to climb Nun's east ridge in 1981 I was under no illusions; I could help by attracting a certain amount of sponsorship, I could carry loads and assist in other ways, but the success of the expedition would have to be placed before any personal ambitions.

'You're here to make the expedition financially viable,' Steve Berry, the leader, had said. 'It's not a "Get Norman Croucher to the Top" expedition.'

That was fair comment and, though I more than paid my way, I did feel somewhat like a hitch-hiker at the time. When it came down to who had any prior claims to the summit I was last in the queue, because I joined late and thus evaded much of the preparatory work. I would contribute, I hoped, to a successful team effort; and the experience of a Himalayan expedition was something to build on.

The reason behind Steve Berry's choice of the east ridge was interesting: in 1946 his father had attempted the route. After a very long march to reach the mountain he was plagued by trouble with stoves, and was forced to retreat when his army leave of six weeks expired. Even so he succeeded in climbing an adjacent peak, White Needle, about 21,500 feet (6,553 m), which in face of all the difficulties was a satisfactory outcome. From the beginning I wondered if White Needle might be a reasonable target for my Himalayan initiation. So, though the main objective would have to come first, and it was not certain that there would be an opportunity to attempt White Needle, I asked Steve to obtain permission for us to climb this peak too. It was not strictly true, therefore, that I was going just to help on the expedition; a chance, however small, to attempt White Needle

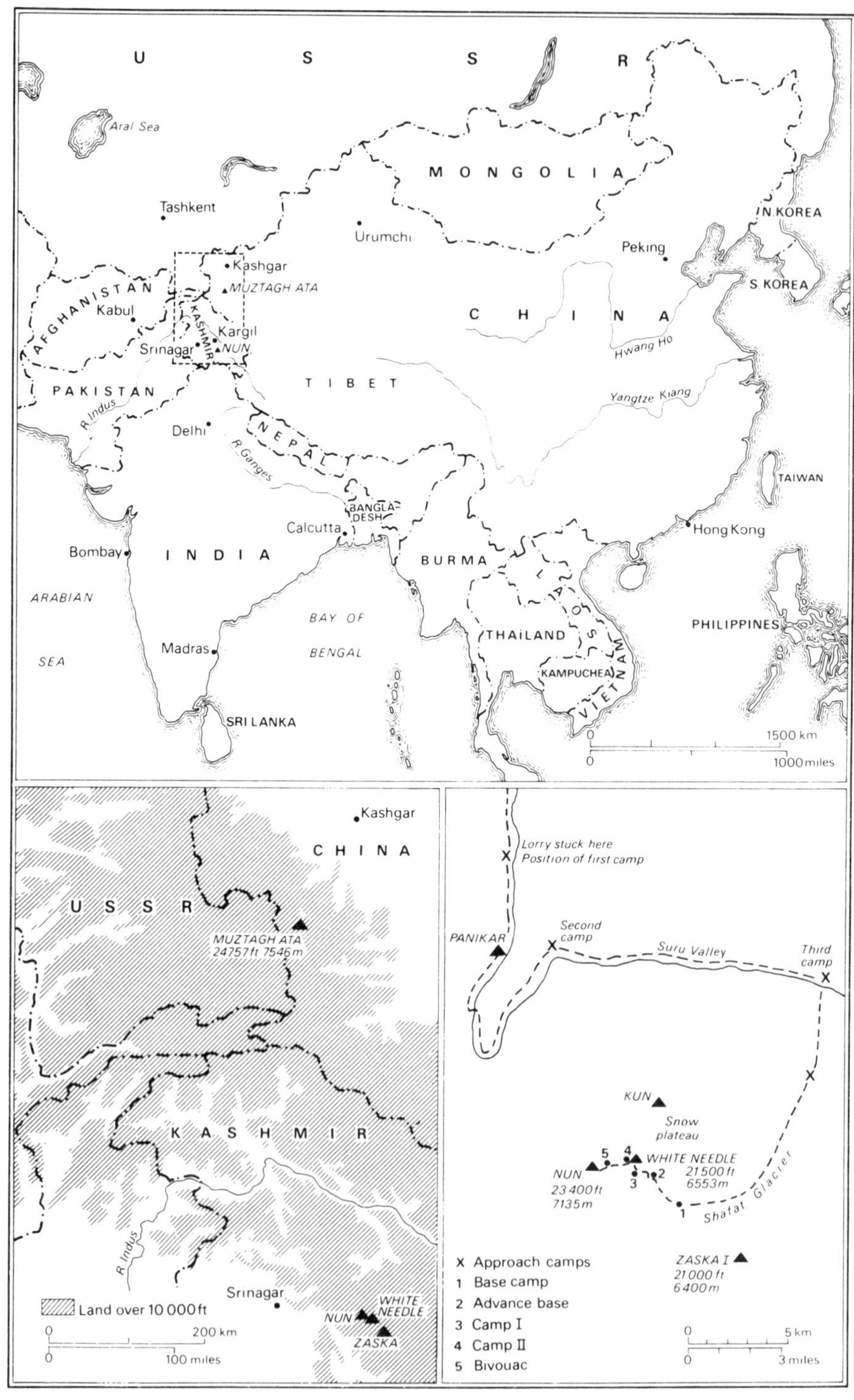
U S S R
Aral Sea
MONGOLIA
Tashkent
Urumchi
Peking
N. KOREA
S. KOREA
Kashgar
MUZTAGH ATA
AFGHANISTAN
Kabul
KASHMIR
Kargil
Srinagar
NUN
C H I N A
Hwang Ho
PAKISTAN
TIBET
Yangtze Kiang
R. Indus
Delhi
NEPAL
R. Ganges
TAIWAN
BANGLA-DESH
Calcutta
Hong Kong
Bombay
INDIA
BURMA
LAOS
ARABIAN
SEA
BAY OF
BENGAL
THAILAND
PHILIPPINES
Madras
KAMPUCHEA
VIETNAM
SRI LANKA
0
1500 km
1000 miles
Kashgar
CHINA
USSR
MUZTAGH ATA
24757 ft 7546 m
KASHMIR
R. Indus
Srinagar
NUN
WHITE NEEDLE
ZASKA
Land over 10 000 ft
200 km
100 miles
Lorry stuck here
Position of first camp
PANIKAR
Second camp
Suru Valley
Third camp
KUN
Snow plateau
WHITE NEEDLE
21500 ft
6553 m
NUN
23400 ft
7135 m
Shafat Glacier
ZASKA I
21000 ft
6400 m
X Approach camps
1 Base camp
2 Advance base
3 Camp I
4 Camp II
5 Bivouac
5 km
3 miles

was a big temptation. If I had seen a good photograph of the mountain the attraction would have been even greater.

'Will my new legs be ready before the twelfth of May?' I asked Brian Campbell, my limbfitter.

'Hope so,' he said, with mock indifference.

They were ready the day before, so I was able to join my first Himalayan expedition with reasonable confidence that the stronger legs would not let me down. I took another pair as well; Argentina had taught me that was wise.

From my point of view the venture commenced on a bad note, for on the departure date I was suffering from bronchitis, an ailment which has troubled me with decreasing frequency since my early twenties. (I was asthmatic as a child.) I took the risk of travelling, fully realising that I might get worse in consequence.

Because it was the International Year of Disabled People Air India had given us two free tickets and sufficient excess baggage concession to take all the expedition equipment free of charge, and they treated us especially nicely on the flight. I remember equally well their free champagne, and their courtesy. There were five of us on board, and two more had gone to Delhi a week earlier to handle the paper work.

In the early morning hours next day we touched down in Delhi. In a stupor from travel and bronchitis, at first I walked off without my spare legs, which had been stowed in a forward cabin. That afternoon we went to take a train northwards to Jammu. We moved by taxi through the crowded streets to New Delhi station. In temperatures up to 41°C (106°F), and with a fever and bronchial burning sensation in my chest, I saw little and remember even less. There is just a vague recollection of being in the land of pyjama-trousered men in the streets, the hungry dogs of India, searching, always searching for a morsel, thin, thin people with skinny, skinny arms, the incongruous conjunction of big bellies created by malnutrition, beggar cries of 'Sahib! Sahib!', dingy cafés with walls covered in old posters (many of religious topics), and lit at night by paraffin lamps.

Every foreign expedition in India is obliged to have with it a liaison officer, who may be very helpful in overcoming language problems, among other things; the one allotted us by the Indian Mountaineering Foundation, Neelam Kumar, joined us at New Delhi station. On the train we found two wooden benches where we sat crushed four to a side, with equipment piled all round, for the fourteen hour journey. Everywhere beside the track, in shanty towns or in the open, adults and children squatted by cooking fires. To a coddled European comes a wonder at where the excess of people find a continuing supply of wood fuel, food, and whether, amongst such an inevitable volume of human excrement, there is any clean water. Shelter is part of the equation of existence too, but less critical in warm climes, and thin, grimy, dusty, sweaty rags sufficed for clothing for the poorest people, while others wore thin but spotless and bright garments. On the flat plains we passed good brick houses and straw-roofed mud huts, tents, lean-tos, hovels of sticks and mud with polythene roofs, and tarpaulins strung between trees, as we clattered along all the hot night.

The transfer from train to bus at Jammu in the early morning was accompanied by protracted argument and haggling about taking our equipment on the bus roof. A crowd of onlookers gathered for the entertainment, and joined in, until money changed hands and the driver smiled again.

Meanwhile, an almost totally blind and ragged woman who might have been thirty or may have been fifty, I couldn't tell, attempted for three minutes to beg from one of our rucksacks which stood upright on the ground. I was unmoved, a sign of how unwell I felt; or was the thick skin of indifference, which you must have in India, growing already?

Through the bus windows we had a view of cacti twenty feet high, vultures, wild peacocks, hovels, and people in foreign dress. With blaring horn the bus chased fast along a good road at first, but it grew worse in the mountains, where muddy rockslides had torn away as much as half the road width in collapses over drops of hundreds of feet. The road itself is a remarkable piece of construction, clinging to cliffs in gorges of enormous proportions, and its upkeep is a tremendous and never-ending task as successive winters attack. At many points slogans exhort careful driving: 'The Icy Hand of Death Grips Speed Kings,' said one, and elsewhere in India we saw, 'Sleeping While Driving Strictly Prohibited,' and, 'Darling, Don't Nag While I Am Driving'! A certain number of serious accidents are inevitable on such a hazardous and busy road; two days after we had travelled the route an army lorry ran off into a ravine and twenty-four people were killed, and eleven seriously injured.

It took twelve hours to get to Srinagar and we would have liked to have rested immediately, but first we had to argue at length with the local taxi drivers, while the police enthusiastically wielded batons to drive away touts for hotels, houseboats and various commodities. We stayed two days in Srinagar, a city in Kashmir, which is in the far north of India. Here we bought rations and made travel arrangements. I felt ill, and guilty at not being able to pull my weight, but some antibiotics began to bring improvement.

From Srinagar airport the next stage was only half an hour by Boeing 737. Forty items of baggage accompanied us to Leh. This town, at an altitude of 11,500 feet (3,505 m), population 8,500 people, has been influenced strongly by Tibetan culture and Buddhism, and is attractive as a result. An eight-storey palace standing two hundred feet up on a rock spur overlooks all, and several hundred feet above that is a monastery. Buildings are of a distinctive Tibetan architecture which helps them blend with the dry, hilly landscape, and prayer flags brighten the place. There are sufficient trees, introduced quite recently I would assume, to give the air of an oasis in the middle of Ladakh's moonscape scenery. Between the Second World War and 1974 the area was closed to foreign intrusion, thus arresting the march of modernisation, but recent tourism has resulted in rapid change. Smiling faces and colourful clothing give a far more welcoming atmosphere than in some other regions of Kashmir, and visiting Leh, however briefly, was a highlight of the expedition; we planned to be there less than a day. The essential gentleness of Buddhism was pervasive, though partially submerged by the infiltration of other cultures, other values, and the attitudes of the rigid Muslim religion.

When accompanied by a lot of baggage, travellers may find movement around India to be far from straightforward, because they are at the mercy of those who provide the vehicles. At first it appeared that the only means by which to complete the next leg of our journey from Leh to Kargil, 127 miles (203 km) away, would be to hire four jeeps with drivers at a very high cost, but then we found a truck driver prepared to do the job much more cheaply. Next the jeep drivers informed us the truck driver had changed his mind 'because of union problems', and he in turn later told us this was not so and he still intended taking us. We believed ourselves the victor until at 8 p.m. two khaki-uniformed policemen presented themselves at our hotel to tell us we could not travel by truck for this was contrary to the law. The next stage saw Richard, Neelam and me accompanying the police officers to discuss matters at the home of the local police superintendent. This gentleman proclaimed that as the verbal contract with the truck driver had come to light he had to insist that we were forbidden to travel by truck. Eventually, after lengthy argument, we managed to extract permission for our equipment to be conveyed by truck and for us to travel in two jeeps instead of four, and those charged at the official rate rather than the high price demanded originally. The affair was settled reasonably amicably, and the night had a genteel ending when the policemen came back to the hotel for tea.

After a 3.30 a.m. start at loading, departure was achieved by 4.20 a.m. Past paddy fields in a hundred glinting mirror steps of the sky, and monasteries, Tibetan faces and the distinctive clothing which went with them, donkeys, horses, cattle, sheep, prayer flags, sparse poplar and willow in arid, stony hill country, we rose, gradually at first, then sharply on scores of hairpin bends and over the Fotu La, a pass at 13,432 feet (4,094 m). On a fine road surface most of the way we made good speed, and Kargil was reached before noon. This small town of 3,000 inhabitants had been more important by reason of it being at an intersection of old trading routes between Russia and India, and China and the west. Now Kargil has a few hotels, mostly scruffy, and markets like rows of wooden lock-up garages raised two feet above the ground and occupied by grocers, ironmongers, tailors, butchers, bakers and other traders. The population is predominantly of the Muslim faith, and apparently the practice of ‘muta’, limited duration marriages of as little as one day, still goes on. Houses are one or two-storied, and mostly built of mud bricks. Streets and homes are illuminated by means of a large diesel electricity generator, which roars like a helicopter during the hours of darkness until about 11 p.m., when the lights go out. Kargil is completely cut off from the outside world for several months in winter, and inhabitants must then rely on stockpiled food. During the summer barley, wheat, peas, tomatoes and potatoes are grown on the outskirts, and extra food comes in by lorry.

Shortly after our arrival in Kargil for an overnight stop the jeep drivers turned nasty, saying we had agreed to employ them to go further, which was not so. Neelam found himself accused of accepting money to take our side (he received no payment as liaison officer, though his employers continued to pay him in his absence). A shouting match, complete with the usual local participatory audience, ensued; a judge whom we met by chance asked if he could help, and told the drivers they were getting the agreed official rate for the distance they had driven. And that was that.

The jolting truck journey next day along a long and deep and fertile valley took us to Sanko village, where we had to sign the register at the local police station before proceeding; amongst those who had travelled up the valley before us, according to that register, was one Mickey Mouse. At the end of six hours following the valley road which deteriorated to a rough track, we were stuck in a cleft carved through old snow as high as the sides of the truck. The gap shovelled clear some days before by local people was wide enough but the back wheels spun impotently in mud and the vehicle leaned over a few degrees to lie on the snow, as if resting after its hard journey. And that was the end of about a week of travel by one form of transport or another.

We were perhaps half a day’s walking short of where we had hoped we might be, but that was not important for we were not pressed for time. Having unloaded the equipment we camped where we were on a meadow at about 10,000 feet, and within half an hour a deal had been struck with local villagers for eighteen ponies and nine porters for the next day. They duly arrived, and under a hot sun our caravan set out to walk eleven miles (18 km) on a rough road through beautiful rocky countryside where the last of the year’s pink roses grew on high ledges. At first the valley floors were taken over by a patchwork of agriculture with poor villages of mud brick houses here and there, but both fields and human shelters grew less and less common the further we progressed. Most of our porters dwelt in these or similar buildings and worked these fields, undertaking porterage only occasionally, when the ties of the land permitted. They were simple men, and might have suffered considerable imperiousness from sahibs, but they set about their work readily. Without a trace of subservience, and with pride but no arrogance, they clearly wished to give fair service for their pay. I took to them right away, though others of our party could not regard them without suspicion, based perhaps on the expectation that porters, almost as if by tradition, would give trouble. Mostly they huddled without complaint at night, thinly clad and under blankets in the open, except for one night so cold that they asked to share tents with us; we managed to find space.

With bronchitis not over, and breaking in a new pair of legs, it was for me an awful struggle towards the end of the day.

'Norm took a battering,' said Barry Needle when we arrived at our camp that evening. He had walked with me all day. A thirty-eight year old engineer who had resigned from his job to be on the expedition, he was our medical officer, and also took charge of rations. (The wisdom behind this being that if he poisoned you he was responsible for curing you.) Barry was very strong, industrious both in the preparatory stages and while on the expedition, and his judgement was good. He had broad mountaineering and rescue experience, was calm, and while not possessed of a great sense of humour was not the sort of person who puts a damper on the fun of others.

Steve Berry was thirty-two, and like everyone else but me, single. He had given up his job to go to the Himalayas, and had formerly been an estate agent, a profession which gives some clue to his personality; estate agents are neither known for shyness nor noted for having sleepness nights worrying about what people think of them. Steve had worked extremely hard to organise the expedition, and he earned the right to lead it by initiating the project and by sheer hard work. He had a bad climbing fall several years ago and as a result of his injuries, which were extensive and included damage to his head, he sleeps with one eye partly open; this had earned him the nickname 'Cyclops'. He had been on one previous Himalayan expedition, and had climbed in the Alps and the USA.

Richard Berry, Steve's younger brother, and known to Steve as 'Titch', was twenty-eight, a surveyor who also had given up his employment to be on the expedition. Good-humoured (sometimes like a naughty boy) and generally constructive and buoyant in his attitude, he had a talent for mechanical repairs, which came in handy putting stoves right; at high altitude, where not only cooking but also the availability of precious drinking water depend on the stoves functioning, this skill is far more critical than might be assumed lightly.

Steve Monks was twenty-two, amongst the top few of Britain's rock climbers and determined to get as much as he could out of his sport; to this end he took only temporary jobs so he had plenty of time off for climbing. He had made many hard ascents in the Alps and Norway.

Damian Carroll was a twenty-five-year-old teacher who had resigned his post on a remote Scottish island in order to go to Kashmir. His red hair went with the usual pale skin, which forced him to protect himself carefully against the sun's rays when high up; the method he chose with a large piece of cloth made him look from a distance like an Arab. He was quick-witted and had a good sense of humour, though his puns were as bad as mine. He was a hard climber who had been on two expeditions to Norway.

John Margesson, aged thirty, had been three years an army officer before becoming a land agent. He had very extensive expedition experience which included a year in Africa, and he had trekked or climbed in Nepal, the High Atlas, Arctic Norway and Central America. He admitted he had little sense of humour and was very serious. I found him to be as he said, and also precise, physically strong, and a very hard worker.

The next stage of the trek, up the left of a steep-sided gorge and along a wide valley, was longer than the previous day's; seventeen and a half miles (28 km) was the estimate of one of the locals, though I felt his reckoning to be on the high side. Whatever the case, we arrived at the ancient camping place of Gulamantongus, having passed over rock avalanches and snow drifts which blocked the crude road to wheeled traffic. With skin rubbed off in various places by the new legs, in the groin, from both buttocks and from both stumps, and with blistered hands into the bargain, the relatively minor but simultaneous pains from several regions were wearing. The pain entered my consciousness in two ways, at different times as component parts from each area of injury, and sometimes as a whole; so now and then I would recognise that a stump was sore at a particular spot, or a palm was telling me it was being rubbed, and when I was not conscious of one or other individual hurt I just felt myself to be generally in pain.

Early next day the liaison officer of a Japanese expedition to Kun (a close neighbour of Nun) passed by, hurrying on his way down to summon a helicopter for a sick climber stuck high up on the mountain.

'Won't take much to lift off a Jap who hasn't eaten for three days,' somebody said, and the liaison officer, understandably, was upset by this unthinking remark. Such a comment may go almost unnoticed in some expeditions, but once overheard by an outsider its nature is transformed from one of resigned, morbid humour to one of insensitive crudity.

Now loomed a river crossing, by pony. Memories of Argentina flooded back as I clambered on the back of a small beast; its size caused me to ponder whether it could carry me, or I should carry it. Having both my legs on this time was a mixed blessing; it was an advantage as far as balancing on the pony was concerned, but they were bound to drag me down if I went in the water. The Suru river spread wide to a quarter of a mile where we aimed to ford it, in two broad channels of sixty and one hundred yards and two smaller ones, separated by pebble banks. The water turned out to be not much over three feet at the deepest, so some waded across; Steve Berry nearly got swept over in so doing. In an hour and a quarter all equipment and personnel were across.

Springy turf, interspersed with muddy, rocky ground, then took us by early afternoon to a camp at 12,500 feet, and next day the porters urged their ponies up very difficult moraine and boulder fields, and across an easy river. On a particularly steep jumble of moraine bank one pony fell and rolled over a couple of times, but still they all kept going. Another intermediate camp at about 13,500 feet was the limit for the beasts, and then we and the porters took everything on our backs for two days to base camp in a snow bowl, at about 16,000 feet. On the first of those days a helicopter arrived to pick up the Japanese casualty but as far as we could tell from the sound and intermittent sightings it did not hover or land to take anyone off from above. It returned early the next day, though, thus adding to the suspicion that no one had been evacuated the previous day; soon after the departure of the helicopter I met the leader of the Japanese expedition descending a snow slope, saying, 'Happy day! Happy day!' and, 'We want you good ruck.' They had had enough and were pulling out speedily, and who could blame them? Their man had almost died, and was saved, and they were hurrying off home.

Not infrequently, expeditions have problems with porters. Our Muslim men from Panikar village neither went on strike nor complained, and worked for what is by local standards a fair rate, and by European standards a pittance. On one day of man-carrying equipment they even made a second carry late in the cold afternoon with inadequately shod feet already wet from being on the snow earlier. The porters were paid and, in keeping with the practice of that area, notes which had been even slightly torn were politely rejected; they had to be near perfect. When the porters left, saluting formally, smiling and waving to us, our liaison officer departed too. He said he would go trekking and would return in two weeks, but he did not come back. Neelam felt unwelcome. There had been a certain amount of personality conflict between him and at least two expedition members; it would be difficult, if not impossible, to properly apportion blame in this, but certainly the fault was not all Neelam's. Having said that, his subsequent behaviour in not returning to the expedition was foolish. He went back to Srinagar, where his wife joined him for a holiday, and this confused his case somewhat as he said he was going trekking. I am sure the whole experience, beginning with a feeling of alienation and ending in a failure to carry out all his duties as a liaison officer, must have been very painful for him.

For three days, in the manner of ants, back and forth we went, carrying to a dump at about 17,000 feet (5,180 m), and on to an advanced base camp at 18,000 feet (5,486 m), before the weather closed in and imprisoned us in a snow and wind blasted base camp for four days. As is natural under such circumstances our interest turned to food we did not have, such as steak and kidney pie, raspberry tart, fish and chips and Cornish pasties. We were also intensely interested in what we *did* have, and our diet of freeze-dried and dehydrated foods higher up, with fresh vegetables and tinned stuff at base camp, was not bad. Powdered milk, intended for babies, proved to be particularly popular, and our eggs, several dozen of them, had survived the journey in. Tinned meat had been scarce in Srinagar, and we missed it. Custard and onions (separately, I should add) were favourites too. We consumed, also, a fair amount of rice, chapatis and dahl (lentils), more from necessity than stoic deference to the local diet. A pressure cooker at base camp helped us to save fuel by cutting down the lengthy period normally required to cook in cold conditions and at high altitude, where water boils at a lower temperature and cooking consequently takes longer. Though we all cooked, Barry did much more than his share.

'Just goin' for a tiddle an' then I'll get t'stove goin',' he would say, or something similar, and he must have cooked twice as often as anyone else. During bad weather in our dug-out snow kitchen this was a lot more work than it may sound, because the kitchen was only partially roofed and therefore rather open to the elements.

As soon as the weather released us on 3rd June we all recommenced carrying food and equipment to advance base camp, known to us simply as ABC, and for a further five days puffing people were tramping up and down, ferrying essentials to ABC and Camp 1. The latter camp had been established by Steve Monks and Damian on 6th June, at about 19,000 feet (5,790 m). Apart from two hundred and fifty feet of snow at forty degrees or more, which is a stiff pull when you are heavily laden and very high, the going to ABC was fairly straightforward. Still, several hours at a time toiling in the heat on soft snow at high altitude was tough work. As Steve Berry put it, 'No words can convey the agony of high altitude exertion.' Those words we did use are best not repeated. On one occasion poor Richard made a carry from base to ABC, forgot to unload everything from his rucksack on arrival there, and gave part of his load a return trip back down to base!

Pressure on the bone at the end of the left stump gave an intermittent pain when I climbed, and I was worried that it might became so bad as to stop me.

From base camp White Needle was a long way away, but even at a great distance the mountain looked elegant. As we saw it the peak, all snow and ice, arched up on the left in a huge gracefully curved back to a corniced summit, from which it fell away steeply on the right side. White Needle had a great simplicity and purity of line. The view we had of Nun, though it was huge, was less impressive than from the west. I knew I should try to resist White Needle's charms, because we were supposedly suitors of Nun, but it was not easy. Much to my delight, it gradually became clear that it was most unlikely a safe route to Nun would be discovered except by going over White Needle. A reconnaisance was required and John and I jumped at the chance. We made our way up to ABC, in my case on snowshoes, which imparted a big-footed Donald Duck appearance.

Steve Monks and Damian had gone down to base for a rest. Richard and Barry were above Camp 1, conveying equipment and supplies part way to Camp 2, and Steve Berry was with John and me at ABC. On 8th

June Steve's first words were, 'Don't think we'll get much done today,' and we spent the morning unzipping the tent and looking out. But hope does not influence the weather.

On the morning of 9th June the three of us were able to go up the gentle glacier between ABC and Camp 1. Though we roped up to cross a couple of crevasses, mostly it was a safe plod. Camp 1 consisted of two small tents pitched on an airy ridge, with a gigantic rock cliff on one side and a crevasse on the other, into which Steve Berry and John dropped up to their waists at different times. Being at 19,000 feet put us in a good position to try White Needle.

John and I, sharing a tent, both woke at 4 a.m., and though the wind was forceful, at 5.15 a.m. we started melting snow for water, in case the weather let us go. But no, a high wind persisted all day and even made us wonder if the tent would blow off the ridge or be torn to shreds, for the material drummed and the little shelter rattled violently and shivered and trembled in furious gusts; the tent survived, however, and we did too, thanks to that. During a brief lull Steve descended to ABC because of a headache.

The subsequent stormy night wailed and howled itself through, and shortly after 5 a.m. we again drove ourselves to prepare. Muesli and tea made up breakfast and not long after 8 a.m., though visibility was not good, the wind had dropped to an acceptable level. Having crossed a crevasse or two, we tackled a short, forty-five degree slope of soft snow, on which Steve Monks and Damian had left a fixed rope. After that rope length we were on the very crest of the narrow, snowy, south-east ridge of White Needle, with a rock cliff of several hundred feet on the left and steep ice and snow and crevasses to the right. With fresh snow everywhere, soft and insecure, it was quite dangerous, though not difficult. The ridge did steepen twice into short steps like a steep house roof, but generally we just had to walk carefully on an uphill gangplank on the long ridge leading towards White Needle. Slithering off to the left was the real danger; in many places the snow cover was such that crampons could not go sufficiently deep to bite the ice. Even where the ridge sloped at as little as twenty-five to thirty degrees on the left we had to beware of sliding over the cliff. There was little chance of preparing safe belays to stop anyone who slipped, and for this reason, as well as for speed, we moved unroped most of the way. Barry, coming this way two days later, slipped, and for a little while Steve Berry watched him slide and expected him to go over the cliff edge. However, Barry stopped himself.

Mist hung over the white ridge most of the time and by two in the afternoon a moderately strong wind had sprung up and light snow drifted down.

'If it doesn't get better soon we should turn back,' John said.

'We could bivi.'

We said no more on the subject, both of us avoiding facing up to the unwelcome prospect of a cold bivouac, but the weather got worse and an hour later we did as suggested, digging a pit for shelter on a large snow plateau and laying out a bivouac bag. At an altitude of about 20,500 feet (6,250 m) we found ourselves in a good location from which either to retreat the next day if the weather remainded bad, or to head for the summit if it was reasonable. In good weather we might have made the summit that day; even in the weather as it was it might have been possible to press on and get there, but time was on our side so we played it cautiously.

The night was cold, minus 20°C (−4°F) at ABC and more like minus 25°C (−13°F) where we were, but at 6.15 a.m. the weather was reasonably clear, though still windy; Nun and White Needle were visible now and then. I woke John, who had suffered a fidgety, restless night through the cold, and who now proceeded to have a paddy at not being able to light the stove in the wind. It can get you that way high up, in dangerous territory, after a less than comfortable night, and I was not immune from feeling ratty either. In the end I managed to get the stove going inside my rucksack. We put some hot milk and muesli inside ourselves.

Soon Nun and White Needle had been swallowed in cloud again. As a precaution against crevasses we roped up and within five minutes John had gone to the top of his thighs in one; he went in twice more soon after.

'I'm going to be desperately slow,' he said when he got out. 'It's killingly hard.'

He was breaking trail on soft snow so had more work to do.

The weather deteriorated again quite soon. Surrounding peaks disappeared in mist and snow, and the wind picked up snow to blow hard at us.

The left stump gave a sharp pain every so often and I was not sure how things would work out in that respect.

The slope increased to a steady thirty- to forty-degree slog. We would have needed half the time had the snow been firm, but we sank to the knee and cursed again and again. So it was not until just after noon that we came upon the equipment left by Barry and Richard three days before. A bivouac bag, a snow shovel, a stove and fuel were added to the little pile on the snow slope.

The elements were not with us and visibility decreased. It had been bad enough, but soon deteriorated even more to a 'white-out', when no division can be discerned between falling snow and the slope you stand on; it is then impossible to judge angles or to see if the slope ends in a chasm, so you are close to blind.

'If it doesn't improve we'd better go down,' John said.

'I think so.'

This was an unwelcome conclusion, obviously, but we had to weigh everything up, and weigh it again if circumstances changed, and weigh it again and again. We delayed, stopping to eat a little, and in half an hour had witnessed only slight improvements in the weather. The dimly-seen slope ahead looked like it reached a tiring forty-five degrees for a short while, then dropped back to thirty-five. Down at ABC the others waited in vain for the weather to clear, and speculated about what John and I were doing. They doubted that we were trying for the summit of White Needle.

'All right, let's give it a try,' John said.

He may have known that was what I tended to favour, though not strongly; I would not have argued if he had said otherwise, for we had time to try in better weather. And from our clear weather sightings we thought we had to go over White Needle to Nun because lower routes were too dangerous.

Though only a few yards ahead John was just a misty figure in the drifting feathers, but the wind did not rise sufficiently to insist that we stop. The slope eased back, and very vaguely, up and to the left, we saw a greenish overhanging ice nose which could have been part of the summit cornice; we headed for it. The summit ridge was at right angles to our path as we came up White Needle's steep back, and we turned left along the slightly rising ridge before reaching what we judged to be the highest point at 2.20 p.m.

Attaining the summit of this elegant white peak was all I wanted. One month to the day after leaving England, I was satisfied with the outcome of my first Himalayan venture, having reached 21,500 feet (6,553 m). (Later Richard and John made a survey of the area and came up with a figure of 22,043 feet (6,719 m), but the survey was based on the only known altitude, that of Nun, when a sighting of that mountain was impeded by cloud. A conservative estimate would put the altitude at 21,800–21,900 feet, so I may just have been on the highest summit I had reached, but I could not be sure.) It was a peak of modest height by Himalayan standards, but a cautious introduction suited me.

The weather cleared for a short while, sufficiently for us to conclude, on the basis of this sighting and what we had seen earlier of the slopes below White Needle, that the way to Nun's summit should be over White Needle. So as well as giving us the ascent itself the reconnaissance had been worthwhile, and a little more essential equipment had been left high up. No matter what happened next, I would not go home with an empty heart.

'White Needle, especially the steep slopes near the top – desperate,' Steve Berry wrote. 'Such a struggle getting up . . . it was pretty scarey moving along the summit ridge with massive cornices on the right and mind-bogglingly big drops on the other.' 'The last stretch up the steep slopes was very strenuous. Knackered!' was Damian's version.

In poor weather again, we did not linger on the summit, but began the descent of ground which was more dangerous on the way down, but less of an agony. Three times I went groin-deep in a crevasse and John admonished me for carelessness; then he walked into one himself (giggle,

giggle). By evening we were back at ABC, to find no one else had done anything that day because of the weather. Now, if we could just get someone up Nun . . .

Over the few days after we climbed White Needle it was verified that the route over that mountain was the way because any lower variations were too dangerous. Steve Berry and Barry had tried to cut out the tiring ascent of White Needle by keeping low, and had come back very scared, having passed beneath insecure ice pillars, on avalanche-prone slopes, on steep and rotten snow and ice, where Barry fell in a large crevasse, but managed to escape without too much difficulty.

Everyone carried towards White Needle and Damian, in company with Steve Monks, descended four hundred feet westwards from the summit to establish Camp 2 on a col there, between Nun and White Needle.

On 15th June Damian and Steve left Camp 2 '. . . and immediately found it very hard going,' Steve said. 'We were only able to take ten steps or so before having to rest and catch our breath. After several hours we had covered only four rope lengths – six hundred feet.' They climbed all day on steep, soft snow to bivouac at 22,000 feet in a bergschrund, which is a large transverse crevasse formed between two snow slopes lying one above the other, where gravity forces the lower slope to part company with the one above purely by reason of mass. Next day they crossed from the lower lip to the upper of the bergschrund, with difficulty, climbed six hundred feet of fifty-degree snow and ice to get on to the east ridge, then followed a long, steep snow ramp, and more snow, to reach the summit of Nun at 5.20 p.m. They descended the same day to their bergschrund bivouac.

'We were totally exhausted and simply crawled into our sleeping bags and went to sleep,' Steve wrote.

The next day was hard too. 'Last section up to Camp 2 is desperate,' Damian wrote. 'Steve almost out on his feet. I'm not much better. Down to five steps at a time; exhaustion, misery. Never again.'

The expedition was successful, and there was the bonus of White Needle. On 19th June, Richard and Steve Berry dragged themselves on to the summit of Nun.

Immediately after going up White Needle for the first time I had told Steve Berry, Barry and John that I was content just to carry loads for them; the appetite was sated for a while, and the left stump was still troubling me. Even so, I tagged along to Camp 2 with Barry and John on my own condition, that I would turn back if the need arose.

In biting early morning cold we roped together and descended fifty-five degree snow and ice from the col for a hundred and fifty feet, crossed a bergschrund and lost three hundred feet or more while traversing forty degree snow to reach Nun's flank below the east ridge. Then began the wearying height gain on soft snow and under threat from avalanches all the time.

'I feel bloody weak as a kitten,' Barry commented at one halt.

At 11.15 a.m. we met Steve and Richard, victorious and elated on their way down.

'I was like a zombie,' Steve said. 'Titch did all the leading. Hey, Norm, didn't expect you to get this far. It's bloody hard.'

We parted company, with those who had the slope in their favour able to move three times as quickly as the unfortunates who had to go uphill on snow which collapsed underfoot and took them in thigh deep. In eight hours we covered the route to the bergschrund, which had taken Richard and Steve nine hours. So, we were not going too badly.

Our bivouac at about 22,000 feet lay under ten-foot icicles hanging from the bergschrund's upper lip; the lower lip rose like four feet of parapet, giving the feeling we were on a balcony. Good weather was what we needed now.

We did not get it, however. Barry went up over the bergschrund next day and stood in heavy hail on the snow and ice slope, while I had a tremendous struggle to get over the big gap which ran like a horizontal groove gouged along the whole south face by some giant with a V-shaped chisel. I made it after expending an enormous amount of energy.

I recover quickly from exertion, and had worked out what to do next to get further up the ice; but as I rested I knew there was a decision to be faced. We were walking an extremely fine line with the weather so bad, us so high, the route so serious and retreat so difficult. We stood at the junction where daring and recklessness took different paths, it seemed. A violent inner battle took place, for in the prevailing conditions it was debatable whether two should try for the summit, let alone three – moving one at a time on ice and steep snow it was obvious that three would take half as long again as two. A party of three would be sticking their necks out and risking two bivouacs above where we were, and real problems if worse weather caught us out higher up. We knew that well enough, for even with tents and adequate food and fuel, the storm at base camp had been a reminder of what the mountains can do to a group which did not even have to go anywhere. We were out on a limb where a shortage of fuel or rations could be a real danger. The overriding argument of all was that though I was self-sufficient I was unable to carry much in the way of the extra fuel and food and equipment which were required; I did not deserve the ascent because the route was too serious. I had known all along that it would almost certainly turn out that way, and all those who had gone before had been extremely hard pressed to make it.

I must quote an outside view, to show that excuses were not creeping in but reasons were being weighed.

'I thought after his supreme effort on White Needle that he would be content with that,' Steve Berry wrote afterwards. '. . . His thoughts were for his companions, and his attitude throughout was that if he felt he was impairing anybody's chances he would bow out gracefully.'

By now the glimmer of hope I had nourished of reaching the summit was almost extinguished, though the ice and snow climbing ahead was likely to be less trouble than the soft snows of the previous day. With the right equipment, medium-angled snow and ice gave me the best possible chance of moving quickly; time and again I was to prove this in the ensuing years.

In the end I made my decision coldly, as if someone outside was looking at it all objectively. I did what I felt I should, and accepted the responsibility as a member of a team and as the hitch-hiker of the group. Having climbed White Needle, it was easier than it might have been, to do as I should.

'I'm going back down,' I said to John, and called the same to Barry.

The two of them hesitated for some time, debating whether they should go on, even as a faster two-man party. Eventually they went.

Alone on the bergschrund balcony I waited, half expecting the weather to chase them back, but they did not reappear. I began to wonder if I could have carried on if the expedition had not commenced with bronchitis, and if the left stump had been less troublesome. Would I have gone a bit better, sufficiently to make a difference?

During the night spindrift showered like a waterfall into the crevasse, burying me three feet deep, and with the advent of morning I found the stove defunct.

Over twenty-four hours after I had last seen them, Barry and John puffed in, having reached the summit at 8 a.m. There they said a prayer for a climber who would have been with us but who disappeared while climbing the previous summer, in the Alps.

Six out of seven on top, and a double leg amputee to 22,000 feet; we had not done so badly by comparison with the team before us.

Could I have got up Nun if I had carried on? Quite likely, I think, for there was no technical difficulty to stop me, but judging from the state of exhaustion of those who got there, if I had been successful it would have been at the cost of speed through being a larger party, and further slowed in all probability by my pace. As the weather turned out better, the actual, hindsight risk was not as much as it might have been, but we could not know it would go that way. If it had worsened, three might have died, and the east ridge of Nun was not worth that.

In the afternoon the descent began on snow so soft we went unroped, for no one could have stopped anyone who slipped on that treacherous cover. Above, the snow was poised, ready to slip. The slopes beneath fell away from hundreds and hundreds of feet, interrupted in places by ice cliffs which would have been a terrible hazard if anyone went. Visibility was poor and small avalanches slid down with great frequency, obliterating tracks made a minute before.

A 'never again' feeling seized me several times, but that is common enough among climbers. Twenty minutes away from the steepest slope leading back up to Camp 2 on the col, John, who was in front at the time, fell in a crevasse. Dropping up to his armpits, he could feel nothing beneath his boots. He managed to get himself out before we reached him but he was very shaken by the experience.

Next day we gasped over White Needle and down to Camp 1. The following day we were reunited with our contented companions at ABC, and descended together to base camp where, to our great annoyance, we discovered several items had been taken: a passport or two, some money, chocolate bars, a jacket, exposed and unexposed film, a plastic bucket and, most serious of all to a group bent on celebration, two bottles of whisky. Brown bears have been known to raid base camps in the area (one Czech report says, 'In the time of their unpresence the Himalayan bears visited their camp and destroyed it.') but we found it difficult to picture a bear wandering off with a bottle of whisky in one paw and a bucket of film and passports in the other. The culprits, it transpired, were members of a thirteen-strong Austrian expedition from near Salzburg, attempting Kun, and camped well below us. Suspecting our base camp to be abandoned, they had searched through and come across Steve Monk's diary, in which the last entry was one month old and said he was about to go off to set up ABC. Since four weeks had elapsed the Austrians reached the wrong conclusion that the camp was abandoned, and their leader explained that apart from the whisky and confectionery all items had been removed for forwarding to the British Embassy in Delhi. Once having reached the wrong conclusion many expeditions might have tucked into the consumables rather than transport them all the way to Delhi; these items were paid for, and most or all of the other property was returned. In a further attempt to make amends the leader lent us a stove, as several of ours were not working properly.

There was one other objective left, a peak of 21,000 feet (6,400 m) called Zaska 1, which had had only one previous ascent, in 1980. Steve Monks, Damian and I thought the risk from avalanche was too great. Steve Berry, Richard, Barry and John wanted to try it, though. I agreed to carry a load towards the mountain for them, as they would not change their minds, and a morning passed in carrying with them and getting back to base camp.

Damian and Steve Monks had descended so I was alone, but not for long; in the late afternoon John appeared, on his own.

'We got caught in an avalanche,' were his first words. 'Tell you about it when I've had something to drink.'

I waited to hear whether anyone had been injured or killed. One sentence would be enough. He related what had happened. Not long after I had left them they had stopped to eat and were just commenting on how nice it was to be there when they heard a crashing noise above; it went on for some time, the obvious roar of an avalanche. A massive cornice had collapsed and fallen four hundred feet down a steep slope towards them, where they sat beneath an ice cliff. The cliff cut them off from a view of the deadly threat which was headed towards them, and someone had remarked without any concern, 'That's a big one.' But suddenly the avalanche reached the lip of the cliff and spewed over, hard ice spreading out in a wide fan and showering down towards them. Somebody shouted, 'Run!' Steve wrote, 'Instantly I got up and started running down the slope. I thought sickeningly, "I am a dead man, this is it, there's no chance." I fell on my face and thought, "I'll be flattened any second," got up and ran again. The crampons I'd just put on were sticking in the snow, threatening to make me fall again. I looked around, chaos, the avalanche coming towards me. Blocks of snow and ice flying past me, two of the others off on the left, it looked safer so I ran left. Then I was out of it and stopped, looking round for the others. Two safe, a third (was it Richard?) in the middle being tossed up and then out of view. Oh no, he's buried! I shouted something like, "Oh my God, not Richard," and immediately saw he was OK and yelled, "Barry!" Then miracles, he sat up and we got him out.'

It had been a near thing. Barry escaped with bad bruising of one leg. They dug out most of their buried equipment.

'What had made me unclip from the rope at lunchtime?' Steve wrote. 'Richard was on the other end of it and running in a different direction.'

If I had been there, I could not have run as fast as they. The likelihood of being killed or injured would have been high.

Laboriously, we hauled everything lower by carrying and dragging. Some of the equipment taken part way and left to be collected the next day was inspected first by a brown bear or two; one cooking pan had a tooth or claw hole right through it, and other things were strewn about.

The liaison officer of the Austrian expedition enquired what my OBE stood for and wanted to know upon what the British honours system was based. I began by explaining that the basis was not all good, and that in the early days some awful people had received high honours, by oppressing others. Suddenly, John was jumping up and down, stamping one foot and shouting 'Slanderous! Slanderous! One of my uncles is a baron!' I thought at first that the clown was joking, but he was deadly serious. Perhaps he knew nothing about land clearances and the slave trade, for instance, upon which the wealth and position of many a 'noble' was based. Perhaps he was unaware that Lloyd George sold titles, and that the granting of honours for party political reasons suggests that the system is flawed. Did he really believe that all persons of high position were worthy? I suggested he should inform himself better, and grow up, and this had the fortunate result that he did not speak to me for some time. I should add that I have a great respect for many who receive honours, and was very pleased with mine.

A happy consequence of meeting the liaison officer of the Austrian expedition was that he talked with me about adventure sports for disabled people, became enthused and was soon instrumental, with the Mysore School of Adventure, in organising a two day adventure camp for physically handicapped people. Twenty-five residents from a home and ten instructors gathered together in December, 1981, for activities which included camping and rock climbing. The event was known as the Croucher Camp, and I had the honour of having named after me the eighty feet of rock up which the participants climbed.

At the arrival of our porters and two skinny ponies we withdrew to the valley. On the way down the porters treated us to freshly caught trout cooked over their little stick fire. We crossed the river by means of a yellow rubber dinghy belonging to the Austrians – pulled back and forth by rope – and took a belly-shaking, bone-rattling, dust-swallowing ride by truck to Kargil. Then on to Srinagar by way of an exceptional 'My God, look at that drop!' road over the Himalayas.

Judy joined me there for a holiday. The surrounding natural beauty was the main attraction, and in particular the adjacent lake area was extremely pretty; there we saw swallows and ducks and ducklings in abundance, bright kingfishers, bold hoopoes, geese and goslings and dragonflies, massed water lilies and bright pink roses, poplar and plump willow, reflected green mountains, yellow-green reeds, flat islands supporting little thatched houses a mere foot and a half above the clear water, floating island vegetable gardens, tourist houseboats galore, dugout boats, and shikaras, which look like brightly painted gondolas and perform the same taxi function.

I did not feel at all well, and soon Richard and I learned that we had contracted salmonella and shigella, very unpleasant and occasionally fatal forms of dysentery.

The Jammu and Kashmir Mountaineering and Hiking Club put on a reception for us, and in Delhi we had a press conference at the Gymkhana Club, with representatives of the Indian Mountaineering Foundation and Air India. They had all reacted very helpfully towards us; we were befriended, too, by Ghafoor Wahid, an almost blind young man who ran an orchard. He put us up in his bungalow in Srinagar and his kindness added a great deal to our enjoyment of the holiday. Back in Delhi, Renee Chandola, a befriender of foreign and native expeditions alike, put us up and helped in many, many ways.

Thanks to Steve Berry most newspapers described the decision to turn back on Nun as 'sporting' and 'in a spirit of sacrifice'. The expedition began for me with bronchitis and ended with salmonella and shigella but no illness could lessen the pleasure of what had come about in one year: the east summit of Ameghino on one leg, taking part in a successful expedition on a hard route, getting up White Needle, and the right decision, the most valid of my climbing life, at 22,000 feet. How much more could I expect from this splendid sport? Would not the time soon come when I would have to abandon the more ambitious projects, which brought such joy? Increasingly, friends told me that time was here. But to my mind it was far away.

In April of the following year we held a reunion of the team at Richard's home in London, where we met the senior Berry who started it off so many years before by attempting Nun and climbing White Needle. Richard was not well mentally, and was heavily under the influence of drugs he had been prescribed. Next day he amused those who had stayed on after our celebration meal by writing to the Prime Minister, Margaret Thatcher, about how to solve the Falkland Islands crisis, which had just come to a head. His naughty boy streak came out, and there was a funny side to what he wrote, in a way. He began his letter with, 'This little incident with Argentina has caught you with your knickers down,' and went on to propose a solution which included kidnapping the Argentinian football team. But behind anything which might have been interpreted as amusing there lay a deep, impending tragedy, for shortly afterwards Richard was admitted to hospital suffering from depression and suicidal feelings. He wrote a letter explaining that he thought he had an incurable mental illness, and, typically, that he did not wish to be a burden on anyone. Then he killed himself by jumping from a very high building.

He had always seemed so resilient. I believe it possible that the salmonella and shigella which he caught at the same time as I was a trigger of his depression. If that is so, then as we stood at a scruffy roadside café in Kashmir, craving meat and deciding whether to take the risk, we were unwittingly treading ground far more dangerous than we imagined. Did he say, 'How about it?' and I, 'Well, I'm not sure. It's a risk, but then we've faced a lot of risk lately.'? Or was it the other way round? I cannot remember, but neither of us would have been so foolish without the company of the other in this silliness. There would be no point in recrimination nor guilt feelings, but I do regret that such an innocent indiscretion may have triggered a chain of events which led to the death of a likeable man.

# 8

# *Aconcagua*

With regard to employment, uneasiness crept insidiously over me. After a near two-year stint raising money which was spent largely on segregated sports for disabled people, I had to ask myself what the hell I was doing. And I had to accept that my heart was not in it.

The strongest of my reservations was that it was all too separate, a backwater, and I wanted to take part in the real world. I did not want the top two thousand feet chopped off any mountain for my benefit. I was not a blind disciple of the principle of integration, but preferred to lean away from segregation whenever practical options for integration existed.

Sport for disabled people had gone wrong way back through too much emphasis being placed on mimicking prestige athletics. When some of us started looking into the possibilities in outdoor pursuits, there was a great resistance from one or two of the leaders of segregated sport, perhaps because outdoor pursuits were seen as a threat to their empire if they were a means of integration. People were expected to fit in with certain sporting categories and rituals, decided for them.

Integrated, segregated, competitive, non-competitive – it was not for me to say one form of sport is invariably preferable to another, but fulfilment is more likely to lie in a wide choice. Opposition came more from those supposedly concerned with the interests of disabled people than from those who understood adventure sports. From some of the former, but by no means all, there were scare-mongering and faint-hearted tales based on nothing but prejudice and poorly-founded guesswork. There was, too, a certain amount of trying to hide behind a shield of medical 'authority'. Among those who were well-informed about adventure sports, reactions were varied: enthusiastic cooperation and encouragement, cautious consideration of the possibilities, reluctance, some of this based on genuine concern about safety. All these reactions helped us to go forward on the right and careful path between overprotection and foolhardiness. I had no intention of encouraging any disabled person to indulge in unsuitable activities, nor see them needlessly barred from something which, if it gave them a tenth of the fulfilment I'd found in climbing, could greatly enrich their lives. The campaign was complicated, not just because there are many adventure sports, several of which require a great deal of knowledge if participation is to be acceptably safe, but also because there are so many types and degrees of handicap. I can only think that the opposition failed to understand the subject but were still prepared to give negative opinions. They have had to come round, or look foolish, because at the end of the campaign anyone who said that outdoor pursuits were unsuitable was choosing to ignore a vast amount of evidence to the contrary. In a few years the face of sport for disabled people in Britain, and as a result in many areas of the world, changed a great deal. The position, particularly with regard to integration, had improved somewhat, but I could compromise no longer. I resigned my job.

Then, too, 1981, the International Year of Disabled People (IYDP) came to an end. What a relief, after a tidal wave of voluntary commitments.

'It was wonderful, a fantastic success,' said ninety-five per cent of those asked about IYDP in a street poll, according to a newsletter published in early 1982. However, I must admit that according to the newsletter the question was, 'Was IYDP wonderful or do you want a knuckle sandwich?' The author of the spoof newsletter had worked very hard for IYDP and was one of a small group of us who found some relief from the serious side of the work in irreverent humour.

Opinions about IYDP were mixed; there would be no point in saying otherwise. Such a campaign cannot be quantified, but my impression, gained from those whose opinions I would respect, was very favourable. Discounting perpetual malcontents and moaners, and ignoring those who did not comprehend what it was all about, it had gone well. In my view there had been too many stunts, too much exhibitionism, which did nothing to foster the image that disabled people were normal human beings with normal needs and hopes and a few bits missing or not working in the way one might expect, but on the whole it was a successful campaign.

We ended the year with access improved in scores of places, with schools having made very special efforts to help children to understand, with information services having sprung up, with useful publications being brought out, with more volunteers involved, with advances in relevant technology and prevention of disability in the third world, with hundreds of fund-raising efforts, scores of conferences on important topics, with increased attention paid to integrated housing for disabled people, with improvements in transport. Special attention was given to religion, leisure, employment, family life, residential care, sport, and several other aspects of life which are of importance to disabled people. Scores of youth, women's, religious and philanthropic organisations paid particular attention to disabled adults and children. And no one who was involved was complacent, for we realised it was a beginning, not an end.

I had enjoyed the privilege of having worthwhile things to do for so long that I seemed to be taking that privilege for granted; or was it simply that I was spiritually tired? The dilemma all along had been this: to get the outdoor pursuits campaign going with sufficient momentum my commitment had to be deep. There were no half measures. So, for a decade, one or two days voluntary work a week would not have been enough; at least half my time was spent working for nothing, and that was the only way to get the job done. That is not said in any way as a boast, for I was doing what I wanted to do and brought much on myself by encouraging demands on my time when it suited me. But when I began to feel resentful sometimes about those demands, it was time to take stock; I learned that I did not have it in me to give like that any more, at least for the time being.

1982 heralded two major climbing objectives. Time was running out and the mountains had to be taken soon. And how was all this to be afforded when it would cost more than I earned in a year? To begin with, the deposit saved for a flat on which Judy had set her heart was commandeered. She moped and made me feel shameful for only a couple of days, then encouraged me to carry on with my pursuit of dreams. What a woman! 'The time is ripe, cherry ripe,' I told her, and once she had got used to the idea she said, 'Yes dear,' and was affable again.

I began to wonder if I could be sane, for climbing weighed so heavily on my mind and was almost all I wanted in life; mountaineering was my destiny and my delight. The prospect of more adventure was both temptation and trap, and could not be resisted. How could my response be that of a rational person? Well, though now I seemed more like an impatient, greedy gourmand than the gourmet of earlier years, this was only a continuation of that behaviour which had so far brought sublime rewards, and there was not the slightest doubt that so far my course had been proper. Nothing had changed except my limits, which had expanded with experience and, particularly, because of the crutches. If earlier climbs had been within the bounds of sanity, then so were those to come.

The first of 1982's expeditions was a return match with Aconcagua. The expedition was scheduled for mid-January 1982. In December 1981 a letter arrived telling me it had been cancelled because too few people had shown an interest in joining the team. There I was back at square one, by now not an unfamiliar position. Fortunately Pete Cummings (the doctor on the first Aconcagua expedition) was able to give me the addresses of leaders of two other expeditions aiming for the same route. At his suggestion I wrote to them and in late December was accepted on one, once more an American expedition.

By stages Judy and I negotiated away from spending a few days over the

Christmas period training on Dartmoor. We had bivouacked in snow a couple of thousand feet up in the Lake District the previous Christmas night. Non-climbers felt this to be somewhat eccentric.

'It'll be easier this time because I'll get a tent,' I coaxed.

'How kind,' she remarked. Over a few days her resistance grew, and she jumped at the alternative suggestion that I would stay home for Christmas, then go to the Alps alone for a couple of weeks. Then it seemed even better to go to Argentina three weeks early, instead of to the Alps, so three days on Dartmoor turned into three extra weeks in the Andes.

There were, of course, plenty of people who said it was not fair to impose such separations on Judy, though at the same time they accepted that men and women might be absent from home for business and career reasons or when involved seriously in sport. I can only say that climbing was in a way part of a vocation. And though she had in some ways enjoyed being in Kashmir, Judy was very much a home bird. She showed little interest in travel, and did not wish to visit remote areas, primitive villages, or base camps amidst boulders or on snow. Though it might have been pleasant, we saw no reason why we should share identical interests. Any Olympic athlete, round-the-world sailor or less ambitious athlete or sailor, or golfer or musician or tennis player, amateur or professional, male or female, is open to the accusation that frequent absences are not fair to the spouse; but what is the alternative? Many a marriage of constant companions is bland, claustrophobic, and death to any freedom of expression, for one or both partners. Men and women may have deep needs which cannot be contained within the constraints of someone else's concept of ideal or proper behaviour.

For those first three weeks in Argentina there might be no one to climb with. Yet it seemed the best way to go about things, so I booked a flight and resigned myself to the tide of events which would carry me to whatever mystery lay ahead. Last minute purchases were made, and equipment sorted, in the first two weeks of 1982. At the limb centre a second pair of strengthened legs was ready.

'They fit very well,' I told Dr Fletcher.

'Must be somebody else's,' he remarked wryly.

An icy 15th January 1982. I had felt like asking, 'Aconcagua return, please,' at the underground station. The destination was Buenos Aires via Paris and Rio de Janeiro. Rio was half a day away from Paris. Apprehension about failure, and the fluttery excitement of going by 'plane to a foreign land, to climb, thrilled me and at the same time made me nervous, and I felt alive. As the doors of the aircraft swung closed in Paris I felt even better, for I had a row of three seats to myself, room to stretch out and sleep the night away with my legs off.

Setting off on the march to the base camp below the Polish Route at about the time I left England were six climbers whom I was destined to meet, and though I would not climb with them they were to have an influence on the outcome of my trip. They were Jim Wickwire, George Dunn, Marty Hoey, Frank Wells, Chuck Goldmark and Dick Bass.

Buenos Aires. That slight fear: would we land safely? We did. Then the next little anxiety: will my baggage appear on the conveyor belt? Yes, we were reunited. The customs officer was perplexed when the Englishman with the worn climber's rucksack on his back opened his cardboard box for inspection; he was perplexed because he found a pair of legs in the box, and he looked from legs to rucksack to Englishman and back to legs again. It did not tie up, but he waved me on.

I have never seen so many friends and relations hugging and kissing and weeping as when we got through the barrier; it was very moving. At least half the people there, men and women, had tears streaming down their faces. There more than anywhere I felt alone, and wondered if the lack of a friend, or at least a companion, would lead to three wasted weeks. Well, I could do a bit of lower altitude walking, I supposed, for the sake of acclimatisation and fitness.

In my notebook was the address of an Argentinian climber who had introduced himself during the mule ride beneath Aconcagua; at the time he had invited me to stay at his place if ever I happened to be in Buenos Aires, but hasty arrangements had not allowed sufficient time to confirm that he had room, or even that he still lived in Buenos Aires. I telephoned. He was there. 'Come here,' he said, and put me up in a room off a courtyard complete with palm tree, and close to the small factory where he made sleeping bags and down jackets. Thus Hector Vieytes, his family, friends and staff became the first of many Argentinians to help me out on this visit, and Hector in particular started off a chain of events aimed at ensuring my three weeks of training would be well spent. We were in the land of mañana, where Hector and his friends might well choose to have half a day off to cook asado (meat done over an open fire) and drink wine, but on the issue of finding me a climbing partner Hector wasted no time. He telephoned Ulises Silas Vitale several hundred miles away in Mendoza, and the latter rang the president of the local climbing club to ask him to make some enquiries on my behalf. Ulises invited me to stay meanwhile at his home, simply because we were both climbers. He was very experienced, having climbed three times in the Himalayas as well as in his local Andes.

I flew almost the width of Argentina in one and a half hours to Mendoza, to stay with Ulises and his family, who lavished upon me typical Argentinian hospitality, and soon his efforts to find a climbing partner brought to his home Miguel Angel Sanchez. Miguel was twenty-four years old, swarthy, dark-haired and bearded, of medium height, and known affectionately and accurately to his mother as 'Flaco', which means 'Skinny'. He was unemployed, a condition he accepted with resignation rather than distress as unemployment was quite high in his country and he was a member of a fairly large family who had a reasonable income between them; formerly he had been a carpenter and a cashier, among other things. His formal education had ended at the earliest age the law allowed him to escape from school, when he was twelve. His interests lay mostly in pop music, jazz, the opposite sex, his family and climbing. He had the Argentinian passion for soccer, but only as a spectator since climbing had displaced this sport some years earlier as far as participation was concerned. Miguel was eager to climb right away, and it was soon settled that we would spend about two weeks in the mountains. It looked as if taking a risk had paid off.

As I would later be joining an expedition with communal tents, ropes and stoves I had not brought such items with me, but had an address from which they could be hired in Mendoza. However, Ulises insisted on lending us these things; climbing equipment is very expensive in Argentina, and suffers some wear and tear in two weeks, so this was a particularly generous gesture. Ulises' wife, Christina, drove me to the centre of Mendoza to buy fuel and to change some money. When I left the bureau de change it was as a peso millionaire, for there were over 17,000 pesos to the pound. It was a strange experience to see menu prices, complete with the same sign as used in the USA for the dollar, when sandwiches were 7,000; and if you got a taxi there would be 5,500 on the clock before you started.

Ulises drove me several miles to stay the night with Miguel's family on the outskirts of Mendoza: father, mother and four sons in all. From the hospitality of one family I was enveloped warmly within the next. Of course, it could not have occurred to me at that time that before long some would regard all the people of this country as enemies, but I must record what happened to me. Father was a watchmaker, a kindly man who made a big effort to use the few English words he knew, and the brothers, aged from twelve to close to thirty, said, 'Now this is your home.' Not having learned Spanish at school, and having only a few days' exposure to the language in Peru and Argentina, I had only 'struggle-by' Spanish. As well as a dictionary I resorted to a phrase-book. At Miguel's we were greatly helped by the dictionary and the place resounded with laughter at a television comedy sketch involving two robbers; they were unable to communicate to an English-speaking lady victim that they wanted her money, so she lent them her dictionary. Mama, a bouncy, rounded, ample lady laughed and laughed and laughed, and said, 'See, he understands! Mistair Norman understands!' each time I grasped the meaning of something one of the family said.

Next morning a neighbour gave us a lift to the modern bus station which, like all South American bus stations, is a place of bustle. We, however, drew a blank; we were there at 10 a.m., but Miguel had got the times wrong and our bus had left four hours earlier. Back to Mama.

'Quick ascent,' I said.

'Supersonic,' she said, and laughed and shook, and put the kettle on for tea.

Our lift next day was on schedule, and we took to the road for 106 miles (170 km) by bus to a hostel at a ski resort called Los Penitentes. In this summertime season no snow lay in the deep mountain-hemmed valley at 8,530 feet (2,600 m), but the hostel warden, Fernando Grajales, and his wife, looked after the many climbers who came to tackle Aconcagua. At Los Penitentes Miguel and I met six Americans who had just descended from that mountain. Jim Wickwire, who was the first American to climb K2, the world's second highest mountain, had climbed the Polish route with Dick Bass, and they gave a serious account of the difficulties created by long stretches of hard, steep ice where in most years lay easier snow. Marty Hoey and George Dunn, who were both professional climbing guides, had started up the Polish route but traversed right to escape the ice, and had reached the summit. Frank Wells, who was President of Warner Brothers, and Chuck Goldmark, had not continued to the summit on the advice of their more experienced companions. This was not a good year to try the route, and what they said put me in a gloomy mood. There was worse to come, when George asked with whom I would be climbing after training with Miguel.

'With an expedition that Eric Simonson's leading.'

'That surprises me, because I don't think Eric's coming. He's never mentioned it to me, anyway.'

'I had a letter three or four weeks ago saying he was.'

'Eric's one of my best friends, and I can't see him not telling me he was coming when he knew I was.'

Training to climb a route which was much more serious than usual, with an expedition which was not coming! I went into the lavatory and pulled a pained, grimacing smile at myself in the mirror, the sort of smile which made Judy laugh at times like this when fate seemed to be conspiring to play a peculiar joke. It had happened all too often in work and climbing, largely because I often trod where there was an absence of precedents, I suppose, and we needed to laugh for relief, and she would say, 'You poor thing.'

However, it was not necessarily all black, for if the expedition had been cancelled perhaps Miguel and I could do the normal route, or climb something else. Even if the expedition did turn up, it was wise for me to bear in mind the option of the traverse to the right to which George and Marty had alerted me. Not for the first time, flexibility, a change of objective, might be the answer; meeting those Americans put this notion firmly in my mind so the encounter had certain positive aspects. As well as that they let me join them to listen to their story, about how Frank had gone under twice trying to cross the river; about how they had been overwhelmed by the military hospitality at a tented camp on the way down and Jim had given a lieutenant two tents and his down jacket; about how the soldiers fed them guanaco ('Probably tortured it first,' Chuck said) and about how the lieutenant had presented Marty with a pair of spurs. They told of how army mules brought some of the rucksacks down while two or three of the climbers ran a day's march in two hours. I was pleased to be listening to English again after a week of struggling by in Spanish, and it was good of them to share their experiences with an outsider. They told me something of the future too: George, Marty, Jim and Eric Simonson were soon off on another big adventure, attempting Everest from the Chinese side, in March. (They did not complete the ascent and Marty did not return from China because she died in a fall; she was the third person I knew to be killed on that mountain in a period of six weeks.)

Shortly before they dashed away to go home next day, George left us a large amount of freeze-dried and other lightweight food, and gave me his address in the USA in case I wanted to climb where he lived. Wherever I went to climb it was always the same, addresses, addresses changing hands all the time, opening up opportunities for further fun. That same day I received another invitation to climb in someone else's country when the last of a party of Basques arrived at the hostel, but what was more important at the time was that five or six of the group of nine had reached Aconcagua's summit by the Polish route; in other words, three or four with a proper pair of legs each had not. Soon after, I was to meet two more Americans who failed, then two who succeeded out of a party of five, then three Italians who failed. What brought home most that the route was not to be under-estimated, though, was the fact that Miguel had attempted it in 1980, and had seen his twenty-year-old companion slip and fall several hundred feet to his death. His body was never found.

Miguel and I set out over rolling hillocks, wave after wave, where big hares bobbed away in fast uphill slaloms. Not far past the blue Horcones Lake we came upon the cocoa river chasing down, sufficiently strong to sweep us away or prevent us crossing. It was full, and we decided not to try to cross yet but to keep to our more difficult scree left bank, as we looked uphill.

In looking for a climbing companion for me, my friends had borne in mind my poor Spanish and sought someone who spoke English. It transpired that Miguel's English was little better than my Spanish, but between us we were able to find sufficient real or made-up words. For instance, Miguel invented 'glug, glug' for boiling water, and when stuck for 'hen' I used 'senora pollo' (lady chicken). We mimed and finger-spelt in the air, and eventually managed so well we stashed the dictionary behind a rock for collection on our descent.

'OK?' he asked frequently, watching me closely all the time.

'Si,' I would say, even if it was a bit of a struggle on loose ground.

We OK'd and Si'd our way up, with eroded peaklets, folded and layered in geological origin and split by extremes of climate, to right and left. Four hours elapsed before the bank we followed refused to let us by a steep and very loose section. A long detour might be a waste of effort, so we decided to halt; we would cross the river in the early morning when the night freeze would have reduced the river's dangerous volume. Rigging a fly-sheet for shade from the intense afternoon sun, we settled down like desert dwellers, on a sandy bank. There was no lack of time; we had not picked an objective so were not subject to the pressure of a timetable. We would walk up the first part of the normal route of Aconcagua and pick one of the lower peaks, of the order of 17,000 feet. Approaches to the normal and Polish routes both began from the south of the mountain, from a road running roughly on an east/west line. The former approach started further westward along the road and passed under the west face, while the other approach brought one in on the east.

At first light next day we got the rope out and Miguel crossed thirty feet of water, up to crotch deep; that may not sound deep but the force made it difficult to maintain a footing. I followed without mishap, and while he lit our little gas stove to warm his chilled feet I drained the water from my legs; we must have looked a strange sight.

We took two and a half days to walk to Plaza de Mulas, 13,120 feet (4,000 m). Here was a stone military outpost which doubled as a climber's refuge. We put up our tent nearby.

Two of Miguel's climbing friends turned up next day, intent on Aconcagua's normal route. We followed them to a hut only six hundred feet higher, where amongst the names written on the wooden walls and beams were those of Ulises Vitale, Hector Vieytes and Cesar Morales-Arnao. All had been helpful to me at one time or another, the last of them having assisted my 1978 expedition in Peru.

Wisdom triumphed over impatience, so we rested at the hut until the next day, before aiming for about 17,000 feet (5,100 m). It was just a breathless slog on a faint, narrow track up dust and scree, producing exclamations from Miguel such as 'Bastard!' and 'Sonofabitch!' Yet five hours for that stretch was satisfactory. Three Spaniards descended, forced to retreat from Aconcagua through the illness of one.

After enduring a fiercely windy night we set out for the chosen summit, Cerro Manso, 18,231 feet (5,557 m). Manso means mild, and that certainly characterised this gentle hump. We put on crampons to cross patches of ice. There followed scree and easy snow, and we were on the top. We were away from the tent less than three hours. In its own right the ascent of Cerro Manso seemed hardly worth the effort, but as an acclimatisation and fitness exercise it was just what I had come for. Four small postage stamp patches of skin had been rubbed from my stumps and would be healed before the next climb, with any luck, and then the legs would be as comfortable as I could expect.

The descent was uneventful, except we covered about twenty-two miles (35 km) in one day, and, though this was mostly downhill, on rough terrain and laden with rucksacks, it was a long, long way for me.

The river, coffee-coloured now in the early morning, was too full; even Miguel did not want to risk it. We waited in the hope that some mules might come by, and in not much over an hour half a dozen mules ridden by soldiers and one civilian appeared, going up the trail. They crossed the river to us, and the civilian greeted Miguel warmly with the customary hugs of Argentina. We forded the river on one of the animals and the mules departed up the trail.

'Flaco! Mistair Norman!' Mama shouted as she saw us getting out of a taxi outside their simple, one-storey concrete house. She hugged us tight and giggled, and everyone had a look at my trouser belt, pulled in two holes. Mama said if that was how much weight you lost she would come too next time. However, she did not want me to attempt the Polish route.

'No Polacos,' she said many times, shaking her head and pouting.

Nine days of training felt just right, so the first stage was completed satisfactorily. Now I had to find my expedition, if they were coming. There was time for one day of relaxation before I set out to patrol the coach terminus, observing passengers alighting from buses from Chile. According to my information this was the day they should leave Santiago for Mendoza, having arrived by air the night before. Late in the afternoon several dusty coaches groaned in, but there was no group resembling an American expedition. Miguel, who had been helping, left at 6 p.m. to meet his girlfriend. He had not been gone long when nine people climbed from a coach and started unloading rucksacks. I had found my expedition.

There was a simple explanation for George Dunn's suspicion that they were not coming: Eric Simonson was no longer the leader because the date of his Everest expedition had been advanced and various commitments meant he could not come to Argentina. John Smolich had taken his place.

Contrary to all we had been told, it took only an hour or so next day to obtain official permission to attempt the climb, and with final purchases such as fuel completed, we were free to take the bus next day to Los Penitentes. Not until we were there was it noticed that a kit-bag was missing, so we were short of a tent, a stove and two days' food. We borrowed a stove, hired a tent, and bought a day's food, all from Fernando.

The three-day march of near forty miles to base camp revealed much about the characters of my nine companions. John Smolich, the soft-spoken leader, was good at seeking opinions on how the expedition should go, without in any way giving up his responsibility for decision-making. He was adamant that everyone should stay together, and though he had the usual share of early greyhounds, others whose pace varied (in two cases because of illness) and me in the party, he coped firmly and pleasantly on this issue. John had been a guide for three or four years, having abandoned a career as a surveyor.

The other John in the party, John Perone, was thin and looked older than his twenty-eight years on account of his semi-bald head. He was single, a chemical engineer who lived in California. What stood out most about him was that he was very funny. Beset by diarrhoea and dragging himself wearily up the long trail, he could still manage to come out with, 'You know, I'm more of a lover than a climber.' And when someone remarked that the presence of our one woman member, Mary, must affect the behaviour of the men, John stood there looking ill, with white glacier cream smeared on his lips and through the five-day black bristles surrounding them, with dust stuck to his face, with black fingernails, with dirty trousers and an old anorak, and said, 'Yes, it makes us all take more trouble over our appearance.'

The woman in question, Mary Michel, was an assistant manager in a climbing equipment shop, and had been introduced to wilderness hiking at a very young age by her father. She had acquired a great deal of hiking, climbing and skiing experience, and was sensitive about doing as well as the males. She was of average height and weight, and much stronger than appearances might have suggested.

Someone else who proved to be stronger than a cursory glance might have conveyed was Ramon Rodriguez Rocca, a Chilean engineering student who in addition to carrying more than his fair share of communal equipment took on board three big honeydew melons for us. He did not reach European or American average male height and lacked any obvious bulges of muscle, but that is often the way with good mountaineers. In consequence of his abilities, Ramon was a leading candidate for a Chilean expedition attempting Everest the following year. His English was about as good as Miguel's.

Mr Muscle of the group was Todd Marlatt, a boisterous ex-marine who worked in the oil business in Saudi Arabia. He could easily have been taken to be too full of himself, but, though he *was* pretty full of himself ('What is the name of the one who talks a lot?' an Italian had asked), his anecdotes were interesting and his jokes funny. He had a dogmatic streak, and when in describing his work he said his firm had been looking for somebody who was not opinionated and was a good listener, John P. stepped in neatly with, 'And that's the guy you work for?'

The oldest person in the group, Ted Mayer, was forty-six, originally from Germany but now, like all but Ramon and me, living in the USA, where he owned a small printing business.

Dan Montague was a soft-drawling, easy-going hospital medical technologist who also ran a raisin farm in California; 'raisin' raisins', as someone expressed it. He was less ambitous than some, and said that unlike the other 'dudes' he would be content to reach 21,000 feet as he had not previously been quite that high.

Paul Slota was a grocery store manager whose interest in photography added a good deal to his enjoyment of the trip. He was a quiet person who blended in unobtrusively.

Vladimir Kovacevic, a Yugoslav doctor, worked as an anaesthetist in Wisconsin. Apart from me, he was the only one of us who was married at the time, and he had two children. Vladimir was fast at the beginning of the expedition and emerged as the person who disliked most the constraints of being in a large group.

Ages ranged from Ramon, twenty-five, and Paul who reached twenty-six during the expedition, through John P., twenty-eight, Mary, twenty-nine, John S., thirty-two, Todd, somewhere around thirty-five, Dan, thirty-nine, Vladimir, about forty, me, forty-one, to Ted. Todd, Ted, Mary and Paul had climbed Alaska's McKinley (20,320 feet, 6,194 m), Dan had been up three peaks in excess of 19,000 feet (5,800 m) and Ramon had many high altitude ascents to his credit. John S., though not having climbed anywhere near as high as Aconcagua, had very extensive experience. Vladimir and John P's experience lay with peaks of alpine proportions rather than Andean.

The march involved a forty feet wide river crossing on the morning of the second day. Most of the others struggled through water up to mid-belly and though none slipped the seriousness of the crossing, even with a rope, was obvious. John S. crossed with me, much to my relief. Facing upstream I entered the clutches of the water and shuffled sideways. As it became deeper I speared the crutches into mucky brown wavelets with dirty white crests, into water which tore even at those thin poles so hard it took all my strength to prevent them being pushed away. My feet conveyed no information as to the contours of the bouldery bottom, so, unlike the others, I had to chance each step and hope that I could remain in balance with the help of the crutches. If the water pulling at my crutches created a problem, what it did to my legs made the crossing the hardest I have ever attempted, for the river worked constantly to sweep me from my feet into rough water. I would sink if I went over, and the river would dash me against boulders, and if I could not get out the cold would soon finish me if drowning did not. The difficulty was reduced a little as the limbs filled with water and became heavier, but when only at knee-depth I thought I would not be able to handle deeper water. A further step to the right, and the water was at mid-thigh, and I fought to get the right leg moved again after its partner had joined it. The river dragged at it as soon as it came off the riverbed and I feared I would not get it down again. For second after long second I thrust as hard as I could, trying to get it on the bottom again while the river wanted to take it downstream, with or without me. I battled, and won a step, but each successive step took me further from the bank and into deeper water. Two, three, four more short steps with the water up to my stomach brought relief in one way: I was in the middle and it was as safe to go on as to go back. John was right behind me, holding my belt. Funny, I thought, I don't know if he's holding me down, lifting me up, or pulling me sideways; we had not worked out what we would do. Another step seemed to take me no further. Don't look at the water, I told myself; it moved so fast it would disturb any balance achieved through the eyes, and I relied more than most on my eyes for balance because my feet told me nothing. With eyes on the hills upstream, I got another step. People on the bank were shouting, 'Great man!' and, 'Go for it!' The water shallowed, it became easier and easier, and I bounded out.

'We got power!' Todd shouted, raising a clenched fist, and John P. reacted more quietly with 'We's funky.'

Much of the early walk took us through prickly, man-high bushes that smelt of castor oil. The river spread wide here, narrowed there, and carved high grit walls and forced us to rise two or three hundred feet to find a way through on slippery grit slopes. There were places where there was nothing underfoot but dried mud and boulders, and other sandy areas, and grassy places, and frightening steep banks of grit. At the end of the second day the wind raged and blew dust at us as we trudged wearily up a half-mile-wide, flat, pebbly river bed.

'You may get a sight of Aconcagua's tip up through the next valley,' I said, playing down the reality.

Then, there was Aconcagua. When they saw the view, 'Wow! Man! Hooee!' they went, dropping rucksacks to rush ahead to a crest for a better view. It was a splendid sight.

The last day into base camp took us first high up the right bank of the Relinchos valley. My first impression was that it was better than the left bank, and I remembered the year before when that bank had made me concentrate on every step, had made me sweat, had made me fear a fall into the river. Now the right bank deteriorated into looseness too, and we were very, very careful.

The uninterrupted view of Aconcagua and Ameghino which was soon ours excited our hearts like nothing else could. We were fired up, and marched quickly. Mostly I was last; skin had been rubbed from the stumps again in several spots.

At Plaza Argentina we stopped to rest, and talked to two people who had attempted the Polish route but had not reached the summit. Their three companions were still up there trying.

The greyhounds pulled ahead, and I stayed with John P., who had what all the Americans knew as 'the trots'. He was weakened, and had to stop frequently to drop his trousers. 'Gonna get a sunburnt butt,' he said, 'with all these trips to the bathroom.'

The mules laden with our food and heavy equipment passed us in the mid-afternoon and I paced John P. for the last couple of hours. We had speculated on how much ribbing there might be when we trailed in an hour or more after everyone else. But as we approached base camp we saw three figures scurrying towards us across the vast flood plain ahead; they had overshot. Since one was our leader and the other a Chilean whose local knowledge we had to rely on, there was considerable banter aimed at John S. and Ramon when five us came into camp together.

So, here I was again in the same base camp, close to where the river we had followed narrowed and its source hid under the ice. My stumps hurt a lot, but I felt well, and the mules had brought up an extra pair of legs this time. 'Have a slug of this,' John P. said, getting out a bottle of whisky. I had a half share in it but he kindly carried it. 'That's for pacing me. How're your wheels?'

'Both feel quite bad. Raw in a few small places.'

John S. heard this, and consequently I was left out of the team of seven who carried to Camp I after we had enjoyed a rest day at base camp. Dan and Paul, both of whom were unwell, stayed behind too, and we agreed it was better that we rested, and we felt terribly guilty at the same time.

Three Americans whose two friends we had met at Plaza Argentina descended; two of them had succeeded, of a total of five. It was serious, and they had passed by three bodies on the glacier, they said. As far as I could gather from various sources, one was of the Argentinian who had died when I was beneath the mountain the year before, and the other pair were Americans who had met their deaths a few weeks earlier.

We started slowly up the moraine where my leg had broken the year before, and up a loose V gully twenty feet deep. Though above the gully the terrain was a jumble of boulders, up to house size, with little frozen lakes in between, and though above that the scree was very steep and loose in places, it was just a matter of slow pace and laboured breathing. Four hours was all we needed. Our next camp was positioned in a wide, grey rock, barren valley between Ameghino's icy walls on the right as we looked upwards, and Aconcagua rising sharply to the left. My prediction that we would find food abandoned on the route had not proved true thus far, so as soon as the tents were up on our flat, stony spot at about 16,250 feet John S. and I went scavenging. We found chocolate, corned beef, sardines, bouillon cubes, sweetened milk, biscuits, tea bags and other commodities in large quantities. Any slight anxiety we might have felt about food was over.

Another carry was executed and the following day we loaded all which remained and made ourselves undertake a purgatorial grind up scree, steep scree, steeper still, to Camp 2. Now the altitude really punished us for coming up there, encumbered by heavy packs. Reluctance, altitude and heavy loads were overcome by the positive, earnest desire to go up, and the balance in our minds and bodies was sufficient to produce the next step up, and the next. Just.

As we rested at about 17,000 feet a ruby-throated hummingbird flew up the way we had come, landed for a few seconds on one of Dan's boots, and took off somewhat to the right of the way we would go.

Having missed out on two carries, and having been near the back or last on the march in, I had begun to wonder whether overall I would be a weak link. I was going well on this carry, among the leaders and, though it was a race, I found no need to push myself as hard as I had thought might be necessary. So I allowed myself the hope that I would perform comparatively better the higher we went.

John P. began to lag a little; at each rest stop he flopped in that slumped attitude which told all and made us wonder whether he would get up again. He stopped more than the rest of us and time and time again got himself up. I dropped back to pace him, and having taken a rope from his pack offered to lighten his load further.

'If you take any more I'll blow away.'

Vladimir and Todd went ahead as we urged our bodies to zig-zag up scree which wanted to slide, so it was gasp and slide and rest and gasp and slide for another hour. The leading pair reached the site of our camp and Vladimir came down and took John P's burden. Todd called down to me, 'How about you, big boy? Take your pack?'

'No, I'm all right thanks, Todd.'

In the shelter of a fifty foot high amphitheatre above the steepest scree our three tents were well protected. Judging from our altitude relative to Ameghino, I thought we were at about 18,500 feet. At least one more camp would be necessary before we could try for the summit.

Altitude dictated that progress should be slow, so the next day sped by as we rested. John S. and Ramon scouted ahead a little and when they got back John looked serious and said, 'It's gonna be hard.'

On Aconcagua, the weather alone could reduce our chances a great deal; this mountain stood so high it was frequently swathed in bad weather cloud while the surrounding area enjoyed the sun. We had not had much in the way of serious climbing so far, though the river and loose banks were not to be treated too lightly. Now the altitude and potential bad weather were serious enough, and on top of that the ice would be difficult.

Our little group had been moving only fifteen minutes up steep stony ground on the way to Camp 3 when the altitude claimed its first victim: John P. could not carry on. His speech was a little slurred and his gait unsteady, and the decision to stop was entirely his own. He descended alone to base camp.

The more difficult part of the route started for the rest of us, on the steep glacier. As we sat to put on crampons the body of the Argentinian was visible two hundred yards to our left and only a few score feet higher up the glacier. It lay in the snow, a vague bundle, and perhaps wrapped in a sleeping bag; the distance was too great for us to tell, and no one mentioned it.

Having started up a snow slope which turned icy higher up, we were in no doubt that from now on great caution would be called for. While load carrying, even short stretches of thirty degree ice are not only tiring but dangerous too; every foot gained is one down which the fragile human could slide and bounce and tumble at an unbelievable speed, and a high proportion of accidents which occur on Aconcagua stem from slips on moderately steep ice. Two more bodies seen at a distance were evidence of this; these were the Americans.

Ted, impatient as ever, took the lead in his jerky, turkey-strut manner, as if every step was dragged out of himself by a distinct mental effort rather than as part of a slow rhythm. That was his way, and he preferred to take slopes in very gentle zig-zags. Before long John S. resumed the lead and Ted took the gradient more gently than John.

'Stay in my steps, Ted!' John shouted at him in tight words tinged by tension. No wonder; I would not like to have taken on the extra burden of leading nine people on a mountain like this. To keep yourself going was more than enough for one man.

To our relief, within two hours we were finding our way up easy angled rock and scree, and looking for somewhere to pitch the tents.

'Wouldn't want to do any snow and ice harder than that without a rope,' Dan commented in his temporarily husky voice (he had a cold), and Paul said, 'I didn't like it but at least I really felt like I was climbing.'

The essential plod of getting poised to climb was over; nine days from the road to the glacier had earned us an attempt at the summit. Yet I was troubled; I had joined the expedition because Camp 3 was planned at 20,500 feet (6,250 m) and I estimated we were a long way below that, leaving too ambitious a summit day for me. The original intention of ascending two thousand three hundred feet had been reasonable, but we were too low by several hundred feet. I made a half-hearted attempt, half-hearted because I was uncertain of our precise altitude and because I was reluctant to question his decision or appear to be complaining, to get John S. to go higher that day. If we were too low, we all deserved to share the blame, for we had surrendered to that awful sluggishness of high altitude which flooded over us after not much more than four hours on the go. We would all pay for it.

It fell to Dan and me to prepare dinner that evening, and breakfast the next day, so we were obliged to start the big day much earlier than everyone else. At 3.30 a.m. the cold was intense but we had to get started on melting the snow. One stove which had been working the day before did not want to start at first, and took half an hour to coax into action; two more hours went in melting sufficient snow for nine people. Our 6.30 a.m. departure was made in the last remaining minutes of that night's darkness.

Once our crampons were put on at the glacier's edge, five minutes away over steep scree, we roped ourselves together in three groups of three. I followed John and Mary and we set off in front, traversing from the right to the left across and up the glacier ice, at angles of up to forty-five degrees. To the sound of crampon rasp and ice axe clunk and heavy breathing we made reasonably good progress, drawing gradually ahead. It would have been easier and safer climbing straight up, using two ice axes, but we had to cross using one axe on the higher right side. (Or in my case, a crutch.) For an hour, two, three we traversed with the icy slope to the left, a constant reminder that tragedy could be just one slip away.

Moving across steep snow John hammered in three snowstakes, to which the rope was clipped for safety. I had used spiked crutches up to that point, but found it better to use an ice axe and one crutch on a particularly steep bulge of snow above a crevasse.

By 10 a.m. we were nearing a shoulder which marked the beginning of a very long snow ridge to the summit, and we sat to wait for the others.

Half an hour went by as we watched them creep in funeral procession across the slope. There was a delay when someone had trouble with their crampon straps, and then someone else lost a crampon, which was recovered from further down the slope where it had come to rest fortuitously on rough ice. Somebody else came to a halt, leaning his head on his ice axe buried to half its shaft length in the slope, and behind him a figure moved slowly with very long pauses between steps. Paul and Ramon looked like the only ones making progress without problems of one form or another. Eventually the group came together.

'It's clear not everyone in this party can make it,' John said, and we all talked over what we should do. What with the waiting and the talking, three-quarters of an hour was irretrievably lost; the stove which worked had cost at least half an hour, and the other which failed to function had set us back a further hour. Whatever the cumulative factors to delay us had been, it was plainly too late to launch out from this point. Boiling clouds higher up revealed the presence of high winds. We had bivouac equipment for only two people. Everything was weighed, and we descended. (Later I read an Argentinian description of the route, in which an extra higher camp was suggested; there is something to be said for dividing the route in that way.)

John, Mary and Ramon had gone well, with Paul and me next in line. However, when it was decided back at Camp 3 that four or five people might try again next day, I agreed with John that the route was too ambitious for me from this low camp. Therefore, I volunteered with Dan to cook again and to get the water ready very early next day. The plan was to be awake by 3 a.m., or earlier.

What a gloomy night it was; thoughts stirred in my head more than I wanted. Two trips to Argentina had left me with the one-legged ascent to about 17,000 feet, and Cerro Manso; an ascent, even by the normal route, of Aconcagua in addition would have put quiet that feeling of dissatisfaction which now bothered me. If only I could have had Aconcagua as well, I would have been overjoyed. The normal route and the one-legged jaunt together would please me as much as the Polish route on its own. If only, if only, if only . . . Enormous disappointment was crowding in. Now I would get up early to send four or five of the others on their way, and I would sincerely wish them good luck, and whether they succeeded or not we would go down; they would want to descend as soon and as fast as they could, and John would do his best to see that the whole group stayed together. What possible relief could there be from this disappointment? I could think of nothing which could ease it. The imminent end of the climbing season precluded an attempt on the normal route in Miguel's company.

No one got up that night. I shared a tent with Dan and was unaware of what went on in the other tents, but it was reasonable to assume that the weather was unfavourable. With that thought in mind I drifted back into sleep, and slept till late. Imagine my surprise when I learned that their failure to get up had nothing to do with bad weather but was a result of the lethargy of high altitude; I could hardly believe they had come all this way only to give up when the odds of success were a good deal better for a smaller party sent on its way earlier and minus the slower members. Vicissitudes were to be expected in this high and wild place, and when the mountain shunned you that need not prevent you trying again. Still, for everyone, there are days when motivation has been taxed too much; they had taken a beating, spiritually as well as physically, and some of them had been taken aback at how they managed.

'We still have the resources to get three or four or five people up,' I said to John. 'Somebody's got to go even if others have to sacrifice their chances.'

The last bit of what I said he looked upon as an admirable gesture of self-sacrifice on my part, and I had to put him right.

'After the first three or four candidates I want to be considered too, by lottery if necessary, for the last one or two places.'

John went to his tent to talk it over with some of the others. There had been, and still might be, a risk of the trip slipping from our grasp just when we should not be letting go.

An hour passed and John came to see Dan and me. Putting his hands around my throat he said, 'Now everybody wants to go!'

Even the Bambi-legged men of the day before wanted to join the attempt. Only Dan had decided against. He and I were melting snow a little later when John came back to our tent. 'Dan, if we were to traverse over to the normal route would you come too?'

'Sure.'

Here was the answer; the antidote to disappointment was at hand, if we succeeded. I would have been a little reluctant to attempt the normal route if not for our sortie up the Polish glacier, which had added some quality to the expedition; taken as a whole the trip was more interesting for that. Now we would go on a gradual rise over scree and snow to the right of the glacier, the way Dan's ruby-throated hummingbird had flown. Only three and a half hours of traversing rotten scree and snow patches and a snowfield led us to the highest mountain hut in the world, the tiny Independencia, set at about 21,300 feet (6,500 m). (There are several different estimates of the altitude in various accounts concerning

Aconcagua.) This wooden, wedge-shaped building looks like a piece of cheese left there with the thin end pointing at the sky. It was about five feet high, and became known to us as the chicken coop. Three tents were put up, and I chose to sleep in the coop, where we cooked.

Todd was soon bent over a stove and shouting, 'Come on bitch!' He and Vladimir would share the extra burden of getting breakfast next day. I was pleased the second summit attempt would not begin that way for me, but as it transpired I did not get it easy on this eve of expectation, or in the first hours of the next day; my water bottle, kept inside my sleeping bag to prevent freezing, leaked. One-and-a-half pints of water distributed itself through the down filling, resulting in frequent awakenings and a lot of shivering, huddle, huddle, all night. This was hardly the start I had hoped for to a very hard day.

Vladimir crawled into the chicken coop at 5.30 a.m. and cursed a troublesome stove. Oatmeal cereal, bland, unwelcome and unappetising, but necessary. Away at 7.30 a.m. Weather: cloudy, low wind. Up easy snow to a slightly rising crest of snow and stones. A traverse on scree, and across an easy snowfield for two hundred yards.

Soon our pace was broken by boulders, loose boulders which made us wary that one of our number might set one rolling on to someone else, so we tried not to get in line below anyone. We were in a gully which gave loose scrambling like some of the harder routes on British mountains, but the extra 20,000 feet made any further comparison meaningless. The steepest snow was only thirty degrees; it felt more like sixty, and demanded considerable effort from us all, making every step a little battle against inertia. Effort, effort, effort, effort.

Following a fifteen minute halt at 11 a.m. John and I went ahead, with Ramon well in advance of us. The top of the gully was not far away and it was likely that from there we would see where we had to go. I feared we might be faced with a distant and high summit which would lead John to say we would have to turn back. Not so far away was a storm. Still, I was in no mood for turning back.

At 11.45 John was twenty feet ahead as we weaved between boulders lying on steep ground. He stopped, and said, 'Come up here and take a look.'

His voice had betrayed nothing, neither elation nor dismay, but as I scrambled towards him he gave me the obvious clue by saying, 'You deserve this. You've worked hard enough for it.' Unless he turned out to be a surprise sadist, the news was going to be good.

I reached him, to discover that the gully ran at a right angle into the ridge which linked Aconcagua's twin summits, with the higher north one to our left and the south to our right as we came up. The south summit looked more interesting, snowier, and showed us a fine ridge, but it was the bigger one we were after, the highest of all the Andes. The north summit was a rock chunk which I estimated to be five hundred feet above us.

'Be there in an hour,' John said.

I felt good, with a belly full of warm hope.

'I was worried it might be further away and a lot higher and I might have to say it was too far,' John said.

Progress was slow but inexorable. Ramon was soon waving at us from the summit, while John and I waited a hundred feet short vertically for the others to catch up. Paul was right behind me, Dan going well behind him, and forty minutes separated him from our tail-ender, Todd. He was just behind Ted and Vladimir. So with the exception of Ramon and John, who were in a class of their own, the early greyhounds were finding it hard. We must beware of seeing that as a judgement, rather than as the observation it is intended to be.

At 1.15 p.m. we dawdled like a single file, exhausted army patrol and flopped down on the summit, a flat brown rock area bigger than a tennis court and almost free of snow, presumably because of high winds. We took photographs of each other alongside a two foot high tubular alloy cross.

'Congratulations,' Ramon said to several of us in turn. 'Congratulations.'

'Pity John Perone's not here too,' I said.

The training ascent, three weeks to the day before, had paid off. At 22,834 (6,960 m) we were all at the highest altitude we had reached. I felt not pride, but a splendid surge of satisfacton. That dissatisfaction which just over a day before had seemed beyond relief was now banished. I had risked much again, not just life and limb, and had won; I had sought inner serenity, and found it. The results of the two expeditions to Argentina added together were so precious, so much more than I could have hoped for.

If ever the summits give me only a sense of relief from suffering, and permission to go down, without some feeling also of a sense of purpose, then I shall stop climbing. It is not a question of trying to prove anything; that time is long past, if indeed it ever existed. But there must be more to it than just a cessation of the physical and mental suffering brought about by pushing my limits to such an extreme that I need no coach to goad or encourage me further. I could think of Aconcagua and other ascents again and again and again, bringing them to mind at any time to relish the thoughts, fanning embers into flame as a never-ending source of spiritual warmth.

Twenty minutes on the summit of the lofty mountain seemed like no time at all.

'Touch it and get back down,' Todd had said, but like the rest of us he could not resist a break.

The storm which had been approaching enveloped us within minutes of our leaving the summit. Loose rocks rapidly became slippery too, plastered by an inch of snow. Now our minds turned more to survival than success; the summit was behind, courted, won, and abandoned. Reaching the uppermost snowfield we went silently down amidst the dead cloth sounds of a place of snow. Fortunately, the wind did not rise much; for an hour and a half snow feathered down but visibility was always satisfactory and we had all retraced our steps to the chicken coop within plus or minus fifteen minutes of 4.15 p.m. And there we slumped.

Dan had several fingers frostbitten, and Ted and Ramon each had one finger affected; none of their injuries was serious.

Todd melted a little snow for us, but I was concerned that everyone should get more liquid inside them; lying inside the chicken coop I had plenty, for no one else came to get it and I drank a lot before it refroze. I called out that I would make some soup, or cook something more substantial if one person came to help, but there were no takers. That was the measure of how tired everyone was. For a while the screech of argument sounded between tents, about someone neglecting to cook, I believe, and then everyone was asleep before dark. I would have made the effort to cook had the task been mine that day, because others had bothered when the going was not easy. But we were at the edges of exhaustion, and those who ate made do with a few nuts and 'candies'. It would be downhill all the way now, so this was not as serious as it might have been.

John was eager to get down and we did not melt any snow prior to departure next morning. During a grumbling, swearing, squabbling-like-starlings, muttering descent Ted had to stop to 'go to the bathroom' and Todd told him to hurry up, saying, 'This weather could kill us,' and 'Hey, man, we're all hurting.' The weather was intermittently quite bad, and everyone was tired and a bit anxious, and most of all keen to get off the mountain.

At Camp 2 Todd got the stove going in the early afternoon and we experienced the delight of quenching intense thirst simply with water. The finest wine in the world could not have given more pleasure. At Camp 1 a couple of hours down Ramon cooked a meal, and everyone but Paul and I hurried down to base camp, where they arrived in darkness. My stumps had grown extremely painful, most likely through the cumulative effects of several days on the go. When Paul got home he had infectious hepatitis, a disease which he might already have contracted at this stage, which would account for his feeling unwell.

After a good night's rest Paul and I descended to base camp, met up with the others and went down the same day to the junction of Relinchos and Vacas valleys. My stumps felt even more painful, causing me to go slowly. Soon most of the others were just scurrying, coloured dots, mostly red and blue, and as the powerful words 'going home' drew them down they became black dots and then were too far away to be seen. The two Johns waited for me and accompanied me over the steep, loose and dangerous river banks; I was grateful for that, particularly because John P. had more reason than the rest of us to want to desert the mountain as fast as he could. He remained in good spirits and came out with a joke worthy of a mass groan when someone called out from a tent, 'Is it chilly outside?'

'No, it's Argentina you fool.'

Though I wished to go home too, I did not feel like many of the others, who resembled fugitives fleeing a plague area; no, I liked just to be there, and to look back and savour it all.

Next day the two Johns, Todd, Ted and Dan waited until I had completed the more dangerous section of the trail before all but John S. headed off quickly to the road. I did not like holding them up, but it could not be avoided; the stumps had had enough punishment, and now in the heat they let me know it. In the final stages I was so slow John S. went ahead several times to drop his rucksack and come back to take mine. It was an ignominious end to a highly satisfactory adventure, but I took comfort from the knowledge that I managed worst where speed was of no consequence.

Almost three days to get from Camp 1 down to the road. Pain was no stranger to me, and it was tough going, as ever when I covered long distances. This time will pass, was all I could tell myself; no, there was something else I could say, that it was worth it. Everyone felt the last stretch to be 'endless', but they could not have experienced the same enormous degree of relief which I did at the sight of the trees at the end of the valley. They waved in the wind like friends, and signalled, 'Here it all ends.'

Fernando waited with his pick-up, and hugged me the way they do there, before driving the few miles back. We stank, of course, after all that time without a wash; now we were back in civilisation the shower was a great attraction. We ate beef and salad at Fernando's, and drank beer and wine. We were bound together like other parties I had seen there, and we succeeded in capturing the elusive joy of life.

I bade goodbye to my new-found friends from the expedition, who travelled together to Santiago; I caught a bus to Mendoza and there was received warmly by the Sanchez family. I had for them a few small gifts and one of these, described by a stallholder as a mineral found high on a mountain near Aconcagua, caused an upset. I had given it to Mama, who proudly displayed it on a sideboard, when a heart surgeon friend of the family came to visit and Mama told him that the mineral came from a mountain.

'I think it came from a factory,' he said, and Mama looked close to tears. The substance may have been silicium, but I could not be sure, and a minute later it was pushed surreptitiously to the back of the sideboard, behind a framed picture. There was worse to follow, when one of the sons took a look at the mineral, which fell to bits as he handled it! I looked up the words for 'drop a bomb on the stall' and said them, and Mama laughed again. And next day some artificial flowers put matters completely right.

The surgeon had been to the Himalayas with an Argentinian expedition, and was interested in the exploits of others. He invited us across the street to his home for champagne with his family, so at about 11 p.m. we all trooped across there. He examined one of my fingers, affected by frostbite, and the lack of seriousness of the damage was summed up in the levity of his advice, which was, 'Three times a day dip it in a glass of wine. Then drink the wine.'

We returned to the Sanchez home at 1 a.m. and in the night-owl fashion of that country two more friends came to visit. It was one of those warm homes where friends and neighbours dropped in all the time.

Several letters from Judy had arrived while I was on Aconcagua. One told me that Sir Christopher Aston, who had worked hard as the voluntary Chairman of the International Year of Disabled People, in England, had died of cancer. He had helped me to get to Argentina by arranging for a very generous grant from the Charities Aid Foundation to be used partly towards the various forms of work I did with disabled people and partly towards expeditions. He had died very shortly after I arrived in Argentina.

In Buenos Aires, Hector was genuinely pleased with my success. He invited some friends around and cooked asado, and a radio ham friend of his got me to talk to a lady in Colombia who wanted to hear about the climb. Later, hams called up from Canada, Antigua and Ecuador to send their congratulations.

Out of courtesy to the local people in Argentina, especially to those who had helped, I did an interview with a Mendoza journalist. At home I got away without any interviews; I was put off by inaccuracies, wrong interpretations and exaggeration, and on this occasion I was not promoting any charity so no one would derive any benefit from publicity. (Once a magazine credited me with an ascent of a peak of 50,000 feet in the Alps; Everest reaches a height of 29,000 feet. At the other end of the scale, after getting up one high mountain I was reported as having climbed to a summit of twenty-two feet!) Judy and I liked the feeling of keeping the climbing private; yet there was an uncomfortable reservation that this was selfish, for many people had contributed in various ways and over many years towards this success. They deserved the story too. I have never entirely come to terms with publicity, for I vacillate between tolerance and dislike, qualified by the knowledge that sometimes publicity can be usefully employed to someone else's benefit. Some years back there is no doubt I found a small bit of publicity to be exciting, but that feeling wore off. Even in those early days I regarded publicity as incidental, and I would never seek it.

Were it not for events originating from outside the narrow world of climbing, this sequel to my one-legged ascent would have been perfect. But about two weeks after I arrived home, Argentina's troops invaded the Falkland Islands. (There had been a lot of talk about the Islands this year, and the threat of invasion had been high, obviously.) Clearly, staying there was likely to lead to heavy bloodshed, and stay they did. We all know about the tragic loss of life and injuries which followed. But the issues were complicated and this is not the place for what could be no more than a cursory examination of the rights and wrongs.

The last word, almost, I leave to John Perone, who wrote to me and sent two photographs, one of Ted and me, the other of me on my own.

'I have enclosed two photos. One is the two ugliest people I have ever seen. The second is the ugliest person on earth. Hope someday we can climb together again. Keep in touch.'

People, places and the accomplishment of dreams. I was very, very fortunate. Life would not be frittered away on the mountains, it would be well spent; events had proved this to be so once more.

# 9

# *Muztagh Ata, China*

24,757 feet

An American expedition led by John Cleare, an English photographer and mountaineer, was heading for Muztagh Ata in China in July and August 1982, so I wrote to see if I could be accepted, and received a favourable reply.

My opinion on publicity needed some revision, for a consultant to the Sony (UK) electronics organisation read a newspaper article about the International Year of Disabled People, noticed therein that I was hoping to climb Muztagh Ata, and suggested that Sony might come up with sponsorship. But first he wanted to meet and talk about the expedition in more detail. After a brief telephone conversation with him, I headed hastily to his office near the London Palladium. Being eager and twenty minutes early for our appointment, I waited in the Dog and Trumpet, and there a lavatory door jammed, leaving me hammering to attract rescue. The upshot was that I was late for the appointment, but this was not held against me and the interview went as I hoped it would. Shortly afterwards a cheque for over £4,000 arrived; this was sufficient to pay the high cost of my participation in the expedition. Various costly elements, of the order of a pound per kilometre for lorry transport, about £600 to insure a liaison officer and an interpreter, and long air flights within China, resulted in expenses being five times those of a similar venture in Nepal. Yet, despite my gratitude, it was only fair that I pointed out that I would not allow sponsorship to influence my mountaineering judgement; I would not climb one foot higher than I would if I had paid for it all myself.

John Cleare did have some misgivings about my being on the trip, mostly because there were long distances to be covered on soft snow; we would need to ski, or accept a higher risk of failure through being on foot. Even for able-bodied people the walking option was considered gruelling; in 1947 Tilman and Shipton failed to make the summit on foot, and if two hard and proven expeditioners like them had failed, what chance did I have? In *Two Mountains and a River*, Tilman tells of the snow's 'vile consistency' and said that long hours of cold and fatigue led to their giving up. From his account it was clear they had not paid great attention to acclimatisation, either. Five earlier expeditions had failed on foot. John wanted everyone on his expedition to use skis and he was worried about my lack of experience in this respect. However, he was straight with me and was prepared to be flexible and to treat me as a special case who would work out his own best methods. For ascent, everyone else would have skins on their skis. Originally made from animal fur but nowadays artificial, skins grip the snow very effectively and prevent backward sliding, and the pile lies in such a way that the skis slide easily forward.

In order to augment my meagre skiing experience prior to the expedition, I went to the Dachstein glacier in Austria, in July 1982. Here one can ski year-round at about 9,000 feet. On a pair of hired skis I set off on the twisting cross-country track, and I learned quickly. What I learned I did not like, for it was soon evident that though on uphill slopes and on the level I could cope, going downhill was a different and wobbly procedure. Downhill skiing on one real leg, assisted by small outrigger skis fixed to crutches, is easier than most people believe, but for the double leg amputee it is another matter. The single leg amputee discards the artificial limb and relies on the good leg but, obviously enough, if you have two artificial legs you can't follow suit. It is not a question of lack of determination. I reached the conclusion that after a great deal of training over many months or years a double leg amputee might cope on gentle to moderate slopes, but the risk of injury from downhill skiing on high mountains would be far too great, and the consequences of injury were likely to be dire. Also, the victim might not be the only one to suffer, for companions might be forced to take extra risks and fail on their climb through having to divert their energies to a rescue. Even on the way up Muztagh Ata there would be much traversing to be done above cliffs and crevasses, perhaps on ice, and skiing competence was essential; no, I could not justify going on skis. So was this a reason why I should not join the expedition? Perhaps, but there might be a solution: how about snowshoes for ascent and a sledge made from skis and a rucksack frame for descent? I made a sledge and further strengthened the contraption with a crutch tied across as a strut and footrest, and from two hundred feet up a slope which was beyond my skiing ability I launched myself off. I picked up speed very rapidly and dug my ice axe in the snow as an effective brake. It seemed a better method for me, but I knew the proof of the pudding could only be in the eating, on the mountain, under expedition conditions.

Nearly twenty-four hours of air travel put us on 23 July 1982 in China's capital, Peking (known also as Beijing). The concrete buildings of the airport might have been any modern airport anywhere in the world, and we went through the typical sausage-machine of baggage reclaim carousels, immigration and customs. Then John held up a card bearing characters saying Chinese Mountaineering Association (was he holding it upside-down, we wondered?) and their two representatives stepped forward and greeted us. They had laid on transport for the one hour drive into the city, the first of many acts which cocooned us in this land where lack of the language could have been a great bother. The rest of the team, nine of them, arrived two days later, and we were all taken under the wing of the Chinese Mountaineering Association, who provided an interpreter and a liaison officer, and made hotel and transport arrangements for us, among many other things.

Our accommodation was satisfactory, in large and comfortably furnished, air-conditioned rooms, usually with a settee, armchairs, two or four beds, a table or desk, and always there was a big, brightly-painted thermos flask of hot water, cups, and a tin of tea leaves. Though knives and forks were available in dining-rooms, we mastered the use of chopsticks to tuck into course after course of fish, mutton, kebabs, duck and many cold meats, nuts, mushrooms, boiled eggs, fried cabbage, egg plant, bamboo shoots, rice, peppers, green beans, steamed bread and lobster. There was no shortage of beer, and most meals were rounded off with melon.

What we saw in and around Peking accorded with photographs and descriptions, as if the country had been showered with traditional symbols of Chinese style: straw hats and sunflowers, pony carts of melons, sedate cyclists on three-and-a-half seemingly identical black bicycles for a city population not greatly in excess of twice that number (in Holland there is one bicycle per eleven people and in Britain the ratio is about one to thirty-three); brown, blue and grey trousers and jackets, but bright skirts and dresses too, paddy fields, tall, straight trees, pagodas, chopsticks, rice and noodles and hundreds of varieties of food, modern and simple four-to-ten-storey apartment blocks, wooden scaffolding, a few packed buses, many drab green lorries, the red star, portraits of Chairman Mao, posters exhorting good behaviour and very small families, and even some advertising consumer goods such as radios and television sets. People are placid and civil, and, as everyone knows, there are lots of people. Yet Peking has none of the teeming feel of many cities because the streets are wide and there are few cars, and though China's enormous total of about one thousand million souls amounts to one quarter of the Earth's population they do have the third biggest country in which to spread out. I've heard tales of overcrowded homes and poverty but saw no evidence of this myself, and there seemed to be no slum areas like those in India or Peru. My short stay in civilised areas was sufficient to give me only a cursory impression, however, and leaves me unable to comment in any depth on life in China. Prices everywhere are fixed, so there is no haggling, nor any tipping in restaurants or elsewhere, as this practice is looked upon as corrupt, and akin to what we term bribery.

Anyone who travelled from the USA or Britain to Peking without visiting the Great Wall would be regarded locally as somewhat weird, even rude, and the Chinese Mountaineering Association had left time in our itinerary for a visit. Built two centuries before the birth of Christ (sections were constructed as early as 770 BC) the 3,600-mile (5,800-km) construction stands about twenty six feet (7.9 m) high and nineteen feet (5.8 m) wide at the top. Its purpose was to keep out nomadic marauders from the north but the Wall was not entirely effective since no height could prevent bribery of guards. We were not disappointed with what we saw; when you remember the length of the Wall, rising and dipping and weaving over green mountains (I pictured it as four times the distance I walked from John o' Groats to Land's End) it is impossible not to be impressed.

There was time, too, to see the Imperial Palace, known commonly to Westerners as the Forbidden City because ordinary people were not formerly permitted entry. Graceful names themselves convey something of the elegance of the great buildings there: Gate of Supreme Harmony, Palace of Heavenly Purity, Palace of Earthly Tranquillity, Gate of Divine Prowess.

But we were here to climb. Peking airport, from which we flew westwards on 27th July, had recently witnessed its first hijacking, perpetrated by four men armed with knives. Their cause I do not know, but they were overpowered by angry passengers on the plane, and a few weeks later were executed.

Our progress westwards took place on two consecutive days, on two flights of about three hours each, the first in a jet and the next in a rattling twin-engined prop plane, over brown desert. On the second flight the air-conditioning system was simple: everyone was given a fan. Between flights at the city of Urumchi, at the airport we happened to meet some of an expedition of eleven Austrians who had attempted Muztagh Atà by a route which was a little easier than our proposed line. Three of them (or was it five, as stated in a later newspaper report?) had reached the top, and several had been halted by the altitude. One had become very ill and was in hospital. The Austrians were not the only expeditioners we met at the oasis factory city of Urumchi, for we also came across an unfortunate group of rafters who had come all the way from the USA to discover that the river they intended descending, and for which privilege they had paid a large fee to the Chinese authorities, was dry!

The second flight brought us to ancient Kashgar city, by which time we had flown about 2,250 miles (c. 3,620 km) from Peking back towards England; John and I had back-tracked almost the width of this huge country and our companions from the USA had completed a journey almost half way round the world. We stepped from the aircraft into a hot early afternoon in a land which in some ways seemed a thousand years behind the times. Adults and children in Muslim dress rode two-wheeled carts drawn by diminutive yet strong and resigned-looking donkeys, between mud-walled houses set along irrigation ditches lined by poplar. In other ways progress had touched the place, bringing in good roads and a few motor vehicles, including tractors, and lots of bicycles and concrete buildings.

Casual tourists were not permitted in Kashgar, so our rare-bird presence created great interest among the local inhabitants. They clustered around in polite, curious, smiling hundreds whenever we stopped in the city. Whether we were in a vehicle or not, we were mobbed in a respectful, orderly way as knots of where-the-hell-did-all-these-people-appear-from? spectators grew tight and vast. Yet when we were on foot they never pushed in on us, and our eager audience would swarm around, a step or two away, as we rich strangers moved. When in our stationary minibus there was a slightly menacing undercurrent as dozens of faces were pressed to the windows, like we were Martians on display in a glass cage and they were not entirely sure of us. Nor we of them.

We toured the city in a minibus which was driven in the customary horn-blaring fashion of all vehicles there. Cyclists, pedestrians and donkey-cart drivers took no notice, because the horns are always blaring, but we never came across a driver who saw the ineffectiveness of the method as any reason to desist. The abject poverty of India was absent, and the place looked quite well-off as far as the basic necessities of life were concerned. There was no shortage of vegetables, fruit, grains, bread, cakes, spices, cloth, shoes, boots, lamps, knives and other ironmongery, and there was quite a lot of meat available. Most of the trading took place from the shelter of little roadside and marketplace stalls; and scribes sat outside the post office to assist those who could not write, or who could not cope with Chinese characters. There was less of the uniform Chinese dress in evidence, for the Kirghiz and Uighur people there have retained traditional dress of bright skirts and blouses and headscarves for the women, and more sombre trousers, jackets and shirts for men. In Kashgar, as in Urumchi, our accommodation consisted of guest house rooms inside a compound, and meals were always rich and satisfying. Bathrooms were shared with local residents: large frogs which hopped around the floors.

From Kashgar we set off on an early-morning chartered bus ride to try our fortunes on Muztagh Ata. The gravel road soon left behind the trees, mud buildings and sunflowers, and took us out into flat desert spotted with occasional oases, before running us along parallel to and in sight of the Silk Road. This formerly important trade route stretched about 4,350 miles (7,000 km) from eastern China to the Mediterranean and was used to transport the products of silkworm cocoons to Greece before the birth of Christ.

For hours we bumped up a deep canyon road, where gangs of men and women worked to counter the ravages of sliding rubble, rockfall and river. A hundred and more miles and nine hours went by, and rock walls, rock walls, rock walls, and high snowy peaks, and a huge, shallow, silted lake surrounded by sand dunes, in a broad valley. We were drowsy from the heat. Then someone shouted. 'There she is!'

Our view across flat green pastures was of a massive domed mountain with a benign appearance, but no mountain of close to 25,000 feet – Muztagh Ata is 24,757 feet high – can be climbed easily, as we were to discover. For all of us, bar John, this would be the highest summit we had attempted, and it was nearly 2,000 feet higher than Aconcagua. Soft snow and altitude would make it hard, while crevasses and bad weather and altitude sickness would be the biggest risks.

We drove on for a while and pitched camp on a meadow at 12,500 feet, in sight of Muztagh Ata, the Ice Mountain Father. The full name is probably incorrect, as it is likely that the mountain was known simply as Muztagh, or Ice Mountain. The longer name is said to have originated when an explorer asked a local resident the name of this lofty peak and was told, 'Muztagh Ata', the 'Ata', or 'Father', being appended as a term of respect to the explorer himself. But he got it wrong in his account so from shortly before the twentieth century the wrong name was reported, and perpetuated in subsequent documents. The mountain's isolation in treeless grassland succeeded by almost barren foothills made it look huge, as indeed it was, and it appeared every bit as awesome as Kongur, twenty-five miles away and 568 feet (173 m) higher.

Several dozen Kirghiz people lived locally in tents and rectangular flat-roofed, mud-brick houses in the vicinity of two large lakes, the Karakol Lakes. Large audiences congregated to watch us.

On the evening of our first full day at the meadow camp, a day occupied with sorting and packing food and equipment, the leader of a five-man expedition from Colorado appeared with his interpreter. They were attempting Muztagh Ata.

'Got two missing,' he said. 'They went for the summit three days ago. Should have got back the same day.'

Being unacclimatised, there was nothing we could do but offer qualified optimism and sympathy, some food and beer, before the two men went on their way in a truck flagged down on the nearby road. They would report what had happened, to the authorities. They had talked of hiring a plane for a search, and someone had voiced our scepticism about the possibility and practicality of such a proposal in this remote corner of China. It would have been preferable for at least two of them to have remained high and searched, weather and rations permitting, but the altitude really had drained them and I could to some extent understand how they felt. Next day we met the remainder of their expedition and learned that one of the missing pair had turned up, with considerable frostbite injuries after two bivouacs. The companion who had reached the summit with him, he said, had disappeared in bad visibility on the descent, and was presumed to have fallen over a cliff or into a crevasse. They achieved two out of five on the summit and lost one of them. So much for Muztagh Ata's benign look;

it was just like any other big mountain. From a diary we found later it was clear that on setting up a camp at 21,000 feet the Coloradans had not been in good shape physically, and in consequence their morale was low. Three of the five said they could not go on, and two made the questionable decision to try to climb 4,000 feet to the summit in one push. In the Alps that height gain is commonly made in a day, but there are few climbers who can manage it safely above 20,000 feet, and they should be acclimatised and feel strong before setting out.

A week later, back at home in the flat we had bought recently (a nice place which Judy loved and had waited for for a long time) someone told her about a newspaper report concerning a man who had died on Muztagh Ata. His age was put at forty-one years, which was my age, and though the name reported was not mine she had a slight nagging doubt that the name was wrong. I had always impressed on her that she should not put too much trust in newspaper versions concerned with climbing, and that it was highly improbable that any newspaper would fail to mention my lack of legs if an accident befell me. Though she knew this to be true the death report reminded her that we were undertaking a serious venture. She had three worrying weeks to face.

On 2 August we laid out our luggage before sixteen ruminant, reeking, twin-humped Bactrian camels which continued grazing from a kneeling position while loading went on. A wide-nostrilled, looking-down-the-nose attitude gave them a haughty appearance. After loading, they ambled a sure-footed way through areas of grass, then dusty sand, then rocky slopes, to our base camp at 14,500 feet (4,440 m). The beasts groaned and snorted and squeaked complaints, but went obediently where they were led; small wonder, for each had a piece of rope attached to a hole in the nose and tied to the camel in front or held by the man at the head of a three or four camel column. Capable of carrying over 300 pounds (135 kg) each, they were a valuable link in the chain intended to get us to the summit, and saved us several days of carrying.

We settled in a grassy, stony depression by a stream, at the foot of the west flank of Muztagh Ata. In a day we could have walked into the USSR. Fourteen black or black and white yaks grazed quietly there by our camp. Yak: 'Long-haired humped grunting ox' says one dictionary descriptively. Tilman and Shipton planned to use one such animal to carry equipment and food to base camp, and Tilman extolled their virtues at some length; he even listed as an advantage the fact that the yak's short legs and rapid steps give the rider the comfortable though false impression of getting somewhere quickly! He went on to say that their particular animal must have been the exception which proved the rule, or like all mountaineers yaks have their off days, for he 'very sensibly struck and sat down at the very first hint of what was expected of him.'

One other animal inhabited the environs of the camp, a shaggy, black-coated sheep which had walked up with the camels. Like another of its kind which had gone the same way a day or two earlier, it was destined for the stewpot; at least, that's what we thought, but the creature had other ideas, got loose from its tether, and escaped for ever in land where the grazing was good.

After the first six failed attempts on Muztagh Ata, a combined Russian and Chinese expedition made the first ascent in 1956. The second success went to the Chinese in 1960, and one of the participants in it was Mr Qui Yin-Hua, who later joined a successful Everest expedition; he was our liaison officer. Mr Qui had no toes as a result of his climb on Everest, but gave the impression that he felt he had received good value in exchange for his extremities. Since the Chinese ascent Muztagh Ata had received no more human attentions until an American ascent in 1980, when foreign climbers were permitted into the area for the first time since 1949. In 1981 two expeditions, one American and one Canadian, put members on the top, and the Austrians I mentioned had three (or five) there. No Briton had succeeded.

The performances of the Austrians and the Coloradans had influenced our thinking and brought about a revision of our opinion of the mountain. It was not going to be as easy as the earlier American and Canadian reports had portrayed, and the sense of John's plan to have four camps above base had been reinforced by what we had heard recently. The trend is towards alpine-style ascents in which climbers do not follow the up-and-down, up-and-down pattern of establishing camps at intervals, but instead carry everything and gain altitude without ever dropping back. There is a lot to be said for this approach of breaking new ground every day, but on a very big peak it may allow insufficient time for acclimatisation. Storms rage in climbing teacups about the two methods; there need be no bitter argument for the different philosophies of style can co-exist. On our first evening at base camp John emphasised that to put just one person on top was success; that was not what most of us had in mind, for each carried strong summit ambitions in his or her heart.

Next day. We must carry to Camp 1. Loads had been prepared the night before. My load, a tent, food and skis. Straightforward going on a steep slope of stones and dirt, but oh, the altitude! And the sun sucking the liquid out of us. Janet Jensen, one of the two women on the trip, carried on for a long time despite frequent vomiting, but was eventually persuaded to turn back. The rest of us dumped our loads as planned at 16,700 feet (5,100 m), after a climb of between three and four hours, then set about laying out flat stones in a crazy paving base for tents. With a couple of tents up, we scurried down to base to eat and relax. The early days are hard at altitude; then it gets worse as you go higher.

Next day was similar: the haul amid small five-petalled flowers like primroses, others that might have been buttercups, then the pull up loose dirt and stones. Three carries to Camp 1 were required, but vomiting and stomach pains and back pains and diarrhoea disqualified me from the third. This was worrying because we were due to go up and occupy Camp 1 that day. From there the others would make three more excursions upwards, the last of these to occupy Camp 2. Two or three days of sickness could leave me weakened and, worse, I would fall behind in our acclimatisation programme. Our interpreter, Mr Su, fell ill too with a similar ailment to mine. He was a tall, slim and remarkable man aged thirty who, wishing to visit Urumchi from his home in Hanchow, had decided to equip his bicycle with a large water container and pedal his way there. The fact that he had over 3,000 miles to cover did not deter him, and in fifty-seven days he cycled across fertile plain and desert to Urumchi. There he soon found himself employment as an English interpreter with the Chinese Mountaineering Association, and this in itself was no mean feat because, during the cultural Revolution, he had been sentenced to 'primitive work' rather than study, and his English was largely self-taught. He'd climbed his form of mountains against the odds, and we could not fail to respect this man. As well as the liaison officer and interpreter, the Chinese Mountaineering Association provided us with a cook for base camp.

The three Chinese personnel at base camp looked after me solicitously for two days. I dozed a lot, and dreamed that I had gone home for a rest and only when there did I realise that I could not travel back in time to join the others. The dream felt so real and the feeling of panic and disappointment hung over me when I awoke because in truth my chances were shrinking while the illness lasted. Two days with hardly any food was poor preparation for what might lie ahead.

Two days saw me right, and Mr Su insisted on coming with me to Camp 1 to carry my crampons, sleeping bag and water bottles. We had been going for an hour when a figure appeared on the skyline. It picked its way down the stones and turned into Don Brown, a doctor, our oldest member at the age of sixty-four, and still very fit. Within the previous few years he had climbed Aconcagua and Mt McKinley. Don was the only other person trying the mountain on snowshoes, and he had some devastating news for me.

'It's no good. It can't be done on snowshoes.'

'Why's that?'

'You just slip back on the slopes. It's too steep and too soft.'

'Good gracious me, what a shame,' I said – or words to that effect.

I stood on the stone slope with Don just three or four feet above as the news sank in, and I remembered that his snowshoes covered twice the area mine did and were therefore much more efficient. The Coloradan leader's verdict had been that it was virtually impossible without skis, owing to the soft going. After getting on the expedition and receiving Sony's generous sponsorship I was going to look silly, because I had been too ambitious. Any mountain of this altitude would force failure on to a large proportion of experienced, able-bodied climbers; I had not researched the route sufficiently and had not paid enough attention to how I might get up the soft snows. Hope had been allowed to lead, where soundly based experience should have been my guide. Don had made a mistake too, or had been given the wrong guidance, had recognised this, and had reached his decision: he was going home.

My conduct was different because I wanted to salvage anything I could from this personal fiasco. I would at least carry as much as I could as high as possible, and share a little of the victory of anyone who reached our objective. So I headed up to Camp 1 and soon met another descending figure, this time a haggard Ted Mayer, with whom I had climbed Aconcagua earlier in the year. He was ill and was therefore descending to base camp, and it sounded like he had the same bug as I had had. He told us that of ten people who had set out the day before from Camp 1 to Camp 2 at 19,100 feet only six had made the full distance. The others had to leave their loads part way. (So what chance was there for me? I couldn't help wondering.) At base camp Ted became so ill he was unable to ingest even water, so Don put him on an intravenous drip.

At Camp 1 the others descended from their second carry to Camp 2. The following day they would occupy that camp, but I agreed with John that it would be premature for me to stay there because I would be gaining altitude too quickly and risking altitude sickness. After carrying next day I would have to return to sleep at Camp 1 before carrying again the next day. 'To be quite honest,' John said, 'if you get to Camp 2 I don't think you'll get any further.'

He was not being unnecessarily negative. He had seen what was ahead. John had supported my case for an attempt at the mountain even in the face of someone who had failed the year before and who had on the basis of that experience maintained it was absolutely beyond me. When I first planned to climb in the Alps, John had written me a very encouraging letter, and I knew he had an open mind.

It looked bad for me, but hope was not entirely extinguished. If the snow froze hard enough during the night and I started very early and reached Camp 2, I might still be in the running. I had been ill and was less well acclimatised and the ascent of the next 2,400 feet (730 m) had stopped four out of ten of them, including the only one on snowshoes, but if I did not make a good showing on the next carry it was clear that my hopes could be extinguished altogether.

Now I was committed to snowshoes because I had left my ski boots at base camp. Without them it was not possible to wear the skis, and I could not afford another day descending and re-ascending to and from base.

A three-quarter moon lit the chilly way and I was off two hours or more before the others. China has no time zones, just the same time throughout the whole vast country, but making an allowance of two and a half hours for our being so far west of Peking my departure was at the equivalent of 4 a.m. The early start up a rib of small, sharp rocks got me at dawn on to easy-angled ice where crampons were necessary; firm snow slopes followed. There was no more rock between here and the summit. By 10 a.m. the first sliver of sunlight flashed over the mountain which stood ahead of me; the orb appeared rapidly to banish blue shadows and soften the snow. Sun, you're softening *my* snow. Go and put on a cloak of cloud, there's a good sun.

An hour later I was sinking to the knee and forced to resort to the snowshoes. With them strapped on all went well for a few minutes on level snow, and then came a gentle slope of thirty degrees. I went at it, but the front edges of the snowshoes broke through the crust and I floundered again at knee depth. The baskets (rounds, like those on ski sticks) on my crutches sank a foot, two feet, sometimes so deep that my hands were buried in the snow. Many a time a step up resulted in collapsed snow and I would drop back to where I had been. Don said it was impossible; for twenty minutes I fought to rise forty feet and I knew that at that rate I would have to give up and accept what he had said. On top of that, *if* I reached Camp 2 John doubted I would manage what followed. Was it worth this unequal struggle?

I stumbled on, up to the knees in snow, and dragged the big feet out, and went in up to the wrists and sank occasionally to the top of one thigh and battled to get that damned leg out and then went in to crotch level on both legs. Oh for a rock ridge or face, quite steep, so effort would be rewarded with height gain! Oh for some ice! When the crutches were laid parallel to the snow like they were skis they did not sink so deep, no more than a foot, and that helped a little, but the altitude would not let me fight all the way up in conditions like these. I was virtually crawling much of the time and that rate of progress was out of the question and in any case this would lead to frostbitten fingers. It was not the sort of thing that fighting could overcome; no amount of determination would bring success, unless I risked stepping from the firm land of judgement into the mire of foolhardiness. Only a man who could walk on water had any chance here without skis. It would be grossly wrong to jeopardise the lives of the others by becoming an exhausted, frostbitten, altitude sick casualty requiring rescue, and even if rescue proved safe it would be selfish to risk adversely affecting their chances of success.

Despair was close upon me, but had not yet seized an unbreakable hold. Try taking the slope at a gentler angle, I suggested to myself, and started on the first zig of what I hoped might be a lengthy series of zig-zags. The snowshoes sank only half as deeply. Oh joy! For the time being I could carry on. Soon the slope eased off to almost level ground and the snow became firm in most places.

There was a crevassed area which could not be avoided because the crevasses came in from the right towards a rock cliff falling away for two thousand feet on the left, and I had to go up a snow ramp in between. This ramp not only sloped down towards me, but was also canted down from right to left, from crevasses towards cliff. The latter gradient was such that anyone who slipped might slide over the cliff edge. Where the ramp narrowed to a hundred feet between the crevasses and the cliff, some of the skiers had been quite scared, particularly on descent.

It was a true Scylla and Charybdis. The higher one went up the right side of the ramp, the greater the crevasse danger. Reducing the crevasse problems involved keeping closer to the big drop; my choice was to keep quite low there and trust to the ice axe pick on one crutch to brake me if I slipped. In some places it was preferable to wear crampons, for there were intermittent patches of ice or hard snow, but mostly it was so porridgy or fluffy that snowshoes reduced the possibility of breaking through into crevasses, of which there were some even low down the ramp near the cliff. Before venturing further I consciously rehearsed in my mind what I would do to hurl the pick into the snow or ice if I slipped: an unarrested slide would have me over the edge in five seconds. A high level of desire for the objective pushed fear, to a great extent, to the back of my mind.

Spikes on my crutches gave considerable security and as long as I kept my eyes open the crevasses did not seem to be too much of a menace. By looking up the ramp rightwards, often I could see where the wider part of the split in the ice showed, being too wide to be bridged by snow, and this gave a clue to the line. On the lower side there was sometimes evidence of the horrible hole in the form of a slight concave trough in the snow. Seven or eight crevasses which were big enough to be dangerous were identified and I went further down towards the cliff to avoid them, or prodded with the crutches and found a firm place to cross, or took a big step-cum-leap across.

In fifteen minutes the snow ramp took me up to where I could rise rightwards and away from the cliff, and the crevasse hazards grew less. Having being going for seven hours I needed to get to Camp 2 soon in order to leave myself enough energy for the descent. Crevasses would be less well bridged then because of the sun's work, and I did not want to go doddering down in a weary state. My pace was falling rapidly through prolonged exertion at such an altitude. Several people had said the trudge to Camp 2 was exhausting, and indeed four had not completed the distance at the first try, so I had a very real fear that I might spot the camp at such a distance that a retreat was the only way. However, I topped a rise and there were the two tents, only fifteen minutes away. I knew then a slender chance still existed that I would go for the top.

Colin and Bob, two doctors who had teamed up and climbed together, arrived at Camp 2 shortly after me. I got the impression that they were very aware of the threat which hangs over all doctors on expeditions: that their chances might be destroyed if they had to attend to a patient over a prolonged period.

Having constructed my sledge I started down, meeting Steve McKinney, the deputy leader, then John, then Grim, Johan and Mary, toiling under huge loads in the heat of the day. Grim, whose real name was Jim Wilson, was a forty-four year old psychology and economics teacher, tall and very strong on his quite spindly legs. He proved to be a reliable and considerae companion, and his good manners caused him to draw apart if others of us became too riotous. Johan Hultin was fifty-seven years old, a runner who kept himself very fit, a wine-loving pathologist who came originally from Sweden before going to live in the USA. I did not have many opportunities to spend time in his company but he seemed to have hidden depths, and though he was slow he looked the sort of plodder who was a likely candidate to be by far the oldest person to climb Muztagh Ata. Mary Laucks was a physics student on the way to a PhD and at twenty-six was our youngest member. She was broad-shouldered and strong, but not so heavy as to prevent her being also a fast long-distance runner. The other woman in the party, Janet Jensen, was an easy-going, smiling accountant, a resident of Honolulu. She travelled extensively, was a pilot and sub-aqua diver, and was at ease with the world because she was at ease with herself.

The sledge worked quite well where the snow was steep, but would go only straight downhill. With no means of steering, this style of transport was of limited use because our route traversed a lot; straight downhill would only take me over the cliff in the upper section between Camps 1 and 2. Still, I managed half a dozen exhilarating runs of up to two hundred yards. I regretted not having brought up my ski boots from base, but my boats were burnt now. Even if I did not risk downhill skiing, ascent on skis and descent by sledge and on foot was looking like the best procedure for me.

At one pointed as I dragged the sledge on a rope behind me across a slope one leg went all the way into a crevasse. With the crutches I was able to prod about and find its line, and roll clear.

Janet had been ill and had not carried to Camp 2 that day, but she intended to go with me next day. At 5 a.m. it was snowing, at 6 a.m. snowing still, and the sky did not become clearer until 10 a.m. The weather was unsettled and the snow would be soft, so we waited a further day and started out at 5.45 a.m. There followed over nine disgruntled hours of thrashing a way up a snow cover much worse than on the previous journey. Despite the early start there was only one short slope where crampons could be used. The rest was just slope after slope of grunts and misery and gasping. On skis, Janet managed much better than I.

At Camp 2 we learned that Bob, Colin and Steve had set up Camp 3 at 21,000 feet (6,400 m) the day before and returned for a day off, while John, Grim and Johan went up. The latter trio arrived back at 7.45 p.m. and one look at their drawn faces told all.

'It's very serious above here, man,' John said.

In poor visibility he had not found Camp 3 so the loads had been dumped (very near Camp 3, as it transpired) and the descent by compass had called for a lot of skill from John. There was talk of awful crevasses and steep ice, and though he did not say it I knew John felt I should not go higher.

'Looks like this may be as high as I go,' I offered, to make it easier for him.

'It would help to have someone in support here.'

I hardly needed to ask my next question.

'You think I shouldn't go any further?'

'Yes. It's serious.'

There was no argument. I had said all along that I would stop if we thought it wise. I could still help by getting breakfast and melting snow to fill water bottles for the six who had elected to go on, Bob, Colin, Johan, Grim, Steve and John. And it might prove useful to have someone rested and standing by at Camp 2, as John had suggested, in case someone was ill or injured.

So I mother-henned a few hours away next day, watched the lucky ones go, and wished I was going too. At the same time I knew if I went higher the soft snow would probably defeat me.

Mary had a bad headache, but her appetite had not failed. She and Janet planned to descend the next day, but their plans were about to be influenced by a third party; in the early evening Ted arrived, glazed-eyed.

'Oh, God, that was tough!' he said in a breaking voice, as he slumped into a tent. 'Janet, can you undo my laces?'

He had been unable to eat for three days and had had his fluids via an intravenous drip, so it was not surprising that he had found it hard between 1 and 2.

'You're not aiming to go higher, are you?' I asked him.

'I'm gonna do it!'

'We'll see. Right now I don't think you should.'

'I know when to turn back.'

'I think that time's come.'

Janet joined in and we tried to impress on Ted that he had been ill and was behind in acclimatisation, that he would have to cross crevasses alone, that we would not know if he met up with the others or not, that Camp 3 was not easily found, that there might be no tracks to follow because of the wind filling them in, that if he became ill some if not all of the others might have to descend with him, and that John had said Ted should not climb any higher. Throughout all this Ted was unbending in his resolution to carry on. He was certainly not short on determination.

Next day when I enquired how he was Ted said, 'I feel great. This will be a rest day. The altimeter shows bad weather.'

We all got together in one tent for a pow-wow. Janet, Mary and I repeated our concern about Ted climbing but he said he was going and why didn't we help by carrying part of his load for him? We said we would not do anything to encourage him and the debate heated up. Mary began to take on an angry, hawklike appearance and to me looked like she was going to give Ted a nasty pecking. Mary and Janet wanted to descend but Janet suggested they might wait one more day in case Ted got ill and needed to be helped down. He had hardly eaten, and vomited during the day. Janet's consideration for Ted was all the more admirable because she had herself vomited and brought up blood during the night. I favoured her going down that day, but she made her decision and stayed, as did Mary. In any case the wind got up.

'I am frightened of the steep bit above the cliff,' Janet confided to me. 'I keep thinking about it, especially at night.'

When you are not well the character of any mountain changes for the worse in your eyes. Muztagh Ata, though in truth neutral, now appeared nasty to Janet.

'I can rope you down,' I said. 'No problem.'

'It's amusing,' Janet said. 'Here you have two helpless females and a sick man and you have to guide them down.'

'Helpless' was a bit strong, but as the day wore on Mary's condition gave greater cause for concern because her headache continued despite sleep and aspirin. That was a bad sign, and her appeite deteriorated.

After Ted had vomited I asked him again if he was going down the next day.

'I'll decide in the morning.'

Though he insisted he would climb, Ted didn't eat supper, and looked grey and ill when I took him a drink.

The night was very windy and I grew concerned that the opportunity for descent had not been grasped at the right time the day before, when there had been no doubt everyone could get along on their own two feet. Anyone who became worse through the altitude could deteriorate very rapidly towards a critical condition. But Ted's presence had complicated the issue.

Friday the 13th dawned.

'Have you got an oven in there?' Ted shouted to me above the wind, from his tent. It took a while for it to sink in that this was not a joke, and he meant a stove. Only rarely did he get a word wrong like that and remind us of his German origins. I passed him the stove and he boiled some water for drinks and cereals. I felt better disposed towards him and asked if he was going down.

'I'm under no pressure.'

This non-committal reply swayed my decision towards seeing Janet and Mary down first. When the wind dropped, around noon, I set off a little ahead of them, down a gently sloping snowfield. Janet and Mary were worried about icy conditions and soon removed their skis, and Mary, troubled by cold feet, hurried on ahead without a rope. I waited where the crevasses lay close to the cliff edge.

'You want a rope here, Janet?'

'I'm scared shitless.'

I took that to mean yes, set up a belay with an anchor known as a 'dead-man' (a metal plate hammered into the snow), an ice axe and a crutch, tied the rope on her and fed it out as she descended a rope's length. After four or five more rope lengths she was on safe ground, half an hour below Camp 2. She joined Mary and they waved goodbye.

Now, what about Ted? I could not know, until I had almost completed the ascent back to Camp 2, that there was nothing to do about him. Just before that camp came into view I looked up and saw a dark figure moving slowly up a snow ridge, three hundred feet above. Ted had 'summit fever', no mistake about that.

Should I follow? I came down on the side of no, because by the time I packed he would be an hour or so ahead. Deciding what to take would be a problem because I did not know what Ted had in the way of food and fuel and stove. The snow would be soft. I didn't like the look of the weather either, with dark cloud swelling in from the south west; it would help no one if we became separated. Above all, the others planned to go for the summit in two days and we could not acclimatise properly nor sensibly ascend nearly 6,000 feet in that time. John had had a bad barking cough and it was quite likely that one or two of the six would be forced to descend and could report whether Ted had found Camp 3. If he had not, then someone would have to go to look for him, if enough fuel and rations remained. I would be fresh.

On Friday 13th and Saturday 14th I sat at the camp on the bottom edge of the huge, tilted snow bowl, and wondered what was going on high on the mountain. I tried to sort out in my mind how I would cope with the disappointment of my failure; if they all failed, too, it would be even worse. It was something I would have to face, though, if I kept pushing my limits on serious expeditions on mountains of this scale; to aim for the extreme of what you can achieve is to court disappointment at the same time. I could not complain about the results of previous expeditions, for on each occasion I had been successful in one way or another. Of course, I did now and then wonder if there was any twist of fate which might result in my having a shot at the summit, but it would need a miracle now. The dream recurred, about going home and being too late to get back, and with my hopes dashed the awakening was as forlorn as the dream itself.

The dead Coloradan's cassette player and some tapes had been left in one of the tents, and I played the theme music from *Chariots of Fire*, which finished with a resounding version of Jerusalem. At first, the words 'Bring me my chariot of fire!' had the deepest effect, for now there was no way I could reach the summit, save through that unforeseeable miracle. But my mood lifted, for the music had a profound effect in such high, beautiful and lonely surroundings. Now I knew better what people meant when they said sometimes that they were inspired, often in an unconnected area of life like work or health or grief, by a runner or a writer, a musician or a mountaineer. If my chance came, I felt able to draw on better reserves.

At 1 p.m. on 15th August Steve skied rapidly down, forth and back, forth and back, steeply across the slope above Camp 2. (He reckoned he did not exceed forty miles an hour!) Why would he descend? Was he ill? Had there been an accident? He drew to a halt by the tents.

'Hi, Steve. You seen Ted?'

'Yes. He missed Camp 3 and spent the night out. There was a big argument with John who said he should go down and Ted said he was going to solo it.'

Steve unfolded the story. While carrying from Camp 3 to Camp 4 they had come across Ted sleeping in the snow, six hundred feet above Camp 3. At first they had thought him to be the missing Coloradan.

'Hello, Robert,' Ted had greeted Steve.

'I'm Steve. Camp 3 is six hundred feet below here. Down there.' He pointed it out. 'You go down there and rest. We'll see you when we get back from this carry.'

'OK, Robert.'

On their return from Camp 4 Ted was still lying in the snow so he was escorted to Camp 3, where he was not made welcome. He had insisted he would solo the climb if no one else would go with him and the argument with John had followed. Steve had stepped in to say that as it was clear Ted was determined to climb he would wait for a day and attempt the summit with him. In opting to do this Steve showed an exceptional spirit of unselfishness, for if the weather turned bad his chance of reaching the summit could disappear. In any case Ted had not had so much time to acclimatise and might prove to be a slow companion. On top of that, as Ted's presence had strained food and fuel resources, Steve chose to descend to Camp 2 to replenish supplies while Ted rested. Steve had shown that there was more to the man than just the will, and the ability, to win. Quite what sort of winner he was, you will learn later.

'Conditions are firm above here,' he said to me. 'Why don't you come up to Camp 3? You could carry some fuel and food for us.'

I was packed in a shade over the time it takes fast runners to cover a mile. At that stage we planned no further ahead than that I should carry to Camp 3 and stay thc night there. But did this change everything? It was unlikely, for it would take a long time to climb 6,000 feet at a pace which would avoid altitude sickness. But still, without being over-optimistic, I once more began to allow myself to toy with the idea that there was a possibility that I might be about to reach my highest summit. Perhaps my chariot of fire had arrived.

With four bottles of fuel and plenty of food, as well as my sleeping bag and other necessities, I set off ahead of Steve, up a steep snow ramp above an awful cliff of ice. Within twenty minutes I was breaking through the snow crust to the knee. For one, two, three, four, five, six steps I sank right in. It can't be done if there's much more of this, I told myself, but it became easier. By 3 p.m. I was starting up the steep back wall of an amphitheatre of snow and ice, and an hour and a half more put me nearly at the top of a second amphitheare. The last hundred yards made me fight and pray for firmness in place of the featherbed stuff which yielded underfoot. Steve easily caught up near Camp 3 and showed me where it was, tucked away in a crevasse thirty feet wide and a hundred long, a navel in a vast snow belly. Four hours and twenty minutes to gain 2,000 feet was satisfactory at that altitude.

As I crawled into the tent Steve had a surprise to reveal.

'I have to tell you now, John asked me to tell you to go down. But things have changed.'

'You did right, taking the initiative when things changed.'

'Hope John thinks so.'

As he had taken the risk of ignoring John's instructions, we concocted several slightly altered versions of what had happened. We found it difficult, however, to settle on the best version, so in the end I said I would explain everything to John when the time was right.

Early differences with Ted were forgotten; Steven's action had poured oil on troubled waters. I had felt no ill will towards Ted, in any case, even though our judgement of what his behaviour should be did differ.

Steve and Ted planned to climb to Camp 4 next day and stay there for the night, then try for the summit. I knew it would be unwise for me to go with them, for that would mean a height rise of 4,000 feet in not much over twenty-four hours. At this altitude that would be asking for trouble. The only comfort was that I had carried up enough food and fuel to give this pair a fighting chance.

Climbing is a game of vicissitudes and the door I thought had closed did open a little again, for next day's weather was bad and forced everyone on the mountain to rest. If it had been fine I would have been left behind.

Our five friends at Camp 4 were not able to make their move for the summit. 'What a storm!' Grim wrote. 'Tents securely fastened to huge blocks of snow and ice. I cannot help but think how the situation could become desperate if the storm really sets in; no way one would want to move up or down.'

Throughout that day we downed hot drinks and took many a swig of water, for this would aid acclimatisation. Our aim throughout the ascent was to pass copious quantities of clear urine, and we often had someone or other announcing happily, 'My pee's clear.'

A nine and half hour test of strength next day started easily enough on firm snow which could be cramponed, but close to Camp 4 at 23,000 feet my happy world was transformed to one of torment as I plunged in to the knee and mid-thigh. With five hundred feet still to gain I had started by trying to do forty steps without stopping, but soon it got so bad I was having to fight for one step at a time. Up to then I had been in front of or just behind Ted all the way, but now he and Steve drew far ahead on their skis. In half an hour they were at the tent on the level space hacked from a slope; I prepared myself for fifty minutes, but that time elapsed and I was still snowploughing a deep trench. There was a long, long way to go.

Five people had been skiing slowly into sight above Camp 4 for some time. They made many, many turns to descend the slope very gradually. Three of them came down further past the camp, and I was able to congratulate each in turn: John, Grim and Johan. With Bob and Colin they had made it to the summit in four hours from Camp 4. In Grim's words, 'John's hands frostbitten; he was beat. Bob very cold – could not get camera out. Johan's camera frozen.' Now the pair of doctors were occupying one tent there while the trio was on the way to the next camp to leave a tent vacant for us, the new arrivals.

'I'm sorry plans have changed without an opportunity to communicate with you,' I told John.

'Changed for the better,' he said. 'Good luck for tomorrow, man.'

I looked at three exhausted men descending on their real legs, and wondered what I was doing there. Without skis, having been ill, and perhaps being behind with acclimatisation, what was I doing there? The collapsing snow was almost impossible to climb and I was gaining less than a hundred feet an hour. A hundred feet an hour! I considered stopping for three or four hours to get the freeze on my side, but if I was to have a chance the next day I had to get some rest, and lots of liquid. So I went on, taking the slope in the gentlest of zig-zags. I would raise the left leg and it would sink eighteen inches, then as soon as I lifted the right leg the left would go in even deeper, to be joined by the other one. I would pull the left one up with the assistance of the left hand and the motion would put the right one in even deeper. I would step up after dragging the right one out, but the snow would collapse and the right snowshoe would come down on top of the left, trapping it. The snow around the hole made by the legs would fall in, increasing the weight to be lifted at the next go, so I needed to pull with a hand again. I would prod with the crutches in an effort to find a firm spot, two firm spots, but as soon as I put any weight on them down would sink and crutches and both feet too, and the weight of my pack would bend me almost double. Oh, God! How could I gain nearly five hundred feet like this when it needed a rest after just *one* step up, when it was so hard to breathe, so hard to take *one* step? For *every* step I had to make up my mind and say, get ready, and now, go! And sometimes a step took me no higher because the snow was crushed underfoot.

This was one of the toughest days I've spent on a mountain. Forget about grades in the normal sense; grade 3 snow and ice would have been easier, even up there. People see the photographs afterwards, pictures of quite gentle slopes, and they say, 'Looks easy.' 'Fools,' you think, but no, they are right. It *looks* easy; no photograph can capture the agonies of altitude.

How long could I go on like this, approaching 23,000 feet? Hell, it was hard, it was hard, it was hard. In a state of utter frustration I muttered and shouted, 'Poxy bloody snow!' and a dozen profane variations. I bellowed, 'I'll be up to my tits in snow!' and was amused at suddenly hearing myself shouting at the unhearing white mantle up there. I calmed down and got on with it. It would have been possible to have deceived myself that I was close to the end of my tether, but experience told me I was not. There was enough 'keep-going' within me for a while.

The last three hundred feet rise did not release me from its grip for over three hours. Steve had some hot food ready but I could not eat. My body shuddered with coughing and retching.

'How about tomorrow?' he asked.

'Day after,' I replied. 'I'm wiped out.'

'Can't. We'd miss the flights back to Peking.'

Our schedule was closing in.

'See how you feel tomorrow,' Steve went on. 'A night's rest can change everything.'

'Right. I recover quickly. If nothing else, this is the highest I've climbed, and I can add to that a bit.'

If I encountered snow like that just below Camp 4, I was doomed to failure. I think Ted was concerned about my holding him back, because he asked, 'Will we keep Norman in sight all the time?'

'Can't say. Depends on the terrain,' Steve replied.

'Don't worry, Ted. If I have to I'll turn back. I'm not going to get in your way.'

We settled down in a very tired state, and Ted started groaning with the cold. It had been minus 10°F (−23°C) at Camp 3, and here it was much colder.

'To think we're all volunteers,' I said to Steve, and we giggled a bit, more than we would have done at sea level.

August 18 was Steve's twenty-ninth birthday. I wanted him to have the summit for a present, and I wanted to be there to see him get it. We were unsure about the weather at first, and made a late start at 1 p.m. Immediately above the tent I sank deep. Hell, this mountain was keeping me guessing to the end. Soon, however, I was walking a firm crust of up to two inches overlying powdery snow. If I sank at all it was only six inches. Steve went ahead and I hung on to Ted's tail, within forty yards.

In two and a half hours I reckoned we were at 24,000 feet. At least I had surpassed my previous altitude best by a wide margin; yet I took little comfort from this. Perhaps within my grasp at last, perhaps not, the very capriciousness of the attempt on this summit had increased the sense of challenge, and I opened my mind rather more to the option of a bivouac if the snow conditions demanded this. The snow remained firm; if only it was like that all the way to the summit . . .

After three and a half hours of uniform, gently-angled crusty snow that looked like slabs of polystyrene, I saw that Steve had stopped two hundred yards ahead. His skis stood up in the snow. Could he be on the summit? Don't raise your hopes, I told myself. It is what it is.

He put his skis on and moved up again, and I was pleased not to have fallen victim to false hope.

The wind began to assert itself after Steve's brief halt. 'In early June on the North Col of Everest one could not experience such cold,' Tilman wrote of his mid-August attempt on Muztagh Ata.

We had been going for four hours when Steve approached a rock hump, big as a large whale, slightly to the right of the line we were taking. Two hundred yards to the left of that hump was another, to our left. First Steve climbed the right hump, then started traversing to the other, which looked higher. Yes, I thought, that's higher. It must be the summit, and I headed for it. Ted, who was a few yards ahead, wanted the nearer hump to be the summit, simply because it was nearer, and he went that way. Within a few minutes, I had joined Steve. He was crying.

'I've just thrown the bones off,' he said.

He had been carrying some of the ashes of a thirty-seven-year-old man who had died in his sleep, and whose brother had asked Steve to throw them from the summit. The successful ascent and this act together had a deep effect on us, for we were still alive, really alive.

'Well done, stormin' Norman,' Steve said.

Ted made it ten minutes later and I let out a Hee-ahh! warcry; just like an American, I thought.

It was too cold for Steve to remove his mittens to operate my little camera, but though all the shots of me on the summit came out framed by wool, I treasure them.

There is a legend among the local nomadic people that an ancient city lies atop Muztagh Ata, dating back to times of peace and happiness. The city has had no contact with the rest of the world, and happiness and peace continue there, without death, cold, darkness or ageing, and fruit trees bear all year round. We felt old and cold, I can tell you, and death and darkness were not far from our thoughts, and we saw no fruit trees; yet it was true that none of the troubles of the lower earth had followed us up there, and none of them could later spoil the experience.

We returned to Camp 4 that day, and set off for Camp 2 or further down next day. However, we had descended no lower than Camp 3 when Ted had had enough for the day. We could not leave him there alone, partly because he had not been doing his share of cooking, and it was essential that he should be encouraged to keep up his liquid intake. Steve decided, and I agreed, that it was best for him to ski down to let the others know we back-markers should appear at base camp next day, and he went swiftly on his way. Since until a few weeks before he had held the world record for speed skiing at 125.7 miles per hour (201 km/hr) Steve was the man for the job. In three or four hours he would be at base camp. 'As time went on, we could see it was Steve coming down,' it said in Grim's diary. 'And with good news – whew!!! I really was expecting the worst – don't know why.' But for Ted and me things were not going to be straightforward; there was a little drama in store for us.

Grim's words tell what was going on at base camp: 'What a scene here tonight. After beer and shrimp cocktail, a huge dinner with about ten dishes. Ne (the cook) had worked all day on this – chicken, peanuts, rice, potatoes and mushrooms, soup, peppers, pork and melon, plus some wine Mr Qui had brought and served now he knew everyone was safe. And a birthday cake for Steve, which Mary and Jan and Ne had made from scratch. John at his best with mountain stories, tales, songs. All this in the middle of Asia. A setting to remember!'

The words 'everyone was safe' turned out to be premature. We were not all safe. Not yet. Not by a long way.

Throughout the night in our dome tent Ted had groaned and muttered, 'Oh, God!' I thought little of it, having heard him when he was cold at Camp 4. But this time it was not the cold which created his discomfort, but something much more serious, as I discovered in the morning.

'Norman, I'm snowblind.'

Snowblindness is a temporary, very painful condition. He was not totally without vision, but would have to be guided down.

'It may take a while but I'll get you down,' I said. 'Did you take your goggles off yesterday?'

'Yes. It was overcast.'

'Fool.''

The weather was not in our favour. Cloud created what we call a white-out, when it is impossible to distinguish between the snow and the cloud. Visibility was as low as three yards. Ted wanted to wait, I preferred to avoid any delay which might cause others to come up to look for us. They had made the ascent with a few resultant minor frostbite injuries and had probably got down safely, and it was time to get away. Any attempts on their part to re-ascend to Camp 2 or Camp 3 would involve a certain amount of additional risk which could be avoided if we headed down. Ted was hardly in a strong position to argue.

Once we were packed and the tent down I moved out of the crevasse into thick whiteness. We had marked the upper part of the route with wands, bamboo sticks supporting thin orange flags, and though they were spaced two or three hundred yards apart and therefore much too far apart for us to follow under prevailing conditions, they would give us reassurance every so often on our long and meandering descent of this white wilderness.

A brief gap in the cloud was enough; I drew an arrow in the snow towards the first wand below Camp 3, then waited for Ted to come towards me. He could not see well enough to pick out my tracks and spotting a wand was out of the question for him, but he could follow my vague outline if I did not get too far ahead. We reached the first wand, and the slope and memory told me which way to go to the next. There it was, and another, and another, but then the slope eased. Visibility was about four yards and it was essential that we maintained contact with the line of wands. Later it would become easier because John had written the compass bearing from one wand to the next on each little flag, but this had not been done in the upper section.

'We'd better sit and wait for a while in case it clears, Ted.'

We sat on the slope.

'I can tell it's getting lighter,' Ted said.

The cloud thickened.

Ten minutes later he said, 'It's getting better,' and it got much worse.

After sitting on the slope for half an hour Ted said, 'It's getting worse, isn't it?' and the cloud cleared briefly. My head was going left, right, left, right, like it was on a swivel, and there, two hundred yards away, was a wand. I took a compass bearing before it disappeared in a cloak of white.

'Right, Ted. Two seven five degrees. Let's go.'

'Can you help me up?'

The past few days had taken their toll and his pack was heavy. Pain is tiring too. His fatigue was not serious at this early stage and at our deliberately slow and cautious pace, but it would have to be borne in mind. Had I known the true cause of his tiredness I would have been more concerned; Ted had amoebic dysentery.

'I'm surprised he had the strength to accomplish what he did,' Don wrote to me. 'For he truly risked his life for that summit.' The ailment which had seized him, as it might have taken any of us, induced in him fever and fatigue, and could get worse, with abscesses on the liver and other complications.

So there I was, descending in a white-out from 21,000 feet, with a snow-blind man who had amoebic dysentery. I opted to go unroped because it was highly unlikely that Ted, on skis, would break through into a crevasse if I had gone ahead on foot without doing so. Also, if I fell into a crevasse when roped to him it was quite likely I would pull him in after me.

'I guess we feel a little like warriors just home from battle, yet there is some anxiety about the others,' Grim wrote. 'Mr Qui perched on his rock, with John's binoculars, looking for signs of them. A storm brewing on the summit. I bet it's wild up there now. The mountain looks *so* big and majestic.'

We walked on a bearing, slid two hundred feet down a slope, walked a bit further, and reached the wand.

'We're at the wand, Ted.'

'You son of a gun! You did it!'

'I know the approximate direction so we might as well go foward on two seven five and see if we come on to the next wand. If we don't we can follow our tracks back.'

We advanced for three or four long minutes but saw no wand. Visibility was at its worst by then. Six feet away, below on a gentle slope, I could just make out a slight trough in the snow.

'Stop there, Ted. Take a rest. I think there's a crevasse in front of us.'

My eyes played tricks in the everywhere whiteness and many times put an instant mirage wand where there was none. Another break in the cloud showed us we had done right by waiting, for there really was a dangerous crevasse just in front of us. We had to detour right, where a sharp change in the line of the wands showed how others had gone around the hazard. Having followed their example we slid easily for three hundred feet, Ted on skis, me on my bottom. By then he was finding it difficult to side-slip down behind me, because he was so weak, so he removed his skis and copied my method of descent.

We struck it lucky with brief breaks in the cloud and several times I was able to get a bearing on a wand and march towards it by compass. Then we came across the first of the bearings John had marked on the little flags, and those took us close to Camp 2 and out of the cloud. Bless you, John.

Picking a way between the crevasses below Camp 2 was a slow business. The ramp was much more icy than previously, and Ted was tired, but his vision seemed if anything improved, and he moved well and without any fuss. It was after 5 p.m. when John and Steve, who had been waiting anxiously, saw us from near base camp. A slide of five hundred feet on a snow-covered ice slope took us on to the stony rib which led to Camp 1. Mr Su waited for us there and took charge of Ted.

I was at base camp by 8.30 p.m., an hour and a half ahead of Ted, who looked fit to drop when he arrived. I had hurried down to let John and Steve know we were all right, but having seen we were safe they had already descended to our meadow camp. Considerately, they had left us each a bottle of beer, and three camels with a driver, so we too could go down to the meadow camp that night. At 10.30 p.m. Mr Su, Ted and I clambered on board the three animals and swayed forth and back for three hours in the near dark. As we picked a way through boulders, Muztagh Ata put on a ferocious thunderstorm, telling us we had been allowed up once, and down too, but not to take any ascent for granted. With the big emu-style head bobbing up and down ahead against the moonscape scenery I could sit back and reflect, and thank God for my good fortune. If John had opted for three camps instead of four, I would not have made it. If Ted had not forced his way up contrary to the judgment of the rest of us, Steve would not have descended to Camp 2 for supplies and would not have encouraged me to go up; Ted's determination had helped me. If I had accepted that as Don could not get by on showshoes I would do even worse – not an unreasonable conclusion – I might have given up. If we had had good weather on one particular day at Camp 3 I would have been left behind. If Steve had been a lesser man neither Ted nor I would have had such an opportunity for success.

At 11.30 p.m. our little caravan reached the meadow. The docs took Ted to a tent, gave him something to kill his pain, and bandaged his eyes. Just about everybody turned out to shake hands or give us a slap on the back or a hug, and fetch a beer or some tea, and our camp was a happy place. There was such pleasure to be found then simply from a mug of hot tea, and from time to relax, to relish the past few days and the friendship of our tiny band which had worked so hard towards our objective, from the time to think about the beauty of where we had been. The sense of joy and well-being! And of relief!

'Well done, Norm,' John said. 'There are not many here who could have got him down in a white-out.'

I passed it off, saying, 'I was only trying to get myself down. Couldn't shake Ted off. Bugger kept following me,' and we laughed, but I did feel very pleased to have had something useful to do.

A bandaged and therefore sightless Ted, insisting on having a window seat, was led on to our bus, and we drove back to Kashgar. The rest is a happy blur; a visit to a market, a department store, gentle crowds around us again; an orchard where young men and women in bright costumes danced and sang and played musical instruments for us; a banquet, a craft shop, the flight to Urumchi, a jade factory, another three hour flight to Peking, a second banquet with officials of the Chinese Mountaineering Association. At both banquets, apart from being served course after course of tasty food, we were introduced to 'mao-tai'. Served in glasses about right for egg-cups, if you like thrushes' eggs, neither the volume nor the appearance betrayed the power lying in this colourless spirit. The tradition is to call out 'Gan-bei', which as far as I could ascertain is the Chinese equivalent of 'Bottoms Up', and down the liquid dynamite in one go. We did. 'Gan-bei' followed 'Gan-bei' in rapid succession, as is the way. Leader, deputy leader, oldest gent, females and amputee received particularly attentive hospitality, i.e. constantly topped-up glasses. I have it from reliable opinion that immediately after descent from high altitude the effect of alcohol is at least doubled, so we as the 'away team' were soon wrapped in the arms of 'mao-tai' and 'Gan-bei' and proclaiming deep friendships with the people of China; those friendships were sincere. And they were reciprocated. Some of the politics of this nation were at variance with those of our individual members, but as ordinary people we were friends.

Ted's bandages were removed and his sight was back to normal. We started putting back on the weight we had lost. John had shed twenty-eight pounds in three weeks and I fourteen pounds. Almost everyone had lost several pounds, but one exception I must mention: Colin reckoned he gained three pounds. What on earth was his normal diet if he could put on three pounds while eating freeze-dried food at high altitude? John and I had both favoured being a little overweight to leave something to burn off, while the weight-watching Americans had a far more stoical approach and at each stopping point en route for Muztagh Ata had disappeared in all directions, running. Our respective performances proved nothing but the enigma of fitness for high-altitude climbing.

Soon we were saying goodbye to our climbing friends who flew to the USA before John and I left Peking. Then we were saying goodbye to our Chinese friends, and embarking on sixteen and a half hours of flying to Paris, before taking the short Paris to London hop. Home.

We had been away for five weeks and two days. If it had not been for the paperwork John had to handle in Peking we could have lopped a few days off that time; not bad, considering we had climbed a mountain of 24,757 feet.

For the first time in my climbing career I had, with John, achieved a British first, for no other Britons had succeeded in climbing Muztagh Ata. It was a climb of great quantity but little quality.

I suffered again the horrible dream that I had come home for a rest and could not return in time to join the others on the ascent. This time I awoke in a sweat, but in seconds I remembered what had come about, and I knew this magic could not be taken away. I had the ascent for ever, and was home too.

# 10

## *Quality and Quantity*

Fortunately Judy had a good Civil Service office job, but I had to pull my weight financially too. I had had some experience in lecturing about my climbing and from late 1982 I turned more to lectures as a source of income in fairly large dollops; lecture agencies relieved me of the need to haggle over fees. To make the lecture business work I had to obtain more slides, and it was quite a committing step to take, to enter the expensive arena of expeditions and to try at the same time to make a living from the results. Much time was spent travelling around the country by train, speaking at a library here, a public school there, at a ladies luncheon club somewhere else, at a sales conference, a literary society, a climbing club. Introductions by chairpersons, and votes of thanks, tended to be embarrassingly glowing, times to keep the eyes down, but there were funny moments too, such as the time when I stood in at short notice for someone who had died; an elderly lady paid me the weird compliment: 'I enjoyed your talk so much! I'm glad the other gentleman died.'

A new lifestyle permitted sufficient flexibility for some voluntary work, but I'm no Mother Teresa, and I found a level at which I was neither overworked nor resentful of the demands made. I had never been one to join committees unless I could see a very good reason for doing so, and once the outdoor pursuits campaign was well established there was no need for me to remain on more than two or three. Instead, working on an ad hoc basis with several projects concerned with disability suited me better than regular commitments.

Partly because of the ascent of Muztagh Ata, there came upon me the deepest sense of urgency about attempting some climbs of quality, some smaller but diamond-bright routes, so in May 1983 I went to the Alps. I had to follow more dreams to reach El Dorado. Simultaneously I began to prepare myself mentally for the time when, through serious injury to a wrist, an elbow, a shoulder, a hip, my back, or through other injury or sickness or disability, my body would no longer endure the severe tests to which it was subjected; if the time came I would accept it, for I had had so much. Soon, a physical problem did loom: my left shoulder became painful when the arm on that side was moved. It hurt even to pick up a jacket. Though I joked about it ('Well, at least I have one good limb left') the seriousness of the injury did not escape me, and I feared my climbing future was threatened.

'We'd better fix you up with an appointment at a sports injuries clinic,' my doctor said.

The specialist there, Dr J. G. P. Williams, was no stranger to me because I had contributed a chapter to a sports medicine book which he edited. Less than ten minutes after walking into his surgery I was out again, having had an injection deep into the shoulder.

I bought an old bike to give myself more exercise and soon came to the conclusion that cycling on London's busy streets was as risky as climbing, so I stuck to back streets. Another element of my training produced some bewildered looks from a neighbour; I took to wearing a forty pound pack around the flat all day when working at home, and one day stepped out of our back door looking like I was headed for the hills, walked fifteen feet, scattered some food on a bird table, and went indoors again!

Remembering the experience of an acquaintance who forgot to post his insurance application form, lost all his fingers through frostbite, and incurred bills for several thousand pounds for medical an allied expenses, I made sure I was properly insured; an accident-free record resulted in my premium being the same as that paid by an able-bodied climber. Some of my insurances were arranged through the London Mountaineering Club, of which I was a member for several years. Though I used the club hut in North Wales occasionally, contributed articles to the newsletter and journal, and gave a couple of talks, I could hardly be described as an active club member. In fact the only record of my involvement during a three year period concerned a one day trip to the cliffs of the Avon Gorge near Bristol; a report which listed the many routes achieved that day concluded simply, 'Norman and Judy took some photographs and then went to the zoo.'

Since I needed material for lectures and writing, many acquaintances reacted differently to my going on expeditions; they no longer queried either my motives or the virtue of my actions, but now viewed the wanderings as acceptable. There were those, of course, who reacted enviously, on the theme of, 'All right for some. Gadding about all over the world. Lucky devil.' But though there had been some luck and many people had helped, it boiled down to continued application more than to luck. You *make* most opportunities happen, rather than wait for luck, and you take risks and opt for sacrifices and apply yourself hard. I have ceased to be surprised at the number of people who tell me they have a climbing or other adventurous ambition but they have never achieved it because no one would give them the money to carry it out. I could advise them that getting there by stages and raising the finances are all part of the job and that securing the finance does not automatically bring the ambition about; anyone can dream up ambitions. Complaining that no one else will come up with the money is a feeble excuse, a sign of lack of commitment, and quite often they could afford to attempt what they had in mind provided they were prepared to make sacrifices. Though I do not mind if people lack ambitions (for there are some ambitious horrors around) I have no time for the windbags who say 'I wish I could' but always find excuses.

Immediately before climbing trips Judy and I seemed to live in different worlds inside our heads.

'I must put some more turf down in the middle of the garden,' she said one day.

'Fine. I'll need a new ice axe for the next trip.'

'Honeysuckle would look nice on that wall.'

'Mmm. Haven't decided whether to take my helmet yet.'

'Mary's given me some nice seeds.'

'Must get some more ice screws.'

'Could you move the trellis on to that wall?'

'Yes. Oh, would you get me another tube of glacier cream tomorrow? You'll be near the shop.'

'All right. Can you put the washing in the launderette and I'll collect it on the way back?'

'Yes. The pick on one of my axes is at the wrong angle.'

'I wonder if there's enough turf at the bottom of the garden that I can shift.'

It did not matter that our thoughts went about like two butterflies rarely alighting simultaneously on the same flower, for when it mattered we listened to each other. Her thoughts centred around her friends and closest relations, the little piece of garden which went with our flat, work and the people she worked with, and cooking, which she had studied for three years at teacher training college. With the exception of infrequent walking excursions we had given up taking mountain holidays together, for the preparations for even the simplest venture assumed the proportions of mounting a crusade; this was because she was not truly enthusiastic about going, and once we stopped trying to fool ourselves about this we had no more problems. She was a home bird, without a doubt.

'A lot of people really do believe I must have deep frustrated ambitions,' she said one day. 'As if ambitions were inevitable and mine have been squashed. They assume everyone wants what they want. Couldn't be more wrong.'

It is only natural that foremost in my mind as I set out on my next climbing trip to the French Alps was a feeling of anxiety about how my left shoulder would perform. On the twenty-four-hour coach journey there, there was plenty of time to wonder about that. Approaching Lyon, we came into a region of sodden fields and forests, flooded so deeply that fences running from high to low ground disappeared completely beneath the water. Farm lanes were submerged, leaving stranded buildings, pretty on their temporary islands. Trees of all sizes stood in the water or on islets, cornfields looked more like rice paddies, and in a sense it was beautiful, as if the water belonged there and had always been there. But of course behind the beauty, the seizure of land was an agricultural tragedy of half-submerged greenhouses and water-filled furrows. The whole scene portended conditions on the mountains around Chamonix: what had fallen as rain here would have left unusually heavy snow for late May on the heights. As we drew into town it was evident that soft snow was going to make the approach to most of the mountains impossible; my only hope was to rise above the fresh deposits by cable-car, to the cooler places. Things seemed stacked against me, for shortly after my arrival the only cable-car which had been operating was shut down owing to avalanche damage. The Brasserie National (known as the Bar Nat or Bar Nash), where English climbers congregate, was shut for several days' holiday, so my chances of finding a climbing partner were greatly reduced. The weather forecast was awful, too. The feeling of farce was reinforcd when I went to book into a dormitory where Judy and I had stayed before I climbed Mont Blanc in 1971, almost a dozen years ago; the place was derelict. The next dormitory I tried was shut, as was the next, so I booked into the cheapest hotel I could find, and began wandering the wet streets and bars, mooching about in pursuit of someone to climb with. The first day produced no results, nor the second, and more snow fell that day. Another day went by without any success, and I contracted a stomach upset. A few wet tourists came by coach, out-of-season animals who did not stay long.

The hunt continued for a partner who would attempt the north face of the Tour Ronde, a grade 4 route on a mountain of 12,441 feet (3,792 m).

Temperatures in the town reached 30°C (86°F) and the place came alive. This was the Chamonix I had seen before, first in 1971. Now it was a Chamonix of busy bars and banks, suntan and sunburn and souvenir shops, postcards and pop music and pommes frites and pavement cafés, dogs and development, restaurants and hasty road repairs and tarmac tipped like black sugar from big lorries, tourists, tourists, tourists, young and old and all ages in between. Coaches, lots of coaches.

Ironically, the fine weather was not all good news, for, though no new snow fell and some cleared, the north face of the Tour Ronde was not frozen and was difficult and dangerous as a result. Two and a half weeks had gone by without results and the forecast was for equally hot weather over several days. I had planned to be there only three weeks and money was running low. To stay or not? Fate intervened when I went to change the last of my travellers cheques, when a bank clerk mistook dollars for sterling and paid out fifty per cent more than she should have; the unsolicited bank loan would tide me over for a few more days.

Three days later I met Dennis Morrod at the Bar Nat. Dennis had been climbing at Chamonix many times. He was a forty-one-year-old motor mechanic who ran a small walking and climbing guiding business during the summer. He wanted to climb with me, not as a client, but as a friend.

Soon we were in the Torino hut (10,896 feet, 3,321 m) and reasonably confident that our chance would come. The night was chilly, just as we wanted it, and at 2.45 a.m. Dennis left the twenty-bed dormitory, of which we were the only occupants, reappeared a couple of minutes later, switched on the dim electric light, and beckoned to me.

'Just take one rucksack,' he said. 'I'll carry it.'

We dressed, packed, drank some tea and followed our head torch beams out into the snow at 4 a.m. The wind was bitter, the sky clear (cloud would have kept the heat in, so a clear sky was what we needed) and underfoot the snow was acceptably firm. From the hut we gained height gradually, lost it and a little more in a vast white valley, and began to regain it all. Crevasses, contours and the need to follow the firmest snow forced us to leave behind a track like that of a drunken man.

Within an hour and a half we were hauling ourselves for three or four hundred feet up a forty degree slope to our first obstacle near the bottom of the face; this was an unavoidable bergschrund, twenty feet high in places, which ran the full length of the bottom of the face. We headed for the only spot we could see where this natural dike narrowed and was bridged between the upper and lower lips by soft snow. While I paid out the rope Dennis struggled up the collapsing seventy degree snow above the gaping icicle-toothed mouth; I would not have been surprised if the mouth had swallowed him, but the bridge held. He disappeared from view over the top lip and the only clue to his movements was the way the rope ran out.

My turn came. The snow bridge took a second body, and held, and the snow above was firm, the right sort of stuff at fifty-five degrees, which gave support to kicked in, forward-pointing crampon spikes.

'Mind if I lead, Dennis?'

'On you go.'

An axe in one hand, a crutch with an axe pick clamped to it in the other. Four limbs shared the work. A hundred and forty feet of rope soon trailed out behind and I was belayed on rock. The leader of an Italian pair who had started just behind caught up; his second had had problems at the bergschrund, but had got up in the end.

The fourth pitch went to Dennis, fifty-five degree snow, finishing up a seventy-degree rock V-chute for ten feet.

'It's half-past nine,' he said. 'Could be on the summit by noon.'

Dennis led again, then I did, on snow which stayed at a little above or below fifty-five degrees. There was no rock belay within reach so I used three pieces of crutch tubing and an ice axe, then Dennis made a short lead of only twenty-five feet to reach a sound rock anchor. My turn again, to reach him and go past up the steep and now softening snow to the very limit of the rope. Before he started moving I spotted a yellow piton hammered into a crack just four feet above my head, and I clipped into it. So while Dennis climbed we were both safe, as he was when he went past me.

Just before he called for me to climb again, there was a noise which made me look rapidly up to the little rock platform where he stood. Something had dropped and was tumbling and making little jumps, end over end in the snow. Dennis could not see it.

'What's that, Norman?'

'One of my crutches.'

He had been using it to belay in the snow.

'I'm getting tired,' he said. 'It must have fallen out of the top of my rucksack.'

The tenth pitch was mine to lead. With a thousand steep and glistening snowdrop-white feet beneath my boots, I was aware of a feeling of seriousness, and told myself to keep cool and enjoy the experience I had waited for so long. I did feel fear, but it shrank in the face of the cause; this escapade was worthwhile. I remembered the headmaster, from a school quite close to where Dennis lived in North Cornwall, who said I was dragged up mountains. I suppose he suffered from what Judy calls 'small man's disease', which has nothing to do with physical size; out of all he might say concerning a varied climbing life his sole comment was not only negative but erroneous too. Judy was referring to a climber who epitomised the small man when he denigrated my early efforts on the mountains, the strugglings of a newcomer who had lacked any precedents to guide him. I did not understand, as I do now, that this pathetic man needed to make me look lesser to try to make himself look greater.

The rope had almost all run out behind when I found the next anchor, a boulder frozen in the snow. Dennis next, slowing down now but still not suggesting I should take the rucksack, and me hoping he would not. The twelfth pitch, mine. The thirteenth, Dennis's. The fourteenth, mine. We had kept to the right of the centre of the face, where protruding rocks provided anchors, so now, at the end of the fifteenth lead up snow, we had to traverse leftwards, because we had reached the top of the snow face which started at the bergschrund and ended abruptly here at a gully cutting straight across. That gully separated us from the final steep rocky summit tower, but by moving left we could reach the top end of the gully and a way to the top.

Dennis had belayed to a rock at the very top of the snowfield's upper lip. Before him, the whole north face, behind, the plunge of the gully. We joined two ropes together so I could move leftwards for nearly three hundred feet to the next anchor; the sixty-five degree slope (at first) I had to edge along, keeping just below the gently rising crescent top, was by this time very soft, for it must have been after 5 p.m. Where had the time gone? It had been spent on care, because of soft snow; the Italians had gone similarly slowly and were only just ahead. We had spent much time sheltering from the ice they dislodged, too, while Dennis bellowed, 'Oi! Bloody watch it!'

A short, easy snow slope, a descent down loose rocks for a little way, a climb up awful snow, and there was a metal Madonna on the summit. Our height gain up the face was not great, about 1,200 feet, but the quality I had sought was there. And I had done my share of leading.

After four hundred feet of descent to the south-east on the normal route's rocky ridge we took stock. A month later, in mid-July, there would not be much snow, but now it was deep, soft and dangerous. It would be soft all the way, and at the bottom walking with one crutch might be hard. In 1979 this route was the scene of an accident in which someone slipped and carried away not only two people on the same rope but several others below. Eight people died, six of them from other parties. Soft snow was given as a reason for the slip. According to a reliable report one survivor, who slid about a thousand feet (c. 300 m) was trapped half way down an eighty-foot crevasse which was blocked by dead bodies. He was then charged with manslaughter, but the charges were dropped.

The weather forecast was excellent. We weighed it all and chose to bivouac. Digging a little cave in the snow beneath a boulder did not take long. We crawled in, but Dennis left the cramped space and passed the night among some boulders on a rock prow above a long and steep white slope.

The bivouac earned us firm snow next morning, and we were soon down.

I had a chat with the driver of a coach leaving soon for London, and though officially I could not book a seat until the following Wednesday, he let me board Saturday's coach.

Despite a warm welcome home, I was received with simultaneously slightly reproachful eyes, like those of a friends' dog when they packed for their holidays, and when they returned. Neither the dog nor Judy would have reacted that way if they had not cared, but they wanted us home with them, safe. That must not, however, be the only and final measure; there is more to life than longevity. There are higher values.

My shoulder was fine and there was only a tiny injury to the left stump, a small raw spot. And I had another little route to yarn about with my climbing friends. And quickly the idea grew on me that I would like to attempt a route of about the same difficulty, but on a bigger mountain, thus bringing together the elements of quality and quantity. I did not have long to wait to find that route.

In November 1982 a letter had arrived to ask if I was interested in joining a US expedition to Peru the next summer. I said yes. John Perone, who had been on the second trip to Aconcagua, telephoned from the USA to say he was going too, and when the full list of the team arrived, there were the names of Dan Montague (the raisin-raiser, Aconcagua),

Vladimir Kovacevic (from the second Aconcagua trip) and Ted Mayer (snowblindness and amoebic dysentery in China). The leader, Phil Ershler, and the Chilean deputy leader, Guillermo Beauchat, I had met in Argentina, so I knew all but three of the members.

Temperatures in England had been nudging the nineties (c. 32°C) for some days around the time I left for Peru. We were up early and Judy was excited because her first poppy, planted because I liked them, had blossomed into the special bright beauty of that flower.

Heathrow, Amsterdam, Zurich, Lisbon, Caracas, Curacao, Panama City, Lima. In twenty-four hours I was in another world, where the high altitude climbing had started; on the way we had passed close by the Eiger, the Mönch and the Jungfrau, where my alpine career had begun. Now fresh and unforeseeable adventures lay just around the corner. Always, something interesting happened when we ventured into the mountains, but I could not begin to guess what it might be. Did I have a date with disappointment, or with delight?

Lima, cleaner than formerly and cleared of hundreds of thousands of shanty dwellings, was better than I remembered it, but I was in a hurry to reach Huaras.

Pepe had a new hotel in Huaras, close to his family's Hotel Barcelona.

'Come and stay in my new hotel,' he said. 'For you, a special rate.'

He had changed little, though at the age of thirty-three he had slowed down somewhat and, at least for the time being, his thoughts centred on only one woman.

In a nearby restaurant I saw something I had not witnessed on the first visit: children begging for leftovers. A boy of about eight, typically dark-skinned and brown-eyed, dressed in grubby grey trousers and shirt, stood silently on the opposite side of my small table as I ate alone. His eyes hardly left my plate. When it seemed I had finished the meal he looked hopefully at me, dropped his eyes to the plate, and back to me again. I nodded, and in small fistfulls he grabbed what remained, chicken bones with a little meat still on them, some lettuce and a few chips, and put them in a polythene bag. He smiled at me and left; most of them did it solemnly, unsmiling.

A man of about thirty crawled along the pavement outside, his legs dragging uselessly; in another country a wheelchair or crutches would have given him mobility. The scene reminded me of an aspect of the International Year of Disabled People which had made me uneasy: the predominant British emphasis had been one of self interest.

Four nights passed. I had chosen to arrive early to spend time acclimatising in Huaras at an altitude of around 10,000 feet. We had no rendezvous point but I was confident I would meet the others in the town, which is what happened. We were ten in all, though two did not arrive until a day later, having spent the extra time in Lima replacing a stolen air ticket, travellers cheques and passport.

The boulder moraine approach to Pisco was even worse than I remembered.

'Some of the worse terrain I've ever crossed,' Dan said. 'Loose as a goose.'

Seven of them climbed Pisco. I opted out because my left foot came loose, but importantly, on the way to Pisco, I met Bob Braun and Glenn Albrecht, two Americans whom I was to encounter again.

Next we headed for Huascaran. Having been up the north summit already, I could muster little motivation for the ascent, and from what I had seen from a distance the route was far more broken and dangerous than in 1978. However, the opportunity to take photographs at up to 17,500 feet, to replace film stolen in 1978, was sufficient to draw me along with the others.

On a narrow moraine spine above base camp we passed the first of the mountain's victims, a small Japanese lady being carried down on the back of a local porter. We did not find out whether she was ill or injured. Then at around 17,000 feet we came across five Peruvian climbers descending with a blue bundle which they lowered ahead of them down the snow and ice, and dragged it on ropes across crevasses. A floppy leg sticking from the bundle at a funny angle, and a bare foot, were the first confirmation that this was a body. The foot, like the bloated face, was the colour of a red tan leather shoe, and the eyes were like glass. We heard it was a Canadian or American man who had died in a fall several days before.

The sight of the corpse cast a cold shadow on our spirits, and in any case my decision to go no higher than 17,500 feet had been made. The dangerous way we had taken, weaving through crevasses and broken cliffs, had provided the long-awaited pictures, and considering the risks to be faced thereafter the reward was too small to tempt me on. Also, the replacement left leg had to be broken in, and was giving a great deal of pain where flesh was squeezed between the leather socket and a bone. Weight loss on expeditions often means that a perfectly fitting leg soon becomes uncomfortable because the whole body, including the stumps, must change shape and volume as fat disappears. The very long distances which must be covered on rough terrain can only aggravate the problems.

One of our team had already gone home after becoming ill and failing on Pisco, and now John, Dan and I had decided that the camp at 17,500 feet, a flat snow space reached at dusk, was as far as we were going.

John and I melted snow for water bottles and breakfast as the remaining six prepared for their early morning start. In an hour and a half they were strung out across a steep snow and ice ramp, and half an hour later they turned back. The place was too serious at that time for the combined abilities of this party.

Our descent through crevasses and ice cliffs, and down five hundred feet of slabs threatened by falling ice, left everyone with a feeling of relief at getting back safely.

My deflated companions had been in Peru less than two weeks and though they had planned to stay three weeks they wanted no more to do with the mountains. Phil gave me a large quantity of leftover rations, and they all departed for the USA, or, in Guillermo's case, Chile. The team's ardour had cooled too rapidly. There were many other relatively safe routes to try around Huaras. I sold some of the rations but retained sufficient to see two or three people through a climb. Alone again; not short of company but lacking a climbing partner.

There was no need to worry, for on the day the others went home, Bob Braun and Glenn Albrecht invited me to climb with them. A New Zealander, Brian Weedon, asked if he could come along, so the absconded US expedition was soon replaced. Bob and Glenn were biologists in their late twenties or early thirties and both had broad climbing experience. Brian was twenty-five years old, had trained as a surveyor and worked in New Zealand as a climbing instructor. He had not been blessed with good fortune while in Peru; he had bought a watch which was wrapped for him and later he unfolded the paper to find a substituted bottle cap, and several low value coins which imitated the strap. Then someone had stolen his passport, money, travellers cheques and camera.

Brian and I took a pick-up truck cum bus a few miles northwards to our rendezvous with Bob and Glenn on the main road through the Rio Santa valley. Having met them on the outskirts of the village of Paltey we flagged down another pick-up truck and bargained for a rough ride of about four miles to Collon, at 10,500 feet (3,200 m). It had been our intention to carry our rucksacks all the way from there, but a local woman approached us as we passed her mud-brick dwelling and told us her husband, Modesto, had a donkey and a horse which would take the loads from our backs for the next ten miles. At mid-day a deal was struck and we set off behind the two beasts. My left leg was extremely painful, so I lagged behind, and Modesto was soon telling my companions I would not make it to base camp; I had other ideas, of course.

We passed through the most beautiful pastoral scenes one can imagine; soft shades of green and cornfield yellow, and nice browns in mellow textures on gently undulating land where streams laid down lush ribbon borders; and patches of darker colour, where mud-brick, thatched dwellings and tall, dark trees and grazing cattle and sheep existed in harmony, before a backdrop of rounded, reddish-brown mountains behind us, distant white ones ahead. It was the kind of scene you can never properly describe. Though I limped painfully, trying to keep my companions in sight, I did not miss the quiet majesty of the place.

Bob, Brian and Glenn were considerate companions, with one or other of them always staying back far enough for me to be in touch with the party. Through a deep U-shaped valley of steep rock walls we followed a river and its forest of quenual trees – thirty feet high and less, twisted branches, peeling papery bark. As we approached base camp our objective started to show itself, and it was a fine looker. Tocllaraju, or Trap Mountain, is 19,796 feet (6,034 m) and was worth going to Peru for on its own.

Modesto, forty-nine years old, father of seven children, married to a woman of forty, made a half-hearted attempt to raise his price by about five per cent, but his will was weakened at being fed copious quantities of an excellent thickened soup concocted by Glenn and Bob, and he gave up. Wearing sandals made from old car tyres, and wrapped in a good poncho, he settled down on the sandy, football-pitch-sized beach where three of us slept in a tent and Brian spent the night out. During the night poor Modesto's animals departed, fortunately almost certainly downhill, but he would have to walk down now. Nibbling at a few biscuits, he padded off over the sand in a resigned way.

From base camp at 14,435 feet (4,400 m) we shared the vague path up a moraine crest with three Austrians. A little scrambling on easy cliffs, a short snow slope which called for crampons, an up-and-down walk on snow, seven hours gone by, and we were preparing to camp on a large, flat snowfield, close to the Austrians. We must have been above 17,000 feet by then.

6.15 a.m. Cold. My mind said my body did not want to move, but I knew the secret: make a small effort, like putting on a stump sock, then you feel a bit more like putting on one leg, which leads to another stump sock and to the other leg and to a jacket, and in three or four minutes you have almost forgotten that you did not want to move. It worked. Now I wanted to go, but there were too many crevasses for me even to begin to think about going alone. I needed the others. Glenn had decided against; like a lot of people, he had had a bad night at altitude. Bob had had an upset stomach the day before, and Brian had hardly slept, but they were going.

The necessary water was melted from snow and drunk as tea, and we started. Walking on easy angled snow up a snaking route, after an hour we roped up for a hundred feet where the way steepened and a crevasse waited at the bottom if we slipped. The Austrians were just ahead, and an Australian party of four, who had approached by way of a variation of our route, were some way in front of them. The south-west glacier and the north-west shoulder, which we were on by now, was the way we should follow, according to a vague description we had read. Other than that, our hastily crystallised expedition had had little time for research except to talk to a Scotsman who said the route was straightforward. Later it was rumoured that he had not reached the summit, and considering how far his view began to diverge from ours, I can believe that.

The ascent was in constant doubt because of the weather. Though not the summer period, this was Peru's dry season, and the weather had been continually good, until now. On this morning dark clouds covered mountains of similar altitude all around us, but Tocllaraju was left alone, at least for the time being. We traversed steep slopes with big crevasses running their length at the bottom, three hundred feet lower down, and moved carefully, unroped; to have belayed would have created too much delay, and we had one eye on the weather all the while.

'Probably just a walk to the top now,' Brian said at one stage, and afterwards we laughed about that.

At eleven in the morning a big decision confronted me. No more than three hundred and fifty feet vertically below the summit the mountain reared up into a formidable last rampart and the real difficulties commenced. First there was a big bergschrund, fifteen feet of mouth, overhanging at the top lip and of considerable depth, running the full length of the mountain's final thrust. Above the bergschrund it looked as if some giant hand had placed a three hundred feet high, layered, steep-sided meringue on the summit, and we had to climb the icy side which faced us. Amidst the large figures we talk of in the mountains, three hundred feet does not sound much, but it equates with the height of a twenty-storey building. We stood and passed rude comments about the judgement of the Scotsman.

The Australians were already part way up, and the Austrians had resigned in the face of such serious territory at more than 19,500 feet.

'How about the last bit?' Brian asked me.

'I'll give it a try.'

'I was hoping you would.'

The trip to Peru needed a good ascent to complete it. Tocllaraju, Trap Mountain, was that ascent, and was worth some extra risk.

A steep ramp of snow and grey ice, like a precarious stepladder, could be reached by way of a very soft snow bridge which spanned the bergschrund; it looked the best (and only) way to tackle the gap. We roped up and set off one by one across uncertain snow. It held for Brian, held for Bob and held for me in turn. The stepladder led to an overhanging lip of snow on which we did not linger, and the rope length of sharply inclined snow which came next was firm and enjoyable. The three of us congregated on a snow platform, wide as a single bed and half as long again, beneath an ice bulge. Looking upwards, we could escape to the right of the bulge. Brian went first and soon disappeared around it. Bob went the same way, up a steep chute of ice. When I followed, the hard ice fractured under my axe, and small chunks, each like a small discus in size and shape, were dislodged. A piece knocked out by one of the Australians, who were on the way down by now, hit me on the head; it could not be helped.

Had we known about this icy section I would have brought a second axe, but had to make do with the pick on one of my crutches. It worked well on snow but did not penetrate ice nearly so well as a proper axe, so I had to be very careful. If I had fallen it was possible that Brian's belay anchor, an aluminium stake, would have been pulled from the snow, and we would both have bounced down the ice into the bergschrund. Crampon points and ice axe picks bit only half an inch or less into the hardest ice, and quite often it shattered. Every move had to be made with caution; before moving a crampon I had to ensure that the other crampon and both picks were firmly planted. Arm muscles had to make up for a lack of leg strength and each move, performed as smoothly and carefully as possible, required both effort and concentration. Ten feet, twenty feet, thirty feet, forty, more.

'That friggin' Scotsman said this was easy,' one of the Australians remarked wryly as he descended past me.

The ice took us up to a narrow snow ridge which plunged ahead and behind. Turning right, we climbed, then walked, in a blasting wind for two or three minutes on gradually levelling snow to the summit. A gem of a climb, on a high mountain. Quality and quantity together, by accident rather than design.

Our descent was trouble-free, apart from Bob dropping my camera down a crevasse. It slid two hundred feet at first, almost came to a halt, and popped over the edge. Bob had insisted on trying to get it back and I had said not if it involved any risk. He went, roped, about a hundred feet down a slope and into a dark hole, to recover the camera, which still worked. And some of the pictures already on the roll of film were the best of the trip.

Next day, for most of the way down the valley, we were able to look back at our gleaming prize. There was a small raw patch on the right stump, and a pressure point on the left stump hurt all the time. By the end of the day I was barely able to walk. No complaints. The approach had been excellent, the peak imposing, the final section exciting, and my companions considerate; the photographs were a bonus.

Climbing has brought in its wake friends and travel and wonderful times when emotions seemed as sweet as a human being could experience. Under the influence of a seemingly bizarre motivation we flirt with death and hope to come back alive, and sometimes climbers are said to have a death wish. That may be true of some but mostly, I think, the reverse is the case. It may at first seem anomalous, but they risk their lives to a greater or lesser extent because life is too precious to waste in appalling dreariness. Through climbing I have discovered my personal path to fulfilment, and feel extremely privileged to have done so. My appreciation of the blessings which have come my way is boundless. Sweet dreams have come true, rich memories spring back; dear God, let it go on and on and on.

*   *   *

And go on it did, on the mountains of Peru, Bolivia and the Canadian Rockies, on Mount Kenya and Kilimanjaro, in Pakistan and Russia and in the Alps, in summer and winter too. But there is no room here for any more tales of mountains. To learn what happened next, of how I fared on three of the most breathtaking mountains it has been my privilege to see, to read of wonderful lakes, to hear about some companions who fell on mighty peaks, to find out how narrowly I escaped death from a falling rock, you must look in my next book, 'Where I Belong'.

# *Glossary*

**Aiguille**
Steep, sharp rock peak (in French, 'needle').

**Abseil**
To slide down a rope.

**Arête**
A sharp rock ridge which may be at any angle between horizontal and vertical.

**Belay**
Noun: an anchor point which may be natural, such as a spike of rock, a tree or a thick icicle, or artificial, such as a piton or nut (see *nut*). Verb: to make use of such an anchor or to hold the rope to safeguard a companion.

**Bergschrund**
A big crevasse (see *crevasse*) which forms between the upper snow and ice of a mountain and a glacier below.

**Bivouac (bivi)**
To sleep without a tent, usually in a waterproof bag.

**Cairn**
A pile of stones set up to mark a point such as a summit, or in a series to mark a route.

**Chimney**
A vertical or slanting crack of sufficient width to get your body in.

**Col**
A pass, saddle.

**Cornice**
Overhanging mass of snow formed by wind action.

**Crampons**
A framework of metal spikes, strapped to boots, to bite into ice and hard snow.

**Crevasse**
A crack in glacier ice. Some are very big.

**Glacier**
A slowly moving mass of ice born from one or more perpetual snowfields.

**Grades**
For our purposes: Britain, on rock – Easy, Moderate, Difficult, Very Difficult, Severe, Very Severe, Extreme.
The Alps – 1 to 6, 1 being the easiest. (To assist the non-climber, in this book numbers have been substituted for the usual French alpine grades such as 'assez difficile'.)

**Harness**
A climbing harness is something like a parachute harness.

**Karabiner (Krab)**
A strong meal snaplink which closes on a similar principle to that of a safety pin. Used for attaching a rope to, for example, a piton (see *piton*) or climbing harness.

**Moraine**
Rock and dust rubble carried down by a glacier and deposited in huge mounds.

**Nut**
A metal chockstone which is inserted temporarily in a crack in such a way that it will not be pulled out (we hope!) when a load is put on it. Used for belays and runners (see *runners*).

**Pack (backpack)**
A modern type of framed rucksack.

**Peg**
See Piton.

**Pitch**
Section of a climb, the length of which is often dictated by the availability of belay anchors. Usually between sixty feet and 150 feet, the upper limit being the length of the climbing rope.

**Piton**
A metal peg which is hammered into a crack. The use of pitons is not generally popular nowadays because insertion and removal damage the rock; nuts (see *nuts*) are much more common.

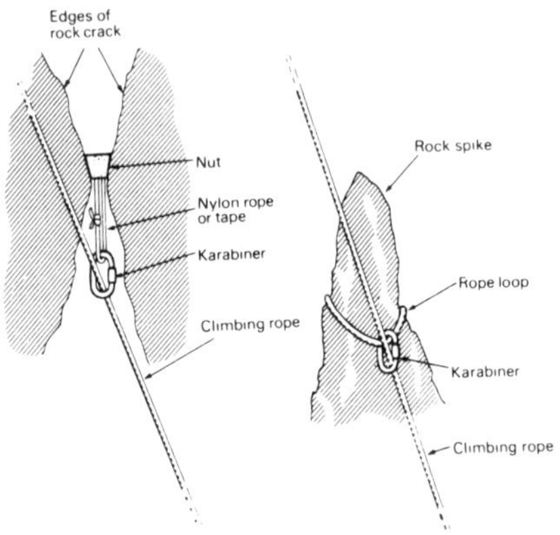


**Runner, running belay**
See first the noun version of belay. In the case of a runner the climber does not attach himself or herself to the belay, but attaches a karabiner and lets the climbing rope run free through it. The karabiner then acts rather like a single pulley wheel. (See Climbing Technique.)

**Scree**
Steep slopes of loose stones.

**Second**
Simply, to climb second. The word is also used as a noun to denote the second climber.

**Snowshoes**
The older type of snowshoe was often described as looking like a tennis racket. Modern types may be made of plastic, or metal frames with nylon strings, amongst other materials. When strapped to boots they distribute one's weight, thus reducing the depth to which the feet sink in soft snow.

**Spindrift**
Particles of wind-blown snow.

**Traverse**
Noun: a horizontal section of climbing. Also a verb meaning, obviously enough, to climb a horizontal section.

**Wand**
A light stick, possibly bamboo, usually with a small flag, left in the snow to mark a route which is complicated and/or in case of bad weather.

# *Climbing Technique*

What follows is intended to teach those of you who know little about climbing just enough about the subject to understand this book. It is greatly simplified and should not be misconstrued as a guide to anyone who wishes to get on to rock, snow or ice.

**On Rock**

The first man to climb is called the leader. He is tied to one end of a rope which is usually between 120 feet and 150 feet in length. One other person, known as the second, is tied to the other end, or there may be two more people, one tied at the middle and one at the end. As the leader climbs, the rope trails behind, paid out by the second; the rope is too thin to climb but is there to save a partner who falls. If necessary and if possible the leader puts on runners (see Glossary) so the next climber can hold him or her in the event of a fall. If a leader falls from ten feet above a runner, the fall will amount to twenty feet before the rope goes tight. Provided the runner does not fail through a nut being pulled out or a karabiner breaking, for instance, the rope will then stretch and help to cushion the fall. The leader may collide with rock on the way down, and there may be long sections of rock devoid of places where runners can be fixed, so runners do not always reduce or eliminate risk.

The leader may climb until the full length of rope between him or her and the second has run out, or may stop earlier, depending on the distances between belays (see Pitch and Belay in Glossary). If possible the leader then sits or stands on a good ledge, and should be attached to some form of anchor (belay). The second climber starts up, to be held like a flying stage Peter Pan if a fall occurs. That may sound fairly safe, but belay anchors may fail, the second may be injured in a sudden fall of a few feet, or, if not climbing in a line directly beneath the leader, may swing about dangerously. On some traverses (see Glossary) the second may face as much risk as the leader. Also the leader may dislodge loose rock on to a second. Generally, however, the leader takes more risk, particularly where runners are widely spaced.

When climbing in a party of two or three, only one person moves at a time, the other two remaining attached to the rock.

As far as possible the legs rather than the arms are used to raise the body, because leg muscles are bigger and stronger. The climber looks for 'holds', which may be small protrusions, cracks of various sizes (which may be big enough to take a boot toe, fingers, a hand, a foot, a leg, an arm or the whole body), and at times will rely on the friction of boots on the rock.

**On Snow and Ice**

On steep snow and ice, in some ways the procedure is similar to rock climbing; the rope is used in the same way and a belay may be a thick icicle, a large, tubular screw driven into the ice, or a metal plate (like a pointed spade blade and called a 'dead-man') hammered into hard snow. If available, rock anchors, such as a rock spike on the wall of an icy gully, may be used too. But whereas on rock one often relies on natural holds for the hands and feet, on ice and steep snow one uses crampons (see Glossary) and various types of ice axes and ice hammers (which are shorter than an axe and have the weight concentrated more in the head), to bite in and give support. (The press often write about climbers using 'ice picks', which is incorrect.)

**Mountaineering**

High mountain ascents may require the rock and snow and ice techniques mentioned above, as well as the additional skills of being able to move safely over glaciers, to perform crevasse rescues, to judge where and when the avalanche risk is high, to assess the weather and to cross rivers. To put up with the sheer slog of carrying heavy loads for long distances, perhaps at great altitudes, requires determination. High altitude mountaineering does not always involve steep rock, snow or ice, but the risks of altitude sickness, bad weather, crevasses, long distances, soft snow, hypothermia, frostbite, loose rock (resulting in rockfalls and tricky climbing) and avalanches can mean that even the 'easiest' routes on big mountains are arduous and dangerous. The severe lack of oxygen distinguishes high Himalayan and Andean climbing from alpine climbing. Because of the differences in performance between people, and because of the need for speed, the rope and belay rules of rock and snow and ice climbing are not always followed; a great many of the world's best mountaineers climb solo at times.

# *Conversion Table*

| Feet | Metres |
|---|---|
| 10 | 3.05 |
| 20 | 6.1 |
| 50 | 15.2 |
| 100 | 30.5 |
| 200 | 61 |
| 250 | 76 |
| 300 | 91 |
| 400 | 122 |
| 500 | 152 |
| 600 | 183 |
| 1,000 | 305 |
| 2,000 | 610 |
| 3,000 | 915 |

| Feet | Metres |
|---|---|
| 4,000 | 1,219 |
| 5,000 | 1,524 |
| 10,000 | 3,048 |
| 15,000 | 4,572 |
| 17,000 | 5,181 |
| 18,000 | 5,486 |
| 19,000 | 5,790 |
| 20,000 | 6,096 |
| 21,000 | 6,401 |
| 22,000 | 6,706 |
| 23,000 | 7,010 |
| 24,000 | 7,315 |

# *Ascents*

| Year | Mountain | Metres | Feet |
|---|---|---|---|
| 1970 | Mönch, Switzerland. | 4,099 | 13,447 |
| 1970 | Jungfrau, Switzerland. | 4,158 | 13,641 |
| 1971 | Mont Blanc, France. | 4,807 | 15,770 |
| 1972 | West Flank, Eiger, Switzerland. | 3,970 | 13,024 |
| 1973 | Wellenkuppe, Switzerland. | 3,903 | 12,804 |
| 1974 | Hörnli Ridge, Matterhorn, Switzerland. | 4,478 | 14,681 |
| 1974 | Breithorn, Switzerland. | 4,165 | 13,664 |
| 1975 | S.S.W. Ridge, Egginer, Switzerland. | 3,366 | 11,043 |
| 1975 | South Rib, Jagihorn, Switzerland. | 3,206 | 10,518 |
| 1976 | Arete des Cosmiques, Aiguille du Midi, France. | 3,842 | 12,604 |
| 1976 | Tete Blanche, France. | 3,429 | 11,250 |
| 1976 | L'Index, France. | 2,595 | 8,514 |
| 1976 | Aiguille, de L'M, France. | 2,844 | 9,330 |
| 1978 | Wallanaraju Sur, Peru. | 5,120 | 16,798 |
| 1978 | Pisco, Peru. | 5,752 | 18,871 |
| 1978 | North Summit, Huascaran, Peru. | 6,654 | 21,830 |
| 1980 | L'Eveque, Switzerland. | 3,392 | 11,128 |
| 1980 | La Luette, Switzerland. | 3,548 | 11,640 |
| 1980 | Point Kurz, Switzerland. | 3,498 | 11,476 |
| 1981 | E. Summit, Ameghino, Argentina. | 5,115 | 16,781 |
| 1981 | Whie Needle, Kashmir. | 6,553 | 21,500 |
| 1982 | Cerro Manso, Argentina. | 5,557 | 18,231 |
| 1982 | Aconcagua, Argentina. | 6,960 | 22,834 |
| 1982 | Muztagh Ata, China. | 7,546 | 24,757 |
| 1983 | Gillman's Point, Kilimanjaro, Tanzania. | 5,682 | 18,640 |
| 1983 | North Face, Tour Ronde, France. | 3,792 | 12,441 |
| 1983 | Tocllaraju, Peru. | 6,032 | 19,790 |

# *Acknowledgements*

As well as all the people whose co-operation and helpfulness in many forms is recorded at various points in this book, there are a great many organisations and individuals who deserve thanks. I hope that between the text and the following list I have included everyone who deserves a mention; and what a lot there are!

W. Adams, Agfa-Gevaert Ltd., Air France, Air India, Alpine Club, Andean Society, Applied Chemicals Ltd., Senor Cesar Morales Arnao, M. Ashraf, Aston Containers Ltd., Sue Bailey, BBC, Berghaus, Michael Bentine, Major R. Berry FRICS, Margaret Billings, Dick Boetius, Walter Bonatti, BP Oil, The Lord Mayor of Bristol, Bristol Evening Post, Bristol Round Table, Bristol and West Building Society, British Mountaineering Council, Buchanan Booth Agencies, The Burgess Twins, Brian Campbell, Canon Cameras, Caravan Ltd., Alok and Renee Chandola, Charities Aid Foundation, Chinese Mountaineering Association, John Cleare, Climbing Gear Ltd., Clogwyn Climbing and Safety Equipment, Collins (Norwich) Ltd., Colmans Foods, Diana Corbin, Mr & Mrs E. Croucher, Peter Cummings, Damart, Dingles (Bristol), Disabled Sports Foundation, Dixons Photographic (U.K.) Ltd., Phil Ershler, Europa Sport, Farillon, Mr & Mrs R. M. Feekery, Richard Fenton, Field and Trek (Equipment) Ltd., Alec Fish, Dr Fletcher, Dr K. Fowler, Fowlers of Bristol, Frenchay Hospial, Gallaghers Tobacco, Jim Galt, Mick Geddes, N. Gifford, Ginsters Cornish Pasties, Glenffiditch, Glorious Twelfth, Chris Grace, John Haig & Co. Ltd., J.E. Hanger & Co. Ltd., E. R. Hemmings, John Hinde, Honeywell Ltd., Bill Hornyak, Indian Mountaineering Foundation, Intermed, Jammu and Kashmir Mountaineering and Hiking Club, J. & K. Department of Tourism, Wanchuck Kaloon, Tourist Officer at Kargil, Karrimor International Ltd., Kellogg, Kingston-on-Thames Association for the Disabled, Bruce Klepinger, Kodak Ltd., Koflach Boots, Lima Tours, Steve McKinney, Mars, Senor Gonzales Mata, Dr John Minors, Dr P. Moffit, Mount Everest Foundation, Mountain Equipment Ltd., Mountain Travel, Mountain World, A. T. Needle, Nelsons of Aintree, Nicholas Laboratories, Nikon U.K. Ltd., N.R. Components, Crompton Parkinson, Pepe Espinoza, Eric Perlman, Peruvian Andean Club, Bob Pettigrew, Pindisports, Pocahontas Ltd., Joan Pralong, Mr Qui, Daniel Quiggin & Sons, Rainier Mountaineering, Ghulm Rasool, Jimmy Roberts, James Robertson & Sons, Roboserve Ltd., The Viscountess Rochdale CBE, JP, Roehampton Limb Centre, Rohan, Alan Rouse, Royal Geographical Society, St Joseph's School, Horwich, Miguel Sanchez, Gerhardt Schwartz, J. A. Sharwood, J.J. Silber, Gary Sillitoe, Smith & Nephew, Jim Smith, Rosie Smith, John Smolich, Sony (U.K.) Ltd., South American Explorers Club, Bill Sparkes, John, Claire, Jack and James Spedding, Dr Peter Steel, Arnis Strapcans, Mr Su, Tefal Ltd., Thornbury Rotary Club, Jens Toft, J. Toogood, Troll Safety Equipment Ltd., Tunbridge Wells Camera Centre, Twickenham Travel, Ultimate Equipment Ltd., Hector Vieytes, Viasa Airways, Ulises Vitale, Ghafoor Wahid, Warwick Productions, Jackie Welham, Norma Welsh, West-croft, Wexas International, Bill & Iris Marks and customers at the Wheatsheaf, Ealing, Dr J. G. P. Williams, Winston Churchill Memorial Trust, Wintergear Ltd., Women's Section of Southfields and Central Wandsworth British Legion, Woodhead Mountain Rescue Team, S. Wooler, Y.H.A., Yousuf Zaheer, Zero Point Nine.